A GUIDE TO
THE ODYSSEY

32 lines a head

A GUIDE TO
THE ODYSSEY

A Commentary on the English Translation of
Robert Fitzgerald

RALPH HEXTER

VINTAGE BOOKS

A DIVISION OF RANDOM HOUSE, INC.

NEW YORK

A VINTAGE ORIGINAL, DECEMBER 1993

FIRST EDITION

Grateful acknowledgment is made to the following for permission to reprint illustrations in this volume:

Illustration 2: Oxford University Press: from *A History of Architecture: Settings and Rituals* by Spiro Kostoff. Copyright © 1985. Reprinted by permission. *Illustration 5:* Harvard University Press: from *Folktales in Homer's Odyssey* by Denys Page, Cambridge, Mass. Copyright © 1973 by the President and Fellows of Harvard College. Reprinted by permission. *Illustration 6:* Oxford University Press: from *A Commentary on Homer's Odyssey* by Joseph Russo, et al. Copyright © 1992. Reprinted by permission. *Illustration 8:* By permission of the Journal of the Royal Anthropological Institute. *Illustration 9:* By permission of the Pierpont Morgan Library, New York. Amherst Greek Papyrus 23. *Illustration 10:* By permission of the Houghton Library, Harvard University.

Library of Congress Cataloging-in-Publication Data
Hexter, Ralph J., 1952–
A guide to the Odyssey : a commentary on the English translation
of Robert Fitzgerald / Ralph Hexter.—1st ed.
p. cm.
"A Vintage original"—T.p. verso.
Includes bibliographical references and index.
ISBN 0-679-72847-3
1. Homer. Odyssey. 2. Epic poetry, Greek—History and criticism.
3. Odysseus (Greek mythology) in literature. 4. Greek language—
Translating into English. 5. Fitzgerald, Robert, 1910–1985.
I. Fitzgerald, Robert, 1910–1985. II. Title.
PA4167.H5   1992
883'.01—dc20   91-58053
CIP

BOOK DESIGN BY JOANNE METSCH
MAP © 1993 BY REBECCA AIDLIN

Manufactured in the United States of America
10 9 8 7 6 5 4 3

Contents

Commentary

List of Illustrations

A GUIDE TO
THE ODYSSEY

Preface

Following is a guide to *The Odyssey* keyed to the translation of Robert Fitzgerald. I had long known, as reader and teacher, that the Fitzgerald translation of *The Odyssey* is astoundingly vivid; it seems to me to capture in English what I appreciate in Homer's Greek. As I worked on the guide, rereading, back and forth, again and again, both Homer and Fitzgerald, I began to appreciate what a truly monumental accomplishment the Fitzgerald translation is, how accurate, how brilliant. But let me emphasize that however much this volume is intended as a companion to his translation, neither publisher nor editor constrained me always to agree with Fitzgerald. Indeed, as users of the guide will see, I introduce discussion of Fitzgerald's translation into my comments at many points, often providing more literal renderings of the Greek, occasionally marking my disagreement with the translator's interpretation and proposing an alternate solution. Obviously, accuracy is my first aim here, but I have brought readers into the interpreter's shop with several other purposes in mind. First, exploring a particular choice on the translator's part is an effective way to highlight differences between Homer's world and our own.

As I explain in the Introduction, appreciating the distances across which *The Odyssey* comes to us is part of the task of the "archeological reader." One aspect of this distance is the translation, which lies between us and the original not as a sheet of plate glass but as a darkened mirror. The work of the translator should be demystified, however much the end product shares in the miracle of poetry (and it does because Fitzgerald is a true poet). If I so often say, "No, it doesn't really say this, the Greek means . . . ," it is because I want readers occasionally to be frustrated that they aren't reading the original, frustrated so that at least some of them will decide to learn ancient Greek for themselves. Homer in the original can be read with pleasure and profit, albeit slowly, after only a year of study. Even if it takes years to become adept at the finer points of Homeric philology, it is well worth the effort.

I had the opportunity of meeting Robert Fitzgerald only once, when he spoke to a group of eager undergraduates about finding the right register for each of his translations of ancient epic (he also translated *The Iliad* and *The Aeneid*). From the passion for the poetry he radiated then, and from the poetry of his translation itself, I daresay that no one would be happier if his work led readers to read and study Homer in Homer's Greek rather than his own English. And while no translation is the equal of its original, Homer is among the more "translatable" of ancient authors: his carefully plotted story, his subtle characters and their eloquent speeches, his vivid descriptions and striking metaphors, in short, the major portion of his infinite invention transfers well into modern English, guaranteeing joys to the reader of a translation comparable to the pleasures of reading the original. As Fitzgerald, himself a consummate student of Homer's Greek, proves, we need not choose between the two.

* * *

Two notes to readers:

In general I employ the spellings for proper names that Fitzgerald himself used—transliterations of the original Greek names—even though English-speaking readers will in some cases be more familiar with the Romanized versions of these names. Thus both translator and commentator refer to Odysseus rather than Ulysses (based on the Latin Ulixes); Akhilleus, not Achilles; Kirkê, not Circe; and so on. However, in the Introduction I use the more familiar English forms for place names where confusion might otherwise arise (e.g., Crete, not Krete), and I do refer to "Ulysses" when I am speaking of the character in the Latin tradition, from Vergil to Dante to Joyce. One note on my own transliteration of Greek words: Greek "u" [υ—upsilon] is rendered "u" except for the family of *poly*-epithets—an element whose familiarity to English readers I did not want to obscure—and for the name "Euryalos" [Eurualos], translated "Seareach" by Fitzgerald (VIII.148), but often appearing as "Euryalos" or "Euryalus" in literature on Homer and his epic descendants.

Finally, I use the abbreviations "B.C.E." (Before the Common Era) and "C.E." (Common Era) in place of the older denominators of the same periods, "B.C." (Before Christ) and "A.D." (anno Domini).

Introduction

Apart from the Bible, it is hard to think of any literary work that, in the world we have come to call "the West," has been so influential through so many centuries as *The Odyssey*, as both a text and a direct source of characters and incidents. This may be a surprising outcome for a poem that seems to have had its beginnings as sung entertainment in the banquet halls of petty chieftains in Greece and around the Aegean basin during a time often named the Dark Age of Greece (roughly the years 1150–800 B.C.E.). Darkness is, of course, relative. Even if the written documents and material culture of the early first millennium B.C.E. in Greece seem meager compared with those of the earlier civilizations of Mycenae and Crete, much less the subsequent brilliance of Classical Greece, both of these cultural moments and all subsequent Western civilization are illuminated by the twin flames that blazed forth out of that darkness: *The Iliad* and *The Odyssey*. No matter what role a bard named Homer had in the final shaping and polishing of the epics, the enduring strength of these two works lies in the fact that they are the living productions of entire cultures, the culmination of the narrative talent of who knows how many generations of bards and audiences, each of which contributed in some way to the drama, the images, the wisdom—in short, the humanity to be discovered in these poems.

Both *The Iliad* and *The Odyssey* were popular as sung stories in their time, and once recorded in written form they were installed by literary scholars and have never been replaced as the twin models of the genre of epic poetry. If *The Iliad* has traditionally been received as in some sense the more epic—in other words, the more fiercely heroic and bloodier of the two—*The Odyssey* has been treasured as the more accessibly human. Even as Odysseus' narrative takes him well beyond familiar geography, the boundaries of the human psyche and human society are drawn and figuratively patrolled. The very border of mortality marks the limits of the human, while at the same time it is presented as penetrable: the poet takes Odysseus once and us twice into the realm of the dead, to speak and listen to the shades of the dead. And even if in *The Odyssey* we see less petty backbiting and infighting among the gods and demigods than in *The Iliad*, the gods of *The Odyssey* are frequently all too human. Learning how to behave toward the gods, in daily piety and ritual, and how to negotiate the incursions of the divine into the human—from interpreting oracles and portents to facing the presence of a god in disguise or in epiphany—all of this tests and defines what it is to be human.

The narrative course of *The Odyssey* presents a wider range of characters than *The Iliad* offers. In the besieged Troy we get a glimpse of family units—men, women, and children—but the thematic pattern of *The Odyssey* demands that both poet and audience enter more often and more deeply into the hopes and fears, the desperation and exultation of individual characters—among others, a fatherless youth, a slave bereft of his master, a husbandless wife, a young woman who fantasizes about a potential bridegroom, an old man condemned to mourn his son, and an older and erotically experienced woman who gives up h...

tionship. It is the variety and depth o...

compelling plot in which they all play the...

kept *The Odyssey* irresistibly alive in the minds...

Poets are readers, too, and many poets have re...
Homer's *Odyssey* to suit their own purposes, not simp...
Homeric vein for foreign riches but adding levels of sigi...
the original poems. In a fragment of the archaic Greek p...
hilokhos often invoked as one of the first individual voices i...
West, the singer describes how he threw away his shield and ra...
from battle. Alkaíos and Anakreon follow suit. Centuries later the...
Latin poet Horace picks up the theme, and it begins to look like part
of the poet's traditional self-deprecation. However, the originator of
this claim is Homer's Odysseus, who says of one particularly sticky
pass, "I wrenched my dogskin helmet off my head, / dropped my
spear, dodged out of my long shield / [and] ran," here not away, but
to beg mercy from the Egyptian king (XIV.318–20). Significantly
for both later poets, this is one of Odysseus' fibs, for this episode is
part of the story the disguised Odysseus tells about his assumed
character of Cretan traveler and fortune seeker. The individual's
and the poet's voices then partake of the voice of Homer's Odysseus
in the very passage where Odysseus is being most himself—lying,
and most poetic—inventing fictions.

This is not the place to explore the manifold transformations that
The Odyssey and above all the character of Odysseus have undergone
through subsequent literature, not least because a good map of
much of the territory exists in W. B. Stanford's survey of the
"Ulysses theme."[1] Some stories concerning Odysseus which cir-
culated in antiquity are lost to us, but many are still extant. We meet
Odysseus in Sophocles' tragedies: *Ajax* (before 441 B.C.E.) and, more
darkly, *Philoctetes* (ca. 408 B.C.E.); briefly in Euripides' *Hecuba* (ca. 424
B.C.E.); in the *Rhesus;* and in the satyr play *Cyclops*. The Odysseus of
the tragedies takes on a life of his own, which will resound down the

century C.E. Latin ad-
speare's *The History of*
doux's 1935 theatri-
Trojan War Will Not
in part on Geoffrey
(1385), which itself
cular Troy poems.
entations in which
ditions, beginning
dually accreted to
en were partially
philosophical tra-
man who survives—

DUCTION

er best hope for a lasting rela-
f character as much as the
ir allotted roles that have
of readers of all ages.

fashioned bits of
ly mining the
ificance to
et Ark-
the

...ength of his character and the subordination of fear and desire to will; for some of the other philosophical sects by his astonishing adaptability. *The Odyssey* had shown Odysseus in both lights and did not apologize for the moments when his infinite adaptability crossed the line into guile and deceit. The Roman comic poet Plautus has more than one character invoke Odysseus as cunning strategist and archtrickster, and it is no surprise that the master wordcrafter among Roman poets, Ovid, chose Odysseus' battle with Ajax over Achilles' arms as the moment in Odysseus' career he would highlight, a battle which was waged and won by skill in words alone (*Metamorphoses,* Book XIII).

As knowledge of the Greek originals faded in the West, reaching its nadir in the Middle Ages, Odysseus became little more than a byword for trickiness, even treachery. This was reinforced by the fact that the Roman Catholic West was inclined to regard in a dim light the Greek Orthodox East, with its center at Constantinople (once Byzantium, now Istanbul), from which the Catholic West had split first politically and then doctrinally. Of course, the theme of Greek "treachery" predates the schism of Rome from Constantinople, running back to the stratagem of the Trojan horse itself, and is kept alive in every retelling of the fall of Troy. This is inscribed in

Vergil's *Aeneid,* the classical text which was most widely studied in the West and one of the few secular texts which was read and recopied without interruption throughout the Middle Ages.

The relationship of the crowning work of Vergil, the Roman Homer, to both Homeric poems is complex (as was noted already in Vergil's own time), but the clever way the Roman challenges his Greek precursor may be well exemplified by the role Ulysses has in *The Aeneid.* In his epic about Aeneas—who, according to legend, escaped the fall of Troy, led Trojan settlers to Italy, and through both battle and alliance established the basis for the founding of Rome by his descendants, Vergil permits Odysseus to appear only at a distance, and in sharp and rather unflattering perspective. In Books II and III, Aeneas—not unlike Odysseus at the court of Alkínoös and Arêtê—responds to his hostess' request and tells Dido of the fall of Troy and his own subsequent wanderings. Within this Vergilian tribute to Homer's strategy of having Odysseus narrate *The Odyssey* Books IX–XII, Ulysses is mentioned. It is from Book II of *The Aeneid,* and with reference to Odysseus' Trojan horse, that we derive the proverbial *"timeo Danaos et dona ferentes"* ("I fear the Greeks even when they are bearing gifts," II.49). Despite such warnings and even more spectacular portents, the false Sinon manages to convince the Trojans to breach their walls and drag the wooden horse within the city. (The Greek Sinon had first established credibility and won Trojan sympathy by pretending to have been maltreated by his comrades, Ulysses in particular.) Although it is never stated in so many words, it is hard not to imagine that Sinon's whole script is the work of Ulysses, whom tradition makes the inventor of the ruse of the horse. In this narrated scene in *The Aeneid,* Odysseus is thus invisible behind Sinon's words (but visible in that invisibility), just as readers know that he is hidden in the horse.[2]

Throughout Aeneas' account of the travels that brought him from Troy to Dido's Carthage, Vergil has him skirt Ithaka, and only once does he bring Aeneas' and Odysseus' itineraries together. At one stop on the desolate coast of Sicily, Aeneas and his companions discover Achaemenides, who turns out to be—so Aeneas reports the story—one of Ulysses' men who had been left behind in Poly-phêmos' cave. The Trojans give him aid and transport, despite his being a Greek and their mortal enemy. The more important point is to highlight an Odyssean episode which shows Odysseus at his most irresponsible. "Pious Aeneas," in contrast, saves his follow-ers—indeed, he even saves one of Odysseus', if, that is, we permit Vergil to interpolate this character into *The Odyssey* and, as it were, correct Homer. Nor do the literary repercussions of this *Odyssey*-inspired scene end here: Vergil's successor Ovid repeats the maneu-ver, interpolating Vergil as well as Homer, by recounting yet another version of Achaemenides' experiences in the land of the Kyklōpês and then presenting a newly invented character, Maca-reus, one of Odysseus' companions who, Ovid claims, skipped ship after hearing of the dangers Kirkê foretold (*Metamorphoses* XIV.154–444).

The Aeneid memorializes the Trojan origins of Rome. In its wake, through the Middle Ages, cities and nations, most prominently France and Britain, put about stories that provided each with a Trojan foundation. In this way an ancient pedigree was provided for their contemporary aversion to the Greeks, with Ulysses stand-ing first in the line of sworn enemies most directly responsible for the fall of Troy, a defeat they now made their own, and his character epitomizing the perfidious Greek at his worst.

The perfidy of the horse and the origin of the Roman people are specifically linked and heightened in *The Divine Comedy* when Vergil answers the pilgrim Dante's query about the twin flames they see in the eighth circle of hell. These are Ulysses and Diomedes, Ulysses' companion on many missions, who together, as Vergil says, "be-moan / the snare of the horse which made the gate / whence issued the noble seed of the Romans" (*Inferno* XXVI.58–60). What Dante knows of Odysseus he knows through the Latin tradition, primarily Vergil's *Aeneid*, Ovid's *Metamorphoses*, and Statius' *Achilleis* (widely read notwithstanding its unfinished state) along with their commentaries, which were the staples of medieval schooling in the Classics or, as they were then called, "The Authors" (*auctores*). Dante conveys his recognition that his knowledge of these figures of Greek epic is entirely mediated by Latin, along with his profound sense of the historical belatedness of his Italian tongue, by staging a Vergilian intervention when it comes time for Dante to question Ulysses and Diomedes. "Leave the speaking to me," Vergil advises, "who have understood / that which you wish: for perhaps they would be disdainful, / since they were Greeks, of your speech" (XXVI.73–75).

Vergil adjures them by his own celebration of both characters in verse and asks one of them to tell how he came to die (XXVI.79–84). Dante makes Ulysses respond, and now it is the Italian poet's turn to make the next move in the literary game of interpolation. The subsequent narrative of Ulysses' last journey is often read, anachronistically, as a remarkable anticipation of romantic, even Faustian, striving. But Dante, like Augustine before him, need only have looked within himself to find the great temptation for an intellectual that the desire for unbounded knowledge represents. Indeed, that temptation, and all the woe born of it, runs back in the Judeo-Christian tradition to the first temptation in Eden. The shipboard address of Dante's Ulysses to yet another set of comrades he will lead to destruction continues the tradition of Odyssean eloquence, and, while it wins over Ulysses' shipmates, Dante expects the reader of the *The Divine Comedy* to be wary of its appeals to the senses and experience (XXVI.115–16). He gives Ulysses these concluding words: "Consider your stock: / you were not made to live like brute animals, / but to pursue manly valor and knowledge" (XXVI.118–20).

But for Dante there is a third way, between brutish existence and undisciplined striving for glory and wisdom: submission to authority and the willingness to brook the limits placed on human knowledge by God. Dante goes far beyond Vergil's presentation of Ulysses as a negative example of irresponsible leadership, against which Vergil highlights Aeneas' self-effacing responsibility. Dante's Ulysses destroys both his companions and himself not merely in striving to satisfy idle curiosity and to see other lands and peoples but in searching for knowledge, on which he, erring, places no limits. It is out of his own understanding of the temptation of the desire for knowledge that Dante could describe in such heroic terms Ulysses' five-month-long sea journey beyond the Pillars of Hercules (i.e., the Strait of Gibraltar), which for Greco-Roman and medieval navigators marked the bounds of the known world. But, as even Dante's Ulysses makes clear when he describes his ultimate shipwreck—"and our prow sank, as it pleased another, / until the sea closed back over us" (XXVI.141–42)—this is a heroism which attracts us at our peril. The "other" mentioned in the canto's penultimate line is, Dante's Ulysses now understands, Dante's God.

While the double-sided nature of Odysseus, explicit already in *The Odyssey*, gave rise to the widest range of interpretations and responses, many of the other players have also left their impress. Penélopê, even if a bit impatient and peeved in the first of Ovid's *Heroides* ("Letters from the Heroines"), became for medieval readers of that very popular collection of poetic epistles the epitome of married chastity. And beyond: "Penelope" became synonymous with "faithful wife" in English and other European languages—with the obvious possibility that the term could be used sarcastically (as in Da Ponte's libretto for Mozart's *Così fan tutte*). Likewise, but with no blot on her scutcheon, her famous ruse has entered the proverbial: a "Penelopean web" is any work that will never be finished.

Diametrically opposed to Penélopê, Kirkê (Circe) became the archetypal temptress. She is the ultimate progenitor of Ariosto's Alcina and Tasso's Armida in the Italian Renaissance, not to mention the various Spenserian temptresses inspired by them. Nor is her afterlife limited to the literary tradition; she too became proverbial. For example, Germans, many of whose proverbial expressions reflect the value their culture has placed on a classical education, may still call a seductive woman a "Circe," and they have even created a verb, *becircen,* to describe Circe-like erotic enchantment. Like Penélopê's web, Circe's cup has become proverbial: it is the draft, literal or figurative, which works enchantment, particularly of the erotic variety.

Mentor too has a proverbial existence as the name of any adviser; indeed, so common is the appellation that in English we no longer even need capitalize the name. *The Oxford English Dictionary* suggests that its use as a common noun, which dates from the eighteenth century, is due largely to the important role Mentor played in the then wildly popular novel *Télémaque* by the French abbé Fénelon (1699). If so, this is yet another indignity inflicted on Telémakhos, who of all the characters in *The Odyssey* has had the least impact on literary and popular traditions. Historically, this is in large measure the result of his having virtually no profile in the Latin tradition, but it is also true that, without a careful and sympathetic reading, he runs the risk of becoming a rather uninteresting prig. Poor Telémakhos! The French novel of which he is the title hero is not only unread today but virtually unreadable, unless one is held by interminable discussions of virtue and theories of moral education.

Less important characters in *The Odyssey* have had better luck. Nausikaa, like Telémakhos a virtual prisoner of the Greek tradition, had to wait until the recovery of Greek to work her charm in the West, but when she did, her champion was none other than Goethe, who sketched and completed parts of a drama about her failure to win Odysseus as a bridegroom. Soon thereafter Eumaios returned in twelfth-century dress as the Saxon slave Gurth in Sir Walter Scott's historical romance *Ivanhoe* (1820), a story of absent lords, usurpers, and disguised returns which clearly shares more than a swineherd with *The Odyssey*. But the most surprising figure to enjoy a poetic afterlife in Odyssean spin-offs is Polyphêmos, the one-eyed Kyklops. Perhaps it was the very challenge of the task which inspired poets to present him hopelessly in love with the nymph Galatea. The mannerist tradition of the lovesick monster begins in

Greek with Theokritos' eleventh *Idyll* and makes its way to the European baroque in large part thanks to Ovid's *Metamorphoses*, where the spurned lover kills Acis, his "rival" for Galatea's affections (XIII.740–898).

I referred earlier to the fact that knowledge of Greek and Greek texts virtually disappeared in western Europe in the Middle Ages, so that poets like Dante and Chaucer were dependent on the Latin tradition. Clearly, knowledge of *The Odyssey* depended on knowledge of Greek, but surprisingly, the reverse seems also to have been true: *The Odyssey* played an important role in the reintroduction of the study of ancient Greek in Renaissance Europe. Petrarch (1304–1374) owned a manuscript of *The Odyssey*, but it was a closed book to him. Having Homer so near and yet inaccessible pained him, and he and Giovanni Boccaccio (1313–1375) hired the Greek Leonzio Pilato to translate *The Odyssey* into Latin in the 1360s.

Pilato's translation was neither distinguished nor influential, but the Italian poets' patronage of him accelerated the interaction of Italian humanists and Byzantine Greeks. In shortly over a hundred years, Italian humanists had learned enough Greek from their Byzantine contemporaries to introduce ancient Greek into the curricula of some of the more advanced Italian academies (e.g., Florence) and to read Homer and other Greek originals in growing numbers. Increasing concern with Greek texts in Greek inspired more humanists to acquire books from the hoard of manuscripts in Constantinople, a transference of cultural goods which proved fortuitous, since in 1453 the Turks finally succeeded in taking Constantinople, ending a tradition of Greek scholarship, much of it devoted to Homer, that ran back all the way to the Alexandrian scholars. From Italy, scholarly study of Greek literature spread across western Europe, and it was on the basis of the manuscripts gathered from the remnants of the Byzantine empire, at first primarily in Italy, that the first Greek texts were printed (*The Iliad* together with *The Odyssey* in Florence by 1488; see illustration number 10).

However, Pilato's was not the first translation of *The Odyssey* made on the Italian peninsula. Not that it remained extant so long that Petrarch could have used it, but around 220 B.C.E. Livius Andronicus had effected for his Roman students a prose translation of *The Odyssey*, a work which can justly be credited with laying the foundation of Classical Latin literature and certainly of establishing the tradition that this literature model itself on Greek literature. Livius Andronicus' version was successful in that it was quickly surpassed in stylistic refinement. Almost at once, Greek literature was not just seen as the stuff from which translations were made but was imitated in ever more creative ways. I have already spoken of many uses of themes or characters from *The Odyssey* in Roman literature, and that discussion came nowhere near exhausting the possibilities. Ovid, describing his trip into exile from Rome, compares his woes with those of no figure more frequently than Odysseus. I have also mentioned how Vergil modeled large parts of *The Aeneid* on *The Odyssey*, from scenes (the hero addressing his companions at the height of a storm; the hero rebuffed by the shade of one he had aggrieved and whose death he had, indirectly, caused) to structural elements (the hero's inset narrative of his own travels and travails).

In more modern times, retellings of all or parts of the actual *Odyssey* have been relatively infrequent. Odysseus' return is the subject of Monteverdi's *Il ritorno d'Ulisse in patria*, written for the Venice opera season of 1641, as it is of Gabriel Fauré's rarely performed *Pénélope* (premiered in Monte Carlo in 1907). Poor Telémakhos again: he was banished from the libretto for the sake of a sharper focus on the married lovers. Even more recently (1954), there is a film version of the entire epic, with Kirk Douglas as a swashbuckling Odysseus. But without doubt the most significant and influential "remake" of *The Odyssey* in the twentieth century, and arguably since Vergil's *Aeneid*, is James Joyce's modernist masterpiece, *Ulysses* (1922). Joyce does not so much retell the story of *The Odyssey* as use the Homeric original as a deep subtext for both structure and characters. The reader's knowledge of *The Odyssey* is taken as a background against which Joyce expects him or her to

read the events of a day in Dublin, and Leopold and Molly Bloom
are drastic revisions of Odysseus and Penélopê. Here, finally, Telé-
makhos comes into his own in the person of Stephen Dedalus.
Besides being an experiment in narrative form and language,
Joyce's *Ulysses* aims to be more encyclopedic of modern culture than
Homer's *Odyssey* is of Mycenaean and Dark Age Greece.

It would be impertinent to pretend to analyze the relations be-
tween Joyce's modern masterpiece and Homer's *Odyssey* in depth
here. Let its existence suffice to testify to the vitality of Homer's
Odyssey in our century. Nor did that vitality exhaust itself in the
mythic modernism of a Joyce or Kazantzakis.[3] The most recent
publication of the 1992 winner of the Nobel Prize for literature,
Derek Walcott, is a long narrative poem entitled *Omeros*.[4] Achille,
Hector, Antigone, Philoctete live and love in a West Indian milieu.
Their characters and story are even more loosely tied to *The Iliad*
and *The Odyssey* than Joyce's *Ulysses* is to the latter. What links the
world Walcott creates to that of Homer's poem is a vision of a
shared landscape and the ethos that emerges from it. I say "land-
scape," but it is as much a shore- and seascape. The shore Walcott
evokes is at once a directly observed Caribbean and a Mediterra-
nean refracted through Homeric recalls. As in *The Odyssey*, a tired
castaway can find rest in a bed of leaves where the sea washes the
land, and Homer, too, after so many centuries of cultural seafaring,
is reconstituted once again.[5]

HOMER AND THE ARCHEOLOGICAL READER

Even without reference to the rich afterlife Homer's *Odyssey* has
enjoyed, reading the original poem in our time involves us willy-
nilly in a project of archeology. This is true, in different ways,
whether we read Homer in a Greek or an English text. In fact, *The
Iliad* and *The Odyssey* have always demanded archeological reading.
Let me explain what I conceive to be the task of the archeological
reader.

Discussions of readers and audiences tend to assume Homer's original audience as the ideal. There is no question that such an audience shared with the poet a code of language, ideas, and assumptions that enabled them to receive *The Odyssey* with a simplicity and immediacy that can never be re-created. It is often presumed that our aim ought to be just such a reception. Leaving aside the obvious consideration that this is not possible, and without considering how close an approximation could be achieved, we ought to ponder whether it is even desirable.

Perhaps in part because it is impossible to recover, the state of the ideal audience is presented as if it were Edenic, a paradise now lost to us. The immediacy of reception that characterizes that lost innocence is, however, by nature unreflective. Masked behind the longing to experience a work precisely as its first audience did is often a desire not to think about the context of its production (as the first audience did not need to); not to analyze the dependency of meaning and interpretation on time, place, and culture; and not to reflect about the work of reading itself. Rather than lament our fallen state, I propose that we consider the benefits of distance, reflection, even—perhaps—objectivity. All of which is not to say that trying to imagine our way back into the mind of the first audience ought not to be one of our tactics in reading. But by making it only one part of the package, we are less likely to overvalue it and, out of desperation, to claim that we have in fact achieved what can only be approximated by an act of informed imagination.

The archeological reader may learn other things about a text by coming to it after a careful process of dis-covery, that is, of uncovering. Nor are the layers through which we dig wholly detritus. Of course, the later accretions and responses to a text are not in any sense part of the original, but they are of interest in the context of a wider cultural history. Even if not part of the text itself, they are a necessary component of our study of it, since we as readers stand at the end of an ongoing process of interpretation. We may of course prefer to ignore our own history as a reading culture, but the archeological reader always chooses the hard work of analysis and discrimination over the fantasy of unmediated response. This is not to deny us moments of such response. I will maintain that at least part of the time we must work to enjoy the spilling of blood in an act of just vengeance as I imagine the first audience would have, and as Homer expected them to. But to know that we should in some sense have this response is already a historically self-conscious position; it can be indulged responsibly only as part of the larger and more complex response I call archeological reading. Archeological reading is the kind we must do whenever we can, and certainly whenever our aim is to study a text in the context of the culture in which it was created.

POET AND POEM, SINGER AND SONG

The Homeric *Odyssey* requires archeological reading at an even deeper level, since it is not simply the creation of one poet for one audience at one time or in one place. So complex is the puzzle of the origins of the Homeric epics that scholars and amateurs alike refer to "the Homeric question." (Indeed, to make it sound yet more portentous, English speakers often use the German *die homerische Frage* in tribute to the nation which has wrestled most earnestly with the question over the past two centuries.) What is the Homeric question? Simply put, it is Who was Homer? The question is as old as the establishment of a literate culture in Greece in the sixth century B.C.E. In the earliest phase, argument centered on questions which now appear simple. For example, Where did Homer live? Many towns vied for the honor. Which poems did Homer write? During this phase, many were willing to ascribe to Homer considerably more segments of the epic cycle than the two major poems alone—*The Iliad* and *The Odyssey*—that have come down to us in their entirety. Finally, which group or guild of rhapsodes recited the authentic version of the Homeric poems? (The rhapsodes were so called from the staff—Greek *rhabdos*—they held while declaiming, reciting the poems by rote, or, more likely, because they "stitched" [*rhaptein*] one song to another.)

By the Classical period (fifth and early fourth centuries B.C.E.), the Homeric poems had long been the backbone of Greek moral education, but even in that increasingly literate and literary time, the vast majority of Greeks would have heard Homer more often than they read him. In the *Ion,* Plato gives us a portrait of a rhapsode who performed in Athens and throughout Greece in Socrates' own day, in other words, in late-fifth-century B.C.E. Athens, the age of Sophocles, Euripides, and Aristophanes (to name dramatists only). Plato's brief dialogue is well worth reading, not only as a portrait of a popular rhapsode and thus evidence for this important stage in the transmission of the Homeric poems but above all for the critique of the claims the educational and cultural establishment made for Homer, a critique that Plato puts into the mouth of his Socrates.

Greek culture and rule were extended far beyond the traditional borders of Greek influence by Alexander the Great, originally of Macedonia. The wider, more cosmopolitan world he left at his death in 323 B.C.E. is commonly known as the Hellenistic world. The small islands of self-rule and limited democracy that characterized the Classical period were overwhelmed by regional satrapies. Under the patronage of local princes, particularly in Pergamum on the coast of Asia Minor and in Alexandria, scholars collected and compared the texts of the Homeric poems. Under this new scientific scrutiny—already Alexander's tutor, Aristotle, had addressed "Homeric questions" at the conclusion of the first book of his *Poetics*—a range of philological problems emerged. To begin with, the assemblage of multiple copies of the Homeric poems made it clear that the texts varied. More than one scholar set himself the task of preparing an authoritative text. How was one to decide which word to choose when different papyrus rolls offered different readings? Which lines should be accepted or rejected when the texts varied radically or when some passages were repeated and others seemed crude to the tastes and expectations of highly literate Hellenistic scholars?

In light of the arrogance of many textual critics in subsequent centuries or other traditions, we can see that the Hellenistic scholars, for all their petty rivalry, worked with admirable tact and skepticism. The Homeric poems had a place in their esteem that approached the sanctity of scripture in sacred traditions. Rather than make copies without the verses that one or more scholars considered redundant or unacceptable, they developed a system of marginal signs meant to alert the reader to the purportedly dubious status of these verses. For this we can be thankful, for while we can reconstruct their principles and to some extent their tastes, the text itself seems to have passed through this period without being diminished or recast. The Hellenistic scholars saw that many words and references in the Homeric poems were mysterious because of changes in the language and culture, but they had neither the historical linguistics nor the archeology to enable them to begin to reconstruct Homer's world. At least they recognized that such a reconstruction would be the first step to an understanding of his poetry.

The Chronology, below, lists some significant moments in the history of Homeric scholarship. My interest here is to visit crucial stages in the Homeric question as it evolved, because our current hypotheses about the origins of the Homeric poems are best understood, again archeologically, as developments in an ongoing process. The Greeks—not only Classical and Hellenistic but their Byzantine descendants—focused on questions of Homer's provenance, the authority of one reading over another, and the need to explicate his meaning. In some instances, the explication led rather far afield, particularly when an exegete adhering to one philosophical or religious sect or another, confident that his doctrine was true and that Homer was the supreme exponent of truth, used allegory to harmonize Homer with his truth. Thus for different interpreters the gods became physical elements such as air and water, gods and heroes became ethical virtues, and the nymphs human souls.

But throughout this period, and even after Homer was reintroduced into the literary culture of western Europe, he was less studied than evoked—as the original Western poet (along with other mere names such as Linus, Musaeus, and Orpheus), as the fount of Classical mythology, and as the first epic poet. As I have described, only in the fifteenth and sixteenth centuries did significant numbers of western European scholars have the opportunity to learn Greek and, with the advent of printing in the second half of the fifteenth century, the texts with which to work. Homer also began to circulate in translations, not only in Latin (at the time the universal language not only of the Church but of scholarship and international affairs) but in modern vernaculars, in English first in George Chapman's rhymed *Iliad* and *Odyssey* (the pair were in print by 1616), then in Alexander Pope's versions in his trademark heroic couplets (*The Iliad*, 1715–20; *The Odyssey*, 1725–26).

Pope's Homer, great as it was, was more Pope than Homer, as contemporary critics were swift to point out. His historical pretensions as well as those of his critics are themselves significant, for they mark incipient scholarly concern with the historical Homer. Starting in the eighteenth and early nineteenth centuries, when, on the one hand, the study of history as a discipline was making rapid advances and, on the other, folktales and the heroic medieval literatures of the various European nations began to be studied and appreciated, substantial new light was shed on Homer. In this, scholarship and fashion went hand in hand. When, in the seventeenth century, the abbé d'Aubignac called Homer illiterate, he intended it as an insult; in the second half of the eighteenth century, which saw the popularity of the pseudomedieval songs of Ossian, the "illiterate bard" was an attractive figure.[6] Working on a more serious level, Vico, Woods, Wolf, Lachmann, and others, with increasingly acute historical sense, led the way in reconceiving the cultural context in which the Homeric poems were created. All were right in this respect: that reconstructing that context was the key to understanding the origins of the poems, and thus solving the Homeric question.

By the end of the nineteenth century, it was not uncommon, at least among literary historians writing in English or German, to assume that the social and political conditions of the culture which produced the Homeric poems were comparable to those observed in "primitive cultures" (as these were then termed) around the world. Some also drew attention to the performance of oral poetry in such cultures and suggested that the Homeric poems were likewise the oral productions of a bard. Scholars were, however, uncertain how to connect this largely ethnographic insight to the analysis of the Homeric texts. At the opening of this century, the remarkable archeological discoveries in mainland Greece and the Troad (the area around Troy in the northwest corner of what is now Turkey) seemed to offer a more fruitful field for Homerists: surely here were the real objects, the material culture which Homer's heroes would have known and which Homer was describing.

Soon, however, an approach based on both ethnographic parallels and a detailed analysis of Homer's poetic language proved more fundamental to Homeric scholarship than the archeological discoveries of Heinrich Schliemann and his successors. In the 1920s a young American doctoral candidate, Milman Parry, wrote and defended a thesis at the Sorbonne.[7] What emerged from this and subsequent studies by Parry and, after his death, by his assistant, Albert Lord, and others, we call the theory of oral-formulaic composition. Both Parry and Lord combined close analysis of the texts of the Homeric poems with on-site study of contemporary oral poets still performing in unbroken oral traditions. Of particular interest was the rich and then still productive bardic culture of the South Slavs.

Singers in this and other well-documented traditions learn their craft by hearing and doing. By manipulation of a repertory of formulae (stock phrases), the singer does not repeat but rather re-creates a certain tale afresh every time he sings it. Armed with the theory of oral-formulaic composition, Parry made sense of Homer's oft-criticized repetitions and fixed epithets. But he did more. By careful analysis of the occurrence of various noun-epithet combinations (e.g., "swift-footed Akhilleus," "wine-dark sea," "rosy-fingered dawn") at different metrical positions in Homer's dactylic-hexameter line (a supple but strictly ruled system of anywhere from twelve long syllables—more normally eleven long and two short—to six long and eleven short syllables), Parry was able to show not only the extent of the formulaic system but its economy. In other words, the practice of oral poets over the centuries had undergone a sort of evolutionary "natural selection," through which the bards' artificial, i.e., conventional, language was so pared down that only rarely did more than one noun-epithet phrase for the same person or thing survive for any particular metrical slot in the line.[8]

This is highly technical, as are the many refinements of the idea that scholars have introduced over the years. Nonetheless, a grasp of even a simplified version of the thesis leads to a realization of its far-reaching implications. Does the theory of oral-formulaic composition undermine Homer's poetic autonomy? That became the central question, for what above all provoked violent resistance to the theory was not only that it appeared to remove originality from the process of creating two of the greatest and certainly the first long poems in the Western tradition—"the bard uses inherited material"—but that it seemed to deny a place to creativity itself. If the singer were working with a strict metrical schema and his cache of formulaic phrases had for the sake of efficiency been reduced to one formula per slot, it seems that composition would have been well-nigh automatic.

But this is an extreme and untenable response. We can, I think, get a reasonable feel for both the constraints and the freedoms available to the singer of formulaic poetry by considering any number of familiar systems, for instance, music. Whether the musical idiom be Gregorian chant, Renaissance polyphony, late-eighteenth-century classical, ragtime, disco, or rap, given a certain bit of thematic material, the living practitioners in each style would think of harmonizing or developing it in only a limited number of ways.

Later students of each style might argue that the system allowed little or no choice. In contrast, practitioners and contemporary listeners, for both of whom the constraints are given and therefore virtually unconscious, focus solely on the range, however narrow, of possible variation. As with so many things, constraints permit freedom.

Indeed, if we analyze it, language itself is largely a formulaic system, albeit with a more generous range of possible variation. As competent speakers of the language, we know the rules of grammar and the range of each word's meaning. We know that one will have failed to construct a comprehensible sentence if the words occur in an incoherent order or if the words themselves cannot be interpreted to make sense. Nor do we often create many of our own words: we take them from a preexisting vocabulary. Nevertheless, we feel entirely unconstrained in manipulating the language. Just as we draw on a vocabulary, the oral poet draws on a "formulary," a repertory of formulae. And just as we sense the freedom rather than the constraint of the system—we do not spend much thought on what it is impossible or nonsensical to say—so the oral poet feels he has enormous freedom to manipulate his poetic diction.

The system works whether the constraints are largely unperceived—as with language, one's native language at least—or they are observed self-consciously. As a living example of self-conscious observation, think of the oral-formulaic system of jokes. When we hear a joke, we don't memorize it word for word. It is usually enough to retain the general context and the punch line. When we want to retell it, we re-create the structure and fill it in with what seem to be our own words but are in reality stock phrases of "joke-ese": an X, a Y, and a Z—it's always three—are at the Pearly Gates—a phrase hardly ever used today in any other context—requesting St. Peter to let them into heaven. Or an A, a B, and a C are in a rowboat. . . .

Formulaic aspects, as Parry suggested and as other scholars have worked out in considerably greater detail, are not limited to the phrase, half line, or series of half lines. Certain "typical" scenes, such as leave-taking and offering sacrifices, have their formulaic rhythms and patterns. These two are of course actions which would have had their standard protocol in any event. However, many other actions, such as arming, which might vary from person to person, are presented according to very strict standards. Many jokes, as the examples in the previous paragraph suggest, have traditional themes and forms as well as a recognizably formulaic diction. We can think of whole families of contemporary jokes, for example, "How many X's does it take to change a light bulb?"

Folktales provide another universe in which the very typicality of patterns makes retelling simple. Once you hear the story of a prince who must accomplish three tasks in order to win the hand of a princess, you can retell it with ease. You can retell it with any set of tasks, so long as there are three. You can tell it in a version in which it is a cruel stepmother rather than a fierce would-be father-in-law who sets the tasks (nor do you need to have experienced "stepmotherly cruelty" to make this substitution: you "know" from other tales that stepmothers can be cruel). And you can tell it in a version in which the princess herself sets the tasks, or asks riddles instead. The possibilities are endless, yet this is in every case the manipulation of traditional story elements. While the teller may feel he or she has complete freedom, the story that emerges will sound as if it were a thousand years old and had never been told in any other way.

The oral poet, then, has patterns at more than one level that guide him or her in the spontaneous re-creation of a story. It may well be that all popular culture is formulaic and generic. From our own experience we know just about all the possible story lines a western or horror movie can take. It is even easier with half-hour TV shows. (The half-hour slot, with commercial breaks, may be for screenwriters what the dactylic hexameter with mandatory breaks at half line—caesurae—was for Homer.) The genre and even the characters are known before the program begins, because they continue from one program to another within the series. So ancient audiences might have known what was likely to come if a tale from the voyage of the *Argo,* or of Heraklês', or Theseus' exploits, had been announced. As soon as the issue is presented, most intelligent viewers know exactly what is going to happen, and how and when the problem will be resolved. True aficionados can look at their watches and know whether, according to the protocol of the program, four minutes before the last commercial break is too late to introduce a new complication or plot reversal. None of this diminishes our enjoyment of our chosen entertainment; indeed, the particular proportion of predictability and variability, of familiarity and surprise, is the essence of such entertainment. I present this not as Homer's equivalent—there are many reasons why the Homeric poems are and were for their day much, much more than television sitcoms are for ours—but as an example of contemporary experience that may help us understand the workings of a popular and formulaic system.

Most recently, it has been argued that a certain inevitability in the entire story set in as soon as a bard determined to sing of the wrath of Akhilleus or the homecoming of Odysseus. If the shapes of story patterns were set at this level, this would of course make it considerably easier for bards to sing a long story, not relying on memory but simply telling the story. While less familiar to us in narrative poetry, such patterned improvising is well-attested in groups of performers, for example, the troupes of *commedia dell'arte* comedians of the sixteenth and seventeenth centuries or, closer to our own time, music-hall vaudevillians.

These analogies are instructive. However, a peculiar and rather obvious problem presents itself when we analyze the Homeric poems as the products of an oral-formulaic tradition. *They were written down.* The essence of the oral tradition is that the participants, singers and listeners, believe in its inviolability, its unchanging nature, so long as it is oral. In the absence of recording equipment, it is not possible to compare two oral accounts by the same singer, and thus not possible to prove the fact of variation. Modern studies of singers in this century, conducted by scholars with tape recorders, have proved that there is a wide variation in subsequent as well as distant performances of the "same" story, just the sorts of differences the entire system of oral composition might predict. But the singers always believe that they are singing the story unchanged.

Two centuries ago F. A. Wolf, in his epoch-making *Introduction to Homer (Prolegomena ad Homerum),* tried to reconstruct the state of writing that could have been known to Homer and his contemporaries. And the introduction, or rather the reintroduction, of writing into Greece is also at the heart of the "Homeric problem." Reintroduction because, as archeologists in this century have made it known, in the later Minoan and Mycenaean periods (roughly 1500–1200 B.C.E.), Greek was written widely around the Aegean, both on Crete and on the mainland, in the script known today as Linear B. Linear B is a syllabary, that is, it represents each syllable by a different character. While a considerable advance on earlier systems of pictographic writing—which represent entire words or concepts by ideograms or hieroglyphs— a syllabary is less efficient than an alphabet, which assigns to each sound, in no matter which combination, a single sign. Nonetheless, despite the comparative inefficiency, Linear B functioned well enough for the purposes of the Minoan and Mycenaean overlords who employed it, or trained scribes to employ it. Granted, the range of texts for which the script was employed was limited—inventories, public inscriptions, commercial documents; there are no literary texts. The very mode and material of writing would make the preservation of literary texts of any length difficult, although despite comparable difficulties a rich and highly evolved literature is extant in contemporary Sumerian, Babylonian, and Akkadian, also written in syllabaries on clay tablets.

Literacy was the province of a trained elite, a caste of scribes, as in ancient Egypt, China, and many other cultures. There was not a broad class of educated persons which could form a "reading public." With the collapse of Minoan-Mycenaean culture, the needs for which the script had been used disappeared, and with them writing itself. The fall of this civilization is often treated as a fascinating mystery, something akin to (and at times linked to) the disappearance of Atlantis, but as in the case of the much later "Fall of Rome," the transformation was likely more gradual. There were certainly wars, there may have been massive invasions and movements of peoples, there may even have been devastating earthquakes and volcanic explosions. But a healthy culture can rebuild and recover from any of these. What clearly happened, over several centuries and under the pressure of these occurrences, is that the old patterns of rulers and ruled, creditors and debtors, importers and exporters, changed.

Nor was the Aegean basin immune from changes in adjacent areas. Crete became less important relative to Egypt and to the new forces setting out from the eastern shore of the Mediterranean. There can hardly be more eloquent testimony to the importance of Phoenician culture and trade than the Greeks' adoption of an alphabet clearly derived from the Phoenician characters. The first examples of writing in what we now call the Greek alphabet date from the last half of the eighth century B.C.E.

It is of course a long way from scribbling a few words to writing down the whole of *The Iliad* or *The Odyssey*. Moreover, the idea of doing so would have to occur to someone, and it would not be likely to occur to an oral poet at the height of an oral tradition. This is the gap over which bridges of various sorts have tentatively been built. According to one argument, in the late eighth or early seventh century B.C.E. an artist, perhaps called Homer (unless that be the name, then already traditional, of some outstanding singer at an earlier stage of the tradition), sang versions of the story of Akhilleus and the homecoming of Odysseus so remarkable, and recognized as such, that at once the practice of oral tradition changed. Instead of learning to re-create epics afresh at each new sitting, the younger generation, recognizing the monumentality of Homer's versions, memorized the poems. Figurative "sons of Homer" (*Homeridae*) and then the rhapsodes described earlier continued to recite the Homeric poems by rote at least into the fifth century B.C.E., by which time writing had been so well established that scribes were able to take down the poems, the texts of which are the ancestors of ours today.

There are difficulties with such a story. For one thing, the oral tradition would mitigate against the recognition of a remarkably different version of a traditional story, although certainly audiences would have said they liked one singer or one song more than another. Moreover, it is hard to imagine a tradition moving from formulaic composition to memorization in one generation.

At the other extreme is the idea of a Homer who, heir to and master of the oral-formulaic tradition, lived when writing was becoming more common. It was Homer then who had the brilliant idea of writing down his own versions of the traditional songs. This theory would have the virtue of guaranteeing that in our texts we have something close to the authorially authenticated written versions of a representative, perhaps the last, of the oral tradition. But participants in a living oral tradition are allegedly unable to conceive of the poems they sing ever being forgotten and thus needing to be written down. A slight modification of this version introduces another individual into the equation, which has the advantage of keeping "the consciousness of Homer" untainted by knowledge of the craft of writing. It is this other individual who will have learned the skill of writing and has taken down the epics, with the cooperation of the poet (by dictation) or on his own. In either case, the assumed primitive state of writing and writing materials would have made this a daunting task. If there was any shorthand at this time, we do not know of it, and many scholars regard dictation as not merely unlikely but impossible.

Gradually, as oral formulaic has matured as a theory and the number of those who would deny that oral poetry has anything to do with the Homeric poems has dwindled, scholars have been able to take more tempered views. One need no longer be a radical proponent or opponent. Among the important advances is the study of the oral-written complex in Archaic and Classical Greece. While living traditions of bardic poetry have been highly suggestive as analogies, we now believe that the devastating effect "literate" culture seems to have on modern oral traditions ought not be posited for ancient Greece. First of all, oral and literate subcultures often coexist in the same society. Moreover, it is one thing when written culture erupts as an explosion of newspapers and books imported from long-literate cultures elsewhere into a society heretofore without writing. But the situation in Archaic Greece would have been different. Modes of exchange were not such that eighth- or seventh-century B.C.E. Greeks were suddenly overwhelmed with copies of Phoenician (or other Semitic) or Egyptian texts. Rather, writing probably began to enter their cultural world at the margins (in Cyprus, perhaps) and then only gradually loom larger in their consciousness. It is also likely that it appeared in relatively limited contexts at first, perhaps in inventories and religious dedications.

Eric Havelock has gone so far as to suggest that the nearly unique interrelation of literate and oral culture in this time and place was largely responsible for the form and quality of Greek literature from Homer to Plato.[9] His argument is worth considering. We don't have to decide whether he is right in order for us to agree with him, and others, that when writing was incipient, tentative, and experimental, there might well have been a moment for the old oral traditions and the new writing to interact in a benign rather than a destructive way. Not yet aware of the paradox formulated by Plato that writing destroys rather than prolongs memory (*Phaedrus,* 274C–275B), perhaps the poets of the eighth century B.C.E. were able to entrust their memories to the new medium without anxiety.

We can carry this speculation—and it is only that—a step further. Maybe it was the medium of writing which inspired one or more singers to create tales of a dimension and structural complexity hitherto unattempted. We will never know. What we do know is that both *The Iliad* and *The Odyssey* are monumental poems and that their author (on the singular, see the following paragraphs) was already admired in ancient times for the economy and craftiness of the structure of the poems. It has often been observed, and I will have occasion to do so many times in the Commentary, that *The Odyssey* shows a particular artfulness in structure, with the "Telemachy" at the beginning, the flashback of Books IX–XII, the paired scenes in Hades, and so on. Other critics and schools have found all or some of these to be "problems" rather than the artful devices I take them to be. These complex emplotments may just show the impress of letters, which can stop and double the flow of narrative as easily as animal skins, papyrus sheets, or even clay tablets, can be shuffled and recopied.

There is not likely ever to be an answer to the mystery of how the Homeric poems were "translated" from the oral to the written state. I would like, however, to point to one aspect of *The Odyssey* which needs to be weighed in our consideration of whether its final assemblage occurred wholly within the oral tradition or over the threshold of a new literate age—not that this can lay the matter entirely to rest. In the second half of the poem, Odysseus tells a famous set of lying tales. As others have noted and as I detail in the Commentary, each of these accounts involves subtle differences from the preceding versions. At each retelling, the narrating Odysseus carefully adapts his tale to its context and to his listener or listeners. This is certainly not the achievement of a poet, oral or otherwise, who thinks all versions of the same story are the same. Are these subtle variations perhaps more characteristic of a culture that knows the fixed form of the written word and hence can track variants and compare versions? Or is it conceivably the final gift of an oral poet consciously at a late point in his tradition, who knows not only that different themes require different stories but—and this he will have learned from his experience as a wandering minstrel—that the same story must be presented differently, to different audiences, and even

to the same audience on different occasions? In either case, it seems
to me, we have a Homer who is aware of the layers and levels of
other and earlier songs to the point that he can play with them, even
to the point that we might call him an "archeological poet."

Homer may be singular in this regard, but that very singularity
leads us to another question: did the same poet write *The Odyssey* and
The Iliad? As early as the Hellenistic scholars there were "separa-
tors," i.e., those who argued that the poet of *The Iliad* and the poet
of *The Odyssey* were different individuals. The arguments of separa-
tors and later "analysts"[10] are transfigured, but not necessarily to-
tally transcended, once we accept, as I and most Homerists now do,
that the Homeric poems are in some sense the product of an oral
tradition. As a scholar I tend to the view that *The Iliad* and *The
Odyssey* are the creations of two different poets. I base this not on
matters of style or the distribution of *hapax legomena* (literally "once
said," the technical term for words used but once in either or both
poems) and not even on the radically different tone of the two epics,
which the choice of theme could go far to explain. Many compari-
sons with more contemporary writers are dredged up, usually to
bolster the unitarian side of this debate: if you didn't know it to be
the case, would you dare attribute both *Love's Labour's Lost* and *King
Lear* to the same poet? Most poets change over the courses of their
careers, others do not. Already the ancient author of the treatise *On
the Sublime* ("Longinus" he is called, although we do not know his
name) proposed to solve the problem by having Homer write the
fiercer and more concentrated *Iliad* as a young man, the more
episodic and romantic *Odyssey* at an advanced age. But while some
poets grow more diffuse and sentimental with age (e.g., Words-
worth), we can easily think of many more artists who grow both
subtler and stronger with advancing years (e.g., Horace, Vergil,
Dürer, Shakespeare, Beethoven, Verdi). Such analogies will never
help us answer the question, because there are too many variables
for the equation. Nor would I base my argument on what I have

described as the more complicated, more artful structure of *The Odyssey*, for that very structure may, for all we know, come with the theme of Odysseus' homecoming.

Ultimately, I see the difference most clearly in what, with conscious anachronism, I would call the "theological." The gods of *The Odyssey* are not the gods of *The Iliad*. They have, to be sure, the same names, and they take the same sides in traditional quarrels. And there is a great deal of overlap, which is not surprising, since the two poems emerge from the same culture. However, in the main action of *The Odyssey*, the gods seem more concerned with ultimate justice. On the whole they exhibit less of the "furious self-absorption" which characterizes, as Bernard Knox so well describes it, the gods of *The Iliad*.[11] This can also, of course, be argued as a consequence of a different theme. But this difference inclines me to believe they were likely composed by different authors.

This division proposed and debated by scholars nevertheless can and should fade into relative unimportance for us as *readers* of either poem. What is important is to realize how the poet of *The Odyssey* depends on *The Iliad* and what differences obtain between the two. *The Odyssey* certainly presents itself as post-Iliadic, just as the story it relates is subsequent to the action of *The Iliad*. As the Commentary will frequently note, the characters and predicaments of *The Odyssey* are regularly presented against a backdrop we know best from *The Iliad*. (We can only speculate on the shape of many of the other epics then circulating.) The Helen of *The Odyssey* must be read against the Helen of *The Iliad*. The same goes for Akhilleus, whose appearance and words in Hades take their very point from their distance from those which characterized the hero of *The Iliad*. Scholars may or may not want to "separate" the author of *The Iliad* from that of *The Odyssey*, but, considering the cumulative and communal working of oral tradition and the intertextual relationships between the two poems (i.e., the allusions and references from one to the other), we are well advised to *read* them as the products of one Homer.[12]

HISTORY AND GEOGRAPHY

It is in light of the archeology of the Homeric poems that the archeological reader must approach the history and geography represented in them. History and archeology can tell us much about the worlds in which the poems took shape, but to go back from the world described in *The Iliad* or *The Odyssey* to reconstruct a coherent picture of Homer's time is not possible. I noted earlier that Parry's oral-formulaic theory outstripped the discoveries of archeologists as a source of insights into the world of Homer's poems. These discoveries are real, but as our understanding of Minoan-Mycenaean and other first- and second-millennium B.C.E. Mediterranean civilizations has advanced, it has become clear that the relationship of the Homeric poems to the actual history and everyday reality of these cultures is one of fictional representation, indeed, layers of fictional representation not unlike the layers of an archeological site. Commentators occasionally still claim to find "memories of Mycenae" in the Homeric poems, in other words, references to artifacts such as a boar's-tooth helmet or the Mycenaean features of a floor plan. Traces of distant memories they may be, but we must remember that for Homer and his poems they were in no sense "Mycenaean": he and his audience had a generalized sense of the glories of their forebears, but this had not yet been given a specific time and locale through the work of archeologists and historical linguists.

Likewise, in an age when travel was difficult, and when no one had the bird's-eye view of the Mediterranean we get easily today from maps and satellite photographs, none of those in Homer's audience would have been able to say where Homeric geography diverged from that of the real world. Indeed, given the localization of knowledge which would characterize such a culture, audiences in different places would react differently to the representation of the world. To judge from the areas which are described fairly clearly, it would appear that the Homeric audience knew the Greek mainland and the Aegean basin, including the western littoral of what we now call Turkey (parts of which were "Greek" into the present century—the evacuation of Smyrna/Izmir dates only to 1921, and possession of Cyprus, just outside the Aegean, is still hotly contested). West of the Greek mainland, the geography seems to have become uncertain very quickly. Even the precise assignment of Ithaka and its fellow islands in Homer to the actual landmasses northwest of Greece in the Ionian Sea engages scholars in controversy, and despite the clever arguments of many students of Homer, I have no confidence that "Homer" ever laid eyes on Ithaka. I am confident that most of his audience had not, and thus would not have cared about the "accuracy" of his descriptions of features of the Ithakan landscape (e.g., cave of the nymphs, bay) that frequently exercise commentators. Still less would they have striven to locate the land of the Kyklopês or the Laistrygônes; we must imagine that even the directions such places evoked in Homer's audiences varied depending on whether they lived in Boiotia or in Pylos, to the north or to the south. By the same token, Homer's audience would not have presumed that his geography was *not* accurate: the point is that accuracy measured by our standards was not and could not have been an issue. To a listener who had never left his mountain village in Arkadia, an accurate description of the currents in the Dardanelles might sound more fantastic than the most outlandish tale of gigantic shepherds living in what would otherwise be a familiar landscape.

Earlier I suggested an analogy between the layers of historical representation or memory in Homer and the multiple horizons of an archeological dig. In the poems, however, the layers are often mixed, unconsciously of course, to a degree that would give a professional archeologist nightmares. Homeric implements and weapons are at times bronze, at other times iron, simultaneous in Homer in a way that does not reflect the revolution in technology and warfare that the introduction of iron actually meant for Mediterranean cultures. The contradictory customs of bride-price and dowry coexist in a manner unparalleled in any culture known to anthropologists. But while Aegean archeology and anthropology cannot explain such features, the archeology of the poems and the anthropology of their performance can. It is common to cite as a comparable case the rewriting of history which the events of 778 C.E.—for which we have testimony in several contemporary or near-contemporary chronicles—underwent in the process of making the *Chanson de Roland*. Neither contemporary witnesses nor modern historians doubt that it was the (Christian) Basques who attacked the rearguard of Charlemagne's Franks as they passed back into France after campaigning against the Moors in Spain. But for reasons of narrative economy, and even more clearly of ideology, the Old French epic has simplified the story, making the "infidel" Moslems responsible for this treachery.

It is important to recognize that casual anachronism and lack of concern for historical and topographical accuracy are by no means limited to prescientific cultures. We may again compare contemporary forms of popular entertainment, which in our world happily coexist with scrupulously historical academic studies widely available in bookstores and libraries. If two or three World War II movies were all that survived from the twentieth century, how accurately could the thirtieth century reconstruct the history of the war, much less all of twentieth-century history? Parts yes, but the reconstruction would be neither complete nor balanced. Such representations become even less reliable as the events or cultures they purport to depict recede into the past and the genre takes on a life of its own. How accurate a picture of the Old West do most westerns provide? Popular entertainment gives a greatly stylized view even of contemporary institutions, processed according to the narrative demands and internal logic of the genre. Police thrillers give a highly glamorized picture of actual police life. Likewise, from watching countless courtroom dramas on television one would not have a very good chance of reconstructing our judicial system with accuracy. How accurate a picture could members of a later culture hope to get?

Such comparisons are not intended to discourage students from research into Bronze or Iron Age archeology, or the study of ancient history or geography (see also Troy, in Who's Who, p. 346). It is important to know as many certain details as possible so that we can better appreciate the complex way the Homeric poems exhibit traces of cultures from the fifteenth through eighth centuries B.C.E. Indeed, in some cases, yet older cultures are likely present in the shape of some inherited stories.[13] The poems "exhibit traces" only to the historically conscious archeological reader, for whom such texts are revealed as palimpsests. Strictly speaking, a palimpsest is a manuscript from which an original text was scraped away so that another, very different text could be written on the newly bare surface. For the bulk of the medieval tradition, it was usually a Classical text that made way for a Christian one. By the use of chemicals and now ultraviolet light we can often make out the words of the original text. Such artifacts are so suggestive of the impact history has on texts that the term palimpsest is currently popular among literary critics to describe a text (i.e., the content rather than the physical book itself) that exhibits multiple historical layers or thematizes the workings of history on the text. The Homeric poems are palimpsests in this sense, as are, by various interpretations, works as diverse as Petrarch's lyric poetry, Shakespeare's history plays, and Cervantes' *Don Quixote*. I do not object to so suggestive a usage, even though we know perfectly well that students of paleography, the field where the term is originally at home, are intent on deciphering two very different texts whose coincidence on one sheet of parchment is, as far as the reconstruction of the original texts goes, entirely accidental.

The final turn in our archeology, however, brings us to note that nothing in the Homeric poems suggests that the author or authors intended the audience or audiences to have any such multilayered sense of the past. For the poet and his audience, the texture of the heroic past is one seamless web, both separated from and linked to the poet's and audience's present: separate, in that the heroes of the past were greater than the mortals of their own day (a vision of continuous human decline made even more explicit in the myth of the successive ages of humanity, starting with the gold age and descending to ever baser metals); and linked, in that humans of the poet's day are supposed to be morally educable by the examples of the heroes of the past.

THE GODS

The heroes rather than the gods are the models of exemplary behavior. It is easier to say what Homer's gods are not than what they are. Historically, the Olympians too are palimpsests and superregional composites. Each embodies traits attributed by local cults to various deities worshiped at different sites over centuries. As something like a pan-Hellenic culture was forged (and at the time Homer lived, this national culture was still at a relatively early stage of formation), traits were added so that Aphroditê, to take one example, combines elements of a graceful and pacific sky deity, traces of whose cult can be found on the island of Kythera, with those of a fertility goddess worshiped in Paphos on Cyprus. (Among her other eastern Mediterranean/Anatolian connections, note that she favors the Trojans in *The Iliad*.) Not as many of the Olympians have important roles to play in *The Odyssey* as in *The Iliad*. Athena, Poseidon, and Zeus are the only three gods who are important throughout *The Odyssey*. Hermês functions as messenger of the gods; as far as the machinery of the plot is required, we could do without the rest of the divinities. But they are there. Apollo and Artemis are invoked, and Hermês is also mentioned in his guise as the guide of souls to Hades. Hêra, Zeus' consort, is relatively marginal in *The Odyssey*. Were it not for the amusing story of the dalliance of Aphroditê, goddess of love, with Arês, god of war, they, along with the aggrieved husband, Hephaistos, god of fire, would hardly appear at all.

Lesser gods and goddesses play important roles in *The Odyssey*, such as Leukothea, the sea nymph who helps Odysseus land among the Phaiákians, and Eidothea and her father, Proteus, with whom Meneláos has traffic. These may have been gods of local cults that were not internationalized in religious practice, but they achieve that wide renown, in mythology at least, thanks to Homer's poems. Figures such as Kalypso and Kirkê were probably never actually worshiped as even minor divinities; in other versions of the homecoming narrative, the females who delay the hero's return might be sorceresses or merely mortal temptresses.

It is important to note that despite the range and significance of roles the gods play in *The Iliad* and *The Odyssey*, the Homeric poems were never sacred texts in the way that the Jewish or Christian scriptures, or the Koran, were and are. Many of the gods' quarrels and battles recall divine battles and interventions preserved in the Hindu Vedas and the ancient Near Eastern texts (in Babylonian, Akkadian, Sumerian), as well as in the myths of Africa, the pre-Columbian Americas, and the European North. (Many scholars have found traces of such battles in early books of the Jewish Bible, but these are submerged as deeply as possible by the redactors and subsequent interpreters, for whom any implications of polytheism are distinctly heretical.)

Homer's gods partake to some extent of the nature of these fierce and autonomous deities known from a wide range of cultures. Their battles may originally have represented the imagined wars of various natural forces (light and dark, land and sea). But they are also members of a polity not unlike an ideal monarchy (which is not to say that none of the other pantheons just mentioned exhibits a political structure). While each of the Olympians has rights over aspects of the lives of men and women everywhere, each has special privileges in his or her domains as well as favorites among mortals. Like a king ruling over his nobles, Zeus is the supreme god, who under ideal circumstances hopes to keep his nobles in line by persuasion but can also threaten the use of force. All the gods at one time or another appeal to "justice" or what they perceive as justice (often a very self-serving view). But although he has his "private" favorites and interests, as ruler of the gods Zeus is expected to be held to, and in a certain sense to embody, justice. Hence, in *The Iliad*, no matter how many diversions he permits the other gods to introduce and how many delays their mortal subordinates may effect, Hektor must die and Akhilleus must surrender his body to Priam just as, ultimately (i.e., beyond the limits of *The Iliad*), Troy must fall and Helen return to Meneláos. In *The Odyssey*, while for offenses both old and new[14] Odysseus may be tested, detained, and stripped of his ships and comrades, Zeus wills that he return to Ithaka and recover wife, house, and status. Athena, Zeus' daughter and Odysseus' special champion, knows this, and when her doing everything she can is not enough, she reminds Zeus and has him renew his promise. Poseidon may interfere, but only within limits.

Zeus does embody justice, but at times this seems less like "Zeus wills only what is just" and more like "whatever Zeus wills is just." This is as handy a narrative device as it is a theological one. The whole logic of *The Odyssey* is based on the premise that the suitors are so evil that to a man they deserve death at the hands of Odysseus and his allies. But there is nothing in the procedures of Ithakan justice that would compel the kin of the slain suitors to admit this, nothing that would put a stop to a never-ending series of acts of vengeance. Homer's solution is simply that Zeus wills the quick and virtually bloodless final settlement between the suitors' kinfolk and the house of Odysseus. That this is Zeus'—and Homer's—will makes it just.

All the gods, Zeus included, are subject to fate. Like justice, which has a name *(dikê)* separate from Zeus', fate is *moira*. It is often close to the will of Zeus, but palpably separate. Homer at times personifies fate with the plural "Fates" *(Moirai)*. Fate is not, however, to be conceived along the lines of Christian foreknowledge, much less predestination: there is no eternal mind of God which knows before the creation of time everything that will happen in time, even if the

Olympians, and Zeus in particular, are often presented as regarding some events (e.g., the fall of Troy, the homecoming of Odysseus) as certain. Mortals have an even more limited insight into fate, via oracles, prophecies, prophetic dreams, and omens. Since these are open to misinterpretation (even outright manipulation), only the most credulous or benighted characters would rely on them for knowledge of the future. Significantly, neither fate nor divine intervention is assumed to relieve mortals from the responsibility of doing all they can to achieve their ends. The Homeric pantheon helps those who help themselves. In a sense, fate functions not unlike justice: fate is in the end what happens. Something is only finally known to have been fated after it has occurred.

Only fairly recently has European tradition become aware of the global distribution of epic poems and myths describing the internecine struggles of divinities and their activities as opponents and allies of heroes. The recovery of tablets and the deciphering of dead scripts and languages have brought to light the mythological literature of "old world" cultures and have allowed Europeans to explore the cosmography of "new world" civilizations. Previously, European tradition had regarded Homer's as *the* gods of poetry (as both Pope and Goethe put it). The epic machinery of an Olympian pantheon was adapted by the Roman poets, and via Vergil and his successors it was imitated in some fashion by every European epic poet. Leaving aside for the moment the essences they would have had for those who took part in their cults ("belief" is a misleadingly anachronistic concept; most ancient religions were based on practice rather than faith), the gods provided the poet with opportunities to sketch another set of compelling characters. They also helped him effect transitions of time and place, and with their superhuman perspective as well as their shape-changing capabilities they provided him endless opportunities for dramatic irony. But the gods were not merely plot devices or colorful figures to vary the landscape. The Homeric poems are ultimately grounded in the serious concerns of humans: as later Greek ethics put the question, How is life to be lived? The gods, who are immortal and for that reason have no mortal cares, are not held to human standards of conduct. Excellent forebears, not the gods, are presented as examples for mortals aspiring to greatness. Where the gods play a role in the life of a good man or woman is simply this: it is right to sacrifice to the gods, to hold them in honor, to hope for their aid.

In other words, it is in the relationship of mortals to immortals, rather than that of immortals to mortals, that the gods have the most importance for *The Odyssey*. Despite all his trials, and his offense or offenses notwithstanding, Odysseus is presented as a pious man, and when he gets to Ithaka we see him fostering piety in his son. Heroes can, in their excellence, be "godlike," which seems to mean that they are supreme in a particular branch of excellence; the term "godlike" is appropriate because whatever a god is, he or she is that absolutely (on "godlike" epithets, see the Commentary, Book I.92, below). Odysseus displays excellence in many spheres, and in that he resembles his patron, Athena. Or, as it is also presented, it is because of these qualities in Odysseus that she is so fond of him. Like Athena, Odysseus excels in prudence, craftiness, and battle, as does Penélopê (battle excepted). Although there are specific Homeric virtues that overlap with those we today would consider virtues (for example, charity to beggars, hospitality), "goodness" is not in itself a relevant concept. Neither, as we will have occasion to see, is honesty. The Greek concept of "help your friends, harm your enemies," is very much in force, and if guile can be employed to this end, Odysseus and Athena—and Penélopê—will be among the first to use it. Nor is there anything inherently good about perpetual restraint from violence, a point which deserves particular emphasis.

VIOLENCE

The ideal reader of *The Odyssey* will weep in Book XVI at the meeting of Odysseus and Telémakhos, and will laugh with joy in Book XXIII when Penélopê's craft finally provokes Odysseus to burst forth, a self-revelation which permits their reunion. But I maintain that no one can truly appreciate *The Odyssey* for whom Book XXII—in which Odysseus and Telémakhos take back their home by force—is not the real climax. There is considerably less bloodshed in *The Odyssey* than in *The Iliad*, but when it comes it must be thoroughly appreciated, even enjoyed. It is not considered proper in many circles today to condone violence in any form, but an inability to suspend such a reservation while reading *The Odyssey* will prove a detriment to appreciation. When at the conclusion of Book XXI Odysseus strings the bow and sends his arrow through the twelve axe heads, a thrill of excitement should shoot through our breasts, the same kind of thrill the makers of Robin Hood or *Star Wars* movies aim to inspire. Telémakhos and the two loyal herdsmen arm, and as they get ready to take on the suitors, we should be looking forward to the massacre. The first arrow kills Antinoös, and the suitors in their folly still have not recognized that Odysseus is before them. Homer describes the deaths of all the named suitors; it is for this episode that he reserves his fullest, most detailed account of virtually every one of them. And, in true heroic fashion, our hero bests them despite overwhelming odds.

If this scene might be compared with the violence in a contemporary film, *The Odyssey* as a whole cannot be. Homer has established that the suitors are bad. That they have gorged themselves on Odysseus' property is the least, if the most chronic, of their ills. They have plotted to kill Telémakhos, and they continue plotting after their first attempt fails. Homer shows that they are cruel to beggars and suppliants; in short, they are impious, and the presence of Athena herself ranged against them in Book XXII shows us exactly where divine justice falls. While there may be some suitors who are not as actively evil as the notorious ringleaders, they have nonetheless willingly participated in evil and are punished. This too is an important and sophisticated lesson of justice. The twelve serving maids who have betrayed the household are bad, and their end is by definition to be considered just.

What readers of *The Odyssey* take pleasure in is not violence or bloodshed in itself, but the exacting of justice. That evil characters meet violent ends must be satisfying in the narrative universe of *The Odyssey*. As is clear, this does not solve all Odysseus' problems. Violence almost always breeds more violence, and it takes one council in Ithaka and another on Olympos, as well as one more death in a small skirmish in Book XXIV, to convince the suitors' families to regard their murders not as acts requiring vengeance but as just punishment. The easy composition of the feud between Odysseus' house and the slain suitors' kin may seem a sleight of hand by the poet; its necessity and occurrence are part of his poem, even if a realistic explanation of the resolution is not. More important is the fact that Odysseus himself must go on what later ages would call a pilgrimage to atone for previous, albeit justifiable, violence. This is very much on our minds, for at the moment of regained bliss in Book XXIII, Odysseus himself apprises Penélopê of the journey Teirêsias told him he must make. This journey is required to settle accounts with Poseidon for the earlier blinding of the god's son, but reemerging in Book XXIII it doubles, poetically at least, as the deed Odysseus must do to atone for killing the suitors in the previous book.

FATHERS AND SONS

For many, the charm of *The Odyssey* lies largely in Odysseus' time in the land of the Phaiákians, from the moment he sees Nausikaa through his narrative of his fantastic adventures. And indeed, the adventures are memorable, as are Sindbad's. But *The Odyssey* is ultimately about family relationships, and Odysseus' voyages, however brilliantly they showcase his fortitude (and consummate narrative skills), constitute in some ways the least Odyssean episodes in the epic. They mark the point most distant from the central issue, just as his exotic ports of call are most distant from his goal— home—and must, however great the temptation to appreciate them as set pieces, be read in the larger context of Odysseus' return. It has often been lodged as a charge against *The Odyssey* that the epic begins with four books focused on Telémakhos, the so-called Telemachy. Let us leave aside the point that by means of this narrative device we easily learn of the sad state of affairs in Ithaka, the deep moral depravity of the suitors and Penélopê's antipathy to them, and the fatal homecoming of Agamémnon. We observe the loving couple in Sparta—Meneláos and Helen. The Trojan War is well and truly over. Leave this aside, because, albeit with less elegance, the poet could have told us of all this directly.

But the Telemachy makes sense if we understand that *The Odyssey* is from the start about the mutual discovery of father by son, and of son by father. Not mere recognition, mind you, but discovery: Telémakhos has never seen his father, he has never had as a present exemplar the great hero he knows it his destiny to emulate. Likewise, Odysseus has never seen Telémakhos (at least not since he was an infant in swaddling clothes) and has thus not fulfilled the role of a father, which means in part guiding and training his son, in diplomacy, battle, and piety. Homer presents us first with the son in search of his father, then the father in search of—his home. Having no acquaintance with Telémakhos past infancy, Odysseus could not have focused his longing on that aspect of his home. Nonetheless, it is not by accident that in Eumaios' hut, his first lodging in Ithaka, he finally meets the young man who is his son, reveals his identity alone to him, and with him begins to plot the final resolution. Nor is Telémakhos' itinerary, in this regard parallel to Odysseus' more fantastic voyage, complete until their moment of mutual recognition in Book XVI.[15]

Odysseus is father; he is also son. He must make peace with his parents before the epic plot can be fully resolved. His mother has died of grief over his long absence. Fortunately, given the economy of the poem and the tradition of the *nekuia* (visit by the epic hero to the land of the dead), his mother's death does not preclude an interview. It is in Book XI, the first *nekuia*, that he speaks to her. From her he learns that while she has died, her husband and his father, Laërtês, is suffering a living death of grief at his son's absence. Again, it is not by accident that Homer reserves the reconciliation of this father-son pair for Book XXIV, where it serves as a capping episode of the poem. This reconciliation is linked to the composition of the nascent feuds between the kin of the suitors and the house of Laërtês and Odysseus. The artful arrangement cannot go unnoticed: the epic opens with a son in search of his father and concludes with a father who has regained his son. The complicating, or rather enriching, factor is of course that the father in the first equation is the son in the second. We have an unbroken chain of generations. The fact that we move from young to old is of a piece with the fact that, as we will have many occasions to see, *The Odyssey* is an epic of maturity. Maturity, the ripeness of adulthood, even of age, is privileged over the rashness of youth. Not that there is any sentimentalizing or softening of the harshness of extreme old age: Laërtês is grievously weakened in spirit and in body. But it is somehow deeply fulfilling that Athena lets him fight yet one more time with the younger men, with his son and grandson. In the generations of Odysseus' family, *The Odyssey* addresses all the ages of human development.

The father-son recognition and the drawing together of the generations rounds out this theme, so central to *The Odyssey*. It is worth remarking that, despite the many differences, *The Iliad* too in its final book stages a father-son reconciliation. As in *The Odyssey*, this involves multiple fathers and sons, and in fact the situation is more complex than in *The Odyssey*. In *The Iliad* we are dealing not with generations within one household but with different families, indeed families on opposing sides of the conflict. As you may recall, the final episode of *The Iliad* is Priam's visit to Akhilleus, in the latter's tent, behind enemy lines, a visit the Trojan king makes in order to beg for the now mutilated body of his son Hektor. Akhilleus is moved to accede to Priam's request only when he thinks of his own absent father, and how he will grieve for his imminent death. The passing of time, in other words inevitable aging and death, is thematized in both Homeric epics by the transfer of power from fathers to sons. In the final moment of each poem, a temporary halt to this process provides a respite from the ineluctable slide toward death at the same time that it reminds us of its inevitability.

MEN AND WOMEN, FAMILIES AND COUPLES

The transfer of power in battle and in governance from father to son to grandson, for all its importance to the history of a single family, is ultimately a public act. It is in the public sphere that fathers and sons, as males, have a place. *The Odyssey* is remarkable among epics for the wide scope it gives to private relationships, which it figures in relations between men and women. This is not to say that these do not also have their public function. A couple need not be so prominent as Odysseus and Penélopê for their partnership to have ramifications in the common weal. Their marriage represents a joining of two clans or kin groups, and, by the exchange of money or other property, a new economic unit is formed. Or rather, in Homer, the woman joins the economic unit of her husband's family.

While such social facts provide the background, *The Odyssey* gives a deeper and more nuanced picture. We would not have needed Homer's poem to know that the wife serves as mistress of the household, keeping watch over provisions and property and supervising the slaves. What Homer tells us, particularly in the person of Penélopê and her relationship with Odysseus, is that a woman could be conceived of as having a relationship of equality with her husband. She is at least his equal and perhaps his superior in prudence and craft; indeed, Homer has a special term, *homophrosunê,* which means something along the lines of "like-mindedness" or "harmony of spirits," to describe what Odysseus and Penélopê, and few other couples, have. The compass in which Penélopê can work her wiles is admittedly narrower—no battles or sea journeys for her—but the fact that she cannot leave her home on Ithaka without some man's permission only forces her to be that much more inventive in manipulating the largely symbolic systems at her disposal. The prime example of this is of course the famous trick whereby she holds off the suitors. This is a sincerely pious charade: under the guise of fulfilling a duty that the system of honor (i.e., male esteem and expectations) demands of her, she claims that before she can choose a new husband she must weave a burial shroud for her absent husband's father. She then uses the secrecy afforded her by the male-mandated seclusion of honorable women to unravel each day's pensum. She is foiled in this delaying tactic only by women, those unfaithful maidservants who have formed liaisons with some of the suitors. I need hardly point out the blatant double standard: the suitors' dalliance with these serving wenches is no bar to their suitability, but the least suspicion of infidelity on Penélopê's part might well lead to her destruction.

Women no less than men are represented in *The Odyssey* at all stages of life, from youth to old age, and as slaves and free. Still, apart from the goddesses who from time to time aid Odysseus—and it is probably inappropriate to subsume divine females in all instances under the category of women—and the slaves, who are property and are not strictly marriageable (although they may be used or bestowed for sexual purposes in unions of any duration), all the women are presented in some way with reference to marriage. This is hardly surprising, since marriage was the central event of the life of a woman in ancient Greek society (as in so many other cultures), marking a girl's true coming-of-age.

That I except the goddesses is also not surprising, since besides the fact that goddesses cannot be exchanged by male-dominated mortal families to form alliances, one of the essential differences between mortals and immortals is that the latter, for better and for worse, do not form lasting relationships of mutual dependency. (Marriages between gods are not characterized by dependency.) They need not, and they cannot. Kalypso is the exception, for she attempts to cross this boundary and make Odysseus her own; Odysseus, preferring the mutuality of a relationship with his mortal wife, for all the risks that entails, turns down what is tantamount to an offer of immortal bliss. Of course the will of Zeus seconds his choice, the right and proper one for a mortal. Kirkê is different in precisely this regard and for this reason emerges as a true foil to Kalypso (and not as a mere doublet, as is often alleged). Kirkê uses her divine status to exercise power over mortal men the way males normally do over women. She can enslave them or she can enjoy them as temporary sexual partners, with no second thoughts.

Among free mortal females we see Arêtê, Alkinoös' consort; their daughter, Nausikaa, who is just arriving at the age of marriage-ability; and Antikleía, Odysseus' mother, now among the dead, grieving for both son and husband. Odysseus describes immediately thereafter the shades of many mortal women, a list he introduces significantly as "consorts or daughters of illustrious men" (XI.258), echoing the point at the end of the episode ("daughters and wives of kings," XI.382): in each case their fame or infamy is calculated with respect to the men to whom other men assume the women owe allegiance. This catalog of heroines provides a set of females whose behavior exemplifies either good or bad ways of being a woman, i.e., wife, daughter, or mother. The exemplary function of women also accounts for the importance in *The Odyssey* of Penélopê's famous first cousins, daughters of her uncle Tyndáreus, Klytaimnéstra and Helen, who serve as potential models for or counterexamples to Penélopê.

The first, Klytaimnéstra, never appears in a scene of direct narration in *The Odyssey,* but her name is on the lips of men—by which I mean males—as the central figure in a tale with admonitory messages for all the members of Odysseus' family. The Greeks traveling home from Troy had various fates, and it was a common-place to contrast them, as Nestor and Meneláos do in their accounts to Telémakhos in Books III and IV. The fate of Agamémnon, who reached home only to fall victim to the plotting of his wife, Klytaim-néstra, and her paramour, Aigísthos, is presented not just as a frightening counterexample to Odysseus but as an alternative plot into which *The Odyssey* on several occasions might veer. A medita-tion on what we might call the master antiplot of *The Odyssey* is the subject of the very first speech of the epic, from the mouth of no less a figure than Olympian Zeus (I.42–62). Nor is it merely the fame of Agamémnon as the supreme commander of the Greeks at Troy and the violent treachery of his murder which make this such an apt cautionary tale. There are roles in the Agamémnon story for home-coming hero, wife, rival or rivals, and son, Orestês, mentioned already by Zeus as the slayer of Aigísthos and avenger of his father's murder (I.46 and 59). Later in the first book Athena, in the guise of Mentês, emphasizes Orestês' part in the family drama as "he" exhorts Telémakhos to plot his reckoning with the suitors:

> You need not bear this insolence of theirs,
> you are a child no longer. Have you heard
> what glory young Orestês won
> when he cut down that two-faced man, Aigísthos,
> for killing his illustrious father? (I.343–47)

Focus remains on Aigísthos as sole or prime villain, on Agamémnon as victim, and above all on Orestês as slayer of the first and avenger of the second throughout the Telemachy.[16] Klytaimnéstra takes center stage as the real villain, the adulterous betrayer of her hus-band, only when the story is related to Odysseus by the shade of Agamémnon (XI.471–535), who extensively vilifies all women and explicitly warns Odysseus to take care, even of Penélopê—a warning that Odysseus clearly takes to heart, for he speaks of Agamémnon's fate to Athena soon after landing on Ithaka (XIII.472–85).

While it is up to Telémakhos (ultimately as his father's helper) to see that his part and that of the suitors coincide with the roles of Orestês and Aigísthos in the story of the Argive royal house, it is up to Penélopê to avoid becoming a second Klytaimnéstra.[17] This she does by remaining faithful to her absent husband and not giving in to any suitor. Indeed, she does more, whether consciously or not, by setting up the contest with Odysseus' bow at just the right moment. Only after the suitors' souls have borne report of the massacre in Odysseus' hall to the other dead (in which report Penélopê is presented as actively involved in the plot against the suitors) will Agamémnon bring to a close the cycle of comparisons between his own fate and that of Odysseus, with the ultimate glorification of Penélopê. She is glorious insofar as she is different from Klytaimnéstra. The limits of this praise in the mouth of a man are clear: despite Penélopê's avoidance of the Klytaimnéstrian model, it is still Klytaimnéstra who establishes (male) expectations of female behavior: "A bad name / she gave to womankind, even the best" (XXIV.227–28; see further my note on XXIV.226–28).

To the shade of Agamémnon in its first appearance, Odysseus had described a fatal link between "intrigues of women" and "both sons of Atreus," Meneláos and Agamémnon: "Myriads / died by Helen's fault, and Klytaimnéstra / plotted against you half the world away" (XI.508–12). The fateful and fraught relationship of Meneláos and Helen also serves as a foil to the relationship between Odysseus and Penélopê. In Book IV Homer presents Telémakhos visiting Meneláos and Helen reunited and once more at home, as Odysseus and Penélopê will be by the end of *The Odyssey*, but there is no simple parallel between the pairs.

In the case of the Spartan couple, man and woman alike required a homecoming, since, as we know, Helen's absence from Sparta was the origin of the entire Trojan War. (It is to this of course that

Odysseus' "Myriads died" refers.) In many ways, Helen's case is more like Odysseus' than Penélopê's—and such gender crossing is usually an indication that we should take special notice. Odysseus in *The Odyssey* has been away from Ithaka and Penélopê not just ten years, the time required for the Greeks to take Troy, but nearly twenty years, because he has been traveling ten years since Troy's fall. Helen was separated from her husband for about the same number of years, since some time—traditions vary—intervened between her departure from Sparta with Paris and the arrival of the Greeks to begin their ten-year siege of Troy. Furthermore, Meneláos did not bring Helen back from Troy directly; he had first to visit and make expiation in Egypt, a lengthy process.[18] Helen's foreign travels and erotic detentions, then, are strongly reminiscent of Odysseus' wanderings and dallyings; in neither case is it clear how much the will of each was involved. To complete the symmetry, while Meneláos sailed to Troy and fought there to regain his wife, in his dogged loyalty to his erring spouse he resembles Penélopê more than Odysseus.

The Agamémnon-Klytaimnéstra plot is contrasted with that of Odysseus and Penélopê at the level of dramatic action, while the comparison of the Spartan and Ithakan couples reveals differences in the inner workings of their relationships, as can be seen when we analyze the discordant anecdotes with which Helen and Meneláos regale their guests and from which a final set of uncanny symmetries and asymmetries among the quartet emerge. Helen and Meneláos each tell their guest a story about Odysseus from their time at Troy. Helen begins. She recounts the story of Odysseus' foray into Troy disguised as a beggar. She claims that, although she penetrated his disguise, she did not betray him. This episode, which at first blush might seem more appropriate for a version of *The Iliad* or some other segment of the cycle of the Trojan War, when placed in *The Odyssey* foreshadows Odysseus' disguising himself as a beggar to enter his own house. Helen's reference to her questioning him and his putting her off (IV.270) looks forward to Penélopê's interrogation of the beggar and Odysseus' clever verbal parrying in Book XIX. "I knew him" (IV.268), Helen says, and any comparison of her in this episode with Penélopê will raise the possibility that Odysseus' lady too had penetrated his disguise. (This remains a nagging question in interpretation of *The Odyssey;* see the Commentary on XIX.620–42, XIX.678–99, and XX.69ff.) Helen's anticipation of Book XIX continues, for, so she claims, she "bathed . . . and anointed him / . . . and swore an oath / not to give him away" (IV.271–73). This foreshadows the footbath Odysseus receives at Eurýkleia's hands, just out of Penélopê's earshot. (On the momentous importance of this bath, see pp. lxvii–lxix.)

"An excellent tale, my dear, and most becoming," responds Meneláos with no little irony (IV.287). Too refined to contradict her openly, Meneláos makes his point by telling a narrative in which Helen appears in a considerably more ambiguous light, and in which her behavior seems to give the lie to the pro-Greek stance Helen attributed to herself in her own story. Meneláos recounts a part of the episode of the Trojan horse, in particular the dicey moment when the Trojans, suspecting the truth, have Helen call out to the horse and imitate the voices of the wives of the Greek heroes in the hope that any soldier inside the horse would give the ruse away. Antiklos is on the verge of doing so, but Odysseus stifles him. Meneláos is presenting Telémakhos with a seductive Helen, parallel to Penélopê, potentially seductive throughout and openly seductive when, with the disguised Odysseus already in her house, and even if she herself doesn't fully understand why, she appears before the suitors in all her beauty and asks for their tributes (XVIII.200ff.). If the parallels and foreshadowings are less clear here, that may be the point. Penélopê is unambiguously unlike Klytaimnéstra—it is a simple ratio of opposites. Helen is a more complex and potentially more troubling model: like Helen, Penélopê has her hidden depths and surprises. Like Helen, she is not ultimately predictable. And if Odysseus foiled Helen when she tried to negate his ruse of the wooden horse by causing the Greek heroes to identify themselves to their "wives," Penélopê evens the score when, in Book XXIII, she tricks Odysseus into confirming his identity as her husband by means of another wooden artifact of his devising: their marriage bed.

MEMORY

I suggested that *The Odyssey* centers its treatment of the passage of time on the theme of fathers and sons, but even though the culture of Homer's time led him to display issues in terms of generations of *males,* there is no reason for us not to read *The Odyssey* as a poem more justly about generations, about memory and ideals, and about each generation growing into the ideals it claims to have inherited from its predecessors. As we know from our own century, memories, regrets, and ideals tend to crystallize around wars. Earthquakes and other disasters, however destructive, may punctuate the otherwise undifferentiable flow of time more neatly, but wars and other cataclysmic events of some duration (plagues, famines) seem to gather larger swatches of time into a bundle. It is said of certain countries that they suffer from an excess of history. Wars too seem to pull into their wake more than their share of history, as if time were passing by a vortex or black hole—the new Kharybdis of space—and bent toward it. What wars mean to those who fight them is one thing; *The Iliad* is the first and will ever be the supreme poem about war. Its presentation of the heat of battle, of death of comrades in combat, and of siege and sack ring true, say those who have experienced these things. Digging archeologically into recent response to *The Iliad,* we note that scholars, readers, and poets touched by the epic struggle of World War II have a special appreciation of *The Iliad*—earned at a terrible price.[19]

The Odyssey is set at a cooler pitch, representing a more domestic world, less tragic but no less subtle. As *The Iliad* presents—in the figures of Akhaians—Greeks at war and—in the figures of Trojans—Greeks at home, the first group ravaging and at the edge of order, the latter defending their home and city, a city still very much in order, *The Odyssey* presents the Greek man traveling and at home. In other words, *The Odyssey* is a postwar poem. If World War II is the war that most readily comes to mind to readers of the previous generation when they read *The Iliad,* for my generation (of Americans) *The Odyssey* speaks to many issues that seem to engage us in a society still obsessed with Vietnam and its aftermath. The post–Vietnam War era is doubly postwar: most obviously, the end of that conflict lies now some decades in the past, but, more subtly, that war was already post–World War II. However unjustly, the country constantly compares the two wars. In its own eyes, America emerged victorious over unambiguous evil in the first, but in the second it was forced to walk away from a conflict which was considerably more controversial. The debates that still swirl around our involvement in Vietnam, the wounds and losses still unhealed, sensitize us to a certain dimension of *The Odyssey* which addresses a similar issue, so that we would not be wrong in seeing *The Odyssey* as the quintessential postwar epic.

We can see Odysseus' challenge as that of readjustment to a civil society. Perhaps ten years of decompression is not so bad an idea; perhaps Agamémnon would have acted less arrogantly had he not come directly from the high command at Troy to Argos (not that this would necessarily have saved him from Aigísthos or Kassandra from Klytaimnéstra's ax). Returning veterans too need to become reacquainted with their country, which will have undergone its own development while the fighting forces were away. They need to reestablish contact with their spouses and parents, and often to establish contact with children for the first time. The emotions of those left behind also need to be addressed. Those (usually males) who are too young to have gone to the war or were otherwise unfit for military service need to deal with their diminished prestige. Telémakhos looks up to his heroic father. The suitors, by contrast, while they are not "protesters," are in the awkward position of seeking honor and glory in a sphere where it cannot be obtained, and for personal reasons it is not in their interest to remain ever subordinate to the absent Odysseus. Political candidates whose war records (or lack thereof) remain the subject of public debate will be sensitive to the feelings of all the Ithakans. I take it that the reason feelings run so high in every postwar generation is that all of us are haunted by the question: Would we have measured up?

The Odyssey, which literally brings Odysseus back from the dead after ten years, almost seems calculated to be the perfect story for our time, when stories about those missing in action fill the popular press. The poem offers a way of healing, both for those who come back and for their families. And there are many moments when we see *The Odyssey* healing wounds opened by *The Iliad*. Early on there is the magical, somewhat mysterious visit by Telémakhos to Mene-láos and Helen in Sparta. The woman whose abduction started the Trojan War is now back home, at her husband's side. Questions of guilt and responsibility are glanced at ever so slightly and always politely, and Helen herself administers a drug that can ease the suffering of memory. The action of retaking Odysseus' home offers roles for all those who stayed behind. Telémakhos, though too young to have participated in the Trojan War, can fight at his heroic father's side and win renown. Odysseus' loyal retainers can do the same. The suitors can fight but can hardly win glory; they missed their chance for recuperation into the postwar polity by pursuing the wife of the absent general. The final book of *The Odyssey* offers two moments of closure to this theme. First, in the second underworld scene, the dead from both conflicts (the one for Troy, the other for Odysseus' hall) meet. This is not a happy moment for the suitors' shades: they are condemned by the ghosts of the Trojan heroes to a perpetual belated status. But in the final skirmish, warriors from three generations can stand shoulder to shoulder, and Telémakhos is now not too late to join his father and his grandfather, the latter a veteran from an even earlier set of conflicts.

* * *

What about memory in the poem itself? The Muse, invoked at Book I.1, is, as repository of the community's memory and the acknowledged source of the bard's song, the guarantee that *The Odyssey* draws on and transmits communal truth. The Muse represents sung tradition itself and guides the epic singer in the right paths as he chooses elements from the vast ocean of memory and song.[20]

Along with the invocation to the Muse, which is the traditional appeal to and seal of memory, there are specific epic features woven deeply into the narrative pattern of *The Odyssey* which may be taken as metaphors for the interpenetration of past and present. A visit to the land of the dead and the ghosts of characters past appears in all epics in one form or another; it is the ultimate epic scene of commemoration. In *The Odyssey*, Odysseus evokes and addresses a select group of ghosts in Book XI, and the narrator takes us for a reprise in Book XXIV. It is the function of epic to memorialize the history of a people, and these "descents" to Hades keep the exploits of forebears alive. In such moments the poet records a supreme adventure of his hero and at the same time has him acknowledge the heroic achievements of predecessors. Previous heroes, such as Heraklês, Iason, or Akhilleus, were already the subject of song, and by including them in this way in his poem, the poet also keeps the older songs alive, adding his to their company. The fact that less famous forebears and their exploits are constantly evoked as examples for emulation (or avoidance) further keeps the past a living part of the present.

The Odyssey gives us another image of memory which is no epic commonplace, but one specific to hero and poem. In perhaps the most famous and oft-praised episode in *The Odyssey*,[21] the disguised Odysseus' identity is discovered and his own strategy put at risk when his old nurse Eurýkleia, washing his legs in the footbath Penélopê had ordered for the Cretan visitor, feels a scar on his thigh. She knows this scar, from the past, and it tells her that the man above her is the same man who left the house some twenty years before. Indeed, she knows this scar from a still more distant past, Odysseus' boyhood. Moving the narrative the way I have just described Eurýkleia's mind as moving, Homer leaps back from the moment of discovery, before the discovery becomes word, to the story of how Odysseus received the original wound: on a boar hunt on Parnassos when visiting his maternal grandparents.

A scar is the reminder and the remnant of a wound, and the individual marking of a body. Odysseus' scar as it is rubbed and recognized by his nurse provides Homer the opportunity not just to recall one incident in Odysseus' past but to return to the very roots of his name. For before fulfilling the narrative promise he has made by mentioning the hunting episode, Homer leaps to the time of Odysseus' naming, when Autólykos, Penélopê's father, was visiting Ithaka. Eurýkleia—the person holding Odysseus' leg over the wash-tub in the narrative present but perhaps forty or forty-five years younger—placed the baby on his grandfather's lap and is reported to have said, "It is for you . . . / to choose a name for him" (XIX.473–74). Drawing on his own experience of "odium and distrust" (XIX.480), Autólykos, via a wordplay, names his grandson Odysseus. (For the details, see notes on XIX.328, XIX.477–81, and XIX.480, the second for a possible additional wordplay involving the Greek for "wound.") As the process of naming described makes clear, one's name is meant as a sign of one's identity. One bears one's name as one bears a scar, sign of the original wound. Homer has created a wound in the narrative body of *The Odyssey*, so to speak, in order to go back to Odysseus' naming, the formative moment of his identity.

There is at least one more identifying characteristic of Odysseus—and the Odyssean Homer—to be discovered as we by reading rub our figurative hands back and forth over the textual wound. Before returning to the narrative present to describe Eurýkleia's and then Odysseus' reaction to this unexpected discovery, Homer's narrative moves to a detailed description of the boar hunt on which

the young prince received the wound. As soon as Odysseus arrives
back at Ithaka, so Homer tells us, his parents "[want] all the news /
of how he got his wound" (XIX.538–39). In what is biographically,
according to *The Odyssey*, Odysseus' earliest narrative, "he spun
out / his tale, recalling how the boar's white tusk / caught him when
he was hunting on Parnassos" (XIX.539–41). As much as odium, a
wound on the thigh, and the name "Odysseus" constitute the hero's
identity, so does his readiness to "spin out" memorable tales.

Interrupting the present to bring to light the past through tale-
telling is not only a characteristic trait of Odysseus: it is the task of
the epic singer in all his endeavors, and it is a defining characteristic
of the poet of *The Odyssey*, who has so constructed this work that
Books IX–XII constitute a similar but larger-scale narrative flash-
back. In these books, Homer's singing and Odysseus' recounting
voices are one. In telling tales, both singer and hero are meant to
be transmitting the past, thereby serving and preserving memory.
What is left open to doubt is how much of what is passed on as
"memory" is in fact invention. Odysseus is presented as a perenni-
ally lying narrator, most evidently in the series of tales in and by
which he first assumes a Cretan identity and then alters it in subse-
quent tellings. Who knows exactly when faithful memory stops and
exaggeration or even fabrication starts in the tale of exotic travels
that Odysseus told to the Phaiákians? Indeed, if Odysseus has al-
ways been Odysseus, how are we to be sure that what he told his
parents about the "boar's white tusk" was the unvarnished truth?

But the tale told as memory *is* memory. As such, it can grow and
change to meet the needs of the present, just as Odysseus' scar is
now an adult version of the scar that first formed over the original
wound. Written documentation not only kills the faculty of mem-
ory, as Plato's wise king pointed out, it also falsifies memory in two
senses: it can prove it false and, by holding it to a literal truth, can
render it less suitable for the present. For the present needs its own
past, and it is that past that the epic Muse always provides.

A FINAL WORD BEFORE READING

It is the business of Homeric scholars and literary critics to make
fine distinctions. Some scholars distinguish among multiple histori-
cal levels they have discovered in Homer's texts; others make a
distinction between an oral and a literate Homer, or between the
author of *The Iliad* and that of *The Odyssey*. As students and scholars
we can, and should, explore all the byways of the Homeric question.
As readers, however, it is our duty to be sure that we subordinate
the results of our study to our appreciation of the text before us.[22]
Whatever our views on the history of the poems' genesis, and
however often we may pause to observe the traces of that history in
the text, there are good reasons to read and interpret the text we
have as a whole.

Paradoxically, this seemingly ahistorical approach will replicate
at least in one important aspect the experience of Homer's first
audience. As we now understand the system of oral poetry, the
singer is always involved in re-creating the poem for his audience.
The singer believes he is singing it exactly as he did before, and as
others sang it before him, while the members of the audience
believe they are hearing it exactly as they and their forebears heard
it before (no matter if in the situations where modern scholars can
run tests, it is clear there have been extensive changes). No one
would say, "But this telling varies in this or that detail from the last
time I heard it," and no one could claim that "three generations ago
the story ran otherwise." Given our text-based overview of the
tradition, we might well be in a position to make such observations,
and as students of the tradition we must. As archeological readers,
we can discriminate among the various levels in the textual dig
before us. Reflection on the layering lets us read another, more than
Homeric text: the text of the tradition. Yet the final demand made
of the archeological reader is to put down his or her trowel and, with
knowledge, perceive that the most authentic and most Homeric way
to appreciate Homer is to believe that the teller of the tale now

before us *is* Homer, the only Homer, who tells the tale as it has always been told.

For readers of this English translation, Robert Fitzgerald is Homer, and *The Odyssey* has always been the Fitzgerald translation, just as, for readers of any other translation, in any language, that is their Homer, and they must believe that *The Odyssey* has always been that translation. That is the essence of the oral tradition, which has always incorporated into itself all previous stages and reintegrated them into a whole, no matter what anachronisms or apparent contradictions remain. As Homeric readers we can operate in like manner when faced with the tensions between early Greek concepts of the gods, justice, gender, age, war and peace on the one hand, and our own on the other. We can, indeed we must, endeavor to hold in our minds the entire former series, but such reconstructions are always grounded in our own contemporary judgments and perceptions. This tension, like the tension between one telling of the story and the next, or between the Greek *Odyssey* and any translation, ultimately becomes part of our *Odyssey*. One of the aims of the commentary which follows is to make that tension as productive as it can be.

NOTES

[1] W. B. Stanford, *The Ulysses Theme: A Study in the Adaptability of a Traditional Hero*, 2nd ed. (Oxford, 1963; rev. 1968).

[2] For a fuller account of this scene and this rather audacious argument, see Ralph Hexter, "What Was the Trojan Horse Made Of?: Interpreting Virgil's *Aeneid*," *Yale Journal of Criticism* 3.2 (Spring 1990), 109–31.

[3] Nikos Kazantzakis' *Odyssey* (1938), which Stanford discusses along with Joyce's *Ulysses* in *The Ulysses Theme*, pp. 211–40.

[4] (New York: Farrar, Straus & Giroux, 1990), p. 14.

[5] I have not mentioned representations of scenes and characters from *The Odyssey* in the visual arts. An interested reader might begin by consulting Appendix F in Stanford's *The Ulysses Theme*, pp. 324–27 (to which should be

added, for ancient representations, Odette Touchefeu-Meynier, *Thèmes odys-séens dans l'art antique* [Paris, 1968]).

6 There was one ancient testimony to Homer's "illiteracy": in the first century C.E., Josephus wrote, "They say that not even Homer left his poems behind in writing, but that they were transmitted by memorization, and put together [later] out of the songs, and that they therefore contain many inconsistencies" (*contra Apion* 1.2.12; trans. from A. Wace and F. Stubbings, 241). F. A. Wolf appealed to this, but many scholars remind us that Josephus is here and elsewhere involved in tendentious arguments: as a Hellenized Jewish historian writing in Greek, he was intent on establishing the superiority and authority of the Mosaic texts over Homer. Nonetheless, even though it is not possible to say how such (as we now believe accurate) information could have been transmitted to him, it would be rash to deny that Josephus' barb might reflect traditional information, or at least contemporary speculation. That it so runs against every other assumption of Hellenistic and late antique scholarship on Homer to my mind increases the possibility that it is not simply Josephus' invention. Of course, any unprejudiced reader of *The Iliad* or *The Odyssey*, noting the singing of Akhilleus in the former and the multiple bards in the latter, might conjecture that this was a picture of Homer's own creative mode. Whatever the truth of Josephus' testimony, it is significant that it was an eighteenth-century scholar who first picked up on it.

7 *L'Epithète traditionelle dans Homère: Essai sur un problème de style homérique* (Paris, 1928); English translation "The Traditional Epithet in Homer," in Milman Parry, *The Making of Homeric Verse: The Collected Papers of Milman Parry*, ed. Adam Parry (Oxford, 1971), pp. 1–190.

8 I do not address here the impact this process may be imagined to have had on the quality of the poetry, especially since it is considered rash to tender aesthetic judgment at all, much less of art formed over and for multiple generations in the distant past. On the one hand, given the banality of so much popular narrative, and so much poetry, today, we might well see the advantage of instituting a rule that nothing be permitted that has not been approved, without exception, by eight or ten successive generations of audiences. On the other hand, over the years strict classicism has fallen into bathos and banality as often and as drearily as original effusions. The difference may be that the elements of traditional poetry—episode, formula, simile—had to *appeal* to an audience, had to be popular, in the fullest sense of the word; pleasing the work's author or some academic rule was not enough.

9 For example, in *The Muse Learns to Write: Reflections on Orality and Literacy from Antiquity to the Present* (New Haven, 1986). More recently, Gregory Nagy has proposed that the particular achievements of Greek archaic poetry, from

Homer to Pindar, should be ascribed to a progressive "Panhellenization" of the repertory, in other words, to the establishment of a truly Greek canon, a process which took place largely under conditions of continued oral performance. " 'Homer' and 'Hesiod' are themselves the cumulative embodiment of this systematization . . . of values common to all Greeks . . .—the ultimate poetic response to Panhellenic audiences from the eighth century onward" ("Hesiod," in T. J. Luce, ed., *Ancient Writers,* vol. I [New York, 1982], 46). Nagy's highly persuasive thesis is worked out with great sophistication and immense learning in *Pindar's Homer: The Lyric Possession of an Epic Past* (Baltimore, 1990).

[10] Much later, in the nineteenth century, when the so-called "higher criticism" of the Bible divided the "Old Testament" into strands labeled J, E, P, and D, each reflecting and promoting a peculiar, or group, tendency, Homeric scholars went beyond separating the poet of *The Iliad* from that of *The Odyssey* to full-scale "analysis," whereby each epic was broken up into "lays" and, particularly as analysis developed through the nineteenth and into the twentieth century, a later redactor was posited to have created the version of *The Odyssey* we possess. The observations of the original analysts and today's neoanalysts have occasioned many important insights into the structure and texture of *The Odyssey.* This complex debate cannot be addressed in detail here, and it doesn't need to be, for "archeological reading" can accommodate analytical as well as unitarian accounts of the creation of *The Odyssey.*

[11] Bernard Knox's "Introduction" to Homer, *The Iliad,* tr. Robert Fagles (New York: Viking Penguin, 1990), p. 44.

[12] If, as Gregory Nagy has argued, above all in *The Best of the Achaeans: Concepts of the Hero in Archaic Greek Poetry* (Baltimore, 1979), the stories of *The Iliad* (the wrath of Akhilleus) and *The Odyssey* (Odysseus' homecoming) were traditional choices for bards before the particular textual incarnations that have come down to us, then it is possible to speak not only of *The Odyssey* as post-Iliadic but of *The Iliad* as post-Odyssean. Some of the interpretive ramifications of this paradoxical state have been developed by Pietro Pucci in *Odysseus Polutropos: Intertextual Readings in the Odyssey and the Iliad* (Ithaca, 1987).

   The Iliad and *The Odyssey* are reciprocally allusive creations of one poet according to George Goold, who argues that Homer himself wrote down his verses and inserted successive additions to fixed texts of both epics over the course of his career. Goold explains the contradictions and evident joins in each poem by claiming that, since writing at this time was so laborious, Homer regarded what he had once written as unalterable: he frequently added material, even to earlier additions, but refused to cut or revise what he had once fixed in letters ("The Nature of Homeric Composition," *Illinois*

Classical Studies 2 [1977] 1–34; see esp. 17 on the difficulty of writing). Most scholars have not embraced this view, however novel; they continue to focus on successive oral performances as the context for the gradual concretization of the poems. Once the poems began to be textualized, by whomever, some of what Goold describes may have occurred. The extreme reverence to words once written strikes me as characteristic of an epigone, not an original creator, no matter how hard the physical procedure of writing. But perhaps that is only a modern prejudice. The question of who Homer was remains.

13 Traces of different stages in the historical development of the Greek language, as well as dialectal variants, likewise coexist in the epic idiom, making it in some sense the idiom of no one particular time or place. (The details can, obviously, only be discussed with reference to the text in the original language.)

14 It is clear that by blinding Polyphêmos, the son of Poseidon, Odysseus earns the sea god's enmity. This is the only offense against a god on Odysseus' part so marked in the poem, and it becomes a crucial element in his life. Even after his return, he will have to go on a pilgrimage to make amends; only then, as Teirêsias informs him, will Poseidon be satisfied. Poseidon, a backer of Troy in *The Iliad*, was hardly likely to be well-disposed to Odysseus to start with. There were also the offenses that Odysseus committed at Troy, above all, the theft of the Palladium during the sack of the city, considered significant for *The Odyssey* by Jenny Strauss Clay in *The Wrath of Athena: Gods and Men in the Odyssey* (Princeton, 1983), a fascinating if unconventional reading of the poem. Odysseus would have been a well-known figure to audiences hearing *The Odyssey* for the first time, and not just from previous versions of his homecoming: he was made the subject of *The Odyssey* because he had a prehistory and stood for something. These other stories are always hovering around our Odysseus like a narrative penumbra, but it is still worth noting that Poseidon's wrath, not Athena's, is thematized in *The Odyssey*.

15 Sheila Murnaghan makes the further, subtle observation: "Telemachus' reunion with Odysseus is the culminating moment of Telemachus' growth to a point where he no longer needs Odysseus' return" (*Disguise and Recognition in the Odyssey* [Princeton, 1987], p. 37).

16 Presentations of the example to Telémakhos which follow the one quoted are those by Nestor (III.208–17 and III.328–37), by Athena disguised as Mentor (III.250–54—she had assumed the form of Mentês the first time), and by Proteus, whose account is narrated by Meneláos (IV.554–73). That Orestês also killed his mother is mentioned in only one of these accounts, and then merely in passing (III.335–36).

[17] Marylin Arthur Katz reminds us that the etymology of "Klytaimnéstra"—
"renowned for being wooed"—would fit Penélopê as well or better (*Penelope's Renown*, p. 45, citing the insight of K. Kunst, "Die Schuld der Klytaimnestra," *Wiener Studien* 44 [1924–25], 18–32, 143–54, here p. 26). Actually, both Helen and Penélopê are more famous than Klytaimnéstra for being wooed if fame is measured in the number of wooers. The pact among the suitors of Helen (1) to abide by her choice and (2) to come to her husband's aid if she is ever abducted is presented elsewhere in Greek legend among the necessary preconditions for the Trojan War; tradition has it that this pact was suggested by none other than Odysseus. Helen succumbed to Paris' blandishments, and Klytaimnéstra to Aigísthos'. It is Penélopê alone who in the face of a great number of suitors prevents their success at wooing. From the man's point of view, a good woman can only succeed at being wooed by permitting successful wooing to one man.

[18] According to *The Odyssey* this took some seven years. An alternate tradition would eventually develop that after the sack of Troy, Meneláos didn't simply regain Helen. According to this plot, the Helen at Troy turned out to have been a wraith, while the "real" Helen had long since been wafted to Egypt, where Meneláos had to go rescue her. See, for example, Euripides' *Helen*.

[19] For a superb example, see Bernard Knox's "Introduction" to *The Iliad*, especially pp. 23–43.

[20] For a recent highly intelligent and suggestive study, see Andrew Ford, *Homer: The Poetry of the Past* (Ithaca, 1992). On these "paths," see Commentary, Book VIII. 79–80.

[21] The episode (XIX.451–552) was known as "the bath" or "the bathing" *(ta Niptra)* in antiquity. One of the most famous modern analyses constitutes the first chapter ("Odysseus' Scar") of Erich Auerbach, *Mimesis: The Representation of Reality in Western Literature*, tr. Willard R. Trask (Princeton, 1953), pp. 3–23, although later scholars would be rather more hesitant in drawing the global distinctions between Homeric and Biblical narrative styles that Auerbach does in his nonetheless stimulating discussion.

[22] I intend this pose as "learned" rather than "willed ignorance," but those who see it as the latter might do well to recall the Greek sophist Gorgias' insight that people who willingly permit themselves to be deceived by literary fictions are wiser than those who resist the deception.

CHRONOLOGY

Homer	Greece/Aegean	Egypt/Near East
	Neolithic (from ca. 7000)	
	3300: Early Bronze Age	3400: First Dynasty
	Early Minoan	Early Dynastic
	3000–2600: Troy I	Giza Pyramids and Sphinx constructed
	2600–2300: Troy II	
	2300–2200: Troy III	Hyksos rule in Egypt, 2200–1700
	2200–2050: Troy IV	
	2050–1900: Troy V	
Linear A	Middle Minoan	Twelfth Dynasty
	1900–1340: Troy VI	ca. 1800: Hammurabi
	Crete, Aegean, and parts of mainland Greece controlled by Hyksos Egypt	Hittites conquer Babylon
	1800s: shaft graves at Mycenae	Eighteenth Dynasty
	Late Minoan / Late Helladic	ca. 1550: Hyksos expelled from Egypt
	1628: Thera erupts	

All dates down to ca. 600 B.C.E. are approximate. Most before 1000 B.C.E. are controversial. They are included here to suggest to readers the general pattern of cultural exchange only.

Homer	Greece/Aegean	Egypt/Near East
Linear B (Greek) 1250–1170: Range of traditional dates for the Fall of Troy 1220–1210: Seige and sack of Troy VIIa	ca. 1400: Destruction of Knossos Mycenaean control of Crete 1340–1210: Troy VIIa ca. 1150: Dorian invasion Iron Age 1150–800: so-called "Dark Age of Greece"	1419–1381: Amenhotep III Israelites leave Egypt 1200: Twentieth Dynasty decline in Egyptian power begins ca. 1190: Sea Peoples invade Egypt
Stories of Troy and other legends sung by oral poets 750–700: *The Iliad* and *The Odyssey* after 700: *Homeridae,* rhapsodes after 600: Greek in alphabetic script common; literacy rare	800: Greeks settle on Southern Italy (including Sicily) and coast of Spain 778: First Olympiad 753: traditional date for founding of Rome 561–527: Pisistratus in power in Athens	1000–960: Rule of David in Judah and Israel 9th century: Phoenicians found Carthage 700ff.: Assyrians destroy Babylon, Memphis, Thebes 553–29: Cyrus II forms Persian Empire

1500 B.C.E.

1000 B.C.E.

Homer	Greece/Rome	Egypt/Near East

500–300 B.C.E.

Homer	Greece/Rome	Egypt/Near East
424–14: First evidence of reading for pleasure and book trade at Athens 403/2: Alphabet change in Athens ca. 390: Plato's *Ion* 360–35: Aristotle's *Poetics* late 4th century: Zoïlus, harsh critic of Homer	490–49: Persian Wars 443: Pericles elected Athenian general 431–04: Peloponnesian War 356–23: Alexander the Great	485–65: Xerxes I 458: Ezra to Jerusalem 30th Dynasty: last native house to rule Egypt

300–0 B.C.E.

Homer	Greece/Rome	Egypt/Near East
284: Zenodotus of Ephesus, first director of the library at Alexandria ca. 217–145: Aristarchus, important Homeric scholar 195–180: Aristophanes of Byzantium, chief of library at Alexandria from 150: Vulgate text in circulation 1st century: Aristonicus and Didymus	275: Rome defeats Pyrrhos of Epeiros 264–41: First Punic War 219–01: Second Punic War (Hannibal) 200–197: Romans in Attica; defeat of Philip V of Macedon 149–46: Third Punic War; Carthage defeated 44: Death of Julius Caesar	247–21: Ptolemy III Euergetes 31: Battle of Actium: Octavian (future Augustus) defeats Mark Antony and Cleopatra VII 6: Rome annexes Judaea

Homerica

0 TO 1500 C.E.

ca. 96: Josephus, *Contra Apion*

2nd century: Herodian and Nicanor

After 100: papyrus rolls copied onto papyrus codices

After 300: papyrus codices copied onto parchment codices

9th century: Codices in capitals and uncials copied into minuscule script; compilation of the "Four-man commentary" (Didymus, Aristonicus, Herodian, and Nicanor), the basis of the A scholia

ca. 863–932: Photios' student Arethas of Patrae

10th–11th century: Florence, Laurentianus 32.34, ms. of *The Odyssey* (G)

11th century: Venice, Marcianus 453, commented ms. of *The Iliad* (B; now "Venetus Graecus 821"), and Florence, Laurentianus conv. soppr. 52, ms. of *The Odyssey* (F)

ca. 1110–ca. 1180: John Tzetzes and Eustathius of Thessalonica

12th century: Venice, Marcianus 454, commented ms. of *The Iliad* (A; now "Venetus Graecus 822")

1201–1202: Heidelberg, Palatinus 45, commented ms. of *The Odyssey*

1204–1261: Crusaders sack and occupy Constantinople, establish Latin Empire

ca. 1260–ca. 1332: Maximus Planudes, Manuel Moschopoulos, Thomas Magister

1453: Turks sack Constantinople

1488: Demetrius Chalcondylas prepares and Demetrius Damilas prints first editions of *The Iliad* and *The Odyssey* in Florence (see Figure 10)

Homerica

1598–1616: George Chapman publishes translation of *The Iliad* and *The Odyssey*

1664: François Hédelin, abbé d'Aubignac, *Conjectures académiques ou dissertation sur l'Iliade*

1713–32: Richard Bentley posits the working of the digamma in Homeric metrics (published 1732)

1715–26: Alexander Pope's translations of *The Iliad* and *The Odyssey*

1767–69: James Woods, *Essay on the Original Genius and Writings of Homer*

1788: J. B. G. d'Ansse de Villoison publishes text of the A ms. of *The Iliad* along with the scholia of mss. A and B

1795: F. A. Wolf, *Prolegomena ad Homerum I*

1837–41: Karl Lachmann delivers and first publishes *Betrachtungen über Homers Ilias*

1871–1890: Heinrich Schliemann excavates in mainland Greece and in the Troad

1893–94: Wilhelm Dörpfeld uncovers Troy VI

1900: Sir Arthur Evans discovers at Knossos large numbers of clay tablets in the script known as Linear B

1928: Milman Parry's thesis "The Traditional Epithet in Homer"

June 1952: Michael Ventris concludes that the language of the Linear B tablets is Greek

1956: M. Ventris and J. Chadwick, *Documents in Mycenaean Greek*

MAP AND
ILLUSTRATIONS

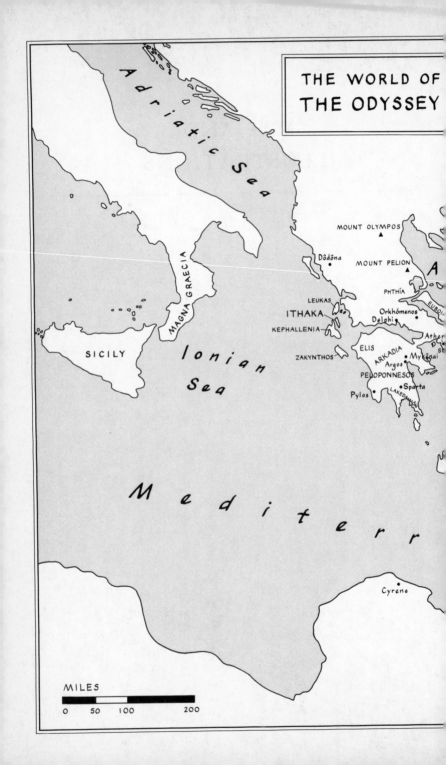

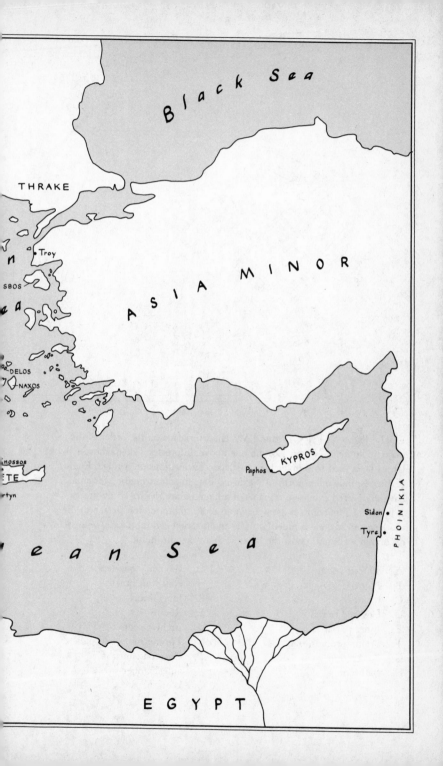

2. The Palace at Pylos. A grand Mycenaean palace on the order of the majestic home of Nestor, like the one above, impresses Telémakhos in Book III, as he is used to simpler life on Ithaka. Excavations on a ridge, Epano Englianos, four miles north of Navarino Bay, in southwestern Messenia, have uncovered extensive remains of a large palace destroyed by fire ca. 1200 B.C.E. The complex grew from an older, more modest palace to the southwest to include a much grander multistoried central palace, with richly decorated walls and floor, the latter with an octopus motif.

A.	Throne room	J–L.	Women's quarters
B.	Portico	J.	Hall with hearth
C.	Court	K.	Inner court
D.	Covered porch	L.	Rooms
E.	Inner porch	M.	Archive room
F.	Waiting rooms, pantries	N.	Throne room, old palace
G.	Storerooms	P.	Covered court or
H.	Bathroom		antechamber
		Q.	Workshops

3. The Homeric ship. A: Mast. B: Yard. C: Sail. D: Braces. E: Sheets.
F: Forestays. G: Pulley-hole and halyard. H: Backstay. I: Rudder-oar.
J: Stem. K: Half-decks.

4. This depiction of Odysseus' escape from Polyphêmos' cave graced a
proto-Attic wine vase painted ca. 675–600 B.C.E. by a stylist so distinctive
that art historians call him or her the "Painter of the Ram Jug." The
illustration is a loose interpretation of the episode (Book IX.463–505) where
Odysseus ties each of his men beneath the middle of three rams while he
clings to the fleece, not the horns, of the largest ram.

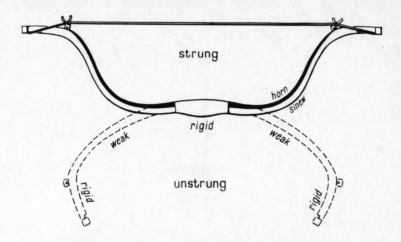

strung

horn
sinew

rigid

weak   weak

rigid

rigid

unstrung

5. A bow like Odysseus' prized hunting bow which Penélopê uses to test the suitors. The amount of tension on the bowstring made it a powerful and effective weapon, and a hard one to string. The suitors fail, but Odysseus has the requisite knowledge, strength, and dexterity. On the peculiarities of this double-torsion composite bow and the trick one needs to know to string it, see the note on Book XXI.12.

6. A fifth-century coin from Thebes shows how an archer is to string the double-torsion bow. Whether sitting (like Odysseus) or crouching (as here), one pushes the bow against the heel of the foot planted behind on the ground. Only in that way can one muster sufficient force to bend the composite bow far enough to get the string around the upper end.

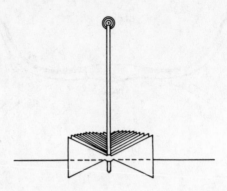

7. This is one possible arrangement of the axe heads through which Odysseus sends his prize-winning shot. Debate continues about the precise arrangement Homer intended us to imagine (see the note on XXI.132–37). One solution, depicted above, envisages Minoan/Mycenaean cult axes with rings at the bases of their handles by which they could be hung up and displayed. In this case, the prize shot would pass through the series of rings at the top of the inverted axes.

8. A second argument has the axe heads fixed in the ground. The challenge is to shoot through the series of holes in the axe heads into which handles would normally be fitted. This is the image that Fitzgerald presents in his translation ("iron axe-helve sockets," XXI.80, and "socket ring(s)," XXI.137 and 483). Visible is the earthen ridge that Telémakhos forms "to hold the blades half-bedded" (XII.134–35). In either case a successful archer would have to be seated, as Odysseus is (XXI.480).

9. This fragment from an early vellum book of the late third or fourth century C.E. displays Book XV.189–210 of *The Odyssey* (corresponding to XV.235–60 in Fitzgerald's translation; on its back are XV.161–81, XV.198–225 in English). Since the oldest extant complete manuscript of the epic dates from the tenth or eleventh century, earlier fragments can give us insight into the history of the text. This fragment exhibits the standardized or vulgate text that was well established by ca. 150 B.C.E. Greco-Roman booksellers, like their later cousins, wished to purvey the most authoritative and popular text.

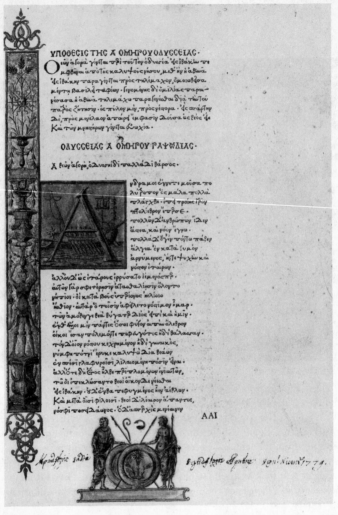

10. A page from the *Editio princeps* (1488), the first printed edition of *The Odyssey* (the original is 12¾ inches high). The Greek text (lines I.1–32 in Fitzgerald's translation) begins with the large initial alpha—the *A* of *andra*, man—which a calligrapher filled in after the book was printed. This artist also decorated the left and lower margins and inscribed the capital O at the top of the page that begins the *hypothesis*: a summary of Book I of *The Odyssey*. Calligraphic initial capitals (majuscules) were among the features of medieval manuscripts preserved in the earliest printed books.

COMMENTARY

A Goddess Intervenes

1 **Sing in me, Muse:** The poet asks the collective cultural memory to sing through him, even breathe into him [*ennepe,* 1]. The Muse, or Muses (on the number of Muses, see XXIV.68, below) are the daughters of Zeus (see I.17, or *Iliad* II.491). Hesiod, Homer's near contemporary—chronological certainty is not possible, but Hesiod (c. 700 B.C.E.) clearly knew the Homeric poems and can thus be placed later than Homer—names Mnêmosynê, "Memory," as the mother (*Theogony* 54). Such divine genealogies provided Greek thinkers a way of expressing the close connections of ideas and attributes. (For a mortal example, see I.142ff., below.) The Muse guarantees that what the bard relates is true memory (on "Memory" and epic, see Introduction, p. lxvi).

Note: Line numbers before each entry and in cross-references refer to the line numbers of Fitzgerald's translation. "Above" or "below" following book and line numbers indicate references to a comment on those lines within this guide.

All references to *The Iliad* indicate line numbers in the original Greek. References to the lines of the Greek text of *The Odyssey* are always placed

For a comparison of this prologue or proem and that of *The Iliad*, with which it has much in common, see West (HWH I.67–69).

2 **skilled in all ways of contending** represents one of the most important epithets of Odysseus, in Greek *polytropos* [1], which means "versatile," "with many twists and turns." This is the first of a veritable family of *poly-* epithets, bound together in the Greek by the shared first element, *poly-*, "many–." Though English has a few such phrases ("many-splendored"), Fitzgerald rightly does not attempt to create a comparably recognizable series in his translation, preferring variety and above all what seems to fit best in the immediate context. When *polytropos* appears next, it is as "O great contender" (X.371 [330]).

The most frequent *poly-* epithets for Odysseus are *polytlas*, "much enduring" (Fitzgerald's "For all he had endured," V.181 [171]), *polymêkhanos*, "much conniving" ("versatile," V.212 [203]), and *polymêtis*, "with many wiles" ("the strategist," V.223 [214]; see also XIX.65, below). Both aspects—Odysseus' creative cunning and his manifold misfortunes—are reflected in the less frequent *poly-* compounds connected with him. Both his nurse ("in his craftiness," XXIII.85 [*polyïdreiêisi*, 77]) and one of the suitors (XXIV.187 [*polykerdeiêisin*, 167]) highlight his wiliness, as does the narrator (XIII.324–25 [*polykerdea*, 255]). Athena will shortly refer to him as "wise" (I.108 [*polyphrona*, 83]).

Odysseus is made to use *poly-* compounds when he refers to his suffering: twice he refers to his *polykêdea noston*, "homeward journey involving pains of all sorts" (to the Phaiákians, IX.41–43

---

between square brackets. I generally cite the Greek words in their inflected form, as they appear in Homer. Readers without Greek should be aware that they are not necessarily the base forms. For readers with Greek, the two major commentaries in English on *The Odyssey* are Alfred Heubeck, et al., *A Commentary on Homer's Odyssey*, 3 vols. (Oxford: Oxford University Press, 1988, 1989, and 1992); and W. B. Stanford, *The Odyssey of Homer*, 2 vols. (London: Macmillan, 1958, 1959). For full citations of other works, see Bibliography herein.

[37], to Penélopê, XXIII.398–99 [351]) and yet another *poly*-compound is behind the words "My heart is sore" that Odysseus, now disguised as a wayfaring Kretan noble, utters to Penélopê (XIX.141 [*polystonos*, 118]). Another member of this *poly*- system is the octopus to which Odysseus is compared (see V.451, below).

Flexibility, adaptability, and trickiness belong to the core of Odysseus' being, as *The Odyssey* shows at every turn (see, for example, XXIII.149–58, below). The first time the narrator (as opposed to a speaker) mentions Odysseus in *The Iliad*, it is with the epithet *polymêtis* (*Iliad* I.311). On the all-important characteristic of mêtis, "cunning intelligence," see IX.394, XX.21, and XXIII.142, below; also M. Detienne and J.-P. Vernant, *Cunning Intelligence in Greek Culture and Society* (cited in the Bibliography, below).

4–5 **after he plundered . . . Troy:** Odysseus, in large measure thanks to his wiliness—the ruse of Trojan horse was his idea (see VIII.84–85, below)—was indeed the key to Greek victory. While not the equal of Akhilleus or Aias in pure killing power, he was a formidable soldier. However, no one could equal him in those qualities which are as valuable at home and in peace as in combat: persuasion and strategy.

7 **learned the minds of many distant men:** In fact, of many different *people* [*anthrôpôn*, 3]. On this aspect of Odysseus' character, see IX.184ff. and XII.193, below.

10–12 **shipmates . . . :** None of Odysseus' shipmates [*hetairoi*] will return. In the proem, Homer emphasizes Odysseus' attempts to save them from their own folly, especially marked in the episode highlighted here (13–16) when they killed and ate of the sun god's sacred cattle (XII.339–555). But many were already lost in other gruesome ways (so claims Odysseus' narrative that begins in Book IX). In fact, Eurýlokhos accuses Odysseus of having caused the deaths of some by just the sort of "recklessness" described here ("foolishness," X.484). On Vergil's implicit critique of Odysseus' irresponsibility, see Introduction, p. xx.

13 **children and fools:** One word in Greek [*nêpioi,* 8], and entirely negative in connotation here (see also XIII. 300–317, below: "great booby," XIII.302). For a striking instance of cultural transvaluation, contrast a considerably later Greek writer's use of the same word: St. Paul's "babes in Christ" (I Cor. 3.1). Long before Paul, Greek writers were marking their distance from Homer by employing words familiar from his texts—for Homer was the staple of Greek education for more than a millennium—in new ways.

13, 39–41 Homeric figures, both gods and humans, take pleasure in feasting, which is one of the central images of the poem as it was a central institution of Homeric society. The feast is a social event, ideally a symbol of harmony, not only among humans but, if the sacrificial ceremonies have been properly observed, between gods and men. However, like all rites, it can be perverted. The theme of eating is remarkably prominent in *The Odyssey,* both good (the meal in Eumaios' hut), and more frequently bad (e.g., monstrous cannibalism, Odysseus' crew's eating of Hêlios' herd, and the suitors' gorging themselves in Odysseus' home on his substance).

16 **The dawn of their return:** The translator waxes slightly poetic to mark the end of his verse paragraph. Homer merely says, "he [*Hêlios*] took away the day of their homecoming" [9]. Which is not to say that Homer is unpoetic, and surely not as prosaic as my literal translation might suggest. He achieves his effects over the longer stretches, that the rhythmic roll of dactylic hexameters makes possible.

17 **Muse, Daughter of Zeus:** See 1, above.

18 **us:** Not just the poet but the audience as well.

19 **Begin:** On the issue of starting points and narrative order, traditional in epic proems, see IX.14–15, below.

19–21 **all the rest . . . :** The other surviving Greeks, most prominently Agamémnon, Nestor, and Meneláos. *The Odyssey* places Odysseus' homecoming [*nostos*] alongside the homecomings of the other Greeks. Indeed, one may regard it as a study in comparative homecomings, in which Odysseus', though the most difficult and longest delayed, is in the end the best. Agamémnon of course reached home only to die at once (see the Introduction, pp. lix–lxi, for extensive comparisons of the two families). We will see Nestor and Meneláos at home in Books III and IV, respectively, and each will relate his own homeward journey and news of others'.

The *Nostoi* belonged to the "epic cycle," a cumulative collection of lesser epic accounts of the entire Trojan War, including the lead-up to it and its aftermath. These poems are extant today only in fragments and summaries. Even in their own day, the two Homeric poems were recognized as the jewels in the cyclic crown; the others were but fretwork.

22 **home and wife:** The winning or regaining of these two characterizes roughly the first and second halves of the poem, respectively. Odysseus places his feet on Ithaka once again at the beginning of Book XIII, and is fully reunited with Penélopê in Book XXIII, the penultimate book of the epic.

28 **ordained for him:** For the conception of fate, see Introduction, pp. l–li. The verb used here draws on the metaphorics of spinning [*epeklôsanto,* "assigned to by spinning," 17]. For the fates, *Moirai,* as spinners, see VII.212, below.

29–30 These lines foreshadow the second half of *The Odyssey,* after Odysseus lands in Ithaka. His is a story not merely of travels in exotic regions and adventures beyond human experience—that justly famous section in fact only occupies Books IX–XII—but more deeply of reintegration, of homecoming. He must not only arrive on the shore of Ithaka but also become a father to a son he has never seen and win back his wife—which in turn involves besting the suitors as well as regaining her trust. Finally he must restore order to Ithakan society, which is on the verge of civil war after he massacres the suitors. As yet, however, there is no mention of the suitors; "trials and dangers" are unspecified.

31–34 **all but Poseidon:** Homer refers to the wrath of Poseidon directed at Odysseus but does not explain the reason for it at this point. It may well have been traditional, in which case the audience would have understood the reference. If not, they would only have to wait until line 92 to find out. Without pre-Homeric texts, we simply cannot say with absolute certainty when Homer was following or adapting tradition and when he was effecting a major innovation.

36 **the sunburnt races:** Fitzgerald quite properly translates Homer's "Ethiopians," whose name in Greek [*Aithiopas*, 23] means "burnt" or "swarthy faces" [*aith-* + *ops*]. According to legend, it is their proximity to the rising and setting sun (37–38) that has rendered them sunburnt, although, as with most such explanatory accounts, we cannot determine whether the name was applied after the story was told or the story was created to explain the name. The same word *aithôn* means "brown" and is referred to iron in I.227 [*aithônan*, 184], where, following an older interpretation, Fitzgerald has translated it as "bright" (see XXII.7, below). In support of the reference to iron, scholars point to the Greek linking of dark, sunburned skin to manly prowess— those who spend much time in the Mediterranean sun become dark. There is thus nothing negative about the "sunburned" or "brown faces" of the Ethiopians here. (See also XIX.290–91, below.) Zeus likewise absents himself from Olympos to visit the Ethiopians at *Iliad* I.423–24, but all the gods follow him.

42ff. **In the bright hall of Zeus on Olympos . . . :** Although the first audience of *The Odyssey* could not be aware of it at this point, this council of the gods begins a transition to the so-called Telemachy or Telémakhos episode (Books I–IV). Analyst scholars (see Introduction, p. xlii) have argued that in an earlier, in their view original, version of *The Odyssey*, the poet moved directly from the proem to the divine council with which Book V now begins. Certainly one could imagine a poet, earlier or later, singing a version which begins from the point Zeus sends Hermês to order Kalypso to release Odysseus (Book V.1–154 in our "monumental" version).

Our poet, however, is preparing the shift of focus to Telémakhos from the very start. Zeus is presented as meditating on the justice Orestês meted out to Aigísthos (45–46), and it is Orestês' position Telémakhos holds in the frequent comparisons of the two families and whose shoes he is repeatedly encouraged to fill (see Introduction, pp. lx–lxi). In the text it is Athena whom Homer presents as speaking to shift Zeus' mind from Agamémnon's murderer, himself in turn murdered, to Odysseus (64–84). Zeus claims he has not forgotten him, but Poseidon has caused delays (86–104). Zeus is willing to entertain discussion now so "that he may sail" (102), but again it is Athena who takes the disposition of affairs into her own hands. Athena cuts short any lengthy discussion suggested in line 101 [*periphrazômetha pantes*, "let us all carefully consider," 76] by proposing that Zeus send Hermês to Kalypso with orders to let Odysseus depart (108–12, with a polite nod to the other gods in 107). It is this request that Zeus will grant at V.32–47, although at that point Athena will have expressed primary concern for Telémakhos' safety (V.9–22, another arrow in the analysts' quiver; see V.9–14, below). In Book I, however, Athena doesn't even give Zeus a chance to act on her proposal before saying that she will go to Ithaka and send Telémakhos on a voyage of inquiry (113–22).

Homer makes Athena do whatever he wants, and he wants her to move the focus onto Telémakhos. It is interesting that the poet presents the goddess so forcefully, as almost willfully stagemanaging the affairs of the gods as Odysseus will in *The Odyssey* the affairs of men—and as Homer does throughout the epic on the level of narrative economy. What Athena and her protégé Odysseus have in common is often stressed (see 63, below). She loves the hero's wiliness, his strategizing, his prudence.

These are all traits long observed and admired in the work of the author of *The Odyssey*. Goddess, hero, poet—they make a formidable trio.

44 **the father of gods and men:** A frequently used formula. Zeus' primacy over the other gods was, according to myth, not original (much less eternal) but hard-won (see 64, below, on his overthrow of his father/predecessor). And the very person of Akhilleus, hero of the *The Iliad*, serves to remind us that Zeus' power is not certain to remain forever: Having heard the prophecy that the son of Thetis would be stronger than his father, Zeus abandoned his suit of Thetis and ceded her to the mortal Peleus.

For all the jockeying for power and battles that went on, at any one time a single male god typically presided over each of the ancient Near Eastern pantheons.

45–46 At many points through *The Odyssey*, the story of Odysseus' homecoming is contrasted with that of Agamémnon. (See Introduction, pp. lix*ff.*, and I.19–21, above.) Agamémnon's wife, the here unmentioned Klytaimnéstra, is a counterexample to the faithful Penélopê. Highlighted here, at the beginning of four books focusing on Telémakhos, is the son of Agamémnon and Klytaimnéstra, Orestês. He is the ultimate avenger of his father's murder at the hands of Klytaimnéstra's lover, Aigísthos, and he is held up as the model of a son who has matured and taken charge of his absent father's house. Fortunately, the parallels are not complete: Odysseus is not dead, although that appears likely to the Ithakans at home. In Aigísthos we have a figure who represents Penélopê's suitors; again, fortunately, none of the suitors is successful and thus in a place to challenge her husband upon his return. But the point of counterexamples is just this: to provide a basis against which to measure the distances. The disastrous story of Agamémnon looms, from the first book to the last, as the nightmare homecoming into which Odysseus' story might develop.

48–62 Zeus defends himself and his fellow gods. They gave warnings, but Aigísthos in his folly ignored them. Throughout *The Odyssey*, the pious characters (Odysseus, Telémakhos, Penélopê) will take heed of divine portents and direct advice, while the impious (the suitors) will not. Like Aigísthos, the suitors will be destroyed.

In *Paradise Lost*, the poet takes on the task of defending divine justice (a "theodicy," as it is later termed), which Homer puts in a god's mouth here. Milton concludes his proem with the prayer, "That . . . / I may assert Eternal Providence / And justify the ways of God to men" (I.24–26).

50 **folly:** The same word in Greek [*atasthaliêisin*, 34] which lies behind "recklessness" (I.12[7]) and the "foolishness" of X.484 [433]. See 10–12, above.

51–52 **double . . . in the lot of man, double portion:** The Greek behind both phrases is *huper moron* [34, 35], literally, "above" or "beyond one's fate"; a common English idiom roughly equivalent is "before one's time." Fitzgerald is right in his rendering to avoid the literal, because the Greeks certainly did not muse on the workings of fate every time they heard this common expression, much less ask themselves, "What is *moros* (commonly translated 'fate' or 'doom') if things that are not fated or are beyond fate can happen?" (On fate and the "fates" see Introduction, pp. l–li, I.28, above, and VII.212, below).

53 **Agamémnon's wife:** Klytaimnéstra remains unnamed until III.285 [266]. For "wife" here, Homer has the phrase *alokhon mnêstên* [36], "lawfully wedded wife" or, even more literally, "successfully wooed bedmate." There are interesting overtones to this collocation. She is his legitimate consort—just as she is *not* Aigísthos' legitimate wife (and as any number of captives, among them Kassandra, are not Agamémnon's legitimate wives). *Mnêst-* is of course a significant component of Klytaimnéstra's name; on her "fame for being wooed"—and the contrast both her name and *mnêstên* would spark with Penélopê, so famously wooed in *The Odyssey* (the suitors are *mnêstêres*)—see Introduction, note 17. On *alokhon*, "bedmate," see XXII.480, below.

56 **Argeiphontês:** See under Hermês in Who's Who.

59 **Orestês:** Homer says, "Orestês, son of the son of Atreus" [40], reminding listeners that the history of enmity in this family goes back several generations (see XI.506–12, below, and the entries for Aigísthos, Atreus, and Thyestês in Who's Who).

63 The goddess Athena is throughout the epic the "special friend" and sponsor of Odysseus (see 42ff., above, and XIII.239–43, below, indeed the whole first scene back on Ithaka).

64 Homer's Athena uses the patronymic "son of Kronos" [45] for Zeus. While entirely conventional, it is also a sly reminder that his own lineage—and ascension—involved intrafamilial violence. The "father of gods" was himself a son who had to supersede his father to gain power. Telémakhos is often referred to as Odysseus' son, and Odysseus, though less frequently, as the son of Laërtês (e.g., V.212). On generations, particularly of males, see Introduction, pp. lv–lvi.

67–68 **is broken for the master mind of war:** Here in the Greek Homer plays with the sound of the words [*daiphroni daietai*, 48]. Alliteration is but one of the many strings to Homer's musical-poetic lyre.

80 **that he longs to die:** This is strong and marks the difference between the mortals and immortals [*athanatoi*—"undying"—in Greek]. The Homeric hero would rather die than depart from what he desires, whether it be home or fame. The Iliadic Akhilleus feels this way but later recants in the underworld to Odysseus (XI.548ff., and especially XI.569–81, below). So also Aias, son of Télamon. Generally, Odysseus is distinguished by his fierce desire to *live*. In this, he is unlike the Iliadic warriors.

84 **hold against:** *Ôdusao* [62], in Greek the penultimate word of Athena's speech, plays on what was taken to be the etymology of Odysseus' name (see XIX.463ff. and 478–81, both below). Stan-

ford has suggested "doomed to odium" as a translation to bring that etymology to the fore, but Odysseus metes out almost as much suffering as he endures, an ambiguity that the verb and the name permit (see XIX.480 on this aspect of the etymology). At line 76 "poor mournful man" [*oduromenon*, 55] may also count as etymological play. (See VIII.70, below, for the fullest list of Homer's wordplay.)

90ff. Now we learn why Poseidon is punishing Odysseus (although Homer's audience may already have known this from earlier tales; see also 31–34, above).

92 **Polyphêmos:** In Greek, the Kyklops is not merely named. He is styled "godlike Polyphêmos" [*antitheon Polyphêmon*, 70]. In fact, Homer has already used the epithet to describe Odysseus [21; Fitzgerald's "brave king," 33] and will apply it with equanimity to Meneláos' shipmates [IV.571; Fitzgerald's "companions," 610], Penélopê [XI.117; Fitzgerald's "your lady," 131], and the suitors [XIV.18; Fitzgerald's "suitors," 19]. To this system we might also add the epithets *dios,* "divine" (frequently reduced to "noble")—applied in *The Odyssey* not only to Kalypso ("ladyship," I.22 [14]), but also to Klytaimnéstra [III.266], Kharybdis [XII.104], and even Eumaios [XVI.56]—and *theoeidês,* "godlike in appearance"—as of Telémakhos [I.113; Fitzgerald's "prince Telémakhos," 142].

This set of examples raises the question of how readers should interpret Homer's conventional epithets. A clever interpreter can explain how each of these figures is in some way "godlike"—Odysseus is like Athena in cunning; Polyphêmos is the son of a god and monstrously strong; the suitors are like the gods in their feasting and single-minded pursuit of pleasure (see XIV.19, below). But Meneláos' otherwise anonymous shipmates? Here "godlike" is clearly being used as a colorless compliment, like "good," which is used just as indiscriminately in modern English. (The adjective "good" does not derive from "God," but a good example of the irrelevance of an original divine referent would be "goodbye"—uttered today with no thought that it's a contraction of "God be with you.") Fitzgerald's decision to leave the epithet untranslated in most places is a sensible interpretation: as a purely conventional element, it would have passed unremarked in one ear of Homer's listener and out the other.

If such epithets are meaningless clichés in some places, are they then to be taken as meaningless every time they occur? One would like to think that if an epithet fits, the figure should wear it. So Odysseus is sufficiently like a god—he is the hero, after all—that at its first occurrence in the epic, Fitzgerald makes something of it ("brave king," I.33; for a significant application of *dios* to Odysseus, see XVI.219, below). And there are instances when an epithet seems so egregiously inappropriate that modern readers wonder if Homer isn't using it ironically, or at least with one of his ten tongues (see *Iliad* II.489) firmly in cheek. Such a case may be Homer's calling the suitors "Akhaian heroes" [I.272; Fitzgerald ducks with "the islanders" (see 321, below, with further reference to VIII.357ff., where, however, the sarcasm is due primarily to the divine speakers' pointedly excessive reverence)].

Other cases bespeaking varying degrees of sarcasm or bemusement may be "divine Klytaimnéstra" [III.266], "the godlike suitors" of XIV.19, discussed above, or the "divine swineherd" [XVI.56]. Fitzgerald passes over the last in silence (XVI.66), but finds a happy solution in the case of the first mention of Klytaimnéstra: he has Nestor refer to her as "the Lady Klytaimnéstra" (III.285). Epithets, like examples, were traditional, but they were also opportunities for audiences trained in comparing one exemplary hero to another to engage in further comparative meditation. In what ways are the suitors godlike, in what ways not? In what ways is the swineherd divine—or noble—and in what ways not? These are questions, I submit, that Homer might well have expected his audience to entertain. As for Klytaimnéstra—well, as Fitzgerald's translation prompts us to say (perhaps anachronistically): she may have started out a lady, but she's a lady no more!

93ff. The love—and importance—of ancestry motivates this brief excursus. Genealogy and familial relationships are part of the "memory" that epic preserves and promotes. Characters are frequently identified by patronymics (see 64, above). Lineage serves an important structural element in portions of the narrative; note "each declared her lineage and name" (XI.266). The most extended and complex genealogical excursus in *The Odyssey* is that introducing the seer Theoklýmenos (XV.282–318); indeed, it precedes the first mention of the seer's name (in XV.320).

95 In Homer the sea [*halos*, literally "salt"] is frequently characterized by the epithet *atrugetos*, the meaning of which still causes lively debate among scholars and which Fitzgerald, scrupulously and diplomatically, forbears to translate. Although the traditional explanation "barren" (already in the ancient commentaries) may not stand up to philological scrutiny (Hainsworth, HWH 1.348), one can appreciate its attractions: the infertility of the sea (fish notwithstanding) highlights the plight of Odysseus, forced to wander across it and more than once to come near drowning in it.

107 See *42ff.*, above.

108 **wise Odysseus** translates the epithet "multi-minded" [*polyphrona*, 83]. It is the second member we meet of the family of epithets with the prefix *poly-*, which Homer characteristically uses to describe Odysseus (see 2, above). It is interesting that one of his most formidable opponents, Polyphêmos, has a name of the same form. (The "phêmos" portion of the Kyklops' name is related to our word "fame"; see 189ff., below, on the name of the bard Phêmios.)

116 **with flowing hair:** In Homer, male gods and heroes are traditionally presented with long hair, and it remained a popular style among the aristocrats or more affluent classes of ancient Greece into the fifth century. Long hair has in many cultures been a symbol of male strength and power, from Biblical Samson to early Germanic warriors and kings ("the long-haired kings") to so many popular hunks today.

117–118 This is the first direct mention of the suitors. Note the emphasis on the economic blight they represent as they take advantage of the hospitality of Odysseus' house and of its master's absence (see 13 and 39–41, above, and 136, below).

122 **renown:** This is the *kleos* [95] which Homer's heroes of both epics strive ever to earn, and which only poetry can confer. In this regard it differs from "honor" or "prestige" attained in the eyes of one's contemporaries, Greek *timê* (see 148, below).

127 On the significance of "bronze" in the archeology of the poem, see XV.407, below. The traveling Athena and the armed Athena are two aspects of the goddess, each of potential aid to Odysseus, one as he wanders, the other when the final battle is fought in the Ithakan hall (Book XXII).

131–32 Athena customarily takes on the guise of someone familiar, here Mentês. The most obvious parallel will come in the next book, when Athena appears as Mentor; both names play on the same root ("to think"), and both are appropriate names for advisers. Mentês is not an Ithakan but a stranger, which makes his surprise and indignation at the outrages of the suitors more significant and carry all the more weight with Telémakhos. Widespread report of the indignity makes it more shameful.

136 **oxen they had killed:** This is a particularly brazen and galling detail. The suitors have truly made themselves at home and are consuming Odysseus' and Telémakhos' property.

138 Note that wine was not drunk neat, i.e., without the admixture of water. That Polyphêmos does so later is a sign of his barbarous, even subhuman behavior (see IX.222–23, below).

141 The amount of meat consumed in Homeric epics, in contrast to the Classical Greek diet at least, reflects at once a memory of more ancient days and some element of fantasy.

142ff. The prompt offer of hospitality, particularly before demanding an identification of the guest (155–56), is a mark of the good breeding of "the prince Telémakhos" [*theoeidês*, "godlike," 113].

(See I.362, III.377, and VI.130–31, below, for more on the sacred duty of hospitality.)

This is the first appearance of Telémakhos' name in *The Odyssey*. He is mentioned in *The Iliad* as Odysseus' son (II.260, IV.354), and the first audience of *The Odyssey* would thus likely have anticipated his having some sort of role in a song about Odysseus' homecoming. The names of the children of heroes often reflect a quality of the hero; Telémakhos, roughly "fighter at a distance," refers either to Odysseus' skill as an archer, which will come into great prominence in the climactic battle with the suitors in Book XXII, in which Telémakhos, too, will prove worthy of his own name, or to the fact that at Troy Odysseus is fighting far from home. (I believe that the first is more likely, although the distance between Troy and Ithaka, and especially father and son, is significant in *The Odyssey*.)

145ff. Telémakhos is always thinking about the potential return of his father; the arrival of any guest, and this one in particular, foreshadows Odysseus' real return. Mentès is a Taphian, a seafarer, not unlike the Kretan Odysseus will pretend to be when he does appear in Ithaka, also in disguise.

148 **Honor** [*Timê*, 117] is key to status in Homeric society. Contrast "reknown" [*kleos*] at 122, above.

153 **Then he said warmly:** Homer has Telémakhos utter aloud "winged words" [*epea pteroenta*, 122], a bit of traditional Homeric translationese which has itself become proverbial. *Epea* ("words"; singular *epos*) is the same as the word for the verses of epic poetry and is the root of our word for the whole genre: "epic." The wings or feathers behind *pteroenta* likely refer to the feathers on arrows, which enable them to fly directly to their target.

154–55 Telémakhos is at once characterized as a direct and sincere young man, a speaker of few and unambiguous words, not the wily rhetorician his father is.

157–60 The spear rack seems a trivial detail, but already the ancient scholiasts or commentators on the poem noted with praise the way Homer prepares the scene for the final slaying of the suitors in Book XXII. It is this kind of linkage, arching over twenty-some books, which argues strongly for a unifying intelligence plotting the whole epic (even though that intelligence might have belonged to a cumulative tradition, not just one poet). On this question, see Introduction, pp. xxxii–xliii.

161–78 The elegance, wealth, and prosperity of Odysseus' court is clear, despite the din of the intrusive suitors.

189ff. The place of singing and of bards such as Phêmios here, or Demódokos in Books VII and VIII, shows the function of Homer or any of the bards who sang *The Iliad, The Odyssey,* portions of them, or the cyclic poems. (On the epic cycle, see 19–21, above.) Phêmios' name could be construed as "the man who spreads report," "the man who is rich in tale" (West, HWH 1.97 [on I.154]). It is, at a distance and via Latin, cognate with our word "fame." Only later (377ff.) do we learn that the subject of the song is the "Homecoming [*noston,* 326] of the Akhaians." Note the ironic fact that Phêmios is "compelled" to sing by the suitors (190).

189 **cithern harp:** This would have been a four-stringed lyre, with "a body of wood and a sound-box made of, or shaped like, a tortoise's shell, with ox-hide stretched over the face and two curved horns rising from it, joined by a crossbar carrying the pegs, to which strings of gut were attached" (West, HWH 1.96–97).

198 Again Homer emphasizes the suitors' leeching, their wasting of Odysseus' (and Telémakhos') resources. And now we know how it rankles Telémakhos.

199–207 Telémakhos believes, or says he believes, that Odysseus is dead. Clearly, he still hopes this is not true, but he pretends to have ceased hoping. It is typical of Greek and much Mediterranean culture of the time to dramatize one's situation and, moreover, to present the worst-case scenario. There are a number of advantages to this, not least being that no one can surprise you with worse news. This is not just a mind game; to be surprised by bad news would involve loss of face.

Telémakhos' report of his father's death is also a sign of the disconnectedness from his father from which he suffers. Compare his avoidance of naming Odysseus (see 199, below), his acerbic remarks at 257–60 (see below), and perhaps also his blunt rebuttal (397–407) of Penélopê's request that Phêmios sing a different song. At the risk of importing modern psychological insights, one might well describe Telémakhos as having erected a range of "defenses" to protect him from really "dealing with" his father's absence and probable death.

199 **a man:** Likely for the reason just noted, Telémakhos does not mention Odysseus by name, as in the periphrases in lines 216 and 278.

206–7 **and there's no help for us in someone's hoping / he still may come:** A more literal rendering of Homer's Greek reveals a subtle difference: "and there's no comfort for us if any earth-dwelling humans should say he will come" [166–68]. The way Homer has Telémakhos formulate it leaves open the comfort such words from another class of being—in other words, a god or goddess such as the one sitting before him—might bring.

212 The wry "I don't suppose you walked here on the sea," although repeated (XIV.227; XVI.70, 266), might here be seen as an invitation for a deity to make her other-than-normal mode of transportation known.

220–29 Odysseus will himself tell lying tales such as this when he returns (XIII.327–65; XIV.229–417; XIX.195–362; XXIV.270–346).

227 On the significance of iron in the archeology of the Homeric poems, see XV.407, below. It appears in a simile at IX.427. "Brown" is now preferred to "bright" by scholars; see above, on I.36. On the particular problem of transcultural understanding of color terminology, see IV.146, below.

231–36 Laërtês is Odysseus' father and Telémakhos' grandfather. It is only after Odysseus reveals himself to Laërtês that the epic concludes. His separation from town, as Athena describes it, is odd and painful, and is yet another sign of the family's disarray. It is one more wrong that must be set right.

240ff. Athena says it quite bluntly: Odysseus is alive and about to return. Although she couches it in the same pious optimism the real Mentês might have employed, we in the audience enjoy the irony of Athena claiming that the gods delay him (239) and then that she believes she can forecast his imminent return (244f.). The first part of the stock disclaimer ("I'm no prophet, no adept in bird-signs," 246) is literally true, for she is a goddess. Telémakhos will miss the irony but not the intended encouragement and inspiration.

241–43 Note Athena's bending of the truth in one particular. In her guise as Mentês she asserts that "savages . . . hold him captive." R.O.A.M. Lyne calls this a "graceful falsehood that it is 'fierce men' not the glamorous Calypso who are detaining Odysseus on a sea-girt island. The truth might have confused the impressionable adolescent, dampening his ardour to preserve his mother against the day of his moral father's return" (*Further Voices in Vergil's Aeneid* [Oxford, 1987], 83–84; he compares Griffin, *Homer*, 64). Though Lynn's version may be too prudish, that stories are tailored to one's audience and even invented to further some greater end is central to *The Odyssey*.

249 **he can do anything:** Behind this lies another of the *poly*-family of epithets [*polymêkhanos*, 205], the third epithet in the *poly*-system (see 2 and 108, above).

253–55 The Kretan in Books XIV and XIX, i.e., the disguised Odysseus, will also claim to have been familiar with Odysseus.

257–60 **And thoughtfully Telémakhos replied:** Homer calls Telémakhos' reply "thoughtful" or "prudent," but "My mother says I am his son" and the misogynistic barb that no one truly knows his father seem callous. Harsh as the reply may be, it

presents the issue of Penélopê's fidelity as significant and shows
clearly how much is at stake. (Indeed, in his "prudence" he is very
much his mother's son; see XIX.65 and XX.79, below.) The
commonplace "Who has known his own engendering?" and the
verses that follow (261–64) reveal not a hard-bitten cynic but a
young man who sorely misses his father (see 199–207, above).
The "proof" of paternity is not either parent's to give; rather the
son's own actions will constitute that proof. As Telémakhos ma-
tures and performs well in a variety of contexts, reflecting his
father's abilities (see 142ff., above), he will be able to be confident
that his father is Odysseus.

266–67 . . . **no lack of honor:** Homer makes clear that the
speaker expects the renown of this family to continue to be
revealed in the future, or, as the Greek has it, "behind us" [*opissô*,
222]; according to the Greeks' conception, one faces the (known)
past and backs into an unknown future. So also "for time to
come" at IX.558 [511].

268 **Penélopê:** This is the first mention of her name in the epic.
Its etymology remains uncertain. Some scholars derive it from
the name of a kind of duck reputed to be faithful to her mate.
Already ancient speculation linked it with weaving. For a theory
that it just might mean "Weaving-Unraveller," see Russo in
HWH 3.81 [on XIX.137]. Of course, that it *might* be so derived
does not mean that it was.

271 **At the expense of all:** Athena states ironically that this is not
"potluck" [*eranos*, 226], where each contributes his own portion
(see IV.668ff., below).

279 **But evil days the gods have brought upon it:** A more
literal rendering of the Greek ("But now the gods have wished
otherwise, devising bad things" [234]) permits the hearer to enjoy
more fully the irony of Telémakhos addressing this to Athena, for
she is in the process of "devising" quite a different outcome.
"Devising" is also one of Odysseus' emblematic activities, and the
verb—*mêtiaô*—displays its connections to *mêtis* (see 2, above).

280–87 Odysseus' present fate is worse than death, both because it is not certain and because, if he is dead, he is unburied, without the honor of a tomb. (On the particular horror of death without proper burial, see III.278–79 and V.321–23, below.) Fitzgerald's "no glory" (286) [*akleiôs*, 241] might be better as "without report" or "without renown" (see 122, above).

291 **Doulíkhion . . . Samê . . . Zakýnthos:** The traditional neighboring isles to Ithaka. On the island's geographical location, and the identity of the other islands, see Fitzgerald's postscript (*Odyssey*, pp. 467–72). On the general issue of geographical accuracy, see Introduction, pp. xliii–xlv.

299 **Pallas . . . was disturbed:** In Greek, Homer sets up one of the most unusual and unusually contrived of puns between Athena's common epithet, Pallas, and the verb [*epalastêsasa . . . Pallas*, 252].

305–12 What is the significance of this brief anecdote? Is it merely a further instance of Odysseus' craftiness? Or is Athena subtly suggesting the use of poisoned arrows, or, on the contrary, advising against it—pious Ilos felt it would inspire divine enmity? The poisoning of weapons is nowhere else described in Homer, and later Greek commentators regarded it as a barbarous practice. Of course, the Homeric Odysseus traverses the boundaries of the civilized.

In ancient Greek literature, largely created and transmitted by and for men, the use of poisons and drugs [*pharmaka*] was generally attributed to women (Kirkê and Helen in *The Odyssey*, or the barbarous Medea).

318ff. Whether or not Odysseus is to return is uncertain (Athena/Mentês says now), so Telémakhos is advised to begin proceedings on his own.

321 **the islanders:** The Greek reads: "the Akhaian heroes" [272], a use of formula so out of place as to function as bitter irony. While there is a danger of overreading, such irony is not at all out of place or character for early epic. (On this question, see 93, above, and VIII.357ff., below, for a clearer example of irony.)

323 Between this line and the next the textual tradition of *The Odyssey* includes four lines that some scholars find spurious, which might be rendered as follows: "As for your mother—if her heart is eager to be married, let her go back to the great hall of her powerful father. They will prepare a wedding and make very many bridal gifts, so much as befits his own daughter" [275–78]. (Fitzgerald notes the excision, his translation, p. 463. My renderings tend to the literal; I would not attempt Fitzgerald's style.) Over the centuries, many lines seem to have been added, for one reason or another, to the Homeric text, and many modern scholars agree with Fitzgerald that these have been interpolated into Mentês' speech. They are based on the words of the suitor Eurýmakhos (II.205–7 [195–97]), but the most cogent arguments involve the contradictions they seem to present: the first words consider a possibility (Penélopê desiring remarriage) that Telémakhos seems already to have given the lie to (295), and they seem very confused about what role the various participants in this action—Penélopê, Telémakhos, Ikários—are supposed to take. In contrast, I.338, later in the speech, offers none of these problems and consequently is regarded as spurious by none. There it is clearly Telémakhos who is to take charge: it was the adult male's responsibility to marry off his female relative, whether daughter, sister, or even mother.

It would be naive to trust the manuscript tradition overmuch, and much can be said in favor of the removal of these lines. However, they are not necessarily so impossibly contradictory as scholars have made out. In her/his implicit contradiction of Telémakhos' assertion that Penélopê does not wish to remarry (295), Athena/Mentês may suggest that Telémakhos himself may not fully know his mother's mind. Nor need these lines contradict line 338. Here Athena will be saying that if in fact (already now, before Telémakhos' travels and contradictory to his expectations) Penélopê wishes to remarry, she should return to her father's house. If she does not, she should remain; but if Telémakhos were to return after learning of his father's death, he should have his mother remarry, the implication being whether she wants to or not.

338 **and give your mother to another husband:** See preceding note. The harshness of this indubitably genuine line is mitigated by the fact that we know that Athena knows that Telémakhos will not learn of his father's death.

339–42 Athena/Mentês presents the idea that the suitors deserve death as a foregone conclusion to Telémakhos and thus to us.

344–47 Athena too presents the example of Orestês to young Telémakhos, to inspire him. While inspirational, it is a somewhat dubious precedent: (1) Telémakhos would need to face many enemies, not just one, and (2) the suitors did not kill Odysseus as Aigísthos did Agamémnon. Still, both young men are to gain fame (*kleos*) by way of the father: the one by revenge, the other by searching for him.

348 **well set-up:** In Greek, *kalos* [301], "beautiful," first in body, then in spirit. Size and beauty were prized, particularly in warriors but in women as well; nor would it have been thought odd for one man to notice this or even say this about or to another man or boy.

356 **like a father to his son** is an apt and touching simile to come from Telémakhos' mouth.

358ff. Telémakhos knows what is due a traveler and guest; on his own travels he receives a bath in Pylos (III.506–8) and gifts from Meneláos in Sparta (IV.629ff.). Odysseus will receive both from the Phaiákians in Book VI. And when he at last returns to his own home, albeit in beggar's disguise, he receives a memorable bath (XIX.416ff.).

362 **such as dear friends give their friends** [*hoia philoi xeinoi xeinoisi didousi*, 313]: The same word [*xeinos*] later describes both host and guest in the guest-friend relationship (see VIII.175, below). "Xenophobia" would have seemed particularly heinous to civilized Greeks, except that unstated in the Greek is the assumption that the unknown guest is a strange Greek, a Hellene of some sort, not a member of a truly foreign people. (On the giving of gifts by hosts to guests, see IV.629–33, below.)

364–67 One can almost sense Athena's pleasure in her polite evasion; while acknowledging Telémakhos' propriety, she slightly mocks his promise of a "precious thing" (in the Greek, she echoes his phrase [312, 318] while, with delicious understatement, she promises a gift of equal value in return—although, strictly speaking, this would have been understood to refer to a future visit by Telémakhos to Mentês).

368–73 Is line 369 a simile, or did she really reveal her godhead by flying off as a bird? Homer prefers to leave this question open but leaves his listener in no doubt that Telémakhos felt encouraged ("in his spirit [*thumos*] she placed strength and courage" [320–21]), that he was more than ever mindful of his father, and that somehow he knew he had been conversing with a god. (*Pace* Fitzgerald, there is no explicit reference to a "dream.")

369 **off and gone:** Other scholars have proposed that the word *anopaia* [320] should be rendered "up through the smoke hole" (in the roof of the hall). But this may be overly concrete and preclude Homer's diplomatic vagueness (see preceding note).

376–80 Song at least can silence the rowdy suitors. Only now do we learn that Phêmios, like the singer of *The Odyssey,* is singing of the Homecoming (*nostos*) of the Akhaians; indeed, he has been since I.192, Athena's arrival, although it is not Homer's style to insist on simultaneity of actions. "There is obvious dramatic irony in the fascinated attention with which the suitors listen to the tale of Athena's vengeance, oblivious to the goddess's actual presence" (West, HWH 1.116–17 [on I.325–27]). Homer does not focus on the suitors' reaction to the topic (although "bitter" or "mournful" [*lugros,* 327] applied to it is proleptic in their case) but rather follows the sound upward to reach Penélopê. A masterful transition, and subtle motivation: the word and idea of *nostos,* and even more the pain it provokes, draw her to the hall.

379 **careful Penélopê:** Homer's epithet is *periphrôn,* "careful" in the sense of "mindful," "prudent," though no doubt her mind was full of "cares" as well. In the extant remains of early epic, this epithet is applied only to women, and Homer uses it often of Penélopê (see XIX.65, below).

385 The "veil" is a further sign of Penélopê's aversion to the suitors, whom she does not receive as guests and from whom she is trying to keep her distance; it is also a token of her virtue.

388 **spells:** *Thelktêria:* Sung poetry was recognized to be like magic in its power to enchant the listener (indeed, note the connection to song in our own word "enchant").

388ff. This is the first exchange we see between Telémakhos and his mother. The independence of mind [*noos,* 347] Telémakhos argues on the bard's behalf (397ff.) is precisely what he himself now claims. We sense at once the new spirit of independence and greater self-reliance that his interview with—from his perspective—the unknown god disguised as Mentês has inspired in him. Indeed, his response astonishes his mother (408), and she goes back into the inner house.

395 Although the terms are applied loosely and with great variation, "Hellas" and "Argos" seem generally to refer to mainland Greece and the Peloponnese, respectively.

402–3 Given the traditional nature of oral epic, the idea that "people applaud and prefer the latest song which comes to listeners' ears" is a notable literary judgment. The fact that the words for both "applaud" [351] and "comes to" or "is about" [352] are *hapax legomena,* in other words, terms not used anywhere else in the two Homeric epics, may suggest that these words are more recent additions to the poet's word-hoard imported to express an idea that is itself new. (This is a complex argument; other *hapax legomena* may be relics of extreme antiquity.) It is tempting to claim that this idea represents "Homer's view," but, before succumbing to the temptation, we should remember that Telémakhos is speaking. It is just as likely that Homer is using this "radical" aesthetic pronouncement to characterize the new Telémakhos. Depending on one's musical preferences, one might compare Wagner's Walther von Stolzing or a fan of the latest style of rock music.

404–7 Telémakhos does not say what he hopes, and has new reason to hope—that Odysseus is alive and will yet return—but rather takes the most pessimistic line possible. Again, these are elements of a characteristic pose calculated to protect oneself from further disappointment and therefore shame in others' eyes, but we must also remember that the suitors are listening, and there is every reason to keep them lulled in complacency.

407ff. Fitzgerald, following some ancient editions and scholars both ancient and modern (again as he notes on his p. 463), omits four lines [356–59] which appear, also in Telémakhos' mouth, in Book XXI and are translated by Fitzgerald there (XXI.394–97). It certainly seems to us that they would be unnecessarily rude here. Nevertheless, these commanding lines would provide more reason for Penélopê's "wonder" (408) and would certainly register Telémakhos' new resolve and sense of self-worth. However rude for him to speak this way to his mother, it is also observably true (although I do not offer this as a compelling argument for the authenticity of these lines here, in Book I) that teenagers often assert their independence vis-à-vis their (loving) parents before they feel capable of asserting it to the rest of the world; indeed, the first is often exaggerated and is often preparation for the other.

411–13 **then she fell to weeping . . . :** Penélopê's grief and longing for her husband are exemplary. It would be an error to infer from these lines that Penélopê is ever the passive victim, although Homer clearly does not mind if we think so at first. He will show her to be active and resourceful, capable of outwitting even Odysseus. The time for her active participation in the plot has not yet come, and Athena at least releases her from waking pain.

417ff. **You suitors. . . . Insolent men . . . :** Telémakhos wastes no time laying down the new law for the suitors and is unwisely direct in his threats (esp. 429–30). This is rash and has no effect other than to focus their hatred directly on him.

432 The suitors, too, are surprised at the new Telémakhos.

439 **Antínoös:** Although the suitors are presented—and ultimately punished—as a group, Homer also characterizes a number of individuals, just as both the Greek and the Trojan fighting forces in *The Iliad* are at once groups and subgroups and very different individuals. Antínoös is, characteristically, first to respond; as his name suggests (*anti* + *noos*, "mind set against" or "opposing mind," highlighted by Homer with *antion* [388], and *Antino'* [389]), he is the most difficult and brazen of the suitors. The patronymic (name in the form "son of x") is traditional as an identifier; the virtually automatic formula, insisting as it does on the proper organization of family and society by generation, here reminds us just how badly out of whack things are in Ithaka. (Telémakhos might have observed, with Hamlet, that things are rotten in the state of Ithaka; there are many points of comparison and contrast between the two young heroes and the situations in which they find themselves.)

447 Telémakhos has obvious reasons here to make the point that since no one has certain proof of Odysseus' death, as far as questions of succession are concerned, he must be regarded as still alive.

448 **I rule:** Telémakhos demands to be lord and master in and of his house, using a particularly important title in Greek, *(w)anax* [397]. *(W)anax* is the highest term for lord or master, applied to both gods (especially Zeus) and men (for example, Agamémnon, leader of all Greek forces in *The Iliad*). The Kyklops Polyphêmos, too, considers himself "lord and master" of his flocks (see "Master," IX.494). On the feminine form, see VI.161, below. The "(w)" stands for the so-called digamma, not represented by any written character in the historic texts of Homer. Whether and when it was actually written, and how late its "w"-like sound was pronounced in the epic tradition, remain uncertain, but its former presence and ongoing force can be inferred from the way certain words behave within the system of Homeric metrics. Indeed, the digamma, whose importance for Homeric verse was first discovered by the English philologist Richard Bentley in 1713, is one of the unmistakable signs of the antiquity of Homeric formulae and the tradition in which Homer's poems participate.

456ff. Although his greeting words are more conciliatory, Eurýmakhos here reveals that he is eager to know if Telémakhos' guest had some news of Odysseus.

465ff. If there had been any doubts before, it is now clear that Telémakhos, like every other character in *The Odyssey*, carefully crafts his words with regard only to his potential advantage over or disadvantage at the hands of his interlocutor. "Truth" is too risky.

472 **So said Telémakhos, though in his heart:** The narrator wants to make certain we understand that Telémakhos has been dissembling. In fact, the Greek makes it clear that Telémakhos knows not just that the visitor was immortal but specifically that she was a goddess [*athanatên,* 420].

482 **Eurýkleia:** The dearest and most trustworthy of the household servants: indeed, having been purchased by Odysseus' father, Laërtês, to serve as a concubine, she was a member of the family. Until recently, one did not need to preface "family" with the adjective "extended"; by the standards of the time, all families were extended.

486 **twenty oxen:** Expensive. In comparison, as West has noted (HWH 1.126 [on I.431]), "a skilled woman slave is valued at 4 oxen" (*Iliad* XXIII.705); "a male prisoner [is] worth 100 oxen" (*Iliad* XXI.79), as is a "set of golden armor" (*Iliad* VI.236); "and a cauldron one ox" (*Iliad* XXIII.885).

488 **for the sake of peace** may be opaque to some readers. A more literal rendering, Homer's "avoided the wrath of his wife" [433], is unambiguous. Such concubinage was not unusual: most of the Greek victors either took or were allotted a Trojan concubine (Agamémnon's Kassandra is the most famous; see Nestor's report at III.167). Odysseus was the conspicuous exception. In another ancient Near Eastern tradition, the Biblical patriarchs Abraham and Isaac had concubines or co-wives. Note also the similarity between the names of Odysseus' mother (Antikleía) and his nurse (Eurýkleia). That Eurýkleia's lineage is detailed (483) indicates that she came from a good family in her homeland. For another example of the fate of enslavement, which could befall just about anyone, compare Eumaios (esp. XV.490–585). The two figures are in many ways parallel.

491ff. **So now she held the light . . . :** The first book has a quiet, restful close. Telémakhos returns to the comfort and safety of his bedroom, with its touches of elegance and luxury. He is loved and cared for in small things by Eurýkleia, as he is—in great things— by the ever-present Athena, whose name forms the last word of the book [444].

The book divisions are later (post-fifth-century; see Hainsworth in HWH 1.315 [on VI.328–31]), but in many instances they may reflect performance tradition of episodization. Russo notes that "thirteen of the twenty-four books of *The Odyssey* conclude with the actors going to bed" (HWH 3.73 [on XVIII.428]) or with some reference to night or approaching dawn, a further indication that the bookends, however much they belong to a textualized *Odyssey,* indeed reflect performance practice.

BOOK II

A Hero's Son
Awakens

2–5 As day follows night, so dressing follows undressing, although now with a difference: whereas Eurýkleia had assisted him as he doffed his tunic, here Telémakhos, alone, puts on traveling clothes and, significantly, arms himself.

7ff. **He found the criers with clarion voices . . . :** As advised and promised, Telémakhos summons the assembly. We note that the Homeric aesthetic in no way seeks to avoid repetition. Doing, even saying exactly what a character or the poet said would be done or said was obviously not regarded as a blemish; rather, it lent unity and architectonic grandeur, even a sort of inevitability, to the poet's song, which extended over hours or, in some cases, days.

12 **sunlit:** Literally, "divinely uttered" [12], frequently used simply to mean "divine."

16–25 Reference to a character's ancestry and in particular his father (often through the patronymic) is common; less common is what we have here, the identification of an older man in terms of his children. Narrative (1) and thematic (2) considerations are paramount. (1) Notably, the story of one of Aigýptios' sons, Ánti-phos, turns the excursus into a little window on a dramatic scene in Book IX. Suspense in traditional tales lies less in the what than in the how, and this foretaste of the horrors to come (in the narrative) is obviously to Homer's taste. (The Alexandrian critic Aristarchus regarded the verses that referred to the events in Polyphêmos', the Kyklops, cave as spurious; even after 2000 years, Aristarchus remains among the most important Homeric scholars, and he is always worth attending to; however, we must remember that he approached the poem with standards and an aesthetic characteristic of the highly literate Hellenistic age, at a remove of nearly 500 years from the time of Homer himself.) The careful listener to Homer's song, even as he or she registers the pathos of Ántiphos being Polyphêmos' last victim, must recall that Aigýptios himself cannot be aware of any element of his son's fate (24–25). While the narrative is focused on Telémakhos' con-cern for his father, in Aigýptios we have a figure of the absent Odysseus, equally ignorant of the well-being of his son.

(2) Aigýptios' sons are, of course, fully grown and accomplished in their own rights, and in him we have an opportunity to look up the ladder, as it were, from the young to the old. *The Odyssey* transmitted to us ends with the return of Odysseus to his aged father, Laërtês. For Odysseus himself, the suitors rather than Telémakhos represent the inevitable challenge every younger generation poses to its immediate predecessor. The question is not whether the younger will replace the older, the question is when and how. Odysseus' answer to the first question will be: not yet.

27–28 **No meeting . . . :** In other words, no such public assembly has been held in nearly twenty years.

31 **Has he had word our fighters are returning:** This is a further reminder that it is not just Odysseus' family who are longing for the return of one man but a whole community that has had no word of its fighting men in something like ten years.

34–35 **The man has vigor . . . more power to him:** Only barely beneath the surface is Aigýptios' frustration at the situation in Ithaka: it is time for someone to take charge.

40 **the staff:** In Greek *skêptron* [37], for us, "scepter," symbolized the right to speak in assembly and, in other contexts, authority itself, traditionally of kings or their representatives.

54 **sons of the best men here among them:** Telémakhos does not shrink from addressing a very touchy problem: any rebuff (not to mention punishment) of the suitors will offend many of the more prominent Ithakan families. Although the suitors themselves are present, Telémakhos consistently speaks as if he is addressing their fathers, who should curb the bad behavior of their sons (here and 78–85). Telémakhos, though aware of political ramifications, here and elsewhere attempts to keep discussion at the level of an outrage to his family. At this point, he speaks as if the suitors were all Ithakans. In fact, from XVI.290ff., it will emerge that the vast majority of the suitors are not from Ithaka, and his inability to exercise any control over the foreigners underlies a distinction he makes in 80–84. However, the leaders and major troublemakers among the suitors are Ithakans, and, on the whole, the issue is presented as an Ithakan problem throughout the poem.

56 **across the sea:** *The Odyssey* is itself quite vague about the exact location of the home of Ikários, Penélopê's father. Tradition of uncertain antiquity (it may well be post-Homeric) puts him on the Greek mainland at Sparta or Acarnania.

60 **beeves:** Cattle.

68–75 Telémakhos, mounting the only argument he can, appeals to his fellow Ithakans' sense of shame vis-à-vis outsiders and a still higher court of justice, the gods, who may yet punish those responsible for wrongdoing.

73 **holy Justice:** In Greek, this concept is conveyed by a second epithet applied to Zeus [*themistos,* 68], based on *themis,* "justice" or "lawfulness." The central terms of any culture's moral and ethical system are notoriously difficult to translate into those of another language.

80–84 If it were only Ithakans who had taken or were consuming his property, Telémakhos would have more opportunity for redress than he does now, when so many of the suitors are from elsewhere. See 54, above. Still, he blames the entire Ithakan community for permitting this outrage against one of their number to go on.

87 **his eyes grown bright with tears:** Tears welling in the eyes, even weeping, would not have been a sign of weakness or an occasion for shame but rather a sign of passion and sincerity.

90 Again, Antínoös speaks first.

95ff. **it is your own dear, incomparably cunning mother:** Although it is from Antínoös' perspective, we now catch a glimpse of the cunning Penélopê (see also 124–30).

100ff. The story of the shroud for Laërtês is told by Antínoös here, by Penélopê at XIX.163ff., and by the ghost of one of the suitors (Amphímedon) at XXIV.145ff. The variations among the three accounts are minor, and there seems to be no adequate reason to get overly exercised over what some scholars consider a discrepancy in the length of time that elapses between the suitors' discovery of the ruse and Penélopê's completion of the shroud.

In all three accounts, Penélopê works on the shroud for nearly four years before a traitorous maid betrays the secret. The suitors have been importuning her for more or less the same amount of time (II.96), suggesting that she must have begun work on the shroud soon after their arrival. The difference is this: Antínoös and Penélopê both give the impression that the trick has been exposed for some time and that she is now holding out longer than expected (obviously, this has a different meaning for Penélopê than it does for Antínoös and the suitors). In contrast, Am-

phímedon gives the impression that Odysseus returns immedi-
ately after Penélopê has been found out and the suitors increase
their pressure to force her decision. This suits his narrative per-
spective (as the ghost of a dead suitor attempting to explain their
defeat), just as an emphasis on the length of time since the foiling
of Penélopê's last plan to avoid choosing a suitor is appropriate
for the very different perspectives of Antínoös and Penélopê,
respectively.

101 **great loom:** With this great loom (also 112) one stood as one
wove. The size of the loom is essential to her argument: it could
not be moved to the home of a new husband.

104 Penélopê is presented as speaking to the suitors as if she is
certain Odysseus is dead, as Telémakhos has, for his own reasons,
done several times.

111 **We have men's hearts:** Less in the sense that "we are
human and therefore sympathetic," than that "we are men and
therefore likely to be outwitted by women."

116 **one of her maids:** She is a traitor to her mistress and the
household, although the suitors will regard her only as one who
levels the field, so to speak, undoing Penélopê's own ruse (see
XIX.163–82, below). As will emerge clearly later, many of the
maids have liaisons with the suitors. Their punishment is among
the most gruesome of *The Odyssey*. The poem insists on the justice
of Odysseus' revenge; thus, it is important that their guilt be
emphasized as often as possible, so listeners will be inclined to
take the part of the house of Odysseus and Penélopê rather than
of the suitors, even when the information is presented out of a
suitor's mouth.

128 **Mykênê with her coronet:** Of Mykênê we know only her
name and a few family connections; there is no extant legend in
which her cunning plays a particular role. Of Alkmênê and Tyro
we know more; they both appear in Book XI (304–7 and 268–95,
respectively). Again, neither is a watchword for cunning, unless
Antínoös means to suggest that any woman who can have a child

by a lover (even divine) and get away with it is obviously cunning. This would be a particularly ironic reading of the story of Alkmênê, who was duped by Zeus' cunning, but it is a revisionary interpretation worthy of Antínoös. Perhaps all three simply belong to a short list of famous women of old.

131–34 Antínoös lays the blame for the very wasting of Telémakhos' property at Penélopê's feet, although he assumes the gods are responsible for her thinking and acting as she does.

137–46 Telémakhos argues that he could never send his mother back to her father for remarriage; of course, this is precisely the course of action which Athena/Mentês advised (under certain circumstances) and which Telémakhos found agreeable in Book I (if the lines are not spurious, see I.323, above).

155ff. **Now Zeus . . . / launching a pair of eagles:** The sending of an omen by a god in epic permits the poet to exploit the disparity of perspectives: between, on the one hand, the god, the poet, and the audience, who share knowledge of the intentions of the gods within the epic in sending the omen; and, on the other, the human actors in the epic, who struggle to interpret the omen, each as his or her heart dictates. In some ways, then, an omen is a model of a poetic text: both must be interpreted at varying removes from the intention of the god/poet. The different interpretations of Halithérsês (170–86) and Pólybos (188–217) efficiently demonstrate this. Halithérsês is basically right, although parts of his forecast (esp. 183–86) seem to exceed the data of this omen. Pólybos accuses him of overreading (esp. 191–92). From our superior perspective as second-time readers, we may take the fact that there are two eagles to portend that Odysseus and Telémakhos together will punish the suitors.

162 **tearing cheeks and throats:** It remains open to question whose cheeks and throats the eagles claw: some of the Ithakans', their own (to symbolize grief?), or (least likely) each other's. Often in parallel scenes the birds swoop down on a victim of the sort they might seize in the normal course of hunting.

179–86 **I am old enough to know a sign when I see one . . . :** Mastor concludes his prophecy with words intended to inspire confidence in his veracity. He may be an experienced prophet, and, from the privileged position of second-time readers of *The Odyssey* (ancient audiences who had known the story all their lives would have been in the same position), we know he is correct. However, there is no getting around the fact that his arguments here are circular: he adduces as support the occurrence of what he predicts will happen. It will happen, yes, but it hasn't yet. In the Greek the illogic of his argument emerges a bit more boldly: he says not "I see this all fulfilled" (186) but "all will now be fulfilled." Later theoreticians, for example, Aristotle, distinguished between the strictly logical argument (syllogism) and the "persuasive augmentation" (enthymeme) of orators. (See also XV.26–36, below.) While the great period of Greek public speaking and the development of conscious rhetorical technique came later, in Athens in the fifth and fourth centuries B.C.E., these very speakers and theorists recognized that Homer's characters exemplified all the basic principles of good rhetoric. Mastor is a minor example; Odysseus is of course the master rhetor.

188–89 **Old man . . . :** In Greek, Eurýmakhos' words are a slightly less veiled threat that Mastor's children may suffer violence, perhaps (here is the threat) because of Mastor's prediction.

197 **Here is what I foretell:** Eurýmakhos mocks Mastor's illogically confident prediction of Odysseus' return, saying roughly, "I'll tell you what will come about," implying "because we suitors will take events into our own hands." The greatness of this minor interchange is that, for all its faulty logic, Mastor's faith in the gods and justice overtrumps the impious cynicism and hybris of Eurýmakhos and the suitors.

222ff. **But give me a fast ship . . . :** Telémakhos must ask for a ship, because the fleet is not the property of the king or his house. Moreover, Telémakhos wants this to be an expedition for the common weal. Twenty is the standard complement of men accompanying someone on a peacetime mission.

236 **Mentor:** The eponymous sage adviser. See Introduction, p. xxiii.

241–43 **Let no man holding scepter as a king:** He is openly sarcastic.

245 **like a gentle father:** Mentor's simile makes explicit the correspondence between Telémakhos' need to find Odysseus and that of the entire populace.

251–53 **What sickens me . . . :** Mentor indirectly urges the assembly to punish the suitors here and now, as Leókritos (255ff.) understands.

257–62 **Suppose Odysseus himself . . . :** Leókritos indeed sees the reality which will face Odysseus and Telémakhos in the second half of the epic: just by landing in Ithaka, Odysseus is far from solving the problems. Indeed, the risks will become greater.

267–69 Whatever Leókritos' purpose in concluding his speech with these derogatory words, they serve to mollify the suitors (Telémakhos won't get anywhere), to spur Telémakhos to action (I'll prove him wrong), and to motivate the rest of the book (Athena disguised as Mentor [282ff.] sees to it Telémakhos sails).

273ff. The young hero goes alone to the seashore. It is perhaps a vocational hazard of commentators on *The Odyssey* always to see *The Iliad* behind their object of primary attention. Homer's original audience would have known a much wider and more varied repertoire and would not always have thought of the one with respect to the other. Nonetheless, there seems to be a special relationship between the two great epics that have come down to us (see Introduction, pp. xlii–xliii and n. 12). Here, certainly, it is impossible not to recall Khrysês invoking Apollo by the sea (*Iliad* I.34ff.) and, even more significant, Akhilleus by the sea (*Iliad* I.348ff.). There, it is the appropriate place for him to call on his sea-goddess mother, Thetis. Here, the sea is less obviously a place to invoke Athena; nevertheless, it is the sea which separates

Telémakhos from his proximate goals of Pylos and Sparta, and, more important, separates him from his father.

275 **then said this prayer:** Fitzgerald removes a distracting reference to Athena as the object of the prayer. Knowledge of the goddess' identity is attributed to the narrator, not to Telémakhos. Still, it is a distraction, for readers at least; one suspects that listeners would be less bothered by this. (See 313–14, where Homer says Athena but Telémakhos seems to react as if only Mentor had been his interlocutor.)

290f. Athena in Mentor's guise here picks up a concern Telémakhos had voiced when speaking to her in her disguise as Mentês (I.258–60) and which she had begun to address there (I.266–68).

292 Although alliteration is not eschewed by Homer, Stanford (1.244 [on II.276]) seems correct in noting that the heavy alliteration in the Greek here [four of the seven words of line 276 begin with "p"] suggests a proverbial ring to the sentiment. Many poets may feel it applies all too well to their standing vis-à-vis our poetic "father," Homer. For all we know, "Homer" may well have felt inferior to one or more of his predecessors in the oral tradition, now utterly lost to us except through Homer's own tribute.

293 **one in a thousand** is Fitzgerald's invention. Homer is more optimistic, repeating the word ("rare" or "few") he had used in the preceding line [276, 277].

306 **barley meal:** These provisions, with grain as the main staple, are more like the regular diet of Homer's contemporaries than the vast quantities of meat he describes as being consumed at banquets. Contrast the sobriety of these provisions with line II.317.

322 **the way you used to:** Antínoös and the other suitors are taking note of the fact that the son of their absent and unwilling host is not the easily manipulated boy he once was (see II.329–30).

333 This is not the cleverest of things for Telémakhos to say. Although he has already shown a capacity to prevaricate, Telé-

makhos is not yet up to his father's ability to dissemble consistently, nor will he ever equal his father in cunning.

341, 349 Note that the next two speakers are nameless. Both suitors are sarcastic, the first more biting in his mockery, the second almost blasé.

357 **Telémakhos:** Homer says merely, "He, however . . ." [337], leaving the listener to understand who is meant.

359ff. Despite the years of consumption by the suitors, Odysseus' wealth is still great, guarded as it is by Eurýkleia, the one true servant of the household.

360 **oil:** Olive oil, in the ancient as in the modern Mediterranean world richly prized. Indeed, after Homer's time Athens attributed its name to Athena's gift of the olive to the then unnamed settlement.

361–65, 372–75 Even the wine can provide an occasion for a thought of the absent Odysseus.

388–89 **Lord Odysseus . . . :** Eurýkleia, too, speaks, when it suits her argument, as if she believes Odysseus is surely dead, although we have just learned that she keeps a special urn reserved against his homecoming.

405ff. That Athena so rapidly dons another disguise, of Telémakhos no less, and the way she so swiftly musters a crew and begs a ship of Noêmon make for a particularly charming and witty passage. Her assistance every step of the way permits a magical ending to Book II.

405 **Meanwhile** is a modern device to permit the author and reader to jump backwards in time and to view a second action as simultaneous with one already narrated. Homer usually presents simultaneous events serially. It does seem likely that Athena went about her business while Telémakhos went about his, but it is an important facet of Homeric narrative that this simultaneity is not insisted upon. We simply are presented with another action, and neither poet nor audience seems overconcerned with accounting for units of time on the narrative microlevel.

In the Greek, both logical and temporal connections are conveyed by means of a rich system of grammatical particles, used by Homer singly and in multiple combinations. They are often impossible to translate "literally," but without them, Homer's narrative web would unravel.

413 That Athena drags the beached ship to the shore herself is of course unusual. It would otherwise have required a number of crew members, whose arrival on board is postponed until after Athena has procured the ship and done much of the outfitting on her own. This postponement constitutes the only deviation that this instance of ship launching exhibits when compared with the "typical scene" of Homeric ship launching.

The fullest standard pattern, constructed by collating and combining all comparable moments in the text, comprises nine stages. Here in Book II we have the first such scene in *The Odyssey*, and, likely for that reason, Homer, who in a number of the later instances abbreviates the scene (IV.831ff.; VIII.52ff.; XI.1ff.; XIII.22ff.; XV.254ff.; 351ff.; also *Iliad* I.478ff.) produces a particularly expansive treatment here. The nine stages of launching are (1) crew selection (here II.407–9); (2) the crew makes its way to the ship (416, postponed as noted above); (3) the beached ship is drawn down to the sea (413); (4) the ship is readied for the voyage (414); (5) the ship is "moored in the harbor" (415); (6) the ship is provisioned (435–40); (7) passengers and crew board the ship (441–42); (8) "the mooring ropes are loosed" (443–44); (9) a favorable wind blows and the voyage begins (445–55). (The above closely follows the summary provided by West in HWH 1.153 [on II.382ff.].)

417–23 Homer has Athena make the suitors drunk and drowsy. We might ask: why not have her kill them and restore Odysseus and order to Ithaka? The Homeric gods do not work that way. They hinder or assist, often at crucial moments, but (as the saying has it) they help those most who help themselves, augmenting each individual's own talents and tendencies. Here we might note that the suitors apparently did a pretty good job of getting soused on their own, and Athena's assistance must have been incremental at best.

426 A particularly "lofty" line in Greek, including one sesquipedalian (i.e., seven-syllabled) word as well as one of five and another of four syllables [300].

434 **now strong in the magic:** The Greek speaks of "the divine force of Telémakhos" [409], although the contexts in which it and comparable formulae appear do not seem as a rule to emphasize either divinity or strength. Presumably the idea is that the hero so described is either now or generally charismatic.

444 **benches** seems to make sense, and the term [*kleîsi*, 419] was long so understood, but we also have here the same "tholepins" that Homer and Fitzgerald give us at VIII.41. Tholepins are "hook-shaped fittings to which the oars were attached for rowing by leather loops" (West, HWH 1.156).

449–55 Homer (and Fitzgerald) knew and loved the workings of sailing ships and sailors, as this vivid, detailed, and technically accurate account indicates. The exacting precision of Homer's imagination and diction, precision without pedantry, is a hallmark of his style and one of the touchstones of his excellence.

BOOK III

The Lord of the
Western Approaches

1–2 **The sun rose:** As in the jump from Book I to Book II, here
we have a contrast between "through the night" (II.461) and the
rising sun.

6 **Pylos town:** There has been much debate about the exact
location of Nestor's Pylos. While there were several sites of that
name, archeological finds have established that there was a major
Mycenaean palace at Epano Englianos, just over ten miles north
of the site in Messenia (in the southwest corner of the Pelopon-
nese), known in Classical times as Pylos. This seems most likely
to have been the palace that at some point in the tradition before
Homer had caused the name "Pylos" ("Pu-ro" in the Linear B
tablets found there) to enter poetry (see illustration 2). Homer's
geographical notions are not to be judged by modern standards
of accuracy, so it matters neither that it would probably have
taken longer to sail to the beach nearest Pylos from Ithaka (if we
can be certain where that was) than the single night that divides
Books II and III in *The Odyssey* nor that it would have taken

43

considerably longer to walk from the shore to the Mycenaean palace of Pylos than III.457ff. suggests. Homer would not have visited the site, and, even if he had, it is doubtful he could have seen much, since the great palace had been destroyed by a fire about 1200 B.C.E., long before his day. In short, at least for *The Odyssey* itself, any resemblances between the Homeric Pylos and the Mycenaean Pylos are purely accidental.

7 **Neleus:** See 36, below.

9 **the blue-maned god who makes the islands tremble:** This is Poseidon, god of the sea, and of course the prime thwarter among the gods of Odysseus' return. The link between Pylos and Poseidon is likely of old standing in the epic tradition: "In the Linear B tablets from Epano Englianos Poseidon is the most important divinity" (West, HWH 1.160 [on III.6]).

13 The smoke from the burning fat rises for the gods. It seems likely, although it remains a point of debate among scholars, that some or all of the worshipers ate the meat after sufficient smoke had "sated" the divinity. The sacrifice of eighty-one bulls is impressive even by Homeric standards, indicating primarily the piety but also the relative affluence of Pylos.

22 **so we may broach the storehouse of his mind:** Instead of "mind," Homer has Athena use the same word for "wily cunning" [*mêtis*, 18] that is so frequently used to characterize Odysseus.

26–29 Telémakhos is acutely aware of his youth and inexperience; the absence of his father forces him to approach Nestor betimes.

32–33 **I should say . . . :** Neither Homer nor Athena tires of their little joke, and, presumably, Homer's audience didn't either.

36 The first picture of Nestor, seated among his sons, emblematizes the ideal. Here and frequently after Nestor is described with the patronymic "son of Neleus." The sixth-century Athenian tyrant Peisístratos, under whom some sort of Athenian edition of the Homeric poems seems to have been made (though the importance of the so-called Peisístratean recension is debated by scholars), claimed descent from the Neleids. Clearly a devotee of Homer, he would have taken particular pleasure in seeing a forebear of the same name presented here as a noble youth.

45–55 Observing proprieties, Peisístratos not only addresses Mentor, the older of the two guests (as he himself explains), first, but also asks the two to participate in the ceremony before seeking to learn their identities.

53 **on whom all men depend:** Literally, "all humans have need of the gods." This sentiment defines the Greek conception of all those who can be regarded as human.

59 **at some length:** Or "earnestly."

60–68 There is an obvious charm to Athena praying to Poseidon (60–66), particularly since he is the major obstacle to her achieving her aim (see the council of the gods at the opening of Book I, at 42ff.); the narrator underlines the irony in lines 67–68.

65–66 **third** Athena cleverly lets her hosts know with whom they are dealing and with great cunning virtually binds them in advance to agree to what they will be asked by including this hope in her public prayer.

75–76 To have waited until after the guests had eaten to ask these questions is yet another sign of Nestor's excellent manners and observation of protocol.

79–81 **corsairs** is an inspired choice, for "pirate" has too negative a connotation. The career of "privateer" or professional raider has been regarded in many cultures and over many centuries as a viable if not entirely respectable option; indeed, "corsairs" have been lionized from the ancient Greek novels to Byron, from Sir Francis Drake to John Paul Jones. Nestor himself refers to sailing for pillage below (114). To the argument that this was a time of war we might respond that the intense competition for goods around the Mediterranean amounted to a virtually constant state of war through much of the second and first millennia B.C.E. and, indeed, for many centuries after. We may well ask if it has ceased yet.

89–90 Though very subtle, this distinction between public and private business is a reminder of what is rotten in the state of Ithaka: were all things as they should be, the affairs of Odysseus' household would be of public concern.

94–99 Telémakhos and his family are suffering the uncertainty that all the loved ones of people missing in action undergo.

111–217 Nestor was noted for the loquacity to which this speech gives ample testimony.

117–20 Note the increasing weight as Nestor goes through this minicatalog: two heroes each receive one half line, one hero receives one line, and finally one hero—Nestor's son—receives tribute of two whole lines, exactly as in the Greek [109–12]. This structure is called *crescendo;* when there are three elements, it is called *tricolon crescendo* (see XI.294–95, below). It is a frequent building block of units ranging from single lines to full episodes.

122–25 **Could any mortal man . . . :** On the one hand, it is a commonplace to convey the immensity of something by claiming it can't be related in speech (the *inexpressibility topos*) and is thus utterly traditional; on the other hand, if we posit one organizing talent as creator of *The Odyssey*, it is hard not to see this as a witty and ironic self-reference. The irony would increase if the poet of *The Odyssey* were also the singer of *The Iliad*. (On the likelihood of both hypotheses, see Introduction, pp. xxxiii–xlii.) If we put the emphasis on "the whole story," this might be a jab at those poets who attempted to do just that. The creator or creators of both *The Iliad* and *The Odyssey* understood the value of selectivity and structure, and later classicizing critics (e.g., Aristotle, Horace) praised Homer and castigated the cyclic poets for just this; the most severe judgment on the latter is of course the fact that their creations survive only in the most meager of fragments and précis.

132–35 **your father?:** Nestor raises the very question troubling Telémakhos—is he really Odysseus' son? (in the Greek [122–23],

this is more explicit than Fitzgerald's question mark alone)—only
to answer with a resounding affirmative.

139 **all the good advice:** Nestor is not embarrassed to voice his
complete self-satisfaction.

146ff. Athena must be gratified that Nestor understands perfectly
well why she grew angry with the Greeks. (For an extended
interpretation of the entire *Odyssey* from the perspective of
Athena's wrath, see Jenny Strauss Clay, *The Wrath of Athena*.)

167 On the taking of slave women and concubinage, see I.482ff.,
above.

183–97 **long sea route:** Pious man that he is, Nestor waited for
an omen (187) before he decided which route to take. He chose
the route that involved more open-water legs, that is, with fewer
nearby ports in which to seek shelter if a sudden storm should
arise. Thanks to his trust in the gods, nothing untoward hap-
pened. Further aspects of his piety emerge at 192–93 and 197.
Contrast impious Aias at IV.534ff., destroyed although he sailed
what would have been considered the more conservative route.

202–11 The whole speech (lines 111–217), but particularly these
lines, serves as partial link and sequel to *The Iliad*, which ends
before the sack of Troy, indeed, before the death of Akhilleus,
much less the journey home.

205–7 Idómeneus' not losing any of his comrades on the voyage
home contrasts markedly with Odysseus, who loses all.

209–17 Again, though the name is not spoken, Orestês appears as
the model for Telémakhos to emulate. The swift conclusion of the
speech, turning from Orestês to Telémakhos, leaves open the way
Odysseus' son will have to avenge the wrongs against his father.

228–30 **My dear young friend . . . :** Now we realize how deli-
cately Nestor refrained from bringing up this painful subject,
waiting for Telémakhos to broach it first.

235–39 Athena's special care for Odysseus was well known to all
the Greeks.

247ff. **What strange talk you permit yourself . . . :** Teléma-
khos' response, not merely modest but verging on despair, now
provokes Athena/Mentor's theology lesson. She does not disagree
with his implication (245) that there are limits to what the gods
can do; she does, however, make clear that only death puts a
mortal beyond their capacity to help (254–56). Returning Odys-
seus from the farthest point of his travels is well within their
powers.

254–55 **as for death, of course all men must suffer it . . . :**
Although, as we will soon learn (V.142–43, 217–18), Kalypso has
offered Odysseus immortality as her consort.

258–61 Here it seems as if Telémakhos is not just being cautiously
pessimistic but rather expressing his most sincere belief.

269–70 Argos here does not refer to the city, whose ruler was
Diomêdês, but more generally the kingdom of the sons of Atreus.
By asking where Meneláos was, Telémakhos suggests that he
imagines Sparta and Mycenae to be more or less contiguous, and
so they may well be in poetry, even if fifty miles separates the
archeological sites.

278–79 **no burial mound:** To lie unburied, prey for birds and
dogs, was the worst fate imaginable for Hellenes (see I.280–87,
above, and V.321–23, below, and compare *Iliad* I.4–5—a very
prominent passage. This is also the fate of the "minstrel" to watch
over Klytaimnéstra, as described immediately hereafter, line
292). Orestês buried both Klytaimnéstra and Aigísthos (see 335–
36).

285–90 Klytaimnéstra is an obvious antitype of Penélopê, who not
only starts out faithful but remains so (and for twice as long). The
"minstrel" or bard makes for an interesting companion and
appears in no other ancient version of the story. Homer may be
prodding his audience (and especially present or prospective pa-
trons) to recall the moral value of his songs and his singing: by
telling of virtuous forebears and their opposites, he reminds his
listeners that their good deeds will be a source of undying praise,

their misbehavior of equally undying blame. For another perspective on the minstrel, see VIII.70, below.

302 **Phrontis** means "foresight" or "prudence." His father's name might be rendered "Benefactor."

325–27 In the next book we will hear more of Meneláos' doings in Egypt. The story of one who, returning from the war, spends some years in trade is not unlike the one that Odysseus, calling himself a Kretan, will put out when he returns to Ithaka.

334 **snake:** Fitzgerald's term is figurative and has no literal basis here in Homer [307–8]. Fitzgerald may be alluding to the snake of Klytaiméstra's dream described in Aeschylus' *Libation Bearers* (523–50) and which stands for the avenging Orestês.

362–67 Even immortal Athena seems to have wearied of good Nestor's lengthy speeches. He has literally talked until the sun set (359).

377 Zeus is the special god of guest friendship, often invoked in this regard with the epithet Xenios. The laws of hospitality, which Zeus safeguards, demand that Nestor provide them quarters in his home (see VI.130–31, VIII.175, XIV.189–90, below).

387–401 Athena/Mentor speaks to Nestor as one elder to another. This whole story (388–401) is a bluff—just the sort her ward Odysseus might improvise—to explain why she will have disappeared by morning. One element is not bluff, however: Athena quite explicitly tells Nestor to send Telémakhos overland (400–401). In her absence, she prefers Telémakhos to stay clear of Poseidon's realm. Then, after her alibi is prepared, she reveals her divinity by flying off as a bird (402–3). This has its intended effect of astonishing and heartening both the Pylians and Telémakhos (404–17).

411 **his third child:** After Apollo and Artemis. This explanation for the epithet *tritogeneia* [378], while possible, is now considered by scholars to be less likely than "true-born" or "legitimate daughter." Since Athena was born from Zeus alone, without a mother's aid, her legitimacy as Zeus' offspring is unquestionable.

414 **dear wife:** The Greek is nearer "chaste consort" [381]. As the diametrically opposed examples of Klytaimnéstra and Penélopê indicate, no Greek wife could be dear unless she was chaste.

430, 432 **showed Telémakhos / . . . to a fine bed near the bed of Peisístratos:** Homer more simply says, "settled Telémakhos in bed . . . beside Peisístratos" [397–400], an unusual practice in Homer, but, then again, Peisístratos is Nestor's only unmarried son.

436–542 In the final hundred lines of the book, two complete days pass from sunrise to sunset. (Indeed, the Greek of lines 436 and 534 is precisely the same [404, 491], as is the Greek of lines 530 and 542 [487, 497]). The sacrifice with all due ceremony was obviously a poetic set piece, the details pleasing to its original audience, and even we, for whom such rites are foreign, can sense the ceremonial splendor and pious grandeur it bestows on the penultimate scenes of Book III. The final scene carries Peisístratos and Telémakhos to the plains of Sparta, with a proper "fade-out" in the final verse.

489 The "wail of joy" is part of the ceremony.

506–8 **Polykástê, a fair girl . . . :** This bathing was an honor for both Telémakhos and Polykástê (see VI.137–39, below). Later legend had Polykástê bear Telémakhos' son, Persepolis (Hesiod, *Catalogue of Women*, fr. 221). West has proposed "that the poet of *The Odyssey* devised this episode to foreshadow a union already familiar in legend" (HWH 1.189 [on III.464ff.]). Even later Homer was named as the child of this union.

516–42 **charioteers:** Note that transport is by horse-drawn chariot; Homeric heroes did not ride horseback (see V.384ff., below). The idea that one could actually have gone from the historic site of Pylos over Mount Taÿgetos to that of Sparta by chariot in Homer's day, much less before, is pure fantasy. Again, it is a mistake to seek geographical and/or topographical realism in the Homeric epic.

BOOK IV

The Red-Haired King
and His Lady

3–16 Telémakhos and Peisístratos arrive at a moment when the splendor and sensuality of Meneláos' and Helen's court is displayed to the full. Sparta's splendor puts modest Ithaka in perspective. Telémakhos has never seen anything like it (see 77–81). But be it ever so humble, there's no place like home (see 186 and 641, below, and for the sentiment, IX.38–40).

The "double wedding feast" is that of Hermionê, the daughter of the royal pair, to Neoptólemos, Akhilleus' son, and of Megapénthês, Meneláos' son by a nameless slave woman, to the daughter of Alektor. Megapénthês' name means "great sorrow" and would refer to Meneláos' distress at Helen's departure with Paris. Homer says that "the gods had never after [Hermionê] granted Helen / a child" (13–14), which sounds to modern ears like a discreet reference to fertility problems. It's more likely an oblique reference to Helen's infidelity: the couple have been apart for most of the past twenty years, during the first ten of which Helen was Paris' lover. Finally, it highlights the fact that, in contrast to Odysseus and Nestor, Meneláos has no legitimate male heir.

For all their superficial congeniality, Helen and Meneláos are not the ideal couple of one mind that Odysseus and Penélopê will eventually be proved to be. Nonetheless, Meneláos, Helen, and Telémakhos form a temporary family structure, something Telémakhos cannot even remember. The encounters with Nestor in Book III and Meneláos and Helen in Book IV bring Telémakhos into physical proximity with the heroes and major figures of the Trojan War, thus indirectly with the father he seeks.

31 **someone free to receive them:** In other words, not already occupied in hosting a large number of friends, retainers, and other guests. As Meneláos' response shows, this was a crassly inhospitable (if practical) suggestion.

35–37 The hardships of the return are never far from anyone's mind, and, in the present context, we must also think of Odysseus, likewise relying on "the kindness of strangers."

67–69 **forebears and families . . . :** This was an aristocratic culture, and one's "breeding" was expected to be evident.

75 An islander from Ithaka, Telémakhos rather than Nestor's son is more impressed by the splendor of the court.

84 Meneláos cannot let Telémakhos' comparison (80–81) of his wealth with Zeus' stand, lest he suffer divine envy. The ancient gods were quick to punish any mortals whose presumption led them to vie with the gods (see also 193, below).

90 **the sun-burnt races:** The Ethiopians [84], whom the Greeks imagined had been darkened by their proximity to the sun (see I.36, above).

91 **men of . . . Arabia:** The "Eremboi" [84] are mentioned nowhere else. "Arabs" may well be intended (the ancient geographer Strabo thought so), but no certainty is possible.

92–96 The travelogue becomes ever more fantastic; the wonders of exotic places hold a perennial fascination, from Homer through the classical and medieval periods up to the present day (we might instance television travel programs).

97ff. **But while I made my fortune . . . :** There is no little self-reproach in this speech. Although he is wealthy, Meneláos' homecoming lacks the joy and satisfaction awaiting Odysseus, even if the latter must wait longer and suffer more.

98 **a stranger killed my brother:** Not so much a "stranger" in the strict sense (murderer and murdered were first cousins) as an "interloper" [*allos,* 91].

114–23 Even before Homer describes Telémakhos' reaction (124ff.), the listener can imagine the emotions—simultaneous pride and grief—that go through him hearing Odysseus praised thus, the speaker unaware of the identity of his interlocutor. In Book VIII (533ff.), an unidentified Odysseus will likewise hear of his own exploits, although he has manipulated the situation to a certain extent.

127 **Meneláos knew him now . . . :** One of the many moving recognitions in the poem: Meneláos knows Telémakhos from his tears (124–27). Homer leaves it open for us to wonder if Meneláos didn't have a strong suspicion and if his speech, though sincere, wasn't calculated to test such a hypothesis.

131ff. The poet cleverly places the entrance of fabled Helen at this very juncture, when the other characters have been reduced to either sobs or embarrassed silence. The Helen of *The Odyssey* is not the Helen who precipitated the Trojan War: beautiful, elegant, loving luxury, yes, but now with a mature and gentle grace (she is after all the mother of the bride, not the bride).

138 **in the treasure city, Thebes:** Mention of the wealth of Egypt and in particular of the fabled upper-Egyptian city, Thebes, very likely reflects renewed trade between Greece and Egypt in the eighth and seventh centuries B.C.E., near Homer's time. It is possibly a reminiscence of the important contacts between Egypt and Mycenaean Greece much earlier.

146 **dusky violet wool:** It is unlikely that the wool is already dyed. Rather, "violet" probably suggests a rich and lustrous sheen. It is notoriously difficult to correlate ancient color terminology with the modern spectrum, much less find entirely adequate translations.

Words describing colors provide an uncontroversial example of how the same "reality" is perceived and described differently in different languages. Scientists can establish the frequency of the light waves reflected by a range of substances, yet speakers of one language will call a certain range red which speakers of another language would insist is orange, purple, anything but red. Ancient Greek color vocabulary suggests that the Greeks responded as much or more to the reflectivity and brilliance of colors as to the frequency of the light waves, as here "violet" seems to describe the wool's tone rather than its tint.

152–55 **Never ... likeness:** A further confirmation of Telémakhos' identity as true son of Odysseus: although Helen didn't witness Telémakhos' reaction to her husband's reminiscences (124–27), she independently and spontaneously recognizes Telémakhos. She is also smarter—and semidivine.

157 **the wanton that I was:** Helen is frank about her shortcomings, indeed, so blunt and cold she might as well be talking about a different person. In fact, Helen pointing out the Greek forces from the walls of Troy refers to herself in exactly the same terms (*Iliad*, III.180), to which the passage here alludes.

170 **gentle:** "Sensible" might be a safer rendering of *saophrôn* [158]; in any event, there is no implication of softness in the Homeric adjective.

182 Meneláos feels a special responsibility, for it was to bring back his abducted but wandering wife that the whole Trojan expedition was undertaken.

186–89 We may well doubt whether the king of Ithaka would have taken up Meneláos' offer (which was probably not meant to be understood as anything more than a conventional compliment).

Odysseus prefers rocky Ithaka to the blandishments of Kalypso in Book V, and he certainly would not have exchanged his Ithakan independence for fealty to Meneláos, no matter how rich the mainland soil.

193 **envious** of "these things" [*ta*, 181], meaning the fantasy Meneláos has just sketched. Meneláos misses the mark in compassing the reasons the gods have not (yet) permitted Odysseus' return.

201 **the son of shining Dawn:** Memnon. His father was Tithonos, a mortal with whom the goddess Dawn fell in love and to whom (in some accounts) she was able to grant immortality. Kalypso has something like this in mind for Odysseus (see V.142–43, 217–18).

208 **Dawn will soon be here:** The implication is not that it is late but rather that on the morrow (and every subsequent day) there will be ample time for further expressions of grief. Given Peisístratos' train of thought throughout the passage, his mention of Dawn (208), however standard, hardly seems casual. The balance of his speech (209–17) is about death and mourning, in particular the death of his brother Antílokhos, killed by Dawn's son.

215 **no mean soldier:** In Greek, "not the worst of the Argives" [199–200]. The figure of *litotes* or understatement occurs frequently in Homer and other epics and may bespeak the same kind of prudence we observe when characters speak as if the worst has already happened or when they seek to avoid envy of the gods.

215–16 Like Telémakhos, who does not know his father, Peisístratos has never known his older brother. Added almost as an afterthought, this fact doubles Peisístratos' loss and brings the depth of his grief home to us.

227 **sons:** Close to the surface is Meneláos' regret that he, unlike Nestor or Odysseus, has no legitimate male heir.

235ff. If there is any real substance behind Helen's magic anodyne, it is more likely to be an Egyptian herbal concoction called *kyphi* than opium. (On the Egyptian connection, see IV.245–46). However, recourse to pharmacology is likely misguided. For all its subtle insights into the minds of its characters, *The Odyssey* is not "realistic" according to modern conceptions of the term. How could it be? Our notion of "reality" excludes the supernatural. Homer's is a true representation of a world where gods and mortals interact and magic is potent. Helen's epithet "sprung from Zeus" [219] (omitted from line 234 by Fitzgerald) recalls to our minds at the very beginning of this passage the fact that she is semidivine. (See also "Zeus's daughter," 243.)

250ff. Although Helen ostensibly ministered her drug to relieve the pain her husband and her guests felt as they remembered their losses, the sequence here suggests that some sort of mind and judgment alteration is the ideal preparation—at least from the teller's perspective—for the somewhat self-serving narrative which follows. As we will see, Helen's picture of her loyalty to the Greeks even while she was in Troy is contradicted by the anecdote Meneláos tells (287ff.).

258–59 Amusing words to come out of the mouth of any singer of *The Odyssey,* even if he has here adopted Helen's voice.

262–68 The disguise in which Odysseus penetrates the Trojan citadel is the same he will employ to return undetected to his home; here the beating is self-inflicted.

271–72 One of the internal contradictions of Helen's account: if, as she seems to imply, Odysseus' filthy condition and rags were essential elements of his disguise, why did he permit himself to be bathed, anointed, and given fine clothes, even by Helen? (She did first swear "on oath not to give him away," 272–73.)

282 **the mad day:** Helen does not deny her guilt but mitigates it somewhat by attributing her culpable behavior to *atê* [261], a folly or overwhelming passion. It is not quite the modern American plea of "innocent by virtue of insanity." "Involuntary adultery" would be closer (on the analogy of "involuntary manslaughter"), or the idea of excusing adultery as the same sort of "crime of passion" which, when it applies to men punishing their wives and their lovers caught *flagrante delicto*, can go unpunished in some societies.

287 **An excellent tale, my dear . . . :** This is deliciously polite irony. No need to have a scene in front of the guests! Meneláos simply relates an anecdote which gives Helen's the lie. The wooden horse (see VIII.533–47) was brought beneath Troy's walls after the scene Helen has just described, yet she had claimed to have "repented" and "come round" "long before" (280) that time. Under the pretense of merely telling another story about Odysseus, he effectively contradicts her. Perhaps through his years with Helen, Meneláos has developed some resistance to her drugs. The young men, under their influence and polite to boot, notice nothing. As listeners and readers, we have only heard of Helen's drugs, not imbibed them, so we can exercise some discretion. Of course, we cannot give more credit to Meneláos' account simply because it comes second or because he is a man and Helen a woman (although many Greek men would have been inclined to do so for the latter reason).

295–98 On the one hand, attributing Helen's aid to the Trojans to some "superhuman power" [*daimôn*, 275] would seem to clear her or would at least mitigate the guilt. On the other, to mention "Deïphobos, that handsome man" is a jab, since after Paris' death Helen took up with Deïphobos.

301 **making your voice sound like their wives:** Ancient scholars ridiculed the implausibility of this idea: among obvious problems, how did Helen know which heroes were inside so that she could know which voices to imitate? How and when had Helen met all these wives so that she knew their voices well enough to imitate them? However, we are not to seek logical answers to all questions: there's something magical about Helen. Nevertheless, it is worth noting that we have only Meneláos' testimony for this; it could be that he and the others heard their wives' voices in Helen's voice and inferred her intent from their experience.

In the 1954 film of *The Odyssey*, with Kirk Douglas as Odysseus, this idea is transferred to the Seirênês. (In Homer, there is no hint of this aspect of the song of the Seirênês, see XII.220–45.) The film is not Homer, of course, but it is great fun and well worth seeing. And it represents a piece of modern mythography that is in essence no different from the transformations that the Homeric material was undergoing all the time at the hands of the bards.

306–11 This brief episode, even down to the detail of Antiklos' name, foreshadows Odysseus' squelching of Eurýkleia, when she almost blurts out his name (XIX.557ff.). It is not in all ancient texts, and ancient scholars advanced reasons to excise it. If it is not original to the conception of the first singer of *The Odyssey*, it has been added along the way to flesh out and harmonize this narrative of the wooden horse with material described elsewhere in the epic cycle—as well as for the sake of the foreshadowing. (This brief excursion into Homeric textual criticism may stand for hundreds of other similar points; the reader, particularly the modern reader, will often be unaware of the fact that behind the text editors print, or a translator translates, lie many thousands of decisions. It seems that we will have to add to the list of questions that cannot be answered with absolute certainty not only "Who was Homer?" but "What was the real Homeric text of *The Odyssey*?" Fortunately, the poem itself withstands the uncertainty, like a painting which is a recognized masterpiece despite centuries of accumulated grime.)

360–61 Fawns . . . lion's . . . doe . . . sucklings: Similes are less frequent in *The Odyssey* than in *The Iliad*, but those the poet employs are almost always drawn (as in *The Iliad*) from nature; animal life is the richest source for similes in both epics.

375 Ancient of the Sea: Proteus, as Menaláos explains in the next passage.

378 Egypt: For the Greeks the source not only of wealth but also of wisdom.

379 hekatombs: Sacrifices, strictly speaking, of one hundred oxen each, but even the gods didn't count the animals per sacrifice, only the number of sacrifices.

394 The seashore is again the site of an epiphany. The wisdom that Telémakhos gleans from Meneláos is greater, not lesser, for coming to him at second hand (like epic tales handed down from singer to singer). Meneláos needs Eidothea's help even to learn how to seize and interrogate Proteus, indeed, even to learn that Proteus exists and has significant wisdom. (The name "Eidothea" may mean either "knowing goddess" or "goddess of many forms"; for both name and helper function, see Leukothea, V.346ff.)

In the "miniepic" of the first four books, the entire episode of Meneláos and Proteus corresponds to the *nekuia* or underworld voyage of the larger structure. As in the case of the underworld journey, the traveler must follow a strict set of prescriptions. (In Vergilian terms, Eidothea is Meneláos' Sibyl, who guides Aeneas through Hades in Book VI of *The Aeneid*.) Proteus himself is a shape changer or djinn—once held, he is compelled to answer Meneláos' questions.

411ff. A young girl, taken to be a goddess, and a marooned sailor meet on the strand, and in response to his request for aid she tells him how to obtain substantive assistance from her father. As we shall see, the encounter here bears an uncanny resemblance to the one between Nausikaa and Odysseus (Book VI), and Meneláos' companions donning sealskins to trick Proteus foreshadows in some details Odysseus in Polyphêmos' cave (Book IX). Story elements serve comparable functions, motifs recur, multiple scenes are of the same type—all this is characteristic of popular traditional literary forms, whether folk- or fairy tales or oral-formulaic poetry. This said, however, the anticipations remain noteworthy and further bind the first four books, the so-called Telemachy, to the story of Odysseus. Indeed, as we have seen, Odysseus is never absent from these books.

471–76 The "stench" of the sealskins may seem a surprising touch of "realism" in so fantastic an episode, but it is not uncharacteristic of authentic folktales, or dreams for that matter. Later critics found the use of divine ambrosia, as a sort of pomade against the foul smell of the sealskins, an even more serious breach of decorum, and Vergil, when imitating the episode, has the goddess Cyrene anoint her son Aristaeus' entire body (*Georgics* IV.415–16).

480 **At noon:** In the hot Mediterranean climate, midday, when sensible people seek shadow and rest, is also a time when spirits walk about. ("Only mad dogs and Englishmen / go out in the midday sun."—Noël Coward)

481 In Homer, we have the further detail that Proteus' seals are "well fed" [*zatrepheas,* 451]. Homer seems to have enjoyed a mild play on words here that cannot be rendered in English: the same form [*lekto*], occurring in the same metrical slot in both lines, means "count" in one place [451; Fitzgerald 481] and, from a different verb, "lie down to sleep" [453; Fitzgerald 483] in the second. Oral traditions on the whole seem to license such wordplay or paronomasia more than written traditions: the pun (as anecdote, not figure) is itself an exclusively oral genre, while neoclassical critics reading Shakespeare feel compelled to apologize for his "indulging in" wordplay, which was an essential part of the spoken theater for which he composed. Although the play on two senses of *lekto* is a minor example, coming as it does in this passage it provides an opportunity to note that, like Proteus, the singer is a shape changer.

493 **Son of Atreus:** It goes without saying that, as a god, Proteus has long since identified the captain among his captors and knows his name. He only feigns ignorance of the god who instructed Meneláos in the way to trap him and the reason for his doing so; in fact, Meneláos calls him on this make-believe (498). This remark by Meneláos also puts Proteus on notice that Meneláos is on the lookout for further trickery.

511 **Nile:** It is interesting that "Egypt" in the Greek serves Homer as the term for both the land and the river which floods it, while the Greek form of "Nile" appears in neither *Iliad* nor *Odyssey*.

530 **Many . . . died, many remain:** This kind of "polar" expression—that is, describing the two extreme possibilities or poles—is typical perhaps of all language, but certainly of ancient pronouncements.

533–34 **One is alive . . . :** Homer actually has Proteus say "and one" [498] rather than just "one," even if he goes on to describe the two "lost" during the homecoming (534–73) and has to be prompted by Meneláos (586–89) to speak of this third, the castaway. Fitzgerald's translation has the disadvantage of suggesting that "Aias" is the other of two, of which the castaway is the first. For this reason I would have rendered the opening of line 534 "Now Aias."

This Aias is not Télamonian Aías, who contended with Odysseus for the right to wear the arms of the slain Akhilleus, lost the debate, and as a consequence went mad and committed suicide (the subject of Sophocles' tragedy *Ajax*). Rather, this is the Lokrian Aias, whose father was Oïleus and who attempted to ravish the Trojan priestess Kassandra, thereby arousing the wrath of the gods, Athena in particular. (The more common English version of the name, Ajax, is based on the Latin form.)

538–40 Aias here is the type or model of the disdainer of the gods, and his impious insolence brings instant retribution.

547ff. **Meanwhile your brother . . . :** Proteus speaks of Meneláos' brother, Agamémnon, who technically reached home safely (557–58) but met foul play there. Although Odysseus is not there to hear it, Proteus' description of what went wrong because of Agamémnon's open arrival is ample justification for the lengths to which Odysseus goes to disguise his own return. While the murder of Agamémnon is news, grievous news to Meneláos at the time Proteus tells him, we and Telémakhos have heard this story repeatedly. Orestês, the example ever held up before Telémakhos as a "role model," appears at 582–83. At the moment of Proteus' exchange with Meneláos described here, Orestês was only a prospective avenger, and Proteus is or pretends to be uncertain whether Meneláos or Orestês will kill Aigísthos.

572 The implication of "of either company," in Greek "of the Atreid" [i.e., Agamémnon, 536] and "of Aigísthos" [537], is that Aigísthos killed all witnesses, even the members of his own retinue.

583 **the feast:** Aigísthos' burial, an occasion for feasting for Orestês and Meneláos but also part of the rites accorded even Aigísthos (see III.278–79, above).

586ff. The news of Odysseus that Telémakhos has sought so long is placed last, for maximum tension. Even then it is excruciatingly brief (591–96). And although Proteus goes on to prophesy Meneláos' safe return, he says nothing about Odysseus, no doubt a disappointment to Telémakhos but obviously very much to Homer's purpose.

599ff. **Elysion** is the Greek paradise, not some heaven but a field or pasture, its most significant characteristic being its temperate climate. This is by no means the standard afterlife destination of Greeks and is accorded Meneláos because he is the husband of Zeus' daughter Helen, as Proteus explains (607–8). The only other inhabitant of Elysion we know of is Rhadamanthos (600; it really ought to be "Rhadamanthys" [564]), of Kretan provenance and inserted into Greek mythology as Zeus' son by Europa. The Kretan connection may suggest that Elysion reflects Minoan conceptions of the afterlife. The name *Elysion* itself refers to the holiness of any place or person "struck by lightning" (*enêlysios*). (On this, see West, HWH 1.227 [on IV.563ff.], following Burkert for the last detail.)

629–33 It was customary not for the guest to bring a gift to his host—that might have seemed like payment—but for the host to exhibit his largess further by giving gifts to his guests upon their departure.

641–51 Telémakhos, with admirable but slightly gauche frankness, asks for something more fitting for Ithaka. In his description of the "island of islands," rockier than the rich plains of the mainland, one catches a sentiment which comes close to being universal to humanity (if anything is): namely, the love of one's birthplace, however poor, simply because it is familiar.

658 **a wine bowl . . . :** An even better gift, because it is the work of Hephaistos (660), the divine smith and metalworker.

661 **Sidon:** Coastal city of the Phoinikians, although in Homer's day Tyre was the chief center of power, as Sidon had been in Mycenaean times. Still, the throwback to the earlier heroic age is probably the result not of Greek traditions, poetic or otherwise, but of current Phoinikian formulae: 1 Kings 16:31 provides roughly contemporaneous confirmation that the rulers of Tyre styled themselves "kings of Sidon." Hoekstra notes that in Homer, Sidonians "are always associated with craftsmanship, whereas the Phoenicians appear as traders" (in HWH 2.239 [on XV.117–18]). The contrasting usage is striking at XV.505–17. The Greeks never caught up with the Phoinikians as seafaring traders throughout the Mediterranean. The Phoinikians established trading factories and settlements in Spain, on the mainland and islands of Italy, and of course in North Africa. Shortly after Homer's time, the Phoinikian settlement Carthage would grow into a mercantile sea power in its own right, playing America to the England of Phoinikia.

668ff. This is a remarkable and remarkably subtle transition from Sparta to Ithaka. (Analytic critics have thought otherwise.) The simultaneous action in Fitzgerald's translation is indeed suggested in the Greek, but indirectly and approximately. There is no phrase which can be rendered "At that same hour" (668, or, for that matter, the "distant" of the following line). Rather, Homer effects the transition by contrast. The final scene in Sparta is the characteristic Dorian feast, where guests supplied the comestibles. Homer then leaps to Ithaka simply with "but": "But the suitors were taking pleasure with the discus before Odysseus' hall" [*mnêstêres de paroithen Odussêos megaroio / diskoisin terponto*, 625–26]. "Taking pleasure" is a key term: unlike the Spartan guests who contribute their produce to their lord to enable his hospitality, the Ithakan suitors continue to consume Odysseus' property, as Telémakhos has often emphasized, abusing the "hospitality" of their lord's family. Fitzgerald renders their hybris with "arrogant lords" (672).

674ff. The appearance of Noêmon at this juncture as motivator of the suitors' plots is delicious in many ways. For one thing, although it is unfortunate that the suitors learn of Telémakhos' trip at all, it is ironic that these noble and arrogant lords had no inkling of a fact that the innocent Noêmon knew all along. The very simplicity of his character is what keeps him from realizing how poorly he is serving Telémakhos by asking Antínoös and the other suitors about Telémakhos' return. (On a larger scale, the sequence of events begun here, which culminates in the suitors' openly plotting the assassination of Telémakhos, prepares the audience to see and feel justice in the eventual massacre of the suitors.) The reason Noêmon now requires the ship he lent Telémakhos—to pick up the mares with the unweaned mule colts at Elis—in its earthy practicality contrasts with the leisured pastimes of the sporting suitors. This contrast may be augmented in our minds (more easily, granted, than in the minds of at least first listeners) if we imagine how little the suitors, shocked as they clearly were (683) at the mention of Telémakhos' trip to Pylos at the opening of Noêmon's speech (677), would have cared about the details of mares and mules Noêmon describes at such length.

685 **the swineherd:** Eumaios, who will play a key role starting in Book XIV. The nameless reference suggests not only that all Ithakans, even the suitors, recognize how important he is to the household of Odysseus but also that Homer's audience likely already knew versions of the homecoming of Odysseus in which the swineherd assumed an important role.

689 **or his own slaves:** The Greek [644] distinguishes between

thêtes, hired hands or day laborers, and *dmôes*, slaves or servants who belonged to the household. Antínoös has obvious disdain for both groups. (On *thêtes*, see also XVIII.443, below, where the other archvillain among the suitors, Eurýmakhos, uses the term to insult the disguised Odysseus.)

693ff. In the face of Antínoös' menacing questioning, Noêmon makes a straightforward reply, giving testimony to his courage, honesty, and loyalty to his lord's family.

699 **or a god who looked like Mentor:** Indeed it was Athena. That Noêmon is prepared to entertain this idea shows he is a pious man, in contrast to Antínoös and all other disdainers of the gods. Of course, Noêmon has good evidence for thinking so, which he shares with Antínoös and Eurýmakhos (700–702), thus making their subsequent plotting even more foolhardy and hybristic.

722 **and trailed back to the manor:** By mere juxtaposition Homer underscores the irony that the suitors head off to consume more food and drink of the man whose son they have just agreed to murder.

730 **they:** "Noble suitors" in the Greek [681]; this is formulaic, but particularly ironic here.

735ff. **you:** In her anger and outrage, Penélopê addresses all the suitors in the person of Medôn.

739–42 Penélopê describes Odysseus' impartiality as superior to the notoriously personal and partial "justice" usually meted out by kings (in the Greek, "divine kings" [691]).

750 **you know:** Medôn of course had no way of knowing that Penélopê was not aware of Telémakhos' trip and that this is the first she hears of it. Her reaction (753ff.) is not to one but to two terrible pieces of news. Her words (758–61) suggest that it is the dangers of Telémakhos' trip itself as much as the suitors' threat that she must come to grips with first.

758 **child:** The relationship in which Telémakhos will always stand to his parents, and thus a keen expression of Penélopê's concern and grief, but at the same time the role out of which he is trying to grow.

771 **a low murmur of lament:** Penélopê's women join her in her lament even without knowing why; it is enough for them that she has reason to cry.

789 **Läertês:** Now that Penélopê knows of her son's absence, Odysseus' father is the one male she can turn to. (Her own family is far away on the mainland, see II.56, above.) Given the suitors, it is not likely that the aged Läertês could have much impact, and Eurýkleia is right for many reasons to dissuade Penélopê (794–808) from this counsel of despair.

797–800 For the oath which Telémakhos had Eurýkleia swear, and the conditions under which Penélopê could be told, see II.395–401. Eurýkleia is indeed not lying.

803–4 **to ask help from Athena . . . :** Not only is Eurýkleia sensible and pious, she is also correct: Athena will save, or at least help save, both Penélopê's son and her husband.

806–8 **the blissful gods . . . :** Just as Penélopê had ended her lament with an expression of concern for the entire line of her husband's father, Eurýkleia ends her speech of consolation with an expression of pious confidence that the gods will preserve the family. Although it is clearest at the end, Eurýkleia's speech has responded to all the points in Penélopê's lament, first explaining why she was not told of Telémakhos' departure and then dissuading her from sending for Laërtês.

815–17 It is standard, not tasteless, to remind a god of the sacrifices given in his or her honor when making a request for aid.

818 **and make the killers go astray:** Penélopê does not ask Athena to destroy the suitors, even if that were richly deserved, only to foil their attempt on Telémakhos' life.

827 Antínoös' caution is well founded but too late.

844–45 A brief but powerful simile. At times Penélopê may seem weak, but Homer shows her great strength by choosing a lion to figure her.

850 **great Ikários' other daughter:** Penélopê's sister.

854 **strap-slit:** Comparable to our modern "keyhole." While the Homeric door had a bolt on the inside and a handle (I.497), there was no knob that could be turned to latch the door. Instead, to bolt the door from the outside one pulled on the "strap" or string referred to here, which ran through the slit from the outside and was connected to the bolt on the inside (I.498). To gain access from the outside, one used the equivalent of a key (although more like a hook), again through the slit.

867–69 **My lord, my lion heart . . . :** Note that these lines repeat 775–77, as in the Greek [814–16 and 724–26]. There are many such instances in the Homeric poems; these "repetitions" have bothered critics since Hellenistic times, and some were no doubt additions well after the poem had been written down, but repetitions themselves were obviously not regarded as blemishes by Homer or his audience. The singing bard likely did not think in terms of repeating so-and-so many lines but rather, responding to a similar or identical situation, fit formulae from his repertory together with the result that the new lines were identical.

883ff. Wise Penélopê even asleep does not miss a golden opportunity for divine wisdom and quickly asks news of Odysseus. Homer's narrative economy, however, requires that she be kept in the dark, even though Meneláos, Telémakhos, and the audience know that he is alive. By presenting her request and the dream image's refusal to respond, obviously obeying Athena's command (or if that seems to grant the phantom too much autonomy, then having no specific instructions to speak on this and being nothing more than an embodiment of those instructions), Homer heightens the pathos of Penélopê's situation; it is against the backdrop of her continued forced ignorance, the mortal condition par excellence, that Homer will, at the opening of the following book, present first the council of the gods at which Athena wins Odysseus' release from Kalypso and then finally bring Odysseus himself "on stage" at last.

894–900 **Penélopê awoke, in better heart . . . :** The actual closing of the book is not, however, dark. Penélopê, even if all her questions are not answered, awakes from the dream happy, for she is reassured that Telémakhos at least will be safe, her greater and more immediate concern. This same certainty renders the final lines almost humorous: the suitors sail and lie in wait for Telémakhos. The audience, however, from an almost Olympian perspective, knows they are engaged in a vain pursuit.

BOOK V

Sweet Nymph and
Open Sea

4ff. A second "council of the gods." This episode takes up the
unfinished business of the corresponding scene in Book I, where
Athena asked Zeus to send Hermês to order Kalypso to release
Odysseus. Athena herself went off on her errand to Telémakhos
before waiting to see that Zeus did what she asked (I.122; see also
I.42ff., above). Since Homeric narration would present simulta-
neous actions sequentially as a matter of course, there is no
inherent reason why the poet would need to reconvene the gods
to have Hermês head off for Ogýgia. Hainsworth, following Page,
observes sensibly: "*The Odyssey* proper calls for some sort of intro-
duction, and an audience (or a poet . . . if we think of him as an
oral composer) needs it after having been compelled to divert
attention for so long to a sub-plot. The second council provides
that introduction . . . and reminds the audience again that the
destiny of everyone in the poem is guided by Olympus" (HWH
1.252). There are a number of councils in *The Iliad*—of the gods
at I.533 (a contentious session), VIII.1, XXIV.31, and of military

commanders (II.53, IX.89), not to mention other meetings and assemblies. The scene here conforms to an ancient pattern of divine council where a goddess initiates a complaint, supplicating the other gods or the chief god. For example, Ishtar takes her complaints against Gilgamesh before her father, Anu (Tablet VI; see *The Epic of Gilgamesh*, Maureen Gallery Kovacs, trans. [Stanford, 1985], pp. 53–54). Likewise, in the Ugaritic *Epic of Aqhat*, the goddess Anat, angered by the hero's refusal to yield her his bow, complains to El (see Cyrus H. Gordon, *Ugarit and Minoan Crete* [New York, 1966], pp. 120–39, esp. 128).

4 **master of heaven:** For Zeus' own assertion that "his power is greatest," see *Iliad* VIII.17–27. (See also I.44, above.)

9–14 **O Father Zeus . . . :** The opening of Athena's speech is striking, no less because it happens to repeat Mentor's upbraiding of the suitors (at II.241–45). (The Greek is an exact repetition [II.230–34 and IV.8–12]). In its present context it suggests a link between the justice of kings and the justice of Zeus. Athena seems to imply that if Zeus wishes kings to act with justice, he should act justly and restore a just king to power. See also Penélopê's outburst (IV.740ff.), contrasting Odysseus' fairness with all-too-common abuse of power. (The abnormally high degree of repetitions of verses or half verses from elsewhere in the poem concentrated in lines 9–22 has aroused critics' suspicions that this is late patchwork, but that is another matter; see I.42 and V.4ff., above.)

16 **the nymph:** Nymphs are secondary goddesses, fully divine but lesser than and subject to the Olympians. Both Kalypso and Kirkê are called nymphs. Homer has Athena name Kalypso here [14]: for Greeks, her name resonates with the common verb "to hide," "to conceal" [*kaluptô*]. Kalypso has, as it were, kept Odysseus in hiding these seven years.

17–19 Note that Homer tells us that Odysseus has lost his ships and his companions before we find out what disasters befell him.

26–27 As in lines 17–19, there is no question whether or not Odysseus will return home and avenge himself on the suitors.

Suspense in such a matter would have been impossible, for even Homer's first audience would have been familiar with the broad outlines of Odysseus' homecoming, his *nostos*. It was a pleasure for them to hear the familiar story again, and their interest would have been in the particular way Homer organized the scenes. The skill he exhibited at every level—the nuances of his plot, description, and characterization, his language and musical performance—would have been the basis of their pleasure.

31ff. Dispatching Hermês, Zeus follows the suggestion Athena made at I.108–12 [and, apart from the adjustment of one verb form, lines 30–31, reproduce I.86–87].

31 **favorite son:** There is no basis for Hermês being called Zeus' "favorite." This is an overtranslation of the Greek *huion philon* [28], which means "dear son" at most, but probably no more than "his son." For Greeks it went without saying that Hermês was *philos* precisely because he was a member of Zeus' family.

44 **his share of plunder:** It was standard and expected that the victors of a war would take away the goods of the vanquished; moreover, the leaders were responsible for properly apportioning shares of the booty according to the soldiers' status and contributions to the war effort. It may be noteworthy that Odysseus' riches are in the end not booty but indirect gifts from the gods, and they differ further from, say, Agamémnon's portion in not including human chattel. We should probably be wary of concluding that this should be seen as a criticism of booty taking. Odysseus, again in marked contrast to Agamémnon, was already noted as fastidious in not taking captives for personal sexual use.

50 **ambrosial:** This can refer to anything of the gods, which is by definition "immortal"—the meaning of the word "ambrosial." The consumable ambrosia is just one among many ambrosial items.

64ff. Fitzgerald's rich and more than usually "poetic" diction here gives an inkling of Homer's lush and enchanting sounds. The entire scene-setting description was clearly an opportunity for the

72 A GUIDE TO THE ODYSSEY

bard to show what he could do. As one small instance of Homer's precision and attention to detail, note that he describes the cedar as "easily split" [*eukeatoio*, 60], applying a word that appears only once in the entire *Odyssey* or *Iliad* [so-called *hapax legomenon*].

79–81 So enchanting is the place that even the immortal gods delight in gazing upon it. Note how Homer uses this sentiment to conclude the set piece and to turn our attention back to Hermês so that both we and the poet can go on to the next segment.

83 **recognized him:** The Greek has the more interesting "did not not know him" [77–78], a type of double negative likely then and ever after a feature of epic and all ornate diction. (For two of the many examples throughout the poem, see "found out" at 133, below—in the Greek, Zeus "was not unknowing" [127–28]— and "tear on tear brimming his eyes" at 158–59, below—"not then were his eyes dry of tears" [151–52].)

92ff. There is a playfulness, even an archness about Kalypso's opening formalities: "why have you come, honored and dear to me as you are?" Homer has her say [87–88]. Her tone is not quite matched by Hermês' more heavy-handed attempts to be diplomatic in an awkward situation. But then, she has so much more to lose, as she knows from the very beginning of the interview.

103–4 Hermês implies that as a goddess she ought to know ("in courtesy" could be rendered "for you ask" [98]).

108 **where gods have beef and honors from mankind:** For the Greeks, it was in no way out of character for Hermês or any of the gods to express the interest they took in offerings made to them. Both their insisting on being honored and the almost sensual pleasure they took from it made them more divine, not less.

114 For more on this "wrong," see the crime of Lokrian Aias (IV.533, above).

117 **and current washed him here:** Hermês may be implying something like "the actions of the gods brought him here, the gods can take him away."

120–21 **His destiny . . . :** The power of Hermês' final words and the ineluctability of the command are greater in Greek as his last two lines [114–15] repeat the final two lines of Zeus' instructions to him [41–42] with only minor adjustments at the beginning of the first; a good example of the value of repetition.

124–35 The gods are often outraged by and jealous of each other's prerogatives. Here Kalypso casts her anger directly at the male gods, whom she accuses of upholding the perennial "double standard": women are prohibited from doing what is permitted men, in this case, to have mortal lovers. The double standard existed in Greek society and was fiercely upheld in public, particularly later, during the Classical period in Athens, at least among the citizen elite. Being immortal, errant goddesses are not themselves punished; it is their mortal lovers who are attacked, and Kalypso gives several instances. It is interesting to note that the actual topic Kalypso believes is the cause of the gods' jealousy is never discussed in the councils to which Homer makes us party, and, moreover, that it is Athena who presses to have Kalypso release Odysseus. Whatever the divine battle of the sexes, though, Athena has an odd place and is traditionally masculinized or at least defeminized: she is a battle goddess; she is fiercely virginal, thus not participating in the role of either consort of a male or mother; and, most significant, as the child of a father only, she has no female forebear (compare with *tritogeneia*, in III.411, above). For a much later and more famous instance of her "taking the male side," see Aeschylus' *Eumenides*, where, in the judicial battle between the Erinyes (representing the ghost of Klytaimnéstra against her murderous son, Orestês) and Orestês (representing his father, Agamémnon, against his murderous wife), Athena's deciding vote acquits Orestês. (Kalypso does note, without comment, Artemis' role in destroying Orion, Dawn's male lover.)

"Sexual politics" was a hot topic in ancient Greece, if not precisely in modern terms. It is significant that Homer has Kalypso make the charge; equally significant, and perhaps typically, he has Hermês ignore it completely in his response.

125 **when we choose to lie with men . . . :** Fitzgerald has left out one important qualifier in Homer: "to lie *openly*" [*amphadiên*, in emphatic position as the first word of 120]. Kalypso's seven-year liaison with Odysseus is certainly quite public, at least among the gods. This is not a tryst or discreet affair but a case in which an immortal takes a mortal "consort" [*akoitên*, 120]. An important detail, at least in Kalypso's view, but not one on which to build a coherent picture of Olympian morality.

130 **Delos:** Homer calls Delos by another name, Ortýgia [123]. He seems to call more than one spot Ortýgia (see XV.492, below).

142 **sang:** In other words, "promised."

144 **there's no eluding Zeus's will:** Kalypso accedes to the will of Zeus, having suppressed any mention of Odysseus' reaction to the promise she has just detailed. Homer has already told us that Odysseus gazes out at the sea with longing (87–89), so we know what his answer was.

150 **and nothing hidden:** A significant promise from Kalypso (on her name, see 16, above).

168ff. Kalypso is most punctilious in her offer of help and advice. She knows that she cannot go against Zeus' will, but is that the only reason she is suddenly so seemingly cheerful? I take it that her love for Odysseus is such that she can't act otherwise with him; moreover, she knows that her only hope of keeping Odysseus is if it is his free choice to stay. Although it is subtle, this may be a slight attempt to seduce him, even as she offers to aid his flight.

179–80 Unspoken remains the fact that it is these Olympian gods who have forced Kalypso to let Odysseus go. Although this is conventional (see Hainsworth in HWH 1.269 [on V.160]), it is a significant suppression. Kalypso has every reason not to share news of Hermês' visit with Odysseus: she wants to take credit for a generous act, and, moreover, to say that she had just received a message from Zeus via Hermês would somewhat diminish the force of the risk of which her proviso (178–79) is meant to make Odysseus mindful. By a mixture of sweetness and admonition, she would persuade Odysseus to choose to remain with her.

183ff. **After these years a helping hand . . . :** Odysseus is characteristically on his guard and in no way shy about confronting her with his doubts, even suspicions. It has often been pointed out that this tendency to imagine that others say one thing and mean another is founded in his own character: he knows very well how to do this himself and often does, to great effect.

195–98 This is a very strong oath.

206–11 As had been the case after Hermês' arrival and initial welcome, here a formal serving of food and drink interrupts the interview. There's a formal quality to the completion of the feast before discussion resumes. Whether it reflects customs of the time or is a by-product of Homer's technique of presenting simultaneous events serially (see II.405, above), Homer makes it an undeniably elegant ceremony.

212 Kalypso begins grandly, trying one last time to persuade Odysseus to remain.

222 **compare:** Homer's Kalypso actually says "compete" [*erizein*, 213]. For a mortal to compete or contend for priority with an immortal is dangerous business, usually fatal for the mortal; Kalypso's speech ends at a potentially precarious point for Odysseus.

224ff. That Odysseus understands at once the goddess' veiled threat is quite clear from his response, and he first asks her not to be angry (224) and assures her that Penélopê is no match for her (226). In a way, Odysseus gives away absolutely nothing of his own thoughts, because to cap his argument that Penélopê seems less than Kalypso, he simply gives back to the goddess her own initial premise. In other words, Kalypso asks, "How can she be more beautiful? Aren't mortals less beautiful than gods?" "Right you are," says Odysseus, but, instead of proving her point, he just repeats it: "she must seem less beautiful, 'because she is mortal, while you are immortal and unaging' " [218]. This logical error is called *petitio principii*. Not unappropriately does the epithet "strategist" (223 [*polymêtis*, 214]) appear to introduce Odysseus here.

At a deeper level, this is not just a clever parody on Odysseus' part. It is the truth. Odysseus is a hero who recognizes and accepts his mortality, and realizes that mortal is mortal, immortal immortal, and while the two may occasionally meet—his career is an example of many such meetings—they may never mix.

233 This is the last conversation between Odysseus and Kalypso that Homer represents, although Odysseus remains on Ogýgia for four more days.

254 **trimmed his puncheons true:** He used a chalk line to make things straight. There is no point in wondering why Kalypso had so marvelous a collection of tools. It is worth noting, however, Odysseus' ability: he is infinitely resourceful and handy. Likewise, it has often been noted that the vessel Odysseus builds is more than a raft and much more than a single worker could assemble in four days. Its greatness reflects on the greatness of the hero, just as the craft's details and complexities provide an opportunity for a great singer or poet (who, by the way, would have had much more experience singing of the building of sailing ships—such as the *Argo* or any of the thousand launched Troyward—than of rafts).

263 **a mast pole, and a proper yard:** The yard is the pole perpendicular to the mast, onto which the sail is attached. The Homeric ship was a square-rigger, and the sail was hung from the yard.

269 **halyards, braces:** These are parts of the rigging, or sheets, the sailor's term for what landlubbers call ropes.

271 **This was the fourth day:** It is interesting that while Homer has described the process step by step, it is only at this point that he tells us it took four days.

272 **on the fifth day, she sent . . . :** Does Homer make it the fifth day because this phrase is a pun in Greek [*pemptôi pemp'*, 263]? It may seem undignified, but we must recall that punning as well as the more dignified forms of paronomasia, playing with words and etymological derivations, have their basis in a belief that language is "natural," i.e., is a true reflection of reality.

Note the absence of any leave-taking: no farewell speeches, no tears. Kalypso outfits him and gives him a good wind, and he's off.

272–73 Fitzgerald has "corrected" the original description of these two events, which put the bathing second, though of course it was first. The Greek [264] is thus an example of the figure *hysteron proteron,* "the latter first" (also called *prothysteron,* "first last"), which is likely an attractive feature of formal poetry simply because it's counterintuitive, in other words, it calls attention to itself and to the craftsmanship of the poet.

280ff. Odysseus sails day and night, steering at night by the constellations. The Greeks of the heroic age preferred to sail during the day and within sight of land, but they did risk night sailing. While night sailing is particularly featured in *The Odyssey,* the present passage is the "sole reference to stellar navigation" (Hainsworth in HWH 1.276, whose discussion on pp. 276–77 [on V.272–77] is a more helpful explanation of the precession of the equinoxes, etc., than any I have found in commentaries to date). The Greeks may have learned some of their astronomy from the more advanced peoples of the Near East and for navigating in particular from the Phoinikians, who were in general more daring long-distance sailors.

Other commentators have found much to discuss in the details of this passage, and, if we knew that such a description was based on observation from a fixed place at a fixed time, we might be able to say that Homer was telling us that Odysseus was making his voyage in the final weeks of summer or the first weeks of autumn. The "if" is of course a large one, and, considering the protocols of traditional epic diction (note that 282–85 [273–75] also appear in Book XVIII of *The Iliad* [487–89]), it seems much closer to the mark to say that by this passage Homer at once conveys a further example of Odysseus' competence and provides himself a further opportunity to display another portion of his poetic repertory and talent. This is not to suggest that Homer and his audience disdained precise knowledge of the stars and their seasonal motions. On the contrary. Such knowledge was crucial for navigation and agriculture alike, and astronomical observations formed part of Hesiod's didactic or perhaps better "wisdom" poem, *The Works and Days,* composed not long after *The Odyssey* and transmitting the values and lore of farmers.

My problem is only with those who go a further step and assume that Homer intends a precise mimesis of contemporary reality, the night sky included, and, further, that he would use such a detail as a hint for his audience to seize on and say, "Aha, it's September." Only after Homer gained a reputation for polymathy and "his" two great poems came to be regarded as encyclopedias did scholars start to worry about such questions. (On the question of time of year, note that Fitzgerald's "autumn" at V.340 ought more strictly to be "late summer" but, more significant, is not conclusive because it occurs in a simile.)

283 **before Orion:** Homer brings the traditional personifications of these constellations to life. In the Greek the Bear actually "watches out for" [*dokeuei,* 274] the hunter Orion, who pursues her through all eternity.

287 **on his left hand:** Holding the constellations to his north, Odysseus sails east.

290 **Skhería:** The precise location of the land of the Phaiákians is no more certain than that of Kalypso's island, Ogýgia. Trying to map Homeric geography is a game that goes back to antiquity,

but we can only say that Skhería is seventeen days' sailing east of Ogýgia. It is closer to Ithaka, but how close is hard to say, since the Phaiákians, who bring Odysseus home overnight (XIII.100ff.), are magical sailors.

292 Homer had noted Poseidon's absence (he was among the "Ethiopians") early in Book I (I.36, above). Now he returns.

314 **Zeus:** Odysseus seems here to be referring to the father of gods and men and not merely the heavens personified. Fortunately for him, Odysseus is wrong about which Olympian is after him.

316 **How lucky:** Fitzgerald clearly wished to avoid a literal translation of what in Homer and then Vergil's wake became a cliché. For the record, however, Homer's Odysseus says, "Thrice-blessed the Danaans, and four times, who . . ." [306], using what was already a well-established and solemn formula. This became Vergil's *ter quaterque beati* (at its first appearance in *The Aeneid*, I.94, the context is the same: a hero faces a terrible storm at sea).

321–23 The wish to have died at Troy is not just pious rhetoric: death on land, in the midst of one's comrades, would net two things—formal burial and formal acclaim—of which death at sea would deprive him.

332 No detail is forgotten: this is the cloak Kalypso gave him as he set out (273).

342 **East wind . . . :** The Greek names are Euros, Boreas, Notos, and Zephyros, although Homer presents them as opposing pairs, first South vs. North, then East vs. West (331–32). On the winds and directions, see XV.238, below.

350–52 Ino knows which god is behind this storm and reveals it to Odysseus. That she doesn't know why Poseidon is angry is not terribly important to either her or Odysseus at this juncture—and he is in no shape to tell her why. However, her "I wonder" does serve to whet the appetite of Homer's audience for a full account of Odysseus' offense (Book IX). Homer had already revealed what it was (I.90–99).

357 Odysseus learns from Ino to what place he has come.

359–63 It is a common motif of folktales for the hero to have a supernatural being help him, most often through the agency of such a talisman. Ino's command that Odysseus throw the veil back into the sea as soon as he reaches land underscores the importance of keeping mortal and immortal, or magical and normal, separate. The concluding injunction that Odysseus "turn away" is the more powerful for Homer's not having Ino explain exactly what will happen, either to the sash or to Odysseus, if he beholds the awesome event (see also X.585–86). At 483–86, Odysseus releases the veil, and it is returned to Leukothea.

Although there are other Greek parallels, the story of Lot's wife in Genesis 19:15–28, as Stanford has noted (1.304 [on line V.350]), makes an interesting comparison, particularly because here too those who have by divine means escaped one danger are still at risk if they look on aspects of the divine machinery helping them.

369–77 As with Kalypso, Odysseus' first reaction is to be suspicious of offers of divine help. His intuition is rather to rely on his own wits, and eyes, and, following the advice given to all sailors, he prefers to stay with his ship, at least so long as it remains afloat.

384ff. Forced sooner than he expected to take the less preferable course of action, Odysseus shows himself to be as always a master of improvisation, riding one plank as if it were a horse. At this point he has nothing to lose, so, following Ino's advice, he discards his cloak and ties on her magic veil.

Ancient scholiasts had noted that while Homer refers to horseback riding and racing, he never shows his heroes doing either one; rather, horses pull them in chariots (see III.517–42, above). It has been suggested that Homer describes contemporary activities in similes but that the nature of the epic tradition (rather than any aversion to anachronism) preserves older forms of behavior in the narrative and militates against the retrojection of later customs.

394 **that race the gods have nurtured:** The Phaiákians, to whom this phrase here applies, were particularly close to the gods, but the phrase (an epithet in Greek) is used elsewhere of both kings and heroes and at least once of a minor god.

399ff. Without warning, Homer has Athena reappear. She helps Odysseus to the end of the book, and beyond. It would not be wrong to imagine, or at least suspect, that she has been watching all along, although we must remember that it is possible for things to escape the notice of Homeric gods, as Odysseus' own progress had escaped Poseidon's notice until he came within eyesight of it. On this occasion, Athena does not reveal herself to Odysseus, who is left to fear the worst (406) even as he strives on.

408ff. There is a "perils of Pauline" aspect to Homer's management of the narrative here, creating a consequent roller-coaster of emotions for the audience. Lines 408–16, particularly the almost sentimental simile of the recovering father (411–14), lead us to believe that Odysseus is out of danger and will make it to land. But, alas, there is more danger: being ripped by the reefs and hurled upon the cliffs. This is indeed a real danger, as any who have boated around Greece or comparable rocky coasts will know, and Homer's audience would have appreciated it. It is also an example of the additive style of Homeric narrative, which permits the poet to add on another scene the way one would add on a building block. As with the arrival of the storm itself and then the appearance of Ino, this new turn of events provides Homer the opportunity to have Odysseus give another speech. This narrative style is of course not restricted to Homer. Popular narratives of many times and now in many media come to mind. I alluded at the beginning of this note to one set of early cinematic cliff-hangers; we might also compare "just when you thought it was safe to go back in the water . . ." or many a television program or series.

424–25 and 307–8 [406–7 and 297–98] **Odysseus' knees grew slack:** The second line of the pair also occurred at 368 [355].

427 and 442 **Zeus** and **he who makes earth tremble hates**

me: Tipped off by Ino, Odysseus now knows which god is helping and which is working against him. As I noted above that Homer gives Odysseus a speech in response to each new stimulus, but each one is very different. Here in particular we hear Odysseus' mind at work, considering the pros and cons of each possible course of action.

443 **During this meditation:** Again, events force Odysseus to react rather than to act. The virtual repetition of line 378 (with only a verb tense changed) underscores the parallelism of the two situations [424 and 365, respectively, in the Greek].

451–52 The simile of the octopus is vivid and brilliant from many points of view, but one feature of its aptness is lost in translation. "Octopus" in Greek is not "eight-" but "many-footed" [*po(u)-lypos*, 432], a word which shares its first element with a range of epithets applied prominently to Odysseus (*polymêtis* and *polytropos*, "of many devices" or "shifts," *polytlas*, "much suffering," and so on).

455–56 The Greek behind "battered inhumanly" (456) is *huper moron* [436] (see I.51–52, above).

456–57 **but he had the gift:** Athena's aid comes in the form of inner fortitude or "self-possession," comparable to the instruction she gave at 446.

467 **O hear me, lord of the stream:** Without prompting, Odysseus appeals to the god of that stream. Normally, it is essential to invoke a god by name in order to get him or her to show favor; in the Greek, Odysseus avails himself of the formula used when addressing an unknown god ("whoever you are" [445]).

473 **servant:** In Greek, *hiketês* [450], the "suppliant who beseeches protection" and a very powerful word. Such technical terms present a particular challenge for the translator, who aims at communicating something of the feeling and not just the lexical meaning of the original. Fitzgerald has clearly attempted to establish a comparably sacral register by echoing Judeo-Christian Bib-

lical and liturgical language with which he imagines his readers will be familiar.

486ff. **Then the man / crawled to the riverbank . . . :** A less prudent man, having gained earth at last, might have just fallen asleep, with no thought of possible risks and the best ways to forestall danger. Not Odysseus.

513–19 **A man in a distant field . . . :** The book's conclusion is simple and quiet, but the simplicity of the effect should not take away our appreciation of the poet's craft. The simile of the "spark" (described metaphorically in the Greek as "the seed of fire" [*sperma puros*, 490]) evokes a civilized man almost beyond the edge of civilization; he has no neighbors and must rely on his cunning to preserve his fire. Just so Odysseus buries himself in the leaves to preserve his "spark of life." Then Athena enters to pour sleep on the suffering Odysseus. She, too, is hiding Odysseus to preserve him. That the action of the mortal is nested within that of the goddess is suggested by the echo and extension of "hid himself" (516 [*kalupsato*, 491]). The last word of the book, which refers to Athena, is built on the same root ["covering round," *amphikalupsas*, 493 (translated as "she sealed," 519)]. The more distant echo of a major character in this book, Kalypso—which sounds here at the end to mark the distance Odysseus has come—suggests that Athena is a better and more productive "hider" than the Ogýgian nymph. Perhaps more significant is the foreshadowing of books to come: at many junctures, but none more crucial than after his return to Ithaka, Odysseus will have to hide himself, with Athena's help, to preserve his "seed of fire."

BOOK VI

The Princess
at the River

5–8 **In days gone by, these men . . . :** These lines at once
establish the Phaiákians as peace-loving people and the Kyklopês
as brutes. The Phaiákians will thus understand Odysseus very
well when he tells them about his experiences in the land of the
Kyklopês.

10 **a New World across the sea:** The Greek "far from toiling
men" [8] sounds less prophetic of Columbus and the "discovery"
of America. The eighth and subsequent centuries, however, were
for Greece, like the fifteenth and subsequent centuries for
Europe, times of intense colonization, expanding commerce, and
war.

11 **Skhería Island:** Although it has almost always been taken to
be an island—the fourth-century B.C.E. historian Thucydides was
not the first to identify it with Corfu (*History of the Peloponnesian
War*, I.25)—and much in Homer strongly suggests this, it must be
admitted that at no point does Homer actually say Skhería is an
island. Granted, it is far off in (or across) the sea (218), and the

city itself has harborage on two sides (280–81). In contrast, Homer is utterly unambiguous when describing Ithaka and the islands near it. There is as little reason to get exercised about this as about the location of Skhería: we have entered again the realm of fantastic geography.

28–29 Athena always chooses to appear in the form of someone who would be likely to speak to the dreamer. Here, she is a close friend the same age as Nausikaa, for whom it would be quite natural to bring up the topic of marriage.

33 **put thy minstrelsy in wedding dress:** In other words, Nausikaa must provide clothes for the male retinue who would escort her home. An ancient scholiast took this as a clever move on Athena's part to guarantee that Nausikaa took men's clothes as well as her own garments to the river; this may be supersubtle, but, on the other hand, we underestimate Homer only at our peril.

36 Would the image of the princess going to the river to do her own washing have seemed fantastic to Homer's audience? To us it seems one of the more naive and charming points of the story, but we must be careful: although Homer's audience may have found it charming, it would have been in different terms. First of all, audiences of folktales know by the rules of the game not to focus on realism or even plausibility at all points in the story; things are "just so" and not otherwise. Furthermore, the Phaiákians inhabit a peaceful land and embody a well-nigh ideal situation. The ancient Greek ideal was not unstructured ease represented in folklore and ballad as the "Rock Candy Mountain" or, earlier, the "Land of Cockaigne." The dangers of such luxury are represented by the Lotos Eaters (Book IX, below). Rather, while the Phaiákians need not work terribly hard to have plenty, they work nonetheless. And, particularly in the eyes of Greek men, the ideal Greek woman would work at certain tasks: weaving first and foremost and running the house, including supervising all the female (and in some cases some of the male) servants. A good example comes just a few lines further on, when we first see Nausikaa's mother, Arêtê (57–59). That Nausikaa would be concerned with washing her clothes is a sign that she is likely to be a good wife, in accordance with the cultural codes of ancient Greek society. Of course, multiple maids—who walk behind the cart while she rides—at the very least assist her with the actual work and may, in fact, do it all themselves.

47–53 Olympos is a mountain, and nothing here contradicts this conception. Yet here and elsewhere in Homer, we see the beginning of its development into a heavenly place.

63 **Papà:** The Greek is *Pappa* [57]—the names for mother and father seem astonishingly close within the Indo-European family of languages, even after millennia of diffusion and development. It is particularly hard to know the exact nuance of such familiar forms; the Greek may well be as familiar as "Daddy," which I personally prefer. Still, if "Papà" seems a bit stiff, at least today, it may nonetheless be right: Nausikaa is, after all, a princess speaking in an epic poem and in perfect control of what she says.

65ff. Nausikaa speaks of doing the household washing and says nothing about her trousseau. But lest we think she is just being cunning, Homer (73–74) tells us that she was too embarrassed to mention her marriage. Her father knows, though, either because he saw a blush (an inference on Fitzgerald's part, quite possible but unstated in Homer [66]) or simply because he is wise.

91 **princess, maids:** Homer is even more clear that Nausikaa is "not alone" [84], her maids present not only as helpers but as guarantors of propriety.

93 **with water all year flowing:** In dry climates like those around the Mediterranean basin, all but the larger rivers dry up in summer, and those that flow are often just dirty trickles. The perennial abundance and clarity ("limpid," 94) of this river is thus remarkable—another admirable feature of Skhería.

102 **sea:** They have come to the mouth of the river, as the story demands. So vivid, detailed, and engaging is the story of Nausikaa's washing expedition that we may well forget for a time that Athena had more than dirty clothes on her mind when she motivated this excursion. The sea is the first reminder of Odysseus and Athena's higher purpose in roughly eighty lines.

110–18 The comparison of Nausikaa amid her maids to Artemis running with her nymphs, the princess and goddess each more impressive than her companions, serves both to conclude a charming episode and to elevate it at its conclusion.

115 Lêto: Artemis' mother delights to see Artemis' superiority. In the immediate context of the simile, it is not the absent Arêtê, Nausikaa's mother, who corresponds to Lêto, but rather the hidden Odysseus, who will soon be awakened to observe the princess and her friends (122ff.)

118 princess: Homer rounds out the line with "unwedded maiden" [109], emphasizing her unmarried state rather than her royal status.

130–31 Any traveler might wonder about the people into whose land he has come, but we will discover when Odysseus narrates the earlier stages of his journey why he in particular would think of "savages . . . , strangers to courtesy." The appearance in this context of the Homeric compound "guest-loving" [*philoxenoi*, 121, almost the exact opposite of the modern English "xeno-phobic"] reflects the fact that hospitality was not only a courtesy but a pious duty enjoined by the gods, Zeus first and foremost (Fitzgerald uses "gentle folk"). One of the epithets of Zeus is "protector of guests" [*Xenios*], as Odysseus reminds the Kyklops in vain (IX.292–93 [271]; on the epithet, *Xenios* or *Xeinios*, depending on the metrical slot in which it appears, see III.377, above, and XIV.189–90, below). And even sooner, in the narrative economy of *The Odyssey*, Nausikaa formulates this principle quite clearly (221–22).

132–35 That was a lusty cry . . . : It is a nice touch to have Odysseus wonder to himself whether he is hearing the cries of mountain nymphs or mortal girls, given the recent Artemis simile. It seems as if here Homer is playing with the division between the two worlds, one of the narrated reality, the other of the simile, a division usually strictly respected. (See also 161–65, below.)

137–39 Odysseus is once again shown to be infinitely resourceful and ever mindful of the perspectives of others, the latter perhaps the key to his famous rhetorical skills (see 155–59). Some have found Odysseus' care to cover his nakedness inconsistent with the fact that Nestor's youngest daughter gave a bath to Telémakhos (III.506–8); however, the bathing of an honored guest whose identity is known, in one's family home and likely in the presence of servants, is a highly structured situation and nothing like the eruption from the bushes of a grimy, unknown man toward a group of girls far from home. As it is, all but Nausikaa flee in fright (149–50). The fact that their menfolk are far away is apparently of no concern in itself, because once she is convinced that Odysseus means her no harm Nausikaa orders her maids to bathe him on the spot (223–24), but neither the maids (230) nor Odysseus himself (232–36) is willing to permit this.

140–51 The branch of course does little to clothe him ("in his rough skin," 145 [*gumnos per eôn*, 136]); it is more important as a sign or token that his intents are not evil and that he is a civilized man. Everything else about his appearance belies this, and Homer effectively shows us how terrifying he looked, first with the simile of the lion (140–44; note another simile in the mountains) and then by direct description of his desperate state (145–48). Their world and their minds are brilliantly and economically caught in the epithet, however traditional, "with pretty braids" [*eüplokamoisin*, 135, and again at 198 (although Fitzgerald eliminates it from the latter, his line 212)].

151 **a bold heart:** Homer sent Athena to Olympos (47–53); here her name stands for the sort of inner confidence or self-possession the goddess often inspires when present in those she would aid (see V.456–57, above).

152–59 Before having Odysseus speak or act, Homer shows him

strategizing, resembling in no way the ravenous lion driven by hunger to which he has just been compared. The main question is this: should he grasp her knees in the formal gesture of supplication or rely on "honeyed speech" (155)? Lest the gesture be considered too forward and thus anger his potential benefactor, he will employ words alone.

161–64 Odysseus' first words are truly "honeyed" and highly complimentary. One might take his professed uncertainty whether he is addressing a goddess or a mortal as a continuation of his thoughts (132–35) and of the earlier simile (110ff.), and, indeed, Homer clearly wants us to recall that simile when he has Odysseus refer to Artemis and her devotees (163–64). But considering the introduction to this speech, in particular the double reference to "honeyed words" [143 and 146], Homer also wants us to be aware that, however large or small the doubt in Odysseus' mind as to the mortal status of his interlocutor, his words are carefully calculated.

161 **Mistress** (w)anassa [149]: The feminine form of *(w)anax* (see I.448, above) is used only for goddesses, and in Homer, apart from this speech, only for Artemis and Athena.

please: Odysseus says literally, "I kneel to grasp your knees," [*gounomai*, 149] while not doing so, thus meaning "I beg you by your knees," the gesture that indicates he is begging for the sacred status of suppliant (see 207, below).

163–4 Another advantage of Odysseus' rhetorical strategy is that in praising Nausikaa's beauty as that of a goddess, he can compliment her without seeming too forward. The first aim of rhetoric is for the speaker to win the audience's goodwill or benevolence (Latin *captatio benevolentiae*). This became a rule in rhetorical handbooks (see also XIV. 229–417, below). But ancient rhetoricians noted that even though Homer wrote long before the systematization of rhetoric, he and his characters "naturally" observed and exemplified its aims. Odysseus became and remained through the ages the master rhetorician, a reputation that can be valued

positively and negatively, depending on an age's attitude to rhet-
oric and verbal craft.

165–69 When he considers Nausikaa as a human, it is in the
context of her family: father, mother, brothers. He wishes to
emphasize his appreciation of civilized social structures, as well as
to lay the groundwork for his request to be introduced to her
family: he knows that if he is to receive hospitality and other
assistance, it will have to come from the head of whatever house-
hold she belongs to.

170–71 It is here that Odysseus seems most forward and runs the
greatest risk in his praise. But he is likely to know, as well as her
father did, what is on a maiden's mind. In fact, it was only
through marriage that a girl in ancient Greece (and in many
other times and places) could take her place as an adult in society.

171 **prevails:** In the Greek the successful suitor "prevails"
through his bridal gifts [159], again a token that the man before
Nausikaa understands and appreciates the fine points of social
organization. She might just think, and Odysseus might mean for
her to think, that he is of better stock than he appears to be.

174ff. Odysseus subtly and somewhat artificially shifts ground to
speak of himself. Casually and in short order, he presents himself
as a man who has visited the shrine to Apollo at Delos, the center
of his cult (175), and a military commander (176) who has suf-
fered misfortune (177).

180–81 **I stand in awe so great:** Through his words Odysseus
can, as it were, both take her knees and not take her knees: by
saying he is fearful to carry out the formal gesture of supplication,
he conveys the intent of the act while observing the punctilious
propriety he has calculated to be wisest under the present circum-
stances.

194–99 Again Odysseus alludes to the marriage theme in such a
way as to emphasize proper social relations. The "harmony" or
"agreement" of man and wife [Greek *homophrosunên*, 181, *homo-*

phroneonte, 183] is an important theme in *The Odyssey,* which is as much an exploration of the "harmony" between Penélopê and Odysseus as it is a story of Odysseus' travels (see Introduction, p. vii, and Books XIII.509, XIX.158–60, and XXIII.69–73, 187, and 189, below). It would not be wrong to imagine that Penélopê is on his mind as he speaks these words to Nausikaa. (Of Odysseus' longing for home and his wife Book V gave ample testimony.)

198–99 **Woe to their enemies, / joy to their friends** is the standard morality of ancient Greece and many other cultures, ancient and modern. It is characteristic of what is often called a "shame culture" as opposed to a "guilt culture." It is against the backdrop of this morality that Sokrates' argument that it is better to suffer evil than to do it seemed so paradoxical—or later, that the idea of praying for and loving one's enemies seemed so revolutionary.

199 **But all this they know best:** This appears to be a puzzling and weak ending to Odysseus' speech, but that may be the point. By this argument, he provides Nausikaa an opportunity to help him, and a rousing and highly impressive ending to his speech would work against the picture of weakness and lack of self-sufficiency he wishes to project. Hainsworth's "they themselves are in high repute" would give the speech a more standard and easily understood conclusion (HWH 1.305 [on VI.184–85]).

207 **comfort due to a poor man in distress:** In Greek Nausikaa acknowledges that he is due special treatment by using the technical term for suppliant [*hiketên*, 193].

216 Piracy and brigandage were common throughout the Mediterranean, and coastal communities as well as merchant ships were at risk.

221–22 **from Zeus:** That is, they are under his protection (see 130–31, above). Understand "a small gift" as "a gift, however small."

234–36 Odysseus' sense of shame may be as much or more the result of a consciousness of his filthy and poor condition than of embarrassment about being seen naked by servant girls.

248 **Hephaistos** was particularly skilled at metalwork and was thus the patron of metalworkers; Athena was patron of all crafts-people.

250ff. **beauty:** Before Odysseus looked admiringly upon the beauty of Nausikaa. Now, with a little help from Athena, the spectator has become the spectacle, and although it would not be permitted to her, as it was to him, to express her appreciation of his appearance openly, she can share her opinions with her maids.

258–60 As Odysseus had at first wondered whether Nausikaa might be a goddess and later expressed this uncertainty to her, Nausikaa very nearly thinks the same of him; certainly he looks like one of the gods. She does think that someone like him would make a fine husband, which some ancient commentators considered a blot on her character. But why not? The subject of marriage has been put into her head by no less than Athena (although Nausikaa thinks it was her friend in a dream), and Odysseus himself has with clever calculation insinuated the idea of marriage any number of times. Finally, she is only speaking her frank thoughts to her maids and confidantes. Shortly she will find a way, as crafty as his, to share this thought with Odysseus himself (see 291ff.).

261 This line is a rapid and seemingly unmotivated shift in Nausikaa's thoughts, so abrupt, in fact, that Homer may be showing her covering her tracks. As Homer does not fail to show us, the same word can mean both "husband" (259 [*posis*, 244]) and "drink" (Fitzgerald's "refreshment" at 261 in the Greek means "food and drink," as at 265 [*posin*, the accusative form of *posis*, 246 and 248]). Considering ancient belief in the power of language, particularly of names and etymologies, I am not certain that we should, with most critics, rule out the possibility of a pun or some sort of intentional linkage on Homer's part. There is no question that Homer plays on such linkages elsewhere and sometimes has his speakers do so. And there is no question that Homer reveals the thought processes of his characters, which he often does by presenting a character weighing several possibilities and choosing one. See XVII.300–304, below. It would be unusual, and astonishingly subtle, if by linking these words Homer was attempting to depict what we would term the subconscious workings of Nausikaa's mind.

280 **Isle:** See 11, above.

285ff. **Poseidon's shrine:** The prominence of Poseidon's shrine and the particularly close relationship between the Phaiákians and the sea, given the location of Skhería, is quite natural. It also prepares us for the way they are able to help Odysseus reach home as well as for the cost Poseidon will exact from them for their service to Odysseus. However, this information in no way inhibits Odysseus from telling the Phaiákians the reasons for Poseidon's anger with him (Book IX).

291ff. Although Nausikaa admires the skill of the seaman, the princess is superior to the dockworkers and sailors. This touch is entirely realistic, and her concern is well founded. Scholars have noted what a clever rhetorical strategy Nausikaa has found: she invents an imaginary gossip, and under the pretense of detailing what she doesn't want bruited about, she conveys to Odysseus: (1) "my name is Nausikaa but I still don't know yours" (294); (2) that she thinks he is very handsome (294), perhaps even a god (298–99); (3) that he certainly looks like a marriage prospect (295) and one very much to her liking (299–300); (4) that she's been courted by many [*polees*, 284] excellent men (302–3); from which he should infer that, if he is thinking of winning her hand, he will have to deal with local competition and perhaps even resentment.

305–7 Nausikaa insists on propriety: she will not and cannot act on her own while her parents are alive, and any potential suitor will have to apply to them. It is a great irony, which at this point even

Odysseus cannot appreciate, that he should be cast even hypothetically in the role of suitor while his wife is fending off suitors at home.

309 **safe conduct:** Nausikaa, however cleverly she has shown the way that her or someone's fantasies might run, properly responds to what Odysseus more likely wants, and indeed does want: to be sent home.

310 **in a roadside park:** That the grove is dedicated to Athena obviously augurs well for Odysseus.

323 **mégaron:** The main feasting hall, although the word is sometimes used to describe other large quarters within the Homeric house. Readers should not, however, be surprised to learn that "just as the geographical descriptions fit many places, so the Homeric house can be drawn in accordance with many plans" (Hainsworth in HWH 1.312–13 [on VI.303]). There was a phase when Homeric scholarship went to great lengths to square epic terminology with the most recent archeological discoveries of Mycenaean architecture, but balance and sense have returned. "Old formulae might preserve a detail, but subject as they were to continuous replacement by new expressions they could not preserve the overall concept with its parts in their proper articulation." This seems quite just.

344–45 Auditors and readers know that Odysseus is wrong here: Athena did help him, if not as much or as obviously as he might have wished. The relationship Homer depicts between Odysseus and Athena is a complex one, strained at times but familiar enough that it can withstand such recriminations. It is because Odysseus expects so much of Athena, without actually relying on her, that he dares to complain.

348–49 **in deference to her father's brother . . . :** Homer gives his listeners an explanation for Athena remaining behind the scenes.

BOOK VII

Gardens and Firelight

10–12 **Years ago, from a raid . . . :** Eurymedousa is a slave in Alkínoös' home, obviously highly valued since she was made nurse to the princess. It appears that, while the Phaiákians may be safe from piracy, they do not abstain from engaging in it. Hainsworth, however, may be right in suggesting that compositorial tendencies make the attempt to resolve such a minor apparent inconsistency irrelevant: "the isolation of the Phaeacians (a special feature) is overlooked in favour of generic ideas about the provenance of slaves" (HWH 1.321 [on VII.9–12]).

Virtually no ancient culture expressed any moral reservation about slavery as an institution. This is a worthwhile observation, despite the fact that we have primarily (but not exclusively) the testimony of nonslaves. It was the lot of some to be born slaves and bad luck for others to be enslaved. But beyond hoping that one would not become enslaved (through capture or debt), or if enslaved that by luck or hard work one would be granted or could purchase one's freedom; and apart from a few ideas that there

95

should be limits to inhumane treatment of slaves, no one thought matters should be other than they were.

22ff. **the grey-eyed goddess:** Almost as if in response to Odysseus' complaints at the end of Book VI (343–46), Athena appears but in disguise—to show proper respect for her uncle Poseidon (see VI.348–51). Athena manifests herself as a young girl, as if she had heard Nausikaa's words (VI.319–20) and wanted to prove her right at once. (There is no contradiction between "boy" there and "girl" here: the Greek [VI.300–301] that Fitzgerald has rendered "any small boy" is using the masculine form as the "unmarked" gender and therefore really means "boy or girl.")

28–29 **here there is no one / known to me:** A small lie, but proper. Athena would appreciate it.

31–39 Even as she helps him, Athena almost seems to mix a bit of teasing with her advice. Out of the mouth of a child, reference to Odysseus' age as a mark of respect is plausible, but it serves to remind him of his no longer youthful appearance. She tells him to go quietly, even though she has concealed him in mist. She might be teasing him, but then Odysseus is probably unaware of the divine envelope. Her description of the Phaiákians as characteristically inhospitable, although it seems to contradict what we learn about them, keeps him on guard and explains certain breaches of etiquette. The mention of Poseidon's favor to the Phaiákians might seem calculated to increase his anxiety unnecessarily, but Poseidon is an ancestor of the royal house (59ff.), and it is best for Odysseus to know this sooner rather than later. Further, by reminding Odysseus of the one god who is set against him, Athena will put him in mind once again of the god who is on his side.

51ff. The second, longer speech of Athena confirms the impression of the first: this "child" is talkative and, above all, wise beyond her years. She gives Odysseus important information Nausikaa had not—above all, the name and pedigree of Queen Arêtê.

57–58 According to the genealogy presented here, Arêtê has mar-

ried her father's brother. If somewhat unusual, this would not
have been considered incestuous or been cause for scandal. The
legendary family trees of founding dynastic families and gods are
characterized by marriages of close relatives, as are the family
trees in historic times of aristocratic and especially royal families.
By this means power remains concentrated.

57 **her name is Arêtê:** In the Greek, Athena actually tells Odys-
seus that her name is "significant" or "etymologically meaning-
ful" [*epônumon,* 54]. "Arêtê" is related to the verb "I invoke, I pray
for" (*araomai*) and thus means "she who is prayed to," or less
likely, "she who is prayed for." It is a name invented for the figure
to whom Odysseus turns for help. The Homeric phrase *onoma
epônumon* ("significant name") not only points again to the natural
power of language but itself exemplifies it: *epônumon* is formed out
of *onoma* ("name"). It is nearly as jingling and circular as "naming
name" would be in English.

71–75 We wonder if Odysseus did not think of Penélopê at this
point.

79–81 The last three verses of Athena's speech are, with one minor
change, a repetition of the concluding verses of Nausikaa's
(VI.332–34 [313–15]; the variation: Nausikaa calls his home
"well-built" [315], Athena calls it "high-roofed" [77]).

89ff. **High rooms he saw ahead . . . :** This is an impressive
palace by any standards, and fabulously wealthy for ancient
Greeks.

101 **undying dogs:** Keep Homer's insistence on the immortality
of these gold and silver Hephaistian dogs in mind. It serves as a
point of comparison with Odysseus' hound Argos (XVII.375ff.),
however unlikely it is that the audience of an oral recitation over
multiple days could have made such a link.

111 **yellow corn:** Not of course maize but wheat or some other
grain (Homer is not at all specific). Our translator is not wrong,
he is simply using "corn" to mean "grain," as the British still do.

113 **like the leaves of a poplar tree:** One of the briefest Homeric similes (not even a full line in Greek [106]), but among the most striking. At least one later Greek poet, Sophocles, thought so too, to judge from his imitation of it.

124ff. The never-failing fruit, even if Homer provides a meteorological explanation (126), is reminiscent of descriptions of the Golden Age, an early epoch when, as in Eden, food was abundant without toil and humans had not yet become desirous of wealth. Obviously, Skhería, though in some ways paradisal, is not a Golden Age utopia in all details (see VI.35, above).

137–41 **and through the garden plots . . . :** The abundance of water was the greatest gift of all for Greeks and other Mediterraneans—the great poet Pindar at the opening of his most famous poem sings "water is best" (*Olympian* 1)—and Homer caps his description of the garden with its two fountains. It is a general principle—not just in Greek poetry—that the two most prominent positions are the beginning and the end.

142–43 A typical Homeric structure. At 86–88 Odysseus was described before the palace, obviously looking about him. Homer now reintroduces him, gazing with wonder. The entire description of what he sees from the threshold, both within and without, is framed by the name "Odysseus." As a structural device, this framing is known as "ring composition. See VIII.499, IX.41–43 (the fullest discussion), XI.192–227, XV.314, and XIX.62–63, below.

147 **before going to bed:** Homer has Odysseus arrive at the very end of the evening.

156 With his first words Odysseus makes use of the information the "little girl" had given him, the queen's name and that of her father.

166ff. **No one stirred:** The lack of response is surprising. It is perhaps best explained by the Phaiákians' complete surprise—Odysseus appeared before their eyes when he was already grasping Arêtê's knees (151–52); this still moment has the further effect of prolonging suspense for Homer's audience: what will happen?

167–68 The counsel of Ekhenêos will carry most weight precisely because he is the oldest. Although he is lower in rank than Alkínoös, his age gives him the right to lecture the king.

194 **A fresh bowl:** That is, for all in the feasting hall [180] (see 198).

204 **seniors:** A gathering of the elders, *gerousia* in Greek (although the noun does not occur in Homer), *senatus* in Latin (from *senex*), whence our word "senate." The respect shown to the wisdom of the elders in Skhería is another indication of this kingdom's good government and social order.

211–13 Alkínoös is wise enough to know what is beyond his ken, and of course, even as the audience learns that Odysseus has reached a safe haven from which he can expect to be conveyed home, it is reminded by these ominous words of the problems he will face on Ithaka.

212 **Spinners:** After Homer, the number of "fates" became established as three, and their tasks were assigned: the "spinner" [*Klôthô*], the "apportioner" [*Lakhesis*], and the "cutter" [*Atropos*] of the thread of life. Something like this must be behind the Homeric image of the "Spinners" [*Klôthes*], but it goes unsaid, and is thus more mysterious and powerful. See also I.28, above.

213 This sounds fatalistic, and although it is characteristic of one mode in which Homer, his characters, and many other ancient Greek writers speak, at the same time Greek heroes strive in the firm belief that their actions can make a difference. If we seek to harmonize these two perspectives, it might be best to imagine that the Fates spun a broad web in which people could act. "In general, *moira* is mentioned as an explanation, more remote and general than the gods, for untimely or unwelcome events, but the decisions a man takes in response to those events remain his own" (Hainsworth, HWH 1.333 [on VII.196–98], with further reference to Adkins [see Bibliography], pp. 17–29). (Certain expressions of fate seem to defy easy systematization: see the Greek *huper moron*, discussed at I.51–52, above.)

We might be less troubled by our inability to resolve all the apparent discrepancies in the Greek conception of fate if we think of a contemporary example, say, the ongoing debate between "nature" and "nurture"—that is, between the role of inherited characteristics and genetic predisposition, on the one hand, and that of cultural education and personal choice, on the other—in explaining a whole range of observed human differences.

214–21 **If, as may be, he is some god . . . :** A significant variation on the commonplace, well established after the speeches of Odysseus and Nausikaa in Book VI, used when one suspects that one's unknown interlocutor might be a god. As Alkínoös explains, the Phaiákians, being kin of the gods, sometimes receive divine visitors. Hence, while entertaining the possibility that Odysseus is immortal—good insurance if he is, a nice compliment if he is not—Alkínoös is inclined to doubt it.

228 **as I might tell you:** This looks forward to Odysseus' long account of his travails (IX.2–XII.580).

230ff. The demands of Odysseus' belly are pressing, a sign—he grimly but humorously notes—that he is all too human, most certainly no god. At the same time, it was a minor breach of etiquette on Alkínoös' part to ask his guest any question before feeding him (see III.46–55, above).

232 **like a dog:** Strongly negative; despite some good Homeric press, dogs in Greek eyes were most notable for the shameless way they satisfied their physical urges when and where they could. They represented the pure "animal," above which "cultured humans" were expected to rise. Odysseus conveys at once that he is cultured, by giving voice to these expectations, and in desperate straits, by being reduced to the level of a dog.

241 **my hall, my lands, my people:** Odysseus makes clear here not only that he is a cultured human but that he is a property and slave owner (ambiguous in English, quite clear in Greek [225]). We wonder why, for the moment at least, Odysseus omits any mention of wife and family.

250ff. Arêtê is a clever queen, and this is a clever turn. Note also Homer's cunning: while he prepares much, he also permits certain surprises. Despite her concern for propriety and her careful instructions to Odysseus, Nausikaa did not foresee this. Or did she? Note also Arêtê's cunning indirection: although Homer tells us that she has recognized the clothes, her words do not betray the exact reason for her suspicions (254–56).

258–319 Odysseus, as he announces, will now recount only a portion of his story. He senses what must be explained, and his narrative ends with an explanation of how he got "this clothing" (318). The departure and seventeen-day voyage from Ogýgia (280ff.), the storm, and his arrival on the shores of Skhería will explain why he was in so obvious a state of need when he met Nausikaa. Here there is clear logic behind the Homeric practice of responding to the questions of one's interlocutor in reverse order. But why does Odysseus begin where he does (261ff.)? Most likely because it explains what he was doing, without his companions on Ogýgia to begin with. The description of his time with Kalypso has at least one and perhaps two further purposes: it presents Odysseus as a man favored as well as pursued by the gods. It also might suggest this contradictory line of thought: if this man turned down an offer of immortality and everlasting youth by a beautiful goddess (1) he is not likely to be interested in remaining here and marrying Arêtê's daughter rather than returning to the home he constantly longs for, and (2) he would be a very attractive catch for Nausikaa.

281 **and word to her from Zeus . . . :** Recall that Kalypso had claimed to Odysseus (V.170) that it was the latter of the two possibilities he now mentions. We see that Odysseus, master of mental reservation (see VII.277) and ever suspicious of others' motivations, has thought of another explanation ("word . . . from Zeus"), and from our privileged perspective as Homer's audience, we know how well founded his suspicions are, and how right his guess is.

294ff. Odysseus intentionally neglects to mention the appearance of Leukothea (V.344ff.) and her magic kerchief.

305 **sacred night:** Homeric scholars debate the sense of this phrase, but the implication is probably that the night, being sacred (a time dedicated to the gods and other spirits), is potentially dangerous for mortals. It is formulaic, and the particular sense of the epithet need not apply specifically to each situation where it occurs (see I.92, above).

314–16 **and her good sense was perfect . . . :** Even as Odysseus praises her daughter (he does not let on that she told him her name, even if she did so indirectly), he is careful to present himself as looking at her from the perspective of the older generation.

317–18 **gave me . . . / a river bath:** Odysseus means that she ordered her servants to give him a bath, and he knows the king and queen will understand it in this sense.

325–29 An out-and-out lie on Odysseus' part, but one of discretion and diplomacy. Even to have explained that it was a sense of propriety that made Nausikaa have him enter the town center after her would not have done; it would have raised the topic of marriage and suggested that it was on the princess' mind. In line 329 we see only a trace of the sarcastic and gossiping workers of whom she had painted an imaginative picture for Odysseus; now, however, the specifics are transformed into a general and intentionally banal observation.

333–39 Seemingly without prompting, Alkínoös speaks of the possibility of marriage, reading with his wonted sensitivity between the lines of Odysseus' account of his encounter with Nausikaa, or out of instinctive (but somewhat rash) generosity.

345–46 That the Phaiákians regard the island of Euboia, which lies just east of the Greek mainland, as "most remote" is one way Homer can suggest that they inhabit a world far from Greece, since for Greeks, nothing was less remote than Euboria.

367–71 **How welcome the word "bed" . . . :** All is well, and Odysseus is tucked into a real bed after three weeks (seventeen nights on the raft, three in the water, one in the leaves). But the story is of course far from over. Mention of Alkínoös' "dear consort" (371), with whom he retires into "his inner chamber" (370), reminds us that Odysseus still must regain his house, his wife, and, as we will see, the right to join her in their bed.

BOOK VIII

The Songs of the Harper

24–25 **mastering every trial:** These lines announce that there will be "contests" or "games" [*aethlous,* 22]. Homer's audience would, upon hearing this word, have looked forward to enjoying the poet's particular treatment of what was a standard feature of both Greek life and Greek epics.

30 **nameless to me still:** It is a mark of Alkínoös and Arêtê's exquisite hospitality that they did not press their guest for his identity. Odysseus, like Homer, knows that certain things, postponed until the right moment, will have the greater impact.

41 **tholepins:** See II.444, above.

48 **Demódokos'** name is the rough equivalent of "esteemed by the people." The role of narrative poetry in heroic society and of the bard in the halls of the wealthier and more powerful members of that society was so well established that, in presenting Demódokos or other bards in his poetry, Homer is not indulging in professional narcissism. This said, there is a great deal of interest in his presentation of the singer, ranging from his repertory to his interaction with his patron and other members of the society. It would not be wrong to look closely into these scenes for a picture of Homer's own vision of his role as poet and his expectations of his audience, always remembering that in creating this picture we should weigh the factors of tradition and idealization, for each of Homer's singers and audiences is different.

65 **tuskers:** Much more likely domesticized pigs than boars.

70 **For she . . . made him blind:** The bard Demódokos, like the seer Teirêsias (see X.547), is blind; in both cases, it is suggested that a greater and more powerful inner vision replaces their eyesight. The legend of Homer's own blindness, quite ancient, is almost certainly based on his description of Demódokos, although, as commentators have pointed out, there are numerous examples of blind poets and singers (think of John Milton, Ray Charles, and Stevie Wonder).

The poet of *The Odyssey* is noted for the wordplay he weaves into his poem. For the most sophisticated instance, see IX.394, below, but note also characteristic etymologizing (see I.299, I.439, VI.261, VII.57, above, IX.104, XIV.144, and XIX.478–81, below) and clever compound nonce words (see XVIII.87, XIX.693, and XXIII.20–21 and 110–11, below). For that reason I venture to suggest as a remote possibility a secondary link between the Homeric bard and blindness, one we could only impute to an inveterate punster like our author. The word for "bard" is *aoidos*, the parallel verb being "to sing" *aeidô* or *aweidô*, if the digamma is pronounced (on the digamma, see I.448, above, and XIX.478–81, below). My suggestion is to entertain the re-etymologization of *aoidos* as *a* + *(w)oidos*, "unseeing" if, that is, one treats *(w)oidos* as a compoundable element deriving from *(w)eidô*, "I see" (cognate with Latin *uideo*), the perfect of which is *oida* (it is common and means "I know [because I have seen]").

Granted, the other alpha-privative ("un"-prefix) compounds involve the verb's root, *wid-* (*aidêlos*, *Aïdês*), rather than a conjugated perfect form. That would only mean that this is not a standard linguistic development, but a (linguistically) uninformed and *ad hoc* coinage—not even a coinage, merely an etymological reinterpretation. If there is anything to this suggestion (which seems daring even to me), we would want to activate it also for the *aoidos anêr* [III.267; Fitzgerald's "minstrel," 288], who was assigned to watch over Klytaimnéstra in Agamémnon's absence and who was "an unseeing man" in another, figurative sense (see III.285–90, above). Finally, twisting *a + wid-* forms further and still more unconventionally, we might note that *aïdêlos* applies to Arês not only in the sense "too terrible to be seen," hence "devastating" (VIII.327 [309]), but also in that particular context as "unseeing" in that he failed to spy Hephaistos' invisible netting before hopping into bed with Aphroditê one more time.

Whether or not "not seeing" is related in some deeper and essential sense to "singing"—in other words, something that stands in for "seeing" in sight's absence—will have to await further exploration elsewhere.

73 **harp:** For a description of the *phormigx* [67], see I.189, above.

79–80 Andrew Ford translates these lines [73–74] "the Muse then stirred up the singer to sing the fames of men [*klea andrôn*] / from that path [*oimê*] whose fame at that time reached broad heaven," explicating the keyword *oimê*, "path" as the way Homer and his fellow bards conceived of "individual themes": "The stability and continuity of individual stories are metaphorically expressed as paths, and the tradition is figured as the great tract in which these stories may be joined end to end" (*Homer: The Poetry of the Past* [Ithaca, 1992], 41).

79 The "Muse" knows that it is better to inspire her singer after the audience has satisfied its hunger and thirst. (On the Muse, see I.1, above.)

81ff. It is obviously a carefully calculated stroke on Homer's part to have Demódokos sing of Odysseus in the presence of the unrevealed hero. Certainly the singer's muse knew, and perhaps the

singer himself sensed, the identity of the stranger. That Homer
has Demódokos choose to sing of "the clash between Odysseus
and Akhilleus" (81) is noteworthy, for it represents a clash be-
tween the hero of this epic and the hero of the other great epic
poem (whether it was the earlier work of the same poet or that
of another). This incident is not found in the extant *Iliad*, and, in
fact, the author of *The Odyssey* never recounts any incident from
the Trojan War also related in *The Iliad*. To a number of scholars
it has seemed as if he studiously avoided doing so, which some
take as proof that the author of *The Odyssey* knew *The Iliad* in the
form in which we have it today. Not a few argue on this basis that
the authors of the two poems were the same person, although it
might with as much certainty be used to support the contrary.

84–85 **joy . . . / for such had been foretold:** There is no cer-
tainty, but the oracle Agamémnon recalls probably ran some-
thing along the lines "Troy will not be taken before there is a
quarrel among the leading Akhaians." There was also a tradition
that the quarrel revolved around the question of whether Troy
would be taken by force or by guile. It is clear that Akhilleus,
greatest of warriors, would argue for the former, the wily Odys-
seus for the latter. And indeed, Homer refers elsewhere in *The
Odyssey* (IV.291–312) to that famous product of Odysseus' cun-
ning, the Trojan horse, by which Troy was ultimately taken.
However, in the present situation, Agamémnon is, as so often,
mistaken. From the perspective of the post-Iliadic *Odyssey*, it is
clear that the quarrel to which the oracle referred as preceding
the fall of Troy did not involve Akhilleus and Odysseus. Rather,
the significant quarrel is the one which breaks out between Aga-
mémnon and Akhilleus at the beginning of *The Iliad*. Agamém-
non's "inward joy" is unfounded.

What is significant here is the way the poet plays with variant
traditions, and in particular the ironies that emerge if we privilege
the Iliadic account.

90ff. Odysseus' tears are likely to give him away and lead to the recognition scene we are all awaiting, but Homer manages to put it off, even after Alkínoös sees and hears Odysseus weeping (101). The king, of course, is polite, and, seeing also his guest's desire to cover his tears, skillfully changes the subject, quite clearly to put an end to Odysseus' distress, whatever its cause (104ff.). Note, too, that Odysseus' quarrel with Akhilleus looks forward to the altercation between Seareach and the hero, 166ff.

113–14 That Demódokos is brought along to the games is probably more than simple kindness. He might be called on to sing at an appropriate break in the contests (and he is, 280ff., although his harp must first be fetched, 268f.). He might also have been brought to create a song commemorating some part of the games. Homer's Demódokos sings of Greek gods and heroes, but bards were also the recorders and repositories of each people's history. A great athletic victory might well be worth remembering (on Pindar's victory odes, see VIII.155–59, below).

117ff. Homer's list of Phaiákian athletes is a tour de force of onomastic fantasy. All the names are invented—or were invented at some time in the telling of this segment of Odysseus' story—and the point is that the poet has composed for the Phaiákians names he imagines a sea-loving people would have. Fitzgerald has quite properly translated the constituent parts into English, so that the names appear as obvious and as fantastic to us as Homer's Greek names did to his original audience. (However, there is nothing in the Greek which corresponds to the phrase "with seaside names" in 118, by means of which Fitzgerald wanted to make sure we understood what he and Homer have done.)

131–33 **mule team . . . oxen:** Homer must have applied this logically unimpeachable but outrageously unsuitable simile to his sprinters (see *Iliad* X.351–2) with no little sense of ironic amusement. It has the further advantage of putting the race into virtual "slow motion," long before film and television gave sportscasters this option.

134–38 Homer devotes two lines (134–35) to the first of the subsequent four events, and one line each to the rest. This is a good point at which to observe Homer's economic structure, quickly setting up a norm for the succession of events, then describing a rather important departure from that norm. First, the list, almost a procession of athletes (118ff.), capped by the three princes (125–26); then one event (the footrace) described briefly (127–33); next, four events for which he gives the winners' names only (134–38). Then there is a pause while Prince Laódamas suggests the young Phaiákians try to involve Odysseus in the games (139–50). Laódamas invites him politely but does not win Odysseus' assent (151–65). "Seareach" [*Euryalos*] puts the challenge in the rudest of terms (166ff.), and Odysseus rebukes the offense. He then decides to compete, not by entering any organized competition but by hurling the discus farther than it had been cast before (195–209), winning the event in an extraordinary heat. He is prepared to enter other contests (214ff.), but Alkínoös prefers (248ff.) to have Demódokos cool tempers with a song.

As a result of the variety of events in this scene, Homer's audience would have had the sense of experiencing these extraordinary games in their entirety. Typically, when the narrative contains a series of events, one of them is treated at length and the rest in summary. The Kyklops episode, for example, gets lengthy treatment in the series of Odysseus' wanderings. (HWH 1.353 [on VIII.104–255]). At the same time, it is obvious how another poet, or the same poet in another performance, could alter the structure by varying events, slotting in others, or actually describing one or more of the competitions for which Homer gives only the final result.

145 **not old:** Or, perhaps, "not past his prime" [136–37]. Laódamas recognizes that Odysseus is a good bit older and will shortly address him with the same *xeine pater* (VIII.153 [145]) used by the "little girl" (the disguised Athena) who met him on his way to Alkínoös' palace. There (VII.31) Fitzgerald translates the phrase as "good grandfer," here (VIII.153) as "Excellency." Both work in their contexts.

This is a convenient reminder that the translator often renders the same Greek word differently in different contexts, and, likewise, that different Greek words may be translated by the same word in English. This is not a license granted only to translators of ancient poetry, who face difficulties of a very particular kind. In fact, it would be wrong to expect a translator of any but the most technical of texts consistently to render a recurring word or phrase in his source with an unvarying equivalent. Why? Because no two cultures—not even contemporary cultures—have exactly the same descriptive methods, and, perhaps even more important, no two cultures break down the world they share at precisely the same points. (For the example of color words, see IV.146, above.) The translator is thus in some sense doomed to only partial success, but one can choose to look at the partial "failures" of translation archeologically, as revealing the slippages between different times and cultures.

155–59 **While a man lives he wins no greater honor:** The importance of sporting competitions and the honor bestowed on participants and above all winners (155–56) was demonstrated by local and national games—not just those at Olympia, which we have revived in this century, albeit in a very different form, but others, such as the Pythian, Isthmian, and Nemean games. The only complete poems we have of the great poet Pindar (late sixth–early fifth centuries B.C.E.) are odes commissioned and sung to celebrate the victors of these contests.

The idea of athletic competition as respite from more serious troubles is expressed directly by Laódamas in the next line (157), which Odysseus, given his war experiences, inflects rather differently (compare 162–3 and 191–2). Laódamas' closing remark only sets up a further irony: Odysseus' arrival in Ithaka now seems assured (the gods willing), but as the audience of Books I–IV knows very well, his troubles are far from over.

165ff. **Now Seareach put his word in . . . :** The confrontation between Seareach [*Euryalos*] and Odysseus and the hero's decisive victory clearly foreshadow the more extended confrontation between him and Penélopê's suitors, also younger men. There, too, an athletic competition of sorts will be crucial (Book XXI, to which Fitzgerald has given the title "The Test of the Bow").

167–73 It is very important to recognize that Seareach does not insult Odysseus by saying that he is too old. It would merely be a statement of fact, given the general respect for elders in Greek society (see VII.203, above). Rather, Seareach's slight is based on social status. He insults Odysseus by claiming that he is not an aristocrat, who would have had the money and leisure to learn a sport and develop skill (168). Seareach charges that Odysseus is the captain of a merchant ship, and traders and all businessmen were despised by the aristocracy and the warrior class, who derived their wealth from tribute or the revenues of inherited property they did not work with their own hands. Even piracy was more respectable than trade.

This social perspective should be kept in mind in the second half of *The Odyssey,* when Odysseus claims to be just such a trading merchant. It is an integral part of his disguise, in all particulars calculated to keep the suitors from seeing him as a threat. Their attitude toward merchants is the same as Seareach's.

175 **friend:** The word Odysseus uses is *xein'* [166]. *Xeinos* is at once "guest" and "host," "stranger" and, in certain contexts, "friend." Odysseus is primarily rebuking Seareach for a violation of the codes of hospitality (see "host," VIII.220). Insofar as aristocrats and nobles were not exempt from the code of hospitality (indeed, as befitted their position and wealth they were expected to uphold it rigorously and ostentatiously), Odysseus sharply throws Seareach's insult back into his teeth. (Fitzgerald's "fool" is on the weak side; the Greek [166] would support "vicious" or even "wicked.")

227–40 Odysseus, having recently had more war experience than time for games, characteristically thinks of contests on the field of battle. He relates his athletic skill in terms of martial prowess, a standard comparison at that time. With all his talk here, it is unlikely that he is threatening any of the Phaiákians.

231–32 **Philoktêtês alone . . . :** In fact, according to another oracle (see also 84–85, above), Troy could not fall without Philoktêtês' bow. If Sophocles' tragedy of the same name represents the stories circulating at the time *The Odyssey* took shape, Odysseus' mention of Philoktêtês verges on bad faith, since Philoktêtês was, for a time at least, treated very shabbily by the Ithakan hero.

235–40 Although it appears an example of scrupulous modesty, in fact, for Odysseus to rank himself with the greatest archers of all time only aggrandizes his claim, especially since the two he mentions were in the same league as the gods, with fatal consequences in Eurýtos' case. According to the story (which follows a very standard pattern), Eurýtos challenged all comers to an archery contest. To anyone who could beat him he would give his daughter Iole. Heraklês took up the challenge and won, but Eurýtos then refused to make good on his promise. Heraklês killed Eurýtos, laid waste his city, and took Iole anyhow.

Note that Odysseus is invoking these names and the story to a king with a marriageable daughter.

255 **wife and children:** Odysseus has not mentioned that he has either. This is probably a matter, as some believe, of little concern to Homer, who sometimes gives characters knowledge of what he has told only to the audience. However, this is not likely to be the case here, given Homer's concern to postpone the identification of Odysseus as long as possible. Moreover, Odysseus does not have *children*, he has one son. It seems that Alkínoös is either fishing or making a likely assumption. A man of Odysseus' status would take a wife if for no other reason than to cement interfamily alliances and have someone to manage his household. And he would want children to take care of him in his old age, to effect beneficial marriage alliances, and ultimately to inherit his prop-

erty and carry on his line. (At 438 Seareach, following the king here, also seems certain that the still unidentified Odysseus has a wife.)

261–63 The Phaiákians, enjoying their blessings, have a luxurious life-style that must have seemed almost fabulous to Homer's original audience. (The Phaiákians have had a reputation as voluptuaries ever since. A generous sampling of post-Homeric Greek and Classical Latin opinions are tabulated by Hainsworth in HWH 1.341.) That they pride themselves on singing, dancing, and poetry means they are cultured and fortunate. It would be anachronistic to imagine that this branded them as "aesthetes" in any negative sense: music, poetry, and dance were enjoyed by and came from the gods, and the great pan-Hellenic competitions included contests in the singing of poetry. (All the great fifth-century B.C.E. Athenian drama, both tragedy and comedy, was produced in competitions at which one of usually three competing playwright-producer teams would be given the prize. In "referees" (272) we see a trace of the competitive context of dance and music in what is to be only an "exhibition game.") Homer, then, is giving Odysseus a highly cultivated audience for his own narrative, to begin in Book IX.

280–392 **Now to his harp the blinded minstrel sang / of Arês' dalliance with Aphroditê:** The tale of Aphroditê, Arês, and Hephaistos, has seemed shocking to some critics over the millennia, blasphemous to others. Such moralizing shafts glance off Homer. The Trojan War itself is a consequence of adultery, and the stories of Greek gods were never intended to provide moral models. The gods were in part enviable because they could enjoy pleasures only dreamt of by humans—virtually without censure. The lovely fable seems appropriate for the Phaiákians, whose existence in Skhería is virtually carefree. Demódokos has chosen the theme and shaped it to end with the composition of a quarrel with an eye to his immediate audience: having witnessed the unpleasant exchange between Seareach and Odysseus, the singer knows why Alkínoös has asked him to perform at this very moment.

Homer, the poet behind the Phaiákian singer, chose the tale with another perspective in mind. In the economy of *The Odyssey*, the story of divine adultery contrasts with the story of Odysseus, Penélopê, and the suitors. On the level of significant detail, marriage beds and weaving are central to both stories. When one reads the one plot against the other, crucial differences emerge: the faithful Penélopê makes no suitor her Arês, and Odysseus is no cuckold. The net with which Hephaistos catches the lovers anticipates Odysseus' trap of the suitors, but the hero's punishment of the suitors is grim and final, as no punishment can be for immortal gods. Precisely because they are immortal their battles are of less moment, less is at stake; while for humans, fidelity becomes a matter of life and death. This contrast runs as a thread through all interactions between mortal and immortal Greeks. The gods inhabit a fantasy world free from death. As a consequence, their struggles are artificial and trivial, lacking the significance that human striving takes on by virtue of the fact that humans must ultimately pay with their lives.

That the gods were such poor models for human behavior troubled Greek philosophers even before Plato, hence the impulse to allegorize Homer and make the greatest poet a spokesman for whatever ideal an individual moralist or culture might prefer. However, the song of the bard is less egregious within the context of archaic poetry than it may at first appear. In scope and tone it resembles those *Homeric Hymns* which tell of the pranks and even deceptions of the gods (though apparently it would be earlier than any of the extant *Homeric Hymns*).

327 **devastating:** Hephaistos means this literally—"destructive," "hateful," even "damnable" (the Greek [309] probably was related by popular etymology to the word "Hades")—not in the sense of "devastatingly good-looking." His reference to Arês' good looks and healthy legs (in contrast to his own) comes in the next line. (For further connotations of this epithet, see 70, above.)

330 **two gods who bred me:** Zeus and Hêra.

337 **Father:** Zeus was not only his father but the father of the bride, Aphroditê. The "wedding gifts" reflect the custom of the bride-price—the groom must give a gift to the bride's father or nearest male relative. The word in Homer [*eedna*, 318] refers half the time to bride-price, the other half to dowry. No explanation for this seemingly undecidable discrepancy has attained wide acceptance (see Introduction, p. xlv).

338 **damned pigeon:** "Shameless bitch" would perhaps more accurately render Hephaistos' harsh words. Literally, the Greek phrase is "dog-faced girl" [319], a good example of how misleading the "literal" can be. Clearly, "dog" could not refer to Aphroditê's physical appearance. It plays off the proverbial shamelessness of the animal (see VII.232, above).

344 **The goddesses stayed home:** A nice touch, but even more another example of the double standard of Greek culture projected onto the gods. The gods of poetry were fantasy figures, almost without exception projections of male fantasy. By "gods of poetry" I mean to exclude the numerous cults, practices, and legends in which women played a real part. Those were part of the real religious life, and we mustn't imagine that Greek religious observance was limited to the Olympians, or even pursued in Homer's time in any form like the practices his poems describe (see Introduction, p. li).

357ff. Note the extravagant massing of traditional epithets in Apollo's first line (357 [335]) and their only slightly less extravagant use in Hermês' reply (361 [339]). Their formality in this very irregular context is part of the cultivated banter in which the speakers are engaged. I take their appearance and function here as important evidence that Homer could use traditional epithets not only consciously, but ironically as well.

366 The ever-serious Poseidon will have a special resonance for Odysseus and the audience.

409–11 Odysseus' words are calculated to signal to one and all that Demódokos' song and the dance have soothed his angry spirit.

414ff. As we saw Meneláos offer Telémakhos gifts in Book IV, here Alkínoös arranges for his guest's gifts. A great king, he can command and specify what gifts the princes or kings immediately under him, sublords in their own right, are to make.

430–32 **this broadsword of clear bronze:** This is a very fine and handsome gift. For him to call it "a costly weapon" (432) is not tactless, since the point is to emphasize not his own generosity but rather the high esteem in which he holds the person to whom he is giving such a gift.

475 Again the expectation is that Odysseus will sail home that night, but his narrative (Books IX–XII) will delay his departure.

478, 482 **Kirkê, Kalypso:** With the appearance of both Kirkê and Kalypso in the space of five lines, not usual under any circumstances in the poem, it is almost as if Homer is showing how Odysseus is preparing to tell of his journey. That may seem to be casting our glance too far afield. The immediate inspiration for these reminiscences is the ministrations of Arêtê, and the reappearance of Nausikaa will soon follow (488). All these figures fit (in some cases ambiguously) under the category "female benefactor." See IX.41–43, below (esp. *ad fin.*) for the rhetorical point of examples of such benefaction.

488 Nausikaa appears for the first time since the end of Book VI to speak but two lines. Homer craftily underplays this scene.

493 **It is worth your thought** seems somewhat cryptic. In the Greek Nausikaa says, "You owe me first the reward for saving your life," [462] leaving it open but suggesting that she will consider his remembering her in the future as satisfactory recompense.

499 **as . . . a goddess:** When Odysseus first heard Nausikaa, he was uncertain whether he was hearing the voices of nymphs or girls, and he initially addressed her as a goddess. His words here recall these moments in Book VI, thus his promise to think of her ever after "as a goddess." By closing the circle, as it were, this makes for a satisfying conclusion to the story of Odysseus and Nausikaa. (On this element of ring composition, see IX.41–43 and XIX.62–63, below.)

504ff. We might well imagine why this scene survived in the tradition: generations of bards would not forget to describe the deference of the throng and above all the generosity of the hero to one of their own guild. Doing so might inspire comparable actions by any would-be heroes in their present audience. (Note especially lines 512–14, which are meant to be universal and further characterize Odysseus as a very wise man.)

509 **crisp with fat:** The best portion.

526ff. **Now shift your theme, and sing . . . :** Odysseus prepares for his recognition by asking that Demódokos sing of the wooden horse, an episode sure to redound to his credit. At 528, Odysseus mentions his own name for the first time in Skhería, although not to identify himself. Again (see VIII.81ff., above), this episode is not told in the Homeric *Iliad*, which ends with the death of Hektor and the return of his body to Priam, well before the sack of Troy that the ruse of the wooden horse made possible. We recall that Homer gave us another perspective on at least part of this episode in Book IV, when Meneláos told how Helen circled the horse and called to the Greeks suspected of being inside in the voices of their wives (IV.291–311).

One critic sees "Odysseus' choice of song evidence of his awakening heroic confidence." He regards the "artistic purpose of the book" as being "to rehabilitate Odysseus, to infuse into him the heroic spirit" (W. Mattes summarized in HWH 1.378 [on VIII.492–93] and 344). Seareach's challenge and his successful discus throw are stages on Odysseus' "spiritual rehabilitation" in the way station of Skhería.

This line of argument has its attractions but is ultimately not persuasive. In Book V Odysseus seems to me to be fully conscious of his identity and his goals, and his appearance as pitiable suppliant is nothing more (or less) than a temporary expedient, with no negative implication for his spirit or self-esteem. In fact, he will don a more wretched disguise for a longer time when he returns to Ithaka. In sum, I see nothing in Book VIII that cannot be explained as the plan of a master rhetorician (Odysseus) and a poet who has determined to postpone as long as possible the moment at which his hero's identity is revealed.

536 **drawing away from shore:** This refers to the story that, as part of the ploy to achieve the final destruction of Troy, the entire Akhaian fleet sailed away, leaving the wooden horse with troops hidden inside. The Trojans were supposed to believe that the horse was an offering to the gods left by the Greeks, who had now abandoned their siege of the city. In fact, the army had only sailed out of sight and would return according to plan under cover of darkness to join the "special forces" in the horse. The story can be almost indefinitely elaborated, and later was.

It has also become the master metaphor in the West for destruction via disguised entry. Odysseus as the inventor of the Trojan horse may be said to be saving lives today, or at least inspiring those who can. Doctors can introduce genetically modified viruses into the body of a sick patient. The baneful viruses, deceived, interact with the modified viruses and are checked or in some cases even destroyed. The modified virus is called—what else?—a Trojan horse. Considering the frequency of its appearance in the popular media as well, the Trojan horse must be judged the single most widely recognized classical reference today.

545 **a cliff:** Troy is not known to have had cliffs, although it was a fortified citadel. Hainsworth observes that this exemplifies the way "the poet's thought is controlled by the context"—the verb "to pitch" suggests cliffs—whether or not they were there for the eye to see (HWH 1.380 [on VIII.508]).

556 Odysseus and Meneláos make for Deïphobos' house because there they will find Helen, who, as they know, after the death of Paris was taken by or took up with (depending on one's view of this most undefinable of women) this one of Priam's other sons.

562ff. **weeping the way a wife . . . :** Demódokos had been singing of the battle in the streets of Troy. So in a way, the "lost field" (563) of this metaphor works as an additional description of the battle scene which Homer merely summarizes. And although the actual scene in the simile is not of fighting within the citadel, there is a continuity with the sack of Troy. The woman of the simile is near enough to see her husband die, as Trojan women would have done. In other words, Homer compares Odysseus' weeping to that of a woman who could have lost her husband in battle with Odysseus himself—his own spear "prodding her back and shoulders" (567). That the simile crosses not only enemy lines but gender lines as well is also significant, but is itself in no way unusual in Homer. (For a study of precisely this feature, see Helene Foley, " 'Reverse Similes' and Sex Roles in the *Odyssey*".)

570–74 This moment recalls a point earlier in Book VIII (99–104). From the point of view of the structure of the entire poem, what happens now could have happened then. For *The Odyssey* that we have (sometimes called the "monumental version"), the poet has chosen to delay the recognition one narrative round and have Alkínoös first stage the athletic contests. It is also clear that in a different context Homer, or another poet, wishing to move more quickly, could omit the games and get on with the story.

587–626 **Now by the same rule, friend:** As Alkínoös says, now that the guest's gifts are bestowed and his request (to be taken home) granted, it is his turn to reveal his identity. Alkínoös asks this with garrulity and love of platitude, and while this is in keeping with his character, Homer uses his speech to effect one more delay. After keeping his audience waiting to hear the hero reveal his identity for so long, just when it appeared inescapable,

Homer stops and says, in essence, "it's been a long session; I'll start at this point tomorrow." If this is "a rather unsophisticated method of heightening suspense" (West, HWH 1.54), then it is the best kind, and it is among the characteristics which *The Odyssey* shares with many popular narrative forms (and which has kept the poem itself popular for so many centuries).

593 **unless a mother bears him:** Homer says "parents" with characteristic wordplay [*tekôsi tokêes,* 554]. The detail is trivial in itself, but it is worth noting that ancient Greek views of generation were very different from our own: for the Greeks, both parents "bore" or "engendered" (*tiktô,* the same verb applied to both father and mother), and in some accounts the argument is advanced that the father's part is actually much more important, he being perceived as adding living form—seed—to the equation, while the mother is just (!) the ground in which the seed grows (see Aeschylus, *Oresteia, Eumenides,* lines 658–666). However nonsensical, counterintuitive, or offensive this appears, the scientific views of ancient (or any other) cultures are always worth studying, for their arguments indicate how differently cultures conceptualize their worlds.

594–600 **Tell me your native land . . . :** Here the Phaiákian ships appear truly magical. Whatever the case, Alkínoös' major point is that Odysseus won't be able to conceal his homeland much longer, since he's going to have tell somebody where to take him.

604–11 An ominous foreshadowing of what will happen at least in part at the beginning of Book XIII after the Phaiákians give Odysseus passage across the sea to Ithaka. That will prove to be the trip foretold by Alkínoös' father which will bring Poseidon's wrath on the Phaiákians. However, this neither causes Odysseus to conceal the fact that Poseidon has good reason to be angry with him, nor do the Phaiákians have any fears about transporting Odysseus after having heard his narrative. The oracle is presented as inevitable (611) not conditional. Odysseus can take comfort in the fact that, even according to the prophecy, the wreck will occur when the ship is "homeward bound" (608), after it has let him off (Compare IX.554, below).

620 **a song for men to come:** This would be self-serving on Homer's part (even in Alkínoös' mouth) were it not for the deeply held conviction that memorable deeds and song are mutually dependent. Heroic deeds achieved in struggle, however vain, against the will of the gods deserve commemoration in song. This commemoration preserves heroic ideals and examples of heroic behavior to which future generations may aspire.

BOOK IX

New Coasts
and Poseidon's Son

2–4 Odysseus' reply is much brighter than our last view of him, weeping, would lead us to expect. We might imagine that he has had time to recover himself, but more is going on here than a change of mood. In general with Homer, what we would call psychologically coherent characterization is subordinated to the formal demands of the situation and above all of the poetry. The situation demands politeness, and the poetry requires a fresh start. Odysseus' prefatory remarks adjust the standard poetic opening to this context; while not a bard like Demódokos and not pretending to sing a song, Odysseus is beginning a narration. Like a poet at the beginning of an epic, he makes a poet's claims. Here, instead of appealing to the Muse, he praises his host's minstrel and all singers, and the joy they give to listeners.

12–13 Odysseus contrasts his own pain, which will be renewed in the telling, with the happy picture of his listeners.

14–15 **What shall I say first? What shall I keep until the end:** Odysseus marks the beginning of his narration with these rhetorical questions. Likewise, the poet of *The Iliad* asks rhetorically, or literally asks the Muse, "Which of the gods drove them [Agamémnon and Akhilleus] to fight in strife" (I.8). A formal question is not necessary, though some reference to a starting point is. At the opening of *The Odyssey*, for example, Homer simply commands the Muse to "Begin when . . ." (I.19). On the ordering of the waystations of Odysseus' travels, see 41–43, below.

20 **I am . . . Odysseus:** Homer does not return to his own narrative voice until XI.387; only then (XI.391–412, 422–37) does he describe the reaction of Odysseus' audience to the hero's narrative and to the revelation of his identity at a point by then many hundreds of lines in the past. We should, however, try to imagine the effect Odysseus' revelation has here; he was just the subject of Demódokos' last song—as Odysseus himself had arranged.

22 **formidable for guile:** Odysseus is proud of this "guile," which he recognizes as his preeminent characteristic. Indeed, the story he requested from Demódokos showcased his mastery of deception. (In the Greek, Odysseus presumes his audience will remember the Trojan horse and does not include "in peace and war," which Fitzgerald uses as a reminder to us.)

25 **Mount Neion:** Fitzgerald follows one tradition going back to Crates; most scholars today prefer to call it "Mount Neritos" [*Nêriton*, 22]. See Neion in the Who's Who, below.

32 **Kalypso:** Odysseus begins here as he had begun his (at the time anonymous) response to Arêtê's question (VII.261ff.). This will be a much longer narrative than that brief summary and will in fact relate material from before his sojourn with Kalypso. The seven years on Ogýgia serve as punctuation within the ten-year period that has elapsed by since the fall of Troy. Beyond giving his audience a point of reference, Odysseus repeats his mention of Kalypso to make his tales sound plausible. Even within fictions, cross-references and consistency enhance credibility.

35 We have met Kalypso and seen Odysseus with her (Book V). As a kind of prologue of what is to come, Odysseus presents Kirkê as a parallel—comparable to Kalypso but much wilder and stranger, as are many of the adventures in Books IX–XII. Odysseus' description of his time with the witch will occupy the bulk of Book X (lines 149–635).

41–43 **What of my sailing . . . :** These are not formal questions in Homer's Greek [37–38]. With these words Odysseus begins the famous account of his travels. Scholars are now in general agreement that the individual episodes are arranged in a "ring" with the *nekuia*—the view of the underworld afforded by Book XI—at the center.

Ring composition is a characteristic archaic Greek device that poets frequently employed to organize their material and that we presume helped singers and listeners to keep both details and the whole clearly in mind. In other words, it functions in part as a mnemonic device. A ring may involve words or phrases within one sentence, thoughts in a paragraph, or, as in the present case, narrative blocks. The classic form involves the treatment of elements a, b, and c, after which the poet takes them or variants of them and presents them in reverse order, c', b', a', so that he or she concludes where he or she began. (For a good example of closure by means of exact repetition, see XIX.62–63, below.)

The structure can be extended to great length, and into any element the poet can insert subordinate rings, as is the case here, so that a graphic presentation is the most efficient way of describing the organization and suggesting the correspondences and contrasts that the ring structure itself sets up. (For example, Lotos Eaters, Seirênês, Kirkê, and Kalypso are all seductive and at least temporarily pleasant detours from the homeward trip; the Kyklops, Laistrygonês, Skylla, and Kharybdis are all man-eaters; the episodes of Aiolos and Hêlios both involve first too little and then excess wind).

Troy (IX.41–43)

Kikonês (IX.44–73)

  two-day storm followed by drifting (IX.74–91)

   Lotos Eaters (IX.91–112)

    Kyklops (IX.113–618)

     Aiolos, including storm (X.1–90)

     Laistrygonês (X.91–148)

    Kirkê (X.149–606)

     Elpênor's death, departs from Aiaia (X.607–35)

      Nekuia, the underworld (XI.1–759)

     return to Aiaia, Elpênor's burial (XII.1–173)

    Seirênês (XII.174–258)

     Skylla and Kharybdis (XII.259–338)

      Hêlios' cattle, then storm (XII.339–547)

      Kharybdis and Skylla (XII.548–72)

     Kalypso (XII.573–580, with reference to VII.261–86)

   two-day storm, followed by drifting (VII.287ff., V.291ff.)

Phaiákians, his audience

Ithaka, his goal

(after Glenn W. Most, "The Structure and Function of Odysseus' Apologoi," *Transactions of the American Philological Association* 119 [1989], 15–30, esp. 21–24). Readers should consult Most's article for detailed interpretation, further secondary literature, and above all for a compelling argument that Odysseus relates these exemplary accounts of hospitality, both positive and negative, monstrous and divine, as parts of one sustained attempt to persuade the Phaiákians to receive him well and return him home.

44–49 In *The Iliad* (II.846), the Kikonês of Thrace are allies of the Trojans. Odysseus does not present this alliance as a justification for his attack (piracy did not require any justification; see III.79–81, above). In the Greek, Odysseus' own account is briefer and even more matter-of-fact. (In two places, Fitzgerald, in his style of explanatory translation, seems intent on white-washing; see 47 and 48, immediately below.) With equal matter-of-factness (as far as piracy is concerned) Odysseus asks the ghost of Agamémnon if he met his death on such a raid (XI.467–69).

47 **men who fought:** In the Greek, simply "the men" [40]. Of course the men fought, but that they resisted Odysseus' men was not the reason they were killed; marauders usually killed as many men as possible as a matter of course.

48 **enslaved the women:** The Greek implies specifically "as bed-mates" [41]. It went without saying that free Greek males could and would use slaves of both sexes, and often foreigners, to satisfy their sexual desires, mostly without recrimination.

51–52 The folly and uncontrollability of Odysseus' companions is a constant theme, until they get themselves wiped out. Homer himself sounds the theme at some length in the prologue to *The Odyssey* (I.11–16), and one cannot help noting that Odysseus' companions bear no small resemblance to that group of fellow Ithakans, the suitors. To wonder how men so foolish and undisciplined lasted for ten years at Troy is irrelevant; the narrative logic of *The Odyssey* demands that Odysseus return to Ithaka alone, so his companions must be dispatched. Since Odysseus cannot be held responsible for this, they must destroy themselves.

56 **on horseback:** Actually, from chariots drawn by horses. Horseback riding appears only in similes (see V.384ff., above).

59–60 Odysseus' repeated mentions of Zeus (also 43, 74) and doom shows him to be a pious man who understands that his trials and tribulations are part of a grand scheme under Zeus' governance.

86 **I might have made it safely home:** Part of Homer's grand strategy of narrative prolongation is that Odysseus nearly comes home at this point, but at the last minute is thwarted. (Note how on a different scale throughout Books VII and VIII Homer nearly brings about the recognition of Odysseus but each time puts it off.)

92 What the "Lotos" itself was, or what Homer meant it to be,

remains unclear. It is not the Egyptian lotus. It is described as "flowery" [84] and as a "fruit" [94] in the most general terms (Fitzgerald's "plant," 101, is appropriate). The eating of flowers or fruit is unknown elsewhere in Homer. Its effects, however, are quite clearly described. As Heubeck aptly puts it, Odysseus has now crossed "the border separating the reality of the familiar Mediterranean world from the realm of folk-tale" (HWH 2.18 [on IX.82–104]).

104 **that native bloom:** Not as a true or even popular etymology (and faintly sounded at that), but Homer may be suggesting some sort of ad hoc explanation for the word "Lotos" where the Greek line begins with *lôton* [97], the fruit, and concludes with a form of the verb "to forget" [*lathesthai*]. They share an initial "l" and second consonant, a "t" sound (unaspirated "t" and aspirated "th")—precious little to go on. Yet Homer seems at pains to sound the pair again in line 109 with different forms of both words [*lôtoio, lathêsai,* 102—this is not a formulaic repetition].

113–24 The land of the Kyklopês is the site of the major adventure of Book IX. As a people, the Kyklopês are, by Greek standards, lawless and uncivilized. The first description of what they eat (115–19) suggests that they simply gather the wild bounty nature provides. But as we will learn, they tend flocks (they are pastoralists rather than agriculturalists). Most significant from a Greek perspective, they do not form a community (120–24) but live in primitive family units. They are literally apolitical, lacking a *polis* (city-state).

"Kyklops" means "round eye," by which Homer seems to indicate that the Kyklopês were as a race one-eyed. I say seems because this is never expressly stated in *The Odyssey,* as it is in Hesiod's *Theogony* (verse 145) and thereafter. If Homer doesn't mean this, he has failed to tell us that the particular Kyklops that Odysseus visits has already lost one eye. Odysseus says singular "eye" without further commnet (at 361 [333]) as Zeus had (at I.92 [69]) where Zeus had named Polyphêmos and revealed that

Odysseus would poke out his eye. The name Polyphêmos does not occur in Book IX until line 438 [403]. Up to that point, Homer has Odysseus call him simply "the Kyklops."

115–16 **Leaving . . . / to the immortal gods:** The Kyklopês are not technically godless, but their attitude toward and relationship with the gods differ from those of the Greeks.

125–93 The major function of Goat Island within the Kyklops episode is to permit Odysseus a place to park his fleet. He crosses to Kyklopês land with only one ship and a few men.

136 **No shipwright:** The Kyklopês are in this respect, as in many others, diametrically opposed to the Phaiákians, Odysseus' present audience. Not seafaring, not land taming, not engaged in commerce, they are also the opposites of the many adventurous seagoers and colonizers among Homer's own contemporaries.

171 **my lot was ten:** As leader, Odysseus receives a special portion (here, ten goats) for himself alone.

184ff. Neither Homer nor Odysseus says explicitly what the motivation for this exploratory foray is: search for hospitality, possible pillage, or just idle curiosity. We should not forget Book I.6–7: it seems that, whether by necessity or desire, Odysseus' "learn[ing] the minds of many distant men" is central to the poet's conception of his hero. Note that when Odysseus' men suggest plundering Polyphêmos' cave after having surveyed its abundance, Odysseus himself refuses. "I wished to see the caveman" (248–49). Nonetheless, in no other episode in his own narrative is Odysseus motivated solely by curiosity.

201–2 Polyphêmos is utterly alone, without even a family. His home is a cave, for which no skill in building is required. Note that in lines 201–8 Odysseus gives a description of Polyphêmos based on full and final knowledge of him, not what he knows at this point in his narrative. This is common, as in the even more detailed description of Goat Island (126–53), which Odysseus could not have given on the night of his arrival (153–61).

211–31 The episode, as it will develop, will require Odysseus to
have abundant wine with him, not necessarily the most likely
item he would haul along as he scouts the Kyklops' cave. Hence
Homer pays particular attention to it: it is a special wine, with its
own history. (In this it is not unlike the famous weapons, usually
swords, of considerably later heroes—folktale heroes always have
their magical props.) In lines 227–31 Odysseus goes out of his
way to explain why he took the wine with him, suggesting that he
expected his Phaiákian audience to wonder at it (as Homer would
have done with his audience).

222–23 **one cupful . . . / in twenty more of water:** This ex-
traordinarily potent Thracian wine was supposed to be diluted
twenty parts to one. To get an idea of the strength of this vintage,
consider that, in Hesiod's *Works and Days* (596), the recommended
ratio of water to wine is three to one. The mixing of wine was
standard practice; to drink wine neat would be considered a sign
of boorishness. Odysseus' remark at the end of this section, "a
wild man, ignorant of civility" (231), although it has a larger
application, also sets Polyphêmos up as being unaware of the
etiquette of drinking. Given that in Greece this included the
knowledge that wines are to be diluted, Odysseus is well on his
way to bringing off another of his brilliantly reasoned deceptions.

This may be the earliest recorded instance of "Western man"
using an intoxicant to trick (and either rob or destroy) someone
who is not acculturated to its use. Compare Osmin in Mozart's
Abduction from the Seraglio: a Moslem and thus officially a strict
abstainer, in a comedy for Christian eyes (Vienna, 1782) he is
presented as an all-too-willing tippler and thus an easy dupe for
the clever (European and Christian) servant Pedrillo. A less liter-
ary and more tragic parallel would be the "firewater" that Native
Americans so easily obtained from European colonists. Of
course, from the perspective of a self-proclaimed "superior cul-
ture," ignorance of the protocol of drinking is just another proof

of the "inferiority" of a "less cultured" people. For the "superior culture," there is nothing wrong with exploiting this ignorance in gaining the upper hand. Still, drugging one's opponent is a plot device in many thrillers today and does not necessarily imply (as it clearly does here) cultural superiority.

235–40 The actual organization of the Kyklops' goods may seem to indicate a higher level of culture than Odysseus at first suggests: milk is processed into cheese, and there is pottery. Not that Odysseus was an archeologist, or that Homer could have known that earthenware pottery had already been around for millennia; nonetheless, he would have observed that even the poorest of backwoods people could live as Polyphêmos does. It is, again, the lack of a social and political structure that marks the Kyklopês as uncivilized.

249 **what he had to offer:** Literally, "if he would give me *xeinia*" [229]—all the rites and appurtenances of hospitality.

250 **no pretty sight:** An ominous litotes.

252ff. It goes without saying that in Homer all beings, even monsters, understand and speak Greek. Most popular narrative forms exploit the convention that one can do without an interpreter, and even an explanation why one isn't needed. Later, when there is an insistence on the congruence of nationality and national language, interpreters are thematized. This in turn can become a convention: consider, in a western, the figure of the "white" captive among "Indians" who can serve as interpreter and, if female, ready-made "romantic interest" for the American cowboy or soldier (to avoid miscegenation).

One of the most illogical but goofily endearing conventions in popular American films is that foreigners speak, even among themselves, in American English with a foreign accent (and the stronger the accent, the more marked that character is in some particular foreign characteristic: evil if we are dealing with a German U-boat captain, romantic with a French or "Latin" lover). But of course, conventions by definition defy logic. Science fiction, which partakes of both the popular and pedantic, will usually thematize the means of decoding and translation between earthlings and extraterrestrials or other intelligences.

252 **took some cheese to eat:** This isn't necessarily robbery. It is part of the ceremony of sacrifice as well as a sort of speculative hospitality, by which Odysseus and his crew act on the presumption that, as guests, they will be accorded proper hospitality upon the host's return. This should have been construed as flattering to one's absent host; the Kyklops thought otherwise.

281–93 In his response to Polyphêmos' rudely suspicious questions (however well founded; see the Kikonês), Odysseus pointedly emphasizes the gods, particularly Zeus, as the motivators of his own travels and the protectors of guests—reminding the Phaiá-kions of it, as well. In lines 288–93 he uses the formal language of supplication [266–67, 269–70] (see also VI.152–207). In saying that he and his men served under Agamémnon at Troy (285), he is for once telling the truth, just not the whole truth: note that he reveals neither his name nor his homeland.

299–300 The Kyklops' apostasy goes far beyond that of an every-day disdainer of the gods (such as Aias at IV.538–40, above). In claiming superior strength (300), the Kyklopês are not unlike the giants who assaulted Olympos in an attempt to overthrow the gods.

312–22 **Neither reply nor pity . . . :** Polyphêmos, a huge, rude, even blasphemous herdsman, suddenly becomes truly monstrous. Cannibalism is the mark of the nonhuman. (See Hesiod, *Works and Days,* 276–78. For cannibalism known to later Greeks, see Herodotus IV.18.3.) Note that Polyphêmos drinks his milk, like his wine, neat ("whey," 322 [297]).

327ff. Homer has cleverly constructed the situation so that simple action will not solve the problem; all of Odysseus' foresight and cunning will be required to escape from the lair of the Kyklops.

337 **another brace of men:** Another two men. Since Odysseus had brought twelve men with him from the ship (210), there are now eight left in the cave besides Odysseus.

361–63 Odysseus is a very wise commander. He could simply have picked the four men he wanted to have as his assistants, but in a situation so desperate he probably reasoned that it was more important for morale to have the eight cast lots.

361 **eye:** Singular (see 113–24, above).

366–68 That the rams come into the cave tonight, as opposed to the previous night (see 259–60), is essential to the plot. At times Homer may seem sublimely indifferent to details, but more often than not he is in complete control. To make Odysseus himself comment on the great good fortune of this unexpected development is brilliant, in part because he cannot explain why it happened. That it might be "a god's bidding" (368) is a good reminder of Odysseus' un-Kyklopean piety, and, in particular, of the care taken of him by Athena, to whom Odysseus had prayed (344). She is not presented here as helping openly, but, then again, we are listening to Odysseus, not the omniscient epic narrator, and some kind of epiphany would have been required for Odysseus to be aware of her assistance.

378–83 Odysseus speaks as if all is lost. Now that he knows how horrid the Kyklops is, there is no hope of escape, and, he says, no need for the wine. He consciously does not flatter Polyphêmos, which might under the present circumstances arouse suspicions that the drink was poisoned, suspicions even the less-than-clever Polyphêmos might have entertained. The calculation works, and Polyphêmos quaffs the drink.

394ff. Odysseus, having sized up his opponent's intelligence (low) and wanting to make a joke at least he can enjoy, claims that his name is *Outis* [366], virtually indistinguishable from *ou tis,* "no one" (as we believe ancient Greek was spoken, there would have been a difference of tone accent on the first syllable only). Likewise, Fitzgerald presents "nobody" in the slightly disguised form

"Nohbdy." This prepares the ground for two verbal jokes, the first fairly sophomoric. The first comes when the other Kyklops understand *Outis* as *ou tis* ("Nohbdy" as "nobody," 446), which emerges from the fact that, according to the standard substitution of *mê* for *ou* in certain grammatical contexts, *ou tis* becomes *mê tis* [410]. (This joke is anticipated in the "noman" of line 440.) This syntactical replacement lays the groundwork for a more sophisticated pun: as *ou tis* is to *Outis*, *mê tis* is to *mêtis* or "cunning intelligence," Odysseus' defining characteristic. Lest this pun escape the notice of his audience, Homer quite pointedly has Odysseus use the word *mêtis* right away [414] (represented in the translation by "deceived," 452), and, again, in the accusative case, *mêtin* [422] ("wits," 460).

400 **Nohbdy's my meat:** Or "I will eat nobody last" [369]. Indeed: he will eat no one else at all.

402–19 **his great head lolling to one side:** Another detail which may seem to be a merely descriptive decoration but is in fact crucial. Given Polyphêmos' size, Odysseus and his men could hardly have put out the giant's eye if he were on his back with his face pointing straight up (and obviously not if he were facedown). As it is, however, Polyphêmos' position permits them to be on the ground and run straight forward with their pole (see 414–16). A number of ancient depictions survive.

This clear picture becomes a little confused in 417–19, which seems to describe a vertical orientation with Odysseus above, his men below. The simplest solution is to recall that this is a simile: the major point of comparison is simply that Odysseus and his men twirl the pike just as shipwrights and their helpers do; the absolute and relative positions of Odysseus/master craftsman, on the one hand, and comrades/helpers, on the other, need not harmonize.

438 **Polyphêmos:** The name occurs for the first time in this book here (see 113–24, above). Odysseus learns it only because he hears the other Kyklops use it, although it is not clear whether or not Polyphêmos was concealing his name from Odysseus the way Odysseus had concealed his from the giant. Likewise, Odysseus will also learn from this exchange the name of Polyphêmos' father (448–49).

440, 446, 452 **No man, nobody, deceived:** See 394, above.

460 **wits and tactics:** *dolous kai mêtin* [422] (see 394, above).

464 **dark violet:** See IV.146, above.

487–93 That Polyphêmos is aware of the abnormal behavior of the largest ram provides a moment of concern to the audience, as no doubt it did to Odysseus himself. Will the plot turn and involve further dangers and complications, requiring further deceptions? Having so often twisted his plot, Homer can achieve nearly the same effect here by merely presenting the possibility of a twist.

502 There is further wordplay in the concluding phrase of Polyphêmos' address to his ram: in Greek, something like "that good-for-no-thing Nohbdy" [*outidanos Outis*, 460]. (Only a line away, and hardly unintended by the poet, is "the floor" (501) [in the dative case, *oudeï*, 459, like another word for "no one," *oudeis*].

519ff. Odysseus cannot resist letting Polyphêmos know that he has been bested. At first it seems a good lesson in piety (522–23), but having spoken at all turns out to have its risks when the Kyklops lobs huge rock masses in the direction of the ship, Odysseus' call having revealed its location. However, despite the warning of his crew (535ff., for once much wiser than their captain), Odysseus reveals his identity (551–52). This, of course, is the means by which the poet of *The Odyssey* motivates Poseidon's wrath (after Polyphêmos' curse, 569–71). This show of pride ends up extending Odysseus' wanderings and proves fatal for all his companions. Odysseus' claim to be acting as the agent of Zeus Xenios and the other gods (523) appears not to be borne out by the plot at all (on Zeus Xenios, see III.377, above).

537–45 Fitzgerald creates five voices to do what the Greek presents as one coherent speech [494–99], which neatly demonstrates some of the differences between ancient epic and modern narrative conventions. It is not that Fitzgerald invents something that is not there; it is simply that Homer conveys the idea more indirectly. He concludes the introduction (535–36) to the sailors' words with a directive: "each in a different way" [*allothen allos*, 493]. This licenses Fitzgerald's solution. Working in print, he can use quotation marks; the reader, who is familiar with this convention, understands how speakers change on the basis of punctuation alone (for other examples, see XVIII.87–90 and 140–45).

Homer tells his audience that the sailors are all pleading in different ways, then presents a speech that sums up and represents the range of arguments and sentiments in a conventional, if not strictly realistic, manner. And yet there is something more behind the differences of technique and convention: it is not epic style, and not epic thinking, to attribute speech to anonymous characters. If someone, even a lowly swineherd, is to speak, he must be presented with a name and perhaps even a patronymic. Fitzgerald and his readers share more democratic assumptions: we are prepared to attend to voices we know are simply those of "sailors."

554 **the weird:** Fate. Polyphêmos' recollection of the oracle is a surprising turn in the narrative. (Since the oracle had foretold the loss of his eye, we might wonder why Polyphêmos didn't assume his assailant was Odysseus as soon as he had been blinded. But then again, Polyphêmos is no rocket scientist.) That Odysseus is the subject of Polyphêmos' oracle might have been particularly interesting for the Phaiákians, over whom the doom of another oracle hangs. Although this bothered ancient commentators, neither Homer nor Odysseus and the Phaiákians seem to be disturbed (see VIII.604–11, above).

558 **for time to come:** See I.266–67, above.

573 **The god of earthquake could not heal you there!:** It has been argued that the irreverence of this understatement, which verges on blasphemy, is the cause of the sea god's enmity toward Odysseus. Certainly, the economy of the passage supports this interpretation, for immediately following Odysseus' words, Poly-phêmos formulates his prayer/curse (the word is the same in Greek, *arê* in Homer's Ionic, although it does not appear in this passage). Polyphêmos calls on Poseidon, and Poseidon hears him. However, it is important to note that Odysseus has already said that he wishes he could have killed Polyphêmos. The Greek behind 573 [525] is quite unambiguously an extension of his wish that Polyphêmos were in Hades and beyond help from his divine father. That once dead, Polyphêmos could not have his vision restored, much less be revived, is accepted Homeric theology (compare Athena's testimony at III.254–56, and see III.247ff., above).

A more fundamental point is that Homeric gods do not need a crime of blasphemy to justify their enmity. Poseidon could just have well have pursued Odysseus simply for blinding his son; he had done harm to one of Poseidon's *philoi* and thus made himself hateful to the god. No excuse was necessary to follow the stan-dard dictum: help your friends and harm your enemies. As we will learn in Book XI from the shade of the seer Teirêsias, Posei-don's anger in fact is due simply to Odysseus' blinding of Poly-phêmos (XI.116–17); Athena will say the same thing (XIII.431).

580–85 For the sake of the whole epic, Homer has Polyphêmos pronounce a second choice: if fate guarantees Odysseus' home-coming, then may it be late and solitary.

605–7 **Zeus disdained my offering:** Odysseus is speaking from his current state of knowledge, inferring backward. There was probably no sign of disdain at the time. The remark is of a piece with his characteristic piety. (See 59–60, above.)

BOOK X

The Grace of the Witch

4 **an isle adrift upon the sea:** The idea of the floating island fascinated the Greeks; according to legend, the very well known Delos, with its shrine holy to Apollo, had been floating before it was anchored.

8 **gave girls to boys:** In this fairy-tale kingdom, the two groups of siblings are of equal number, which works perfectly for the marriage of all the sisters to their brothers. With the continued presence of all his children at daily feasting, Aiolos is the fantasy image of a father in *The Odyssey*. (For both more fairy-tale and realistic elements of this episode, see 22–29, below.)

17–18 **the return of the Akhaians:** Strictly, Odysseus would at this point have known little about the *nostoi* of any other of the Akhaians. Homer is no pedant, and no one in his audience would have gotten stuck on this point.

22–29 The bag of winds with all of them tied up and only one (at first) let out—the favorable west-wind—is one version of a traditional motif. Another example, developed somewhat differently, is Pandora's box, so-called because Pandora (literally "all gifts") opened this box, releasing all woes into the world. She managed to slam it shut in time to retain only one item—hope.

Denys Page cites examples of "rain-makers and wind-control-lers in primitive societies" as well as "professional wind-sellers" in a variety of cultures, arguing that some were familiar to the Greeks. He claims that Homer's audience would not see this aspect of the Aiolos episode as the stuff of fairy tale at all (*Folktales in Homer's Odyssey*, pp. 73–78). But what is realistic as "primitive magic" can be cast into a shape that has recognizably traditional elements (threes, prohibitions violated with disastrous conse-quences, and so on). Here is a brief story also quoted by Page:

In Siseby on the Schlei dwelt a woman skilled in sorcery, who could turn the wind round. The herring-fishermen of Schleswig often used to land there. On one occasion they wanted to return to Schleswig, but the wind was in the west. So they asked the woman to turn the wind round. She said she would, in return for a plate of fish; so the fishermen offered her herrings, perch, bream, and pike, these being all the fish they had. Thereupon she gave them a cloth with three knots, and said that they could open the first and second knots, but must not open the third till they reached land. The fishermen spread their sails, although the wind was still in the west; but the moment the oldest member of the company opened the first knot, a fair wind came from the east. He opened the second knot, and a strong wind came upon them, and they reached their town at high speed. And now they were curious to know what would happen if they opened the third knot too: they had hardly done so, when a terrible hurri-cane fell upon them from the west; they had to jump into the water in a hurry, to drag their ship to the beach.

(Müllenhoff as excerpted in Page, *Folktales*, 77)

57 **a quick finish:** That even the ever-resourceful Odysseus con-siders suicide suggests how deep his despair is at this point. His

moments of despair are coming more frequently as his travels continue (see 552–53).

82–85 Aiolos' response does not constitute a breach of hospitality or of the rights of suppliants. It was proper for a host to refuse to aid someone who was hated by the gods. Underlying this was the belief that those being punished by the gods were foul or stained, and that the *miasma* with which they were infected could be contagious. Has Odysseus forgotten the listening Phaiákians?

93–97 **In that land . . . :** This seems to be a clear reference to long summer days in far northern European latitudes. While there may not be any well-informed geographical knowledge behind the description of Odysseus' travels that would permit us to identify the "real" locations of these way stations, there is every reason to believe that Homer could have heard reports of the midnight sun from traders and incorporated them into his description of a fantastic land. Amber from northern Europe reached the Mediterranean as early as the Iron Age and found its way into Mycenaean shaft-graves (c. 1700 B.C.E.). The first recorded Greek sea voyage to Scandinavia is that of Pytheas (c. 325 B.C.E.).

By contrast, the land of the Laistrygonês may be far to the east, the home of the Dawn, thus (poetically) depicted as a land of never-failing light. The strangeness of this world is further emphasized by the "workaholic" fantasy Odysseus spins. The Greeks well appreciated the fact that night gives respite from the labors and cares of the day. In a poem frequently imitated (though now fragmentary), the seventh-century-B.C.E. Spartan poet Alkman described all of nature, from the mountain peaks to the depths of the sea, asleep in peaceful rest (*Lyrica Graeca Selecta*, ed. D. Page, frag. 34).

99–107 Some scholars have suggested that Homer is depicting a Scandinavian fjord, and this could serve as a good description of one. (Going further down this road, lines 106–7 might be a reference to ice [*leukê galênê*, 94, could be rendered "white calm"] and line 94 perhaps even a yodeling herdsmen's call.) Such a fjord would have been "curious" to the Greeks, and the description may suggest that the harborage is in some way remarkable and noteworthy (the adjective in line 99 literally means "famous" [*kluton*, 87]). Again (see 93–97, above) we must remember that while the poet may be incorporating elements that at several removes go back to a traveler who saw a Scandinavian coastline, neither Homer nor his audience would have the geographical apparatus to put this on a map. Indeed, they had no concept of "Europe" comparable to our own. The problems of literalization are well exemplified in the equation of "white calm" with "ice": the Greeks could not possibly have envisioned a sea frozen over with Odysseus sailing through it.

108–10 **My own black ship . . . :** The separate moorage of Odysseus' own ship will prove important (see 133ff., below).

117–20 It was no doubt quite common, in life as in literature, for travelers heading toward a settlement to meet someone coming out to fetch water (Jacob and Rachel at the well in Genesis 29:2–11, or when Athena appears before Odysseus as the young Phaiákian girl with a "water jug," VII.23). However, although Odysseus' party encounters the king's daughter, as he had encountered Nausikaa in Phaiákia, things will turn out rather differently here.

123 **waved her hand:** She must have answered the questions asked in line 122, for there is no other way for Odysseus to have learned the name of the people or their king. (There is also a possibility of some narrative negligence; see 534, below, with further references.)

125–28 The gigantic Laistrygon couple recall the giants in "Jack and the Beanstalk." Here the husband, Antiphatês, (at least) is the man-eater. We wouldn't speak of *The Odyssey* as being a "source" or "influence" in such a case, but of "analogues" or "folk-tale types." Such tales have wide distribution, and in the mouths of skilled tale-tellers they have infinite power to undergo transformation. They may even be generated anew or reconstituted from common motifs according to a deep structure or pattern (i.e., archetype).

129–38 The cannibalistic, giant, rock-lobbing Laistrygonês are another incarnation of many of the story elements Homer presented in the tale of the Kyklops (Book IX). But instead of criticizing this as mere repetition, it is more appropriate, given Homeric techniques, to appreciate it as theme and variation. The same critique has been made (and the same defense should be mounted) in the case of Kalypso (Book V) and Kirkê, whom we are about to meet (149ff.).

132ff. All but Odysseus' ship, fortunately moored farthest out to sea, are destroyed. Now we see that lines 108–10 were not merely descriptive but preparatory and functional. Likewise, the fjordlike formation of the harbor (see 99–107, above) is best explained functionally: such an anchorage beneath the cliffs permits the rock-lobbing Laistrygonês to demolish multiple ships and provides the narrator a dramatic and economical way to dispatch most of Odysseus' companions and all but one of his ships in one fell swoop, a move that the narrative shape of *The Odyssey* requires. Note that the variation in topography and placement of ships makes this a very different episode from Polyphêmos' rock throwing at IX.524–92.

167–69 **So I took counsel with myself:** After the last episode, Odysseus proceeds more cautiously.

169–71 **No, better not . . . :** This is not only a sound idea but also one of the clearest resemblances to the Odysseus of *The Iliad*. In Book XIX Akhilleus finally returns to the main camp of the Greeks, though it has taken the death of his dear Patróklos to rouse him. Now raging and impatient, he wants to lead the Greeks at once against the Trojans, particularly Hektor, who slew Patróklos. Odysseus in two speeches (XIX.155–83 and 216–37) manages to persuade the other Akhaian commanders (if not Akhilleus) that for the men to march out and fight on empty stomachs is likely to spell disaster. The allusion is all the cleverer, since the present context is so utterly unlike the situation in *The Iliad*. The themes of eating, of life as long as sustenance remains (see esp. *Odyssey* X.192–95), and of feasting, both wise and foolish, are central to *The Odyssey* (see also I.13, above).

173 **some god's compassion:** Although Odysseus had uttered comparable thoughts before (the nighttime landing on Goat Island, IX.153), here (as with "some god," 157), it has special significance, after the disastrous two first episodes in Book X and Aiolos' specific description of Odysseus as being cursed by the gods.

192–93 **Come, friends . . . :** A nice joke on Homer's part, appreciated by connoisseurs of *The Odyssey*. As Kirkê will instruct him, he will have to go to the House of Death (543), which he will report in Book XI. (See also Heubeck, HWH 2.54 [on IX.174–77].)

208–11 Odysseus can hardly mean they don't know where the sun rises—it just rose (205). But since Odysseus and his men have no idea where their present position is in relation to Ithaka, they don't know which way to sail. What Odysseus says is true in general: they are completely and utterly lost.

212 **any least thing to serve:** In Greek, the word is again *mêtis* [193], some stratagem Odysseus can hatch.

223, 227 **two platoons, with twenty-two companions:** In addition to Odysseus, forty-five men remain: Eurýlokhos and two groups of twenty-two each. Odysseus must thus originally have had in his own ship fifty-eight companions, since thirteen have been killed (six by the Kikonês, six by Polyphêmos, one by the Laistrygonês). If the other eleven ships lost in the harbor in that last-named episode each had a captain and a crew of the same size, his total contingent would have numbered just over seven hundred. (Only in Books X–XII does Homer name any of Odysseus' companions, and then only rarely; ultimately, we learn the names of four: Eurýlokhos here, Politês at 247, Elpênor at 610, and Perimêdês at XI.25.)

230ff. If we were to seek an analogue to Kirkê familiar from popular European fairy tales, it would be the witch in "Hansel and Gretel," who, as it turns out, has bewitched many children who are only freed when she is defeated by the heroes of the tale. *The Odyssey* diverges from the popular version of the modern fairy tale in several important ways: as far as this detail is concerned, note that Odysseus has no moral interest in freeing any of Kirkê's previous victims and wins the release of his comrades only (and by persuasion, not by destroying the "witch"). Indeed, simpleminded categories of "good witch" and "bad witch" will not do for Kirkê or any force in *The Odyssey*. She is a goddess (634). Contact with divinity is always fraught with risks, as well as possibility for great rewards. It's also worth noting that Kirkê never works her magic on anyone who has not of his own free will put himself in her power (note that immediately below, 255ff., the wary Eurýlokhos is *not* compelled to enter her house).

260–61 **to make them lose / desire or thought:** This aspect of Kirkê is a variation on the theme first presented in the land of the Lotos Eaters (IX.91–109), a parallel underlined by Homer's use of the verb "to forget" [*lathoiato,* 236] (see also IX.104, above).

283–86 It is somewhat odd that, while Eurýlokhos witnessed the crew's transformation into swine, he does not appear to report any of the specifics to Odysseus. (For other quibbles about the narrative economy of this episode, see 534, below.)

309–40 Odysseus no doubt gives special attention to the words spoken by the youthful helper he encounters in the forest (exactly when he realizes it is Hermês is uncertain), but in the Greek, Hermês' words are not set off either by rhyme (avoided rather than sought in ancient Greek) or by any change of meter or line length. The youthful demeanor of Hermês in particular calls to mind the god's memorable appearance to Priam in *The Iliad* (XXIV.347–8).

321 **as amulet:** One need only have the magic *molü* (see 343) on one's person to be protected.

335 **a pleasure you must not decline:** While the double standard familiar to Homer's audience permitted infidelity to the husband that it firmly denied to the wife, there is some indication that Homer wanted Odysseus to have a reputation for extraordinary fidelity and chastity: he alone of the Greek commanders takes no concubine (see I.488., above), and Hermês warns him that he dare not refuse to sleep with Kirkê. It is an essential part of what he must do to free his comrades. He is, of course, not loath to do so once he has extracted the requisite oath (note "flawless bed of love," 390).

391–413 The pairing of gold and silver runs as a leitmotif throughout the description of the paraphernalia of Kirkê's woodland retreat.

421–24 Given Kirkê's knowledge elsewhere (e.g., 506–7, 543–50), she may very well know the reason for Odysseus' downcast spirits.

456–64 A particularly homey simile, and another involving gender crossing (see also VIII.560–64). The pathos in this case is the greater, since the audience knows that none of these companions will ever see "the crags of Ithaka" (463) again.

476ff. Eurýlokhos' hesitation, bordering on mutiny, is well drawn. He might have some ground to fear that Odysseus is himself now bewitched and may unwittingly be leading his remaining comrades to destruction.

484 **foolishness:** This is the same word [*atasthaliêisin*, 433] as the "recklessness" of I.12 (7; indeed the second half of both lines are identical in Greek). On the issue of responsibility, see I.10–12, above.

534 **keep your promise:** Odysseus has neglected to tell us of any moment when Kirkê made either an implicit or an explicit promise. We are, of course, free to imagine one, and Kirkê does not refuse Odysseus (although she refers to no promise). Homer's organization of this episode is uncharacteristically negligent (see 123, 283–86, above, and 610–19, below).

543ff. A complete surprise. Kirkê has restored him and his men, and will let them go, but she has important instructions, which set Odysseus on a new course and set up the major content of Book XI. Although it is not explicit here, Kirkê's language in 543–44 suggests that the gods require this trip of Odysseus. (See Proteus' directive to Meneláos, IV.509–14, that he must return to Egypt and complete rites there before the gods will permit his home-coming in Sparta. The two episodes are parallel in many respects.) Odysseus certainly never doubts the authority of Kirkê's injunction.

545 Perséphonê may be mentioned so often (550, 565, 591) because she inhabited the world of the living before becoming queen of Hades. She has, thus, a liminal nature—she is a sort of mediator between life and death. In the fully developed form of her story she lives on earth half the year and in the underworld the other half. This unique status plays a prominent role in some of the most important ancient mystery cults.

547 **Teirêsias:** He is the most famous of all soothsayers. Compare the seer's outer blindness/inner vision with the blindness of the bard Demódokos (see VIII.70, above).

564ff. **bourne of Ocean:** See XI.15, below. Gilgamesh, too, reaches the land of the dead by sailing, in his case to the west (see *Epic of Gilgamesh,* Kovacs, trans., Tablet X, pp. 83–94).

573ff. Odysseus is not to travel through the land of the dead but to arrive there and summon the shades or souls with libations. Kirkê's warning to turn away (585–86) recalls Leukothea's warning (V.361–63, obeyed at V.483–86—see the note on V.359–63, above).

600–601 Again, the gold and silver combination seems to be the fashion on Aiaia (see 391–413, above).

619 **But I was outside:** Odysseus clearly did not know of Elpênor's death at the time. In the next book Elpênor's shade appears to Odysseus and tells him what took place (XI.54–90). This serves as a further link between Books X and XI.

Arguments "from silence," i.e., from what is *not* mentioned or described, are generally suspect, but not always invalid: the conventions of Homeric epic are sufficiently consistent for us to confidently assume, as Homer's first audience would have, that, had Odysseus known of Elpênor's demise at the time, he would have undertaken to bury him with all the necessary rites. (The issue of the failure to bury Elpênor is prominent at XI.55–57 and 81–90.)

632 **a black ewe and a ram:** Kirkê supplies the animals for the sacrifice on the shores of Death that she herself had ordered (582–84).

BOOK XI

A Gathering of Shades

15 **Ocean's bourne:** The "Ocean" was envisaged as a band of sea or river ("Ocean stream," XI.23 and XII.1), which encircled the known lands. It seems that one could have sailed across its width (usually an indeterminate distance, but in this case apparently requiring only a bit more than one day and one night's sailing) to reach what is on the other shore: in some accounts the Isles of the Blessed, here, the land of the dead. However, this would contradict the standard view of the encircling Ocean, and it could be that Odysseus sailed from east to west along the southern oceanic circle (Heubeck, HWH 2.78 [on XI.14–19].) This may be more logical, but ultimately, once we have entered a mythical landscape, logic has little to offer.

16 **Men of Winter:** One of the possible interpretations of Homer's *Kimmerioi*, which some Greek scholars located in the Crimea, while others suggest "dwellers in darkness" or simply "a fabulous tribe living by the entrance to Hades." Lines 17–21 certainly suggest a people living in the far north, though again not

literally, since the description would not fit the upper latitudes during summer, when days are extraordinarily long (see X.93–97, above). As in the case of the Laistrygonês, the best answer may be that these people live in the land of night, the setting sun, i.e., the west.

26ff. **the votive pit . . . :** The digging of the trench and pouring of blood suggest offerings to the dead in the earth. Attracted by the blood, they swarm up into the pit as though they dwell beneath it. What the "souls" (*psukhai*) that appear to Odysseus are is not an easy question to answer. Homer doesn't present any coherent theology of the afterlife. These are shadowy, visible, but untenable representatives of the dead, whose appearance resembles that of their former selves. After drinking the blood, they regain memory of their experiences while alive. Line 44 suggests they were imagined as being dressed just as they had been the moment they died.

54ff. Despite Kirkê's admonition (X.592–94) that Odysseus keep all of the ghosts away from the blood, which would enable them to speak with him, until he has questioned Teirêsias, Odysseus addresses Elpênor and Elpênor replies. It appears contradictory, and Homer doesn't tell us what allows this exception, not granted even Odysseus' mother (XI.99). However, it probably can be explained by the fact that Elpênor has neither been cremated nor been buried (55) and thus does not need to drink blood before he can speak.

73–76 **your wife:** However indirect the source, these constitute the first details the Phaiákians learn of Odysseus' immediate family.

79 **. . . upon Aiaia Island:** This is news to us and to Odysseus. Kirkê had implied a direct voyage home (X.596–97), although a second stop on Aiaia does not contradict what she said.

98 **held her off:** In other words, held her back from the blood. It emerges in lines 158–72 that Antikleía does not yet recognize her son and will do so only after she is permitted to sip the blood. ("Through pang on pang of tears" refers to Odysseus' tears.)

100ff. Teirêsias is the single exception to the rules binding the souls of people whose remains have been cremated and ashes buried: he recognizes Odysseus and can speak, but he can "speak true" (107; see also 152) only if he can drink the blood. Again, this is not the doctrine of any sect but merely the "rules of the game." They need make sense only for the purposes of the narrative.

105 **joyless region:** A grim understatement.

130ff. **insolent men:** This is the first that Odysseus will have heard of the suitors, and it is presented as a prophecy. Teirêsias' speech (124–27) seems to imply that if Odysseus could have gone home directly from Thrinákia, that is, if his companions would have avoided violating Hêlios' flocks, causing their destruction and Odysseus' further delay (especially the seven years with Kalypso), Penélopê would not have been importuned by the suitors.

135–51 By means of this prophecy, Homer includes—or creates—a portion of the legendary life of Odysseus that falls beyond the time frame of *The Odyssey*.

139 **oars that fledge light hulls for dipping flight:** The image is one of oars rising and falling in rhythm like the wings of a bird.

148 **seaborne:** Many other scholars interpret "off the sea" [*ex halos*, 134] as meaning "not on the sea" rather than "from the sea." The controversy is ancient.

192–227 Note that Odysseus' multiple questions are taken up and answered by Antikleía precisely in reverse order, so that the exchange becomes another instance of ring composition (among numerous examples, see VII.142–43 and IX.41–43, above, and XIX.62–63, below).

207–10 This would seem to fit the image of a Penélopê as yet unwooed and of a home as yet unmolested by the suitors (see 130ff., above). The only problem is a slight chronological embarrassment: Telémakhos should be only about fourteen or fifteen at this point, yet Antikleía's words suggest a man older by several years at least. This apparent inconsistency clearly did not bother Homer. "The poet almost imperceptibly alters the time-scale quite substantially, allowing the hero to report conversations the content of which really only fits the period immediately before he lands in Phaeacia, in order to prepare the reader for the events of xiii–xxiv" (Heubeck, HWH 2.88 [on XI.181–203]).

256ff. Perséphonê is described as staging the spectacle of souls who approach and speak to Odysseus. The "first act" of her pageant comprises famous women (through 386); after an intermission, during which the narrative returns to the Phaiákians and Odysseus, a "second act" follows, starring a number of the most prominent commanders at Troy (characters well known from *The Iliad*): Agamémnon, Akhilleus, and Aîas (449–674). Then comes an extended procession of selected other denizens of Hades (675–754; on some particular problems of this section, see 673–747a and following, below), concluding with a rapid departure from the land of the Dead (755–59).

258 **consorts or daughters of illustrious men:** The significance and status of these women is presented in terms of their relationship to male heads of households: technically, they are the wards of either their fathers or their husbands. (The phrase is important enough to return at the end of this section, in line 382.) However, in many of the stories about to be narrated, women play far more important roles, as do two who are prominent members of the audience of these tales: one, to whom Odysseus is currently narrating his adventures, Queen Arêtê in Phaiákia, and the other, Penélopê, prospectively (254–55). (To identify all the legendary women presented here, and the heroes who follow them, consult Who's Who in *The Odyssey*, pp. 307–48.) It is obviously important that many of the women who appear are presented as having broken sexual codes restricting their behavior, often but not always with gods as their male lovers. Without presenting a moralizing framework for these "legends of good women" (the title of one of Chaucer's poems, based in part on an even more overtly moralistic collection by Boccaccio), they serve as counterexamples to the perfect wife, Penélopê, and are in this way woven into the thematic fabric of *The Odyssey*.

294–95 **Aison, Pherês, / and Amytháon, expert charioteer:** A good example [as is the Greek, 259] of the tricolon crescendo (see III.117–20, above). Some sort of formal device is often employed to round out a narrative segment; here it marks the end of the section on Tyro and her children.

308 **and Megarê:** Her name is parallel with Alkmênê (305), not Heraklês (306).

315–16 This is clearly not the complete version of the aftermath of the revelation of Oidipous' patricide and incest as told by the Athenian dramatists in the fifth century. For this, see Aeschylus' *Seven Against Thebes* and Sophokles' *Oidipous at Kolonos*. However, any disagreement between the versions is more muted in the Greek: "all through his evil days" (Fitzgerald's line 316) is an inference based on the imperfect tense of the Greek verb [276].

321 **endless agony from a mother's Furies:** This is generally less prominent in the stories of Oidipous than in that of Orestês.

330 **and Pêro, too:** This is another child of Khloris. It is Khloris whom Odysseus saw, not Pêro. Although chronology is one of the first things neglected when legends from different cycles are brought together, it is likely that Pêro, sister of Nestor, was still thought to be alive at the time of the telling. (Fitzgerald's "turned" in the past tense, 330, is an unintended consequence of his expansion of the Greek [287].)

It is an interesting variant on the catalog structure that at this point the greater part of the segment is devoted to a story about the daughter of the woman Odysseus saw, not about the woman herself. The entry ultimately focuses on and concludes with the story of a would-be suitor of that daughter. Many of the entries conclude with and thereby emphasize stories of the women's sons.

336 **a diviner:** Not named here, but it is Melampous (as confirmed by XV.279–318). It is hard to piece together all the details of the story from the two Homeric passages, suggesting that the myth was well known to Homer's audience. From later fragments and allusions it appears that Íphiklos rewarded Melampous with the herd for what seemed to be the seer's prophetic powers. In fact, Melampous understood the speech of animals (a common folk-tale motif) and learned from them what was concealed from other humans.

360–61 If we take these dimensions literally, this would mean they were about fifty-four feet tall and thirteen and a half feet across at the shoulders. And this at only nine years of age! They were expected to get bigger ("As giants grown," 367).

368–69 **the bright son of Zeus / by Lêto:** Apollo.

372–86 As Odysseus and Homer conclude this section, the names form clusters and the entries become briefer. Also, these last six names are of women who betrayed either a husband or a father. The women mentioned previously were perfect only in beauty and heritage; this section provides legends of unambiguously bad women. Perhaps it is out of consideration of this as much as the passage of time that Odysseus, mindful of Arêtê in his audience, decides to cut his narrative short (381–82).

384–86 Odysseus concludes with a diplomatic reminder that what he really wants is the promised trip home.

394 **He is my guest:** Odysseus is Arêtê's guest in particular be-cause he made his first appeal to her (VII.151–64) and because he is a guest of the household of which she is the lady.

398–99 **eldest / of all Phaiákians:** As eldest, Ekhenêos had also spoken first at VII.171–79 (see VII.166–68 and 204, above, on the value placed on age).

414–20 Odysseus' response is in part simply the language of the court, and all who know the rules of such discourse understand that it is not meant literally—we can be quite sure Odysseus would not look on a year's delay with equanimity, much less pleasure—but is understood to mean "you are powerful and I appreciate your kind disposition toward me." The consideration of the gifts and their value sounds calculating to us, but it would not have been deemed at all crass. A guest was expected to receive gifts graciously. To pretend unworthiness was not part of the code and would have insulted the offering host. Odysseus can even say (as he does in 417) that he "could wish" a large quantity of gifts, since it is understood that he is prepared to reciprocate on the same scale. Odysseus' reasoning in lines 417–20 would have won agreement all around: wealth bespeaks power. But the tactic Odysseus will have to choose upon his return to Ithaka is very different from the return envisioned here—an irony to be appreciated at this point by Homer's audience alone.

429 **a man who knows the world:** *Epistamenôs* [368] should rather be taken as "skillfully," "knowing the ways of poetry." The exact sequence of thought behind the part of Alkínoös' speech leading up to this point (422–28) is hard to pin down. There seems to be some sort of frame-breaking humor in line 429: the poem's real audience may well smile at this doddering character who's saying to Odysseus, "Wow, you told that story just like a good poet," since they can see that Odysseus is but a mask for Homer. (Likewise da Ponte's Countess exclaims to Cherubino in Act II of Mozart's *Marriage of Figaro*, after "he" has sung a song to her, "what a lovely voice"; of course: the singer portraying Cherubino is an opera star.) There may well be comparable humor behind the assertions of Odysseus' credibility (422–27), given his own reputation for trickery, even lying. (Behind "many," 424, is a *poly*-compound [365] another *hapax*; also consider the many *poly*-epithets for Odysseus, starting at I.2, above.)

436–37 We might imagine that the generations of bards from whom Homer descended would have wished for such listeners, such patrons who would want them to sing all night.

443–48 **Other and sadder . . . :** Alkínoös had specifically asked to hear of those who "met their doom at Troy" (432). Akhilleus and Aîas, of whom Odysseus will speak shortly, fall into that category. However, as is appropriate for the theme of *The Odyssey* and as a mark of Odysseus' awareness of the perils still facing him, Homer has Odysseus widen the scope, reminding Alkínoös and all the Phaiákians of those "other and sadder / Tales" of those who returned safe from Troy "only to find a brutal death at home— / and a bad wife behind it."

467–69 **or you were cattle-raiding . . . :** Note again the expectation that even great kings and commanders would engage in raids for goods and slaves, as Odysseus himself had done in the land of the Kikonês at the beginning of his voyage homeward (IX.46–73). Odysseus imagines as the most likely causes of Agamémnon's death two things he has experienced on his travels so far: storms at sea and armed resistance of natives.

476–504 Agamémnon's narrative of his murder at the hands of Aigísthos and the treachery of Klytaimnéstra is obviously the climactic moment of the Agamémnon-Orestês theme in *The Odyssey*.

492–94 On the difficulties of interpretation involved in these lines, see Fitzgerald's notes (pp. 472–74 of *The Odyssey*).

500–501 **my children and my slaves / at least:** It seems Agamémnon had imagined that his wife might have had some cause to be angry when he returned, considering that he was bringing Kassandra home from Troy as his concubine and—*if* the story was as old as *The Odyssey*—that he had sacrificed their own daughter Iphianassa (Iphigenia) before going to war. He had in any event not anticipated a murder plot.

501–4 **But that woman . . . defiled herself / and all her sex:** We note that Aigísthos' vile act does not in Agamémnon's perspective defile all men, for Agamémnon is himself a man—a typical gender bias.

506–12 Odysseus' response is diplomatic; he is of course moved by the horror of Agamémnon's fate, but he doesn't concur with Agamémnon's wholesale condemnation of women. Of course he does take precautions when he arrives home. This is hardly the time for a debate, but in lines 507–8, with overt piety, he suggests that Agamémnon's house carried this curse for some time. Indeed, the family had a penchant for both adultery and foul murder.

515–17 Agamémnon describes a relationship that is very far from the *homophrosunê*—"like-mindedness"—which Odysseus and Penélopê share (see VI.194–99, above). Indeed, Agamémnon seems to except Penélopê from his condemnation of women (533–35). The lies and half truths that Odysseus and Penélopê tell each other in Books XVIII–XXIII are not of the type Agamémnon advises here, for they are only temporary expedients used until the danger represented by the suitors can be removed and their full partnership reestablished. In a sense, that they both engage in cunning and calculation shows how deeply their like-mindedness runs.

530, 536–40 **my own son:** Orestês' name is postponed so that it can be the very last word Agamémnon speaks (540 [461]), although everyone would have known exactly who is meant already in 530. The audience of *The Odyssey* and indeed some of the epic's characters (e.g., Telémakhos) know of Orestês' vengeance, but neither Agamémnon nor Odysseus could have any inkling of this at the moment represented here, since at that time it had not yet occurred.

553 Unless we are to imagine a breakdown of the "rules of the game" (see XI.101ff., above), we must assume that Homer simply chose to omit describing the moment at which Akhilleus and shortly Aîas are permitted to drink the blood.

569–81 This is the central interchange and the climax of the encounter between the hero of *The Iliad* and the hero of *The Odyssey*. By his remarks and questions (569–74) Odysseus becomes spokesman of the world of *The Iliad* and of Akhilleus' famous choice in that poem (*Iliad* IX.410–16): glory [*kleos*] even at the cost of one's life. In response, Akhilleus, who now has another perspective, is made spokesman for the worldview of *The Odyssey:* what counts is life, surviving at any cost, and even becoming a different man in the process (577–81). This is of course what Odysseus excels at, so that here, the poet has arranged to have Akhilleus, "best of the Akhaians" and hero of *The Iliad,* implicitly take second place to Odysseus.

582ff. Akhilleus' concerns are for his son Neoptólemos and his father, Peleus.

620 **the lad:** Eurýpulos (also "him" in 621). Line 619 refers to the tale in which Eurýpulos' mother refused to let her son fight but was eventually persuaded otherwise by the gifts of her father, Priam.

651 **Trojan children:** Trojan captives. Aristarchus disputed the authenticity of the line. It is odd.

671 The proud silence of Aîas was already famous in antiquity. The author of the first-century c.e. treatise *On the Sublime* writes, "Ajax's silence in the Vision of the Dead is grand and indeed more sublime than any words could have been" (pseudo-Longinus, *On the Sublime* IX.2, D. A. Russell, trans., in D. A. Russell and M. Winterbottom, *Ancient Literary Criticism* [Oxford, 1972], 468).

673–747a This passage, while ancient (Plato refers to it as Homeric, *Gorgias* 525E), is almost certainly an interpolation or later addition to *The Odyssey.* Clearly it is part of *The Odyssey* we have inherited, and we might do well to ask in what sense the word "interpolation" is used in the context of a poem that is the product of an ongoing process of accretion and development. The problem is that this segment simply does not jive with the underworld as Homer has consistently presented it so far. Until this moment and from line 747b on, Odysseus stands at the edge of the world of the Dead. The souls come to the trough he has dug and speak to him from that point. Suddenly, in the section in question, Odysseus is within the landscape of the underworld, viewing heroes and giants in tableaux, with significant objects in their hands, sometimes performing some action. These are not only souls. Particularly jarring is the fact that Odysseus here sees the dead undergoing punishment, which was not the case up to this point.

For all these reasons, most scholars agree that this section is a later patch with a clearly different "take" on the underworld. It is also a classic case of the "purple patch," a term that goes back to Horace's *Ars poetica*, 15–16. While the diction is not impossibly *un*-Odysseyan, the section is just too densely packed and precious to be fit comfortably into *The Odyssey*. Each of the tableaux presented here is a little set piece and an opportunity to show off, which the poet cannot resist doing. Note in particular the description of Tántalos' fruit tree at 704–8—in the Greek of 705–6 [589–90] there are two consecutive and parallel tricolon crescendos—and above all the *ekphrasis* (description of an object) of Heraklês' belt at 726–31. (On the insertion of the passage into the preexistent text, see XI.747, below. For a defense of the passage's integrity, see Heubeck, HWH 2.110–11 and 114 [on XI.565–67, 568–627, and 601–27].)

699 **weasand:** Throat.

718–21 This is a rather obvious interpolation within the interpolation. Someone, realizing that there was a major problem with a text that put Heraklês in the underworld, since he was known to have been made immortal and taken up to Olympos, added these lines [602–4] to "solve" the problem: this is not really the dead Heraklês but a "phantom" [*eidôlon*] of him or of his soul. (This solves the problem somewhat in the way that the positing of epicycles made the Ptolemaic earth-centered astronomy fit newly observed phenomena.) It is a good reminder that for all the Hellenistic scholars who were eager to remove lines from Homer, there were others, earlier readers no doubt, who were prepared to add lines.

734–45 The last of the figures in the interpolated passage speaks to Odysseus. Note that he, or rather his phantom, requires no drink of blood to recognize and address Odysseus.

Heraklês performed heroic deeds, but from the Archaic period on he became increasingly admired in certain quarters for his fortitude, for simply having endured the labors assigned him, until later still he became the Stoic hero par excellence. In 734–37 the author of this passage suggests in no subtle way that Odysseus shares these qualities; to put this praise of Odysseus in Heraklês' mouth (and in turn in Odysseus' mouth) is particularly unsubtle—another mark of the crass inappropriateness of this section. In lines 741–45 Heraklês points out another parallel between the two heroes: while living they both made forays to the land of the dead, Heraklês to fetch Cerberus, Odysseus now.

747 **but I stood fast:** We return to Homer uninterpolated. To get an idea of how the passage would work before the intervening lines were added, read 671/672/747b/748:

> But he [Aîas] gave no reply, and turned away,
> following other ghosts toward Érebos.
> But I stood fast, awaiting
> other great souls who perished in times past.

(It is also possible, though less likely, that lines 671–72 belong to the interpolation, in which case 746–47a would mark the end of the Aîas scene. Note that "Heraklês" in line 746 is not actually in the Greek, which simply says "he" [627].)

BOOK XII

Sea Perils and Defeat

5 Mention of the sun (*Êelios* in Greek [4]) takes on a special significance at the beginning of this book, since Êelios will be provoked to enter the action all too soon (see 480ff).

12–18 Odysseus and his men fulfill all the requests made of them by Elpênor's restless spirit (XI.83–87).

27 **twice mortal:** Literally, "twice dying," since entering into the land of the dead is normally permitted only to those who have died. Even though the word is based on the premise that Odysseus and his men would enter the land of the dead once again, never more to take their leave, there is nothing ominous about it: the Greeks seem to have been less uncomfortable about the certainty of their mortality than we are.

47 **a god:** Kirkê herself.

48ff. **Seirênês:** Commonly "Sirens" in English. Fitzgerald is right to choose a more accurate transliteration, which both preserves more of the music and, simply by not being the all-too-familiar name, recovers some of the wonder and magic that must have accompanied their mere mention for the Greeks. Homer twice refers to two Seirênês [52 and 185; Fitzgerald uses "two Seirênês" only once, line 218] but more often uses forms which would normally be appropriate for three or more Seirênês. Their number is neither here nor there for Homer or for their significance. The idea of mermaids, attractive but fatal nuisances to sailors, is widespread; having them sing makes the attraction stronger.

57–67 **Steer wide . . . :** The method that Kirkê proposes to keep Odysseus and his men from falling under the sway of the Seirênês—and it is the method Odysseus employs, with great success (190ff.)—is an interesting variation on the way Odysseus had managed in Book X to resist Kirkê's own charms and rescue those of his comrades who had already succumbed. There Hermês had given him the charm to counter the effects of her potions; here it is Kirkê herself who gives the protective advice. There it was Odysseus' men who underwent the transformation and had to be rescued, here it is Odysseus who alone hears the dangerous song, his men who as it were "rescue" him (although it is Odysseus, following Kirkê's advice, who renders them capable of doing so by stuffing their ears with beeswax).

68–71 **One of two courses . . . :** On some points, Kirkê provides only intelligence. Odysseus must choose the course which seems best to him based on that intelligence—whether to go past the "Prowling Rocks" (72–89) or between Skylla and Kharybdis (90–130). The second choice here involves a subordinate choice, whether to sail nearer to the whirlpool or to the monster. It is clear that by lines 132–34 Odysseus has decided not to risk the "Prowling Rocks," and this is no surprise, given the dire terms in which Kirkê describes them.

73 **Amphitritê:** The sea (so also 115).

90ff. Skylla and Kharybdis were traditionally identified with the Strait of Messina, which divides Sicily from the Italian peninsula—Skylla on the mainland side, Kharybdis toward the island—but Homer gives no hints. We are still in the world of the fantastic. The "Prowling Rocks" (through which Jason steered the *Argo*) are usually located along the passage from the Aegean to the Black Sea.

100 **lugger:** A ship with a lugsail; in other words, a rectangular sail.

103–15 Skylla seems to display certain octopus- or squidlike elements but is fantastically elaborated and much more frightening. Her name is connected with *skullein*, "to tear," but there is a further etymology hidden behind "whelp's" [*skulakos*, 86].

109 **six heads** and 118 **one for every gullet** (the latter also 146): See 319, below.

121 **A great wild fig:** The fig tree will play an important but perhaps unexpected role (see 552–64).

122–25 **Kharybdis** might be etymologized "gaping swallower." The latter element of her name ("-rybdis") is echoed in "spews . . . up" (124) and "sucks . . . down" (125) [*anaroibdei*, 105, and *rhoibdêseien*," 106, respectively].

132–49 Odysseus' question shows his concern to protect his men as much as possible, thrown into even greater relief by Kirkê's response, which actually suggests that it is "the immortal gods" (138) who will be behind the loss of his comrades. The emphasis on Odysseus' concern for his comrades, however belated, is particularly important in this book, which will see the loss and destruction of all the remaining men.

150 **Thrinákia:** Traditionally identified as Sicily itself.

152–63 Unlike many Homeric numbers (see XII.319, below), there may be, or have been, a particular sense to the number 350 for Hêlios' cattle: "From ancient times . . . the number 350 has been interpreted as representing approximately the number of days in the solar year. In the Vedic hymns of the Hindus . . . the rays of the sun are called his 'cows' " (Stanford 1.410 [on XII.129–30]). It is well known that even today cattle are sacred to the Hindus and may not be killed for any reason, even to be food for starving people. Sanskrit, the language of the Vedas and still the religious language of Hinduism, is related to Greek (and most of the other European languages, for that matter), belonging, like Greek, to the so-called Indo-European language family. Some scholars have researched formulaic and metrical similarities between Homer and Indic hymns, and it is possible that in the cattle of the sun (which one slays at one's peril) we have an ancient reminiscence of what is preserved quite clearly in the Hindu tradition.

163–70 Kirkê repeats Teirêsias' admonitions (see XI.120–27). Teirêsias did provide Odysseus with prophecy (X.546–47), but Kirkê's directions are more detailed and considerably more useful in plotting his homeward course.

173 **up the island:** Inland, away from the shore.

180 **the singing nymph with sunbright hair:** Kirkê; she is identified by name in the Greek [150].

193 **yet she urged:** Kirkê had in fact said quite explicitly, "if you wish to listen" (61 [49]). The audience understands Odysseus to be involved in a slight fib here, presumably lest his comrades feel envious that Odysseus alone will have the pleasure of the Seirênês' song. This least of Odysseus' lies comes, typically, in a speech which opened with the idea that he was going to share with his comrades what Kirkê had told him (185–90). It is characteristic of Odysseus that he would want to listen. That he "learned the minds of many distant men" (I.7) seems to be an essential part of Homer's conception of his hero. On "curiosity," see IX.184ff., above.

Modern scholars are generally suspicious of conceiving the actors in Homer's epic as having fully-developed psyches, and of course they are fictional creations, with no existence outside literature. Nonetheless, consistent and credible characterization marks Homer from beginning to end, and Odysseus' desire here is in line with his thirst for experience throughout *The Odyssey* (see also I.7, above).

199–200 Note that while Odysseus has Kirkê's advice to follow, he alone must decide how to get his men to do what he wants. His skill as commander—and rhetorician—involves knowing what to tell the crew and when to tell it to them (see 260ff., and esp. 289–90, both below).

218 **two Seirênês:** See 48ff., above.

220–45 Again, note that there is no change from dactylic hexameters in the Greek (see also X.309–40, above).

220–21 In Greek, the Seirênês actually appeal to Odysseus by name [184].

236 **Goeth more learnèd:** The appeal to knowledge is well calculated to attract Odysseus in particular. (For a very different "interpretation" of the Seirênês song, see IV.301, above.)

244–45 Like the Muses, the Seirênês know everything.

260ff. Odysseus very consciously (289–92) does not tell his men about the risks to which they are about to be exposed. Lines 289–90 ("I / told them nothing") are a very good example of the "need to know" policy of sharing intelligence (see 199–200, above).

274 **a way out for us:** Yes, his crew might murmur, for all of "us" who remain, although some of "us" died there. It will be all too similar here.

287 **smother:** Thick, impenetrable fog. The Greek here is much vaguer: "woe" [221].

319 **whisking six of my best men from the ship:** Odysseus' remaining crew is reduced from forty-four to thirty-eight—"one man for every gullet," as Kirkê thought inevitable (See both 118 and 146. At the previous count there had been forty-five, after which Elpênor alone was lost, see X.223, 227, above.) All of this is interesting to note, but it is clear from the text that neither here nor elsewhere does Homer display any particular concern for numerical specificity. The frequency with which Odysseus' companions are picked off in sixes reminds us that this figure as well as the threes, nines, fifties, and other numbers that appear throughout are traditional narrative elements.

346–47 **Teirêsias . . . Kirkê . . . both forbade me:** Another fib: Teirêsias (XI.120ff.) and Kirkê (XII.150ff.) both spoke as if he and his men would land on Thrinákia. Odysseus clearly believes—correctly—that he will have a better chance of avoiding the disaster of which they warned him if his men never make land. He attempts to buttress his own authority with that of both Teirêsias and Kirkê, but his well-intentioned lie is to no avail.

357 **Eurýlokhos cried out:** In Book X, Eurýlokhos urged the men to disobey Odysseus, although in that situation he had legitimate grounds to wonder if Odysseus was in his right mind (see X.476ff., above). After Eurýlokhos had time to see he was wrong, all appears to have been smoothed between him and Odysseus. A hundred lines above he had been one of the two men to carry out Odysseus' orders to tie him tighter to the mast as they sailed past the Seirênês (250). His speech ("Are you flesh and blood, Odysseus," 358–76) makes some good points, whatever the motivation—lines 356–57 are ominous—and it proves impossible for Odysseus to refuse the unanimous demand of his men (377–81). But he clearly holds Eurýlokhos responsible for the final, fatal rebellion he instigates (XII.435ff.). This characterization of Eurýlokhos as independent to the point of mutiny is not inconsistent. Of course, our only witness is Odysseus, who might have reason to minimize his own responsibility for the loss of his comrades.

377–78 **I saw the power of destiny devising ill:** Odysseus feels more "outmatched" (381) by destiny (in Greek, a "daimon [spirit] plotted evil" [*kaka mêdeto daimon*, 295]) than by the men themselves. That's how he presents it to the Phaiákians after the fact (and after the death of all his comrades).

426–78 It is interesting to compare this entire sequence—the leader withdraws upland to consult with the relevant divinity or divinities, there is rebellion among the ranks and prohibited acts are commited, the leader returns at the height of the feasting—to the episode of the Israelites and the golden calf (esp. Exodus 32).

Within *The Odyssey* there is a more distant parallel to X.39–61, where the crew unties the bag of winds while Odysseus sleeps.

497–98 This is an afterthought to explain what Odysseus could not have known without an informant. Even Kalypso needs a divine intermediary, Hermês, to tell her the councils of heaven, since she herself has no direct access to Olympos.

553 **like a bat:** Homer uses the word for "bat" exceedingly rarely (only twice, both times in *The Odyssey*); it is a perfectly apt image, including the fact that Odysseus hangs on the tree all day until dusk (561), like a bat. In fact, the nocturnal habits of the animal were well known: the word for "bat"—*nukteris* [433]—is based on the word for "night," *nuxs*.

561–63 **And ah! . . . with what desire . . . :** This is an astonishingly distant field from which to fetch a metaphor to convey Odysseus' desire to see the mast and keel of his ship reappear. There is probably no cynicism here, namely, that judges are eager to quit working. Rather, there may be some kind of pathos in contrasting Odysseus' experience, which is almost beyond human imagination, with a situation so everyday and ordinary.

577–78 Odysseus refers to his brief narrative at VII.258–319.

580 **with tiresome repetition of a story:** Some critics have wished that whoever divided *The Odyssey* into twenty-four books had drawn the division between Books XII and XIII at XIII.115 or 152, so that the second half of the epic could begin with Odysseus back on Ithaka. Yet the literary-critical comment that concludes Odysseus' narrative—that overlong narratives are hateful—makes a very satisfying book end.

BOOK XIII

One More Strange Island

17–18 Alkínoös promises the Phaiákians that they will be paid back for the additional gifts they are to contribute. The king is obviously not embarrassed to say this; what seems to us to be crass calculation and a lessening of the gesture of giving was not seen that way by Homeric aristocrats. In Homeric society (and other traditional societies), gift giving was strictly regulated; it was an honor for the twelve kings to give Odysseus gifts, and it was an honor of sorts for lesser people to give gifts to the kings.

35 **Demódokos, honored by all that realm:** The second phrase is intended as a gloss or paraphrase of the name itself, which is somewhat clearer in the Greek [28]. (See VIII.48, above.)

51–52 Odysseus is being properly and sincerely pious: it is only because of the blessings of the gods that humans can enjoy the gifts they receive and the goods they possess.

54–55 **god grant I find . . . :** Odysseus had heard from Teirêsias that he will find his hall overrun by strangers (XI.129ff.). Yet as long as Odysseus acts prudently, he can at least hope that reality will be better than Teirêsias' dark prophecy. As we know, his wife is in his hall, and all those he loves best (his mother excepted, as he knows) are alive, but they are sorely pressed.

57–58 **may the gods . . . :** The gods, Poseidon in particular, have other ideas (see 153ff.).

97–99 While it is never stated in so many words, there is something magical about this sleep. We might have expected Odysseus, who was capable of staying awake nearly three weeks when he sailed from Kalypso to Skhería (Book V), to remain awake this one night in anticipation of his first sight of Ithaka in twenty years.

There are, however, other conventions at work. First, this is a passage from "fairy-land" to familiar geography, and mortals are usually not permitted to witness the magic that makes this possible (see V.359–63, above, for the prohibition of watching Ino's scarf return to her). Second, the poet does not want to have Odysseus recognize that he is home until after Athena's intervention. So he exploits the idea of a magical sleep and extends it—Odysseus doesn't awaken until the Phaiákian sailors have carried him and all his treasure onto the island and sailed away.

111 **in twenty years:** Just before Odysseus lands, Fitzgerald's translation reminds us of the number of years he has been away—ten years at the siege of Troy and ten years attempting to come home. But Homer, with considerably less interest in chronology, merely says "before" or "up to now" [90].

116 **the sheer bright star:** Venus, which we still call the morning star and the evening star, is of course actually a planet.

127–37 **a cave of dusky light . . . :** Scholars and philosophers in late antiquity—Porphyry most notably (see Suggestions for Further Reading, p. 353)—interpreted the cave of the Naiadês mystically and allegorically. The original Greek is poetic and mysterious. If Homer says that there are "winebowls" and "amphorai" in the rock, and that the nymphs weave on storm looms, so be it—no one can argue with him in his own poem. But if we want to look for a slightly more prosaic "reality" behind his description, we could well imagine the "winebowls" and "amphorai" to be holes in the rock formed by the water; and in the "looms of stone" either vertical stone ribbing or stalactites and/or stalagmites.

The two entrances (134–37), one for mortals, one for immortals, are also mysterious and awe inspiring, the cave being a liminal space where gods and mortals meet. Homer's poetry only tells us that the entrances face north and south (actually, toward the winds which blow from these directions; see XV.238, below). Reading into this we might imagine a cave which had one entrance above water and another, more secret entrance below the surface of the water (like the famed Blue Grotto on Capri). The former would be for mortals (and would involve descent, 135 [110]), while the latter would be for immortals and would be particularly appropriate for Naiadês.

Other scholars have claimed that Homer was actually describing the cave of Marmarospilia on Ithaka. If he had seen it (which I doubt) or heard an accurate description of it, he certainly rendered it mysteriously.

147–48 It has been some time since we've heard of Athena's help, primarily because Odysseus narrated all but a few lines of Books IX–XII. Nonetheless, just before she reappears this is a good way for Homer to have his audience recall the goddess' role in bringing Odysseus safely ashore (end of Book V), motivating Nausikaa to go washing (beginning of Book VI), guiding Odysseus unseen into the hall of the Phaiákians (Book VII), and making the Phaiákians well disposed to him after his monumental discus throw (VIII.203–9).

153–98 Though brief, this is a "heavenly council" scene near the beginning of the second half of *The Odyssey,* just as there had been scenes shortly after the beginnings of Books I and V, in other words, at other points of narrative departure.

176 **their eldest and most noble:** We should probably understand Zeus to except himself from his words here. On the one hand, Zeus shows himself in this brief speech to be a masterful diplomat. On the other hand, he is, in another tradition, the youngest child of Kronos, whom he deposed (Hesiod, *Theogony*, 453ff.).

180 **as your wrath requires:** The gods are like mortals not only in being concerned about status and honors shown them but in having violent emotions. Later Greek thinkers would find the Homeric gods very much undivine (as they defined the divine) for these and other reasons (see VIII.280–392, above). But at this period, gods were more respected as gods the more they demanded privileges and showed anger. (So also Yahweh, explicitly a "jealous God" (Exodus 34:14, Deuteronomy 4:24; and compare Deuteronomy 5:7).)

188–91 The destruction of the vessel and the ringing of Phaiákia with mountains, thus landlocking a seagoing people, is what Alkínoös had heard as a prophecy from his father, as he reported to Odysseus (VIII.603–10) and will recall to his countrymen (XIII.215–22).

198 Zeus suggests a mitigation of the punishment and urges Poseidon not to encircle the city with mountains. Poseidon says nothing but appears to have been moved to mercy on the second point.

230–35 In the final view Homer gives us of them, the Phaiákians are praying that Poseidon not complete their foretold doom. We, having witnessed the scene in heaven and heard Zeus' request, may feel fairly confident that nothing more will happen, but the Phaiákians can't share our point of view. They have seen the ship petrified and are now waiting for the "other shoe" to drop. We are left thinking that they are a good and pious people, and that somehow the world is a lesser place now that they have had to suspend their tradition of sending home sailors and travelers who have been cast away on their shores. Odysseus, then, is the last person to enjoy this privilege. There is a further implication that in this (as in many other dimensions) no one will be able to follow him on his travels and adventures in fairy-tale realms.

240–44 It is an unexpected twist on the moment of homecoming that the long-desired Ithaka appears so strange to Odysseus that he does not recognize it. This time Athena takes the precaution not only of shielding Odysseus from the eyes of others but of obscuring his surroundings from Odysseus' own eyes. Athena wants to speak with him first. And while it is unlikely that the ever-prudent and forewarned Odysseus would rush to his own house after Teirêsias' prophecy that there may be trouble at home, Athena is taking no chances. There is, as well, an undeniable element of playfulness in her being able to trick Odysseus and to show him that while he may be the cleverest of mortals, she is the cleverest of immortals (see especially 379–83).

243–44 This establishes the basic strategy—Athena's, Odysseus', and Homer's—for the plotting of the remainder of the epic.

253–54 It is a nice irony that Odysseus, having experienced the likes of the Kyklopês and Laistrygonês, should unwittingly ask this question about Ithaka. The irony within the irony is that, as events currently stand, it is justified. The suitors are hardly "god-fearing," and some of them will prove to be in no way hospitable to him when he arrives in his own hall disguised as a castaway.

261–75 It is typical of Odysseus to suspect trickery by the Phaiákians. He even goes so far as to count his treasure. When he finds that it's all there, he may be relieved, but he is really even more deeply perplexed, for he can't imagine what motivated the Phaiákians to act as they did. His prayer to Zeus (266–69) to punish the Phaiákians takes on particularly ironic tones since we know that it was Poseidon who punished them for transporting him to Ithaka. Zeus, tempering justice with mercy, has convinced Poseidon to go light on the Phaiákians.

293–94 **as I might / ask grace of a god:** Surely just a bit of flattery—recall the more elaborate version of this commonplace when Odysseus addressed Nausikaa in Book VI—but here it's truer than Odysseus realizes. When a character acts on the basis of less knowledge than the audience possesses, ironies multiply.

300–317 Athena's speech is delightful teasing. Note especially "else you are a great booby" (302 [*nêpios*, 237])—to describe cunning Odysseus, of all people!—and the way she postpones the name of Ithaka, which gives the whole game away, until line 315.

318–25 Attentive listeners or readers of *The Odyssey* must no longer expect Odysseus to reveal either his true feelings or his identity to a complete stranger.

327–65 **Far away in Krete:** This is the first of several "Kretan narratives" Odysseus tells. The others involve variations that range from minor to significant: the most extensive of the accounts, told to the swineherd Eumaios (XIV.229–417); an abbreviated version for the suitors (XVII.552–82); again an extended tale told to Penélopê (XIX.195–362); and finally to his father, Laërtês (XXIV.270–345). The last two of these involve increasingly more "information" about Odysseus, of whom the "Kretan" claims to have news. This first version seems to be a brilliant improvisation, but we expect no less from Odysseus.

327 **Krete:** Home of Minoan culture before and during part of the great Mycenaean civilizations on the Greek mainland. Any specifics would long since have faded from the memories of eighth-century B.C.E. Greeks. For them, Krete was a way station for traders between Greece, Egypt, and the Levant frequently visited by merchants from all three lands.

There is also an important tradition claiming that Kretans are notorious liars. How far back it goes is uncertain. The earliest extant testimony is a famous dictum of the late-sixth-century B.C.E. Kretan mystagogue and wonder-worker Epimenides: "The Kretans are always liars, evil beasts, idle bellies." Now whether or not we believe a Kretan telling us that Kretans always lie (a logical conundrum), Kretan mendacity did enter the popular tradition and become proverbial. The Greek *krêtizô*, "speak like a Kretan," could be used to mean "lie." The proverb is carried far beyond the ancient world by the Pauline Epistle to Titus 1:12–13, where the author quotes Epimenides, then resumes with sublime naïveté, "This testimony is true." Odysseus' choice of a Kretan mask for his lying narratives may well not be accidental.

331ff. The story Odysseus invents presents him as a tough contender—there is an implicit warning that his unidentified interlocutor had better not try anything untoward, for this Kretan knows how to take care of himself and protect his interests.

332 **Idómeneus:** Grandson of Minos and in his own day king in Krete, he commanded the Kretan forces at Troy. He is mentioned with some frequency in *The Iliad,* although he would hardly count as one of its major heroes.

349 **Phoinikia:** Odysseus' Kretan alter ego ships with a Punic merchant, just the kind of person the Phaiákian "Seareach" [*Euryalos*] had insultingly accused him of being (VIII.167–73).

363 **Sidon:** The geography of the Punic world was well known throughout the Mediterranean (see also IV.661, above).

366ff. This is another surprise. No intervention of a god in the affairs of humans so far in *The Odyssey* has developed this way. Recall that the poet at one point made a distinction—Athena will help Odysseus openly only when he reaches Ithaka, no matter how much she has helped him all along. Now that he is on his home island, she appears.

371–72 **... guileful as a snake:** Homer's Greek does not give us a comparison to a snake but the language of commercial cunning and even thievery, something like "you're always out to get something, you rogue, by all sorts of tricks" [291]. (This vocabulary is also behind line 325 of the English translation [255].) Here, Fitzgerald is clearly drawing on a different tradition, which attributes the primal act of Satan's seduction and persuasion of Eve to the devil in snake form.

387–88 **I who made / the Phaiákians befriend you, to a man:** See also VIII.203–9; and XIII.147–48, above.

398ff. Odysseus has said he is a Kretan, but he is not. His interlocu-

tor now claims to be Athena—is she or is she not? Her change
of appearance suggests she is a goddess, but Odysseus has had
experience with Kirkê, has questioned the motives of Kalypso,
and wondered if he should trust Ino. No surprise, then, that he
demands more assurances from this divinity.

419 **coolheaded:** See 509, below.

432ff. Athena makes Ithaka visible to him, removing the mists she
had covered it with (240–43).

482–84 The counterexample of Agamémnon and Klytaimnéstra is
made explicit by Odysseus' own words.

484–85 Odysseus realizes that the most important help Athena
gives him is this advance report of the situation in his home.

494–98 This outcome is hardly to be doubted now that Odysseus
has also heard this prophecy from Athena. As always, it is a
question of how, not what.

508 **as ever** translates the difficult *homôs* [405]. The scholia take it
"as from the beginning"; "as before" is likely. The point is impor-
tant in judging how well Odysseus knew Eumaios before he left
for Troy (see XIV.4 and XV.464ff., below).

509 **Penélopê:** In the Greek, Athena refers to Penélopê with an
epithet [*ekhephrona*, 406] which means "prudent," "keeping one's
wits about one." This is the same epithet she had applied to
Odysseus (419 [332]), translated there by Fitzgerald as "cool-
headed." Odysseus and Penélopê share epithets as well as quali-
ties of mind.

516 **the great beauty's land of Sparta:** The reference to Helen
is implicit in the Greek, beneath the surface and without mention
of her name [*Spartên es kalligunaika*, 412]. It would be hard for
Odysseus to think of Helen, the cause of "all their woe," with
anything other than, at the least, very mixed emotions.

528–29 **to make his name / in foreign parts:** While there is
some question whether it is right to see Telémakhos' journey as
educative, this seems a clear statement that Athena did think it
important that he undertake some mission to "win his spurs" and

begin to come into his inheritance as the son of a hero, if not yet a hero himself.

535 **I rather doubt they will:** Ironic understatement, in a goddess' mouth.

Athena doesn't respond directly to Odysseus' questions of lines 522–25. Her silence implies that this is something that Odysseus and Telémakhos had better take care of themselves. Without suggesting that Athena or Homer is anything like a modern psychologist, they do seem to have an understanding that for a father and son to be reunited after twenty years (nearly half of which time the son has had to live with the likelihood that his father was dead and the uncertainty that he may be alive, with no end to despair and no period of mourning) requires a catharsis of greater proportions. Athena does assure Odysseus that he need not worry for his son's physical safety.

BOOK XIV

Hospitality in the Forest

3 **the swineherd:** In Greek, the swineherd is called "noble" [*dion,* 3] (see I.92, above). For his own account of his heritage, see XV.441ff. In fact, both men are of higher station than they appear to be. Eumaios, enslaved now for many years, still takes pride in playing as well as he can the unexpected role fate has handed him. Odysseus is transformed and outfitted to play the beggar for a time.

4–24 There is no finer image of the passionately devoted and energetic servant than Eumaios, the swineherd, who has not "hid his talent in the earth" (Matthew 25:14–30 and Luke 19:12–27) by merely preserving Odysseus' goods. Instead, he has improved the facilities and considerably augmented his master's holdings. It would not be at all unusual for the most trusted and skilled slaves in a large household or estate to have this much latitude and responsibility, nor would it be unusual to have them supervise underlings. Female slaves would not operate so autonomously outside the house, but they would have supervisory capacities within the household, always under the executive control of the mistress.

in the old days (4) is an interpretation of the Greek (see XIII.508, above, and XV.464ff., below).

19 In Greek, the suitors are "godlike" [*antitheoi*, 18], and while the epithet is conventional, they are like the gods even here insofar as they demand good food and live a life of luxury (see I.92, above).

32–42 Eumaios' watchdogs nearly savage Odysseus: this episode shows to what point the master has sunk. Even his customary craftiness is of no use—letting drop his staff, with which he might have attempted to beat the dogs back, was supposed to show them that he had no hostile intentions. Eumaios must save him. The canine reception here forms a contrast with the one when Odysseus reaches his own home (XVII.375–417).

46–52 These are of course fine words for the swineherd Eumaios to say in Odysseus' presence, but not so wise before having ascertained the identity—and the sympathies—of the beggar before him. This speech does show, however, the true temper of the swineherd: plain speaking and right thinking.

49 **foreigners:** In Greek Eumaios simply says "others," which is in a sense more accurate, since not all the suitors were foreigners. (For the census, see XVI.294–300.) But "foreigners" conveys better than "others" the disdain Eumaios intends: in his view, anyone who is not a member of Odysseus' household is an outsider; his allegiance would be to his master's family, not to any putative Ithakan nation.

65 **O my swineherd!:** The fifteen times in Books XIV–XVII that the narrator addresses the swineherd (fourteen times with this formula, once with slight variation, XV.325) constitute one of the more curious features of *The Odyssey*. While the poet of *The Odyssey* uses this strange convention only of one character, the poet of *The Iliad* employs it in connection with five males (Patróklos, eight times; Meneláos, seven times; Phoibos, two times; Melanippos and Akhilleus, once each (data from Stanford 2.218 [on XIV.55]). The relative frequency of these apostrophes in *The Iliad* may indicate that they were still a living convention in the poet's repertory but by the time of *The Odyssey* had become outdated, surviving in one, frozen case. Stanford reports that H. Hayman, in his three-volume commentary on *The Odyssey* (London, 1866–1882), suggested that "it may be a vestige of a primitive ballad-singer's phrase." The protocol of ballads to this day requires the narrator to apostrophize one or more figures.

Stanford rightly rejects the idea that this apostrophe "is a mark of the poet's special affection for Eumaeus" (see scholium on *Iliad* XVI.787) as "highly uncharacteristic of Homer's very impersonal style." A translator of *The Odyssey* into English might well be justified in removing this last vestige of the convention.

69–70 Eumaios is pious as well as kindhearted and loyal.

77 Note that property, house, and woman/wife—the word *gunê* has both meanings—are all goods to be given the slave by the master.

78 **that other men . . . courted:** The epithet in Greek is *polymnês-tên* [64] (see Introduction, note 16, above). In *The Odyssey* it is significant that Penélopê too receives *poly-* epithets.

84 **race of Helen:** Not the Spartans but women. Eumaios gives voice to misogyny typical of ancient Greek men, indeed of many men in many societies down to and including our own. Also typical is the inconsistency in the misogynist's position: not ten lines earlier he wished he had been given a woman/wife, and here he's cursing all women and wishing them dead. The illogic of this male mode of thinking wasn't lost on ancient Greeks: Aristophanes has the female chorus of his *Thesmophoriazusae* (performed 411 B.C.E.) pose the question in the *parabasis*, "if we are an evil, why do they marry us?" (v. 789).

100–101 Eumaios speaks even more clearly in the Greek of divine vengeance [*opida*, 82] of which the suitors ought to be mindful: Homer does not miss an opportunity to keep the climactic resolution of *The Odyssey* in his audience's mind.

108–10 **having some word . . . of my lord's death:** This seems to be an inference on Eumaios' part. In any event, it suggests to Odysseus that the suitors' behavior has shifted to a new level of outrageousness.

113–30 Who better than Odysseus' swineherd to give an exact account of Odysseus' property before the suitors started to diminish it, and to note in quantitative terms how much they were consuming? It is Eumaios' professional responsibility to keep such a detailed count and report it. Telémakhos and Penélopê are outraged at the expense but do not go into such detail.

131–33 Three lines which characterize Odysseus: keeping his counsel, he eats, taking care of his immediate human needs while never losing sight of his ultimate goal, to regain control of his home. We may observe—without imagining that this was in the poet's mind—that in his capacity to coordinate means and ends in and through a wide range of situations, Odysseus is not unlike the poet of *The Odyssey*. (A further indication of his mastery may be hidden in lines 134–36 if the Greek [111–13] means, as some argue, that Odysseus filled his own cup and gave it to Eumaios.)

144 **roamed** [*alêthên*, 120]**:** Fitzgerald cleverly re-creates the echo with "rover" (150 [*alalêmenos*, 122]). But Homer's punning stretches even further. He uses another word based on the same root in "Wandering men" (151 [*andres alêtai*, 124]), and, with this ringing in our ears, finally produces the root of his pun: "truth" (152 [*alêthea*, 125]). Eumaios says that "wandering men lie and do not wish to tell true things" [*andres alêthea / pseudont', oud' ethelousin alêthea muthêsasthai*, 124–25], but Homer's wordplay reveals a truth over Eumaios' head: Odysseus is hidden within this wanderer, as "truth" is in the word "wanderer." (Eumaios isn't quite done with this word family: "traveller," 153 [*alêteuôn*, 126].)

148–60 Homer is playing, again, with our eager anticipation to hear the name "Odysseus," the first step toward the revelations and recognition even more hotly desired by his audience. But instead of prompting the praise of Odysseus we might have hoped for from Eumaios, Odysseus' question unleashes "who hasn't claimed to have known my master?" Eumaios suspects that this unknown traveler wants to learn the master's name so that he can make up some story about having seen him, the purpose of which would be to ingratiate himself further with the family and receive gifts and extended hospitality (151–60). That the disguised Odysseus meets this rebuff is of course ironic. Perhaps more significant, Homer shows how suspicious Eumaios is, a quality which can only recommend itself to Odysseus, who, in this situation, needs allies who are cautious, truly loyal to him, and not likely to be misled and betrayed by that most insidious of enemies: hope. Odysseus would not do otherwise in the same situation.

153–60 **Every time some traveller . . . :** Odysseus will play this kind of traveler when he finally appears before Penélopê. Eumaios' words are the truest testimony Odysseus could have that his wife still remembers him, loves him, longs for him.

161 On Eumaios' certainty that Odysseus is dead, see XIV.108–10, above.

170–73 We learn more of Eumaios' past at XV.490–585.

175 **Odysseus:** The name is postponed to near the end of Eumaios' answer [144] and closely follows Eumaios' use of the verb connected with the root of the hero's name, *oduromai* [142]: "I grieve" or "I lament" (technically represented by "I miss" at line 171 of the English, but the force seems to have been transferred by Fitzgerald to the more pathetic "I ache," 174, placed even closer to the name). The two words, "distressed" and "Odysseus," are placed in one line at 208 [174]. On the etymology of Odysseus, see I.84, above, and XIX.463ff., 478–81, and 480, below.

180–93 All this is true, yet it is not a revelation. Eumaios would take this as the wishful optimism that mirrors his own pessimism.

185, 191 As Fitzgerald notes (p. 463), he has omitted three lines from Odysseus' speech which are suspected by many critics to be interpolations. After "his own hall" (185), some manuscripts include a line which reads, "a cloak and a tunic, good clothes, to clothe me" [154; the uncertain and at best awkward syntax is one of the problems of fitting this line in the passage]. And between 191 and 192 Fitzgerald has omitted two lines [161–62] that also appear in a similar passage in Book XIX: "Between this present dark and one day's ebb, / after the wane, before the crescent moon, / Odysseus will come" (XIX.360–62 [306–7]). The issue is that lines 185 and 191 are the best conclusions to the lines that precede them. (It is interesting to consider the way such an error in the manuscript tradition might have occurred. An ancient scholar or scribe, having noticed the three-line overlap between the passages [XIV.158–60 are very close to XIX.303–5 (in Fitzgerald XIV.189–91 and XIX.356–59)], decided that the parallel could be extended, and imported the following two lines from Book XIX into Book XIV. Such occurrences seem endemic in canonical literature: many similar instances of "harmonizing" can be seen in manuscripts of the Greek New Testament.)

187–88 **I hate as I hate Hell's own gate . . .** [156–57]: See Akhilleus' words to Odysseus (*Iliad* IX.312–13). While the formulaic poet and experienced audience would know that this is the "right" way for anyone to talk about lying, there is a richness for connoisseurs of epic poetry who think of the moment in *The Iliad* when similar words were addressed to Odysseus instead of uttered by him [*Odyssey* XIV.156 is identical to *Iliad* IX.312].

189–90 **Zeus . . . , the table, . . . / and . . . hearth:** It is not strange to invoke Zeus to witness an oath, but why a table and a hearth? The ideas underlying this may be multiple: (1) Zeus is far away, the table is very much present and tangible: to invoke the table is to say, "My claim is as certain as this table is a real object"; (2) the table or hearth may be called on as a more active witness of truth—as fire, water, or any object could be—a belief which underlies the trial by ordeal, a type of trial in which the physical world, which could not be out of step with the Truth, was believed to reveal the truth or falsehood of a particular statement; (3) "the table garnished / for strangers" and the hearth (add from the Greek, "to which I've come" [159]) are closely linked to the reception of guests, meaning that they may be being invoked as attributes of Zeus Xenios (see III.377, above), or as objects holy to him. Homer most likely wasn't thinking about all these concepts behind what sounds like a traditional oath: oaths tend to be formulaic (and gain power from that character), and this one recurs in *The Odyssey* (at XVII.194–95 [XIV.158–59 = XVII.155–56]).

How, for example, could we explain, "Sure as God made little green apples" or "Sure as shootin' "?

208 **Distressed:** See 165, above.

213 **god or man:** The audience—and now Odysseus—know that Athena is the tutelary spirit of Telémakhos' expedition.

229–417 The second of Odysseus' four Kretan narratives, of which this is by far the longest and most detailed. Note that during Odysseus' standard preface, "I'll tell you all . . . If we could sit here long enough" (229–35), Homer's audience would have had no idea what story Odysseus will tell Eumaios: one comparable to the tales he told the Phaiákians, or the one Odysseus tried to palm off on Athena when he arrived? Homer resolves that question in line 236 ("Krete"). There are, however, plenty of surprises in store: new details, additions, and variants on the previous version, all brilliantly calculated to win the goodwill of Odysseus' present listener, Eumaios (which is, of course, the aim of all rhetoric; see VI.164, above).

There are indications that not only Odysseus but Homer himself is telling an untraditional story, or a traditional one in an untraditional way. We might make this inference from the *hapax legomena* behind Fitzgerald's "life at home" (263 [*oikôpheliê*, 223]) and "shake to see" (266 [*katarigêla*, 226]), keeping in mind, of course, that these words may be unattested elsewhere in Homer only because Homer had reason to tell this particular story nowhere else, even though they were traditional from some other source. (For more details on *oikôpheliê*, see 273, below.)

239 My mother was a slave: A detail not in the first narrative, and one bound to engage the sympathies of Eumaios, who is likewise a slave.

244 Kêrês: "Fates of death," "ministers of death," often symbolic of death itself (see *Iliad* IX.411).

252–53 The extreme compression of the Greek—literally, "but I think that looking at just the stalk [or husk] you can know me fully"—indicates that Homer is having Odysseus play off what must have been a well-known proverbial expression. The proverb itself refers to practiced agriculturalists, who can judge the quality of the grain harvested from the stubble that remains in the field.

252 Ear: Of grain.

273 my house grew prosperous: It is one of the oddities of Odysseus' account that what he says happened [*oikos ophelleto,* 233 echoes the very thing that ten lines earlier he claimed to have no concern for [*oikôpheliê,* 223]. Fitzgerald there translated it "life at home" (263) but it might more literally be rendered "estate development." (On this word as *hapax legomenon,* see 229–417, above.) It may be too daring to say that Homer is undermining Odysseus' account with little inconsistencies of this sort in order to suggest that it is an improvisation, but then again it may not.

277 See 85. In Greek, the two lines, one belonging to Eumaios, the other to Odysseus [69 and 236], are identical for the concluding four and a half of their six metrical feet. While it is no surprise that identical thought generates identical formulaic expression, the poet of *The Odyssey* is, in my view and that of many others, in full control of his use of formulae. Thus it is part of Homer's strategy to have Odysseus, who is improvising a speech for Eumaios, adopt an idea, however traditional, to which Eumaios had also given voice. For that reason Homer has him repeat the exact words Eumaios used shortly before.

284–85 Evil days . . . / Zeus: The Greek is more punning and

etymological: we could translate *emoi . . . kaka mêdeto mêtieta Zeus*
[243] as "Devising Zeus devised evils for me."

299 **delta:** The Nile delta.

304 **reckless greed:** It is clear from the Kretan's way of life that
he is not claiming that piracy itself is bad; what was "reckless"
about his advance party's "greed" was that it was imprudent.
They ought first to have reconnoitered (as they had been com-
manded) and gathered intelligence, from which they could have
calculated potential gain versus risk. Even in this "fictive" dis-
course we have again the motif of prudent commander (Odysseus
in Kretan disguise) against reckless crew whom no prudence can
save from folly—a motif familiar from Books IX–XII.

314 **but some they took alive:** Those who were taken alive were
enslaved, a common practice. Although the way Eumaios was
enslaved was different, Odysseus may calculate that this is an-
other moment at which he can arouse his listener's sympathies.

320–23 All the elements of the tale so far sound quite plausible in
the world of *The Odyssey:* trade with Egypt, piracy, the natives
striking back. This detail, however, is quite a bit less plausible,
much more the stuff of fairy stories. We note that it puts Odysseus
in the same position—a foreigner thriving under an Egyptian
king—in which Joseph finds himself (Genesis 41–50; Moses is a
more distant parallel). It is not surprising that widely distant
peoples had stories in which some of their heroes made good in
Egypt; well into the first millennium B.C.E. Egypt would have
been regarded as the "land of opportunity," the America of the
ancient eastern Mediterranean basin.

329 **Seven years:** Seven is of course a special number, which
often figures in narratives; note the repeated importance of
"seven years" in the Biblical story of Joseph's Egyptian sojourn.

333 **Phoinikian adventurer:** The first Kretan narrative had in-
volved a Phoinikian merchant sailor who was not evil (see
XIII.349). In the present version the merchant plays a much
more sinister role.

334 **a plausible rat:** Both Greeks and later Romans regarded the Phoinikians as inveterate liars and deceivers. In Latin, *fides Punica*—"Punic faith"—was proverbial for bad faith. The word for deceiver or knave [*trôktês*] is used only twice in Homer, both times of Phoinikians (here [289] and Fitzgerald's "sea-dogs," XV.505 [416]).

345–46 **I could guess the game / but had to follow him aboard:** By this means Odysseus covers over a narrative inconsistency that, if pressed, might reveal his story to be an invention: the Kretan could not have known the Phoinikian's dastardly intentions since a storm prevented them from being realized.

349, 352, 361 **Zeus** and **Kroníon:** "Son of Kronos," in other words, Zeus. While in itself hardly unusual, the frequent mention of Zeus, to whom the guidance of events is attributed, has the function of conveying to Eumaios that his Kretan guest is a pious man and, furthermore, that Zeus is watching out for him, even punishing those who wish him ill. ("The gods," at 403 and 414, has the same function.)

367–71 Odysseus presents Eumaios with another exemplum of generous hospitality, a model to which Odysseus hopes his host will conform. In line 371 he may already be dropping a hint: he needs some clothing even now. But Eumaios will require more prompting (see 464 and 546–612, below).

368–70 Odysseus' "fictive" narrative again seems to offer a variant of Homer's in the first half of *The Odyssey:* here, Pheidon's son plays a part comparable to Nausikaa's in Book VI. Further on (384–86) Pheidon and his Thesprótians play, or start to play, roles comparable to those of Alkínoös and the Phaiákians in transporting Odysseus to Ithaka.

372–86 Here for the first time the "Kretan" pretends to have news of Odysseus. His strategy is to test the waters, in particular Eumaios' sympathy. Homer's strategy is to create irony wherever he can. Although Eumaios cannot know it, Homer's audience will realize that the treasure mentioned (375–76) is not entirely bogus: Odysseus and the listeners will be thinking of the treasure stowed with Athena's help in the cave of the nymphs (XIII.456–64).

376 **Bronze, gold, and iron:** The Greek [324] too is a tricolon crescendo (see III.117–20, above), with wrought iron, a more recent metallurgical discovery and more valuable in war, in the climactic final position.

379 **Dodona:** Oracle of Zeus, where the god was thought to speak through, or inhabit, a sacred oak.

383 **openly, or on the quiet:** A hint that Odysseus might appear in disguise, as well as an invitation to Eumaios to comment on the advisability of secrecy.

391–402 The men of Thesprótia nearly accomplish what the Kretan shortly before had claimed the Phoinikian intended: to enslave him. This too is intended to appeal to Eumaios, for Odysseus must know the details of the enslavement of his sister's playmate, which we will hear about only in the next book (XV.490–585; see also XV.464ff., below).

415–17 Odysseus' penultimate remark ("and with me . . . of one who knows the world") is decently complimentary of his host. His last sentence ("My destiny . . .") emphasizes both his piety and the fact that he has divine protection. It's plain to see why Homer's Odysseus set the standard for eloquence.

421–50 **That tale / . . . :** Eumaios is a hard nut to crack and doesn't believe his guest's story about Odysseus. Indeed, as we soon learn (441ff.), his skepticism has been hardened by deception and bitter disappointment: the Kretan is not the first to pretend to have news of Odysseus. We know that Eumaios is both right and wrong to disbelieve the Kretan.

464 Odysseus' second and slightly less subtle attempt to make the swineherd understand that he's in need of a cloak. (See 367–71, above, and 546–612, below.)

471–78 **a great name** in line 472 is meant sarcastically. In other words, he says, the "compact" Odysseus proposes (460) is out of the question. Again (as at 456) Homer emphasizes the piety of Eumaios.

490 **the outsiders:** The suitors (see 49, above).

494–514 Stanford provides a good summary of the traditional "ritual of . . . preliminary sacrifice before a special feast," whose protocol is followed here with precision and is described in detail: "Its principle was that the gods should have a first share of the meat and cereal food. The first ceremony was to cut off some of the hair of the animal as an offering—"who tossed the forehead bristles," 496–97—to be burnt, with prayer; this formally dedicated the whole animal to the gods. Then when the victim had been killed and prepared for cooking, the thigh bones . . . were wrapped in fat . . . , covered with strips of raw flesh . . . from every limb as first offerings . . . , sprinkled with meal . . . , and burnt. The savour of the burning flesh was thought to rise up to the gods in heaven. . . . After the gods have received their share, the meat is prepared for the guests: they chop up the rest of the meat, spit it on skewers, roast it carefully, draw it off the skewers and heap it on dishes for serving; then the host divides it fairly among the guests" (2.232–33 [on XIV.422–32]).

494–99 **The gods, / as ever . . . :** Here, in the prayer, we see not only Eumaios' piety but also that his hope has not been utterly extinguished, whatever he says in his characteristically pessimistic vein (e.g., 425ff.). He puts his hopes quite rightly in the gods— and in no one on earth.

519 To those who fear that Odysseus might be giving away the game by addressing the swineherd by name it may be answered that by now he will have heard the others address Eumaios. However, it is more likely that neither Homer nor his oral audience gave this argument a second thought. When the poet wants us to focus on a piece of cleverness or stupidity, he generally points the way.

532–33 **bought by the swineherd on his own:** This slave is a good steward of his master's resources.

546–612 The great tale of the cloak, which achieves the end that
Odysseus' hints at lines 371 and 464 (see above) had not. This is
a clever bit of narrative nesting. His opening remarks (esp. "wish-
ful," 547) and the carefully calculated claim that the wine has
inspired him to tell a tale best left "untold" (551) will alert his
listeners that the tale has some point to make beyond its enter-
tainment value. For Eumaios and his crew, that point is clearly
that Odysseus needs a cloak, but Homer's audience can appreci-
ate that fact and enjoy the even more deeply hidden secret:
Odysseus is himself here, in all senses of that phrase. Of course,
this irony has applied throughout the book, but it comes to a head
at this point: the fictive Odysseus in the tale of Troy, created by
the disguised Odysseus in Ithaka, tells a deceptive tale in order (so
the story claims) to conjure up a cloak for the freezing Kretan
(541ff.). The Kretan is now employing the identical ruse. It is left
for anyone to conclude that the identities of the authors of both
ruses are one: the Kretan and Odysseus converge on a point. In
both cases the same man ends up with a cloak. Homer's game is
not over, however, because he has set up this equation through
a nested series of out-and-out fictions. At what point do the
fictions and fabrications of tale-tellers and liars become truth?

547 **wishful:** The Greek can also have the sense of "boasting" (see
557, below).

557 **and I ranked third:** A very daring comment for a Kretan of
whom no one has heard. For an audience who knew every
episode in the Trojan War, this is the Homeric equivalent of
Woody Allen's *Zelig*, in which the hero inserts himself into well-
known historic moments.

562–80 It has been pointed out that one very un-Iliadic feature of
this story is that it turns on the hardships associated with cold
weather. The heroes in *The Iliad* are never reported as being
influenced by something so mundane as natural climatic condi-
tions (see Hoekstra in HWH 2.226 [on XIV.473–7]).

594 **Thoas . . . , the young son of Andraimon:** This hero *is* in fact mentioned in *The Iliad* (II.638, IV.527–31). Here, as he runs off to the fleet, he acts out the root of his name—*thoos,* "swift," from *theô,* "to run" [appearing in the Greek in the infinitive form, *theein,* 501].

602ff. **That was a fine story:** Eumaios passes the test ("Odysseus / began to . . . test the swineherd," 541–42) with flying colors: he understands the story as a "story" (*ainos* [508], in Greek a story with a point or moral), and the Kretan gets his cloak.

609–12 **When our prince arrives:** The cloak, as it turns out, will only be on loan for the night. Here at the end of this crucial first day on Ithaka, also the end of Book XIV, Homer prepares a link to Book XV and the return of Telémakhos—thus to the long-awaited meeting of father and son, skillfully delayed to Book XVI. Homer's skill in careful arrangement and prolongation is never more apparent than in the second half of *The Odyssey,* with its carefully graded crescendo of recognitions and revelations leading up to Odysseus' terrible epiphany—one may almost speak thus—before the suitors (Book XXII). The volume diminishes but (to continue the musical analogy) the harmony becomes more complex for the final and full reunion with Penélopê (Book XXIII), while Odysseus' meeting with his ancient father, Laërtês, provides a return of the recognition theme, with new variations (XXIV.333ff., below) in a minor key.

BOOK XV

How They Came
to Ithaka

1–5 Homer must now bring Telémakhos back to Ithaka—a process
that reveals the complex narrative structure of *The Odyssey*. We
have not seen Telémakhos since Book IV. 663 (Telémakhos is not
mentioned in the last tableau in Meneláos' Lakedaimon, IV.663–
67, before the quick scene change to Ithaka). To prepare us to see
all the narrative threads come together, Homer had had Athena
tell Odysseus (XIII.515–17) that she was going to go fetch Telé-
makhos from Lakedaimon. First, however, Homer devoted Book
XIV to getting Odysseus settled at Eumaios' cottage, where the
long-awaited meeting of father and son is to take place, and
where all three can hatch their plot against the suitors. Homer
uses Athena as an elegant figure by means of which he can shift
his own narrative from place to place.

4ff. We left Telémakhos with Meneláos before he bedded down for
the night, but these sleeping arrangements are the same as those
described at the end of his first day in Sparta (see IV.325–26).
Gods often appear to those deep in sleep—Athena appeared to

Nausikaa at the opening of Book VI—but it is a nice touch to have Telémakhos lying in bed wide awake thinking of his father while his friend Peisístratos, who has no comparable worries, sleeps soundly beside him.

13 **what he had heard about his father:** Homer doesn't make this strong a reference to the little news Meneláos had imparted about Odysseus. The Greek only mentions that "cares for his father kept him awake" [8]. Fitzgerald's elaboration, harmless in itself, is instructive in bringing into relief Homer's more consistent focus on the moment at hand. Homer is in no way concerned to suggest links with Telémakhos' experiences in Book IV, which a modern translator, however sensitive to Homer's style, may, perhaps unconsciously, tend to infer and introduce. Indeed, at the opening of this book Homer shows himself uninterested in patching what might seem to be a serious problem for those concerned with continuity. Stanford's summary is excellent: "The chronology of the poem is uncertain here. Two nights intervene between Telemachus' departure and his arrival in Ithaca. It seems simplest to assume that neither Homer nor his audience would vex themselves with considering the possibilities that Athena's summons to Telemachus had occurred on the day before the end of the last book, *i.e.*, on the same day as Odysseus' arrival in Ithaca, or else that a day and a half had passed unrecorded at the swineherd's hut before the supper mentioned" at lines 373–75 (2.238 [on XV.1ff.]).

24 **press him to send you back:** It would be an unthinkable breach of etiquette for Telémakhos to depart without his host's permission.

26–36 **It seems . . . / Eurýmakhos . . . :** There is no reason to believe that this is anything other than a clever invention on Athena's part. Like a good rhetorician (or poet, for that matter), she knows that a vivid picture of one suitor in the lead will be much more alarming and likely to galvanize Telémakhos into action than a more accurate description of the whole gaggle of suitors still jockeying for pride of place. Note that even in this tale Penélopê is presented as still holding out. The goddess cannot and will not blacken her character. In lines 32–36 Athena evokes the image of any woman, not Penélopê specifically. The argument is a rhetorical one, an enthymeme (see II. 179–86, above): since "you know" women act this way, your mother, being a woman, will too. And you will be cast in the role of stepson in your own house. It may seem that the goddess Athena is slandering women in general here, but she is often on the side of men and is trying to persuade one here.

29 **in gifts to her and made his pledges double:** The gifts are to the bride, the pledges to her father.

42ff. If what Athena has said about Eurýmakhos were true, it seems unlikely that the suitors as a group would be involved in a plot against Telémakhos, but he least of all is likely to be troubled by this trifling inconsistency. Homer's audience knows this part is true.

148 Fitzgerald omits roughly five lines of the Greek, which also appear in Book IV. 656–62 (an omission not noted on his list on p. 463). [In the Greek, lines XV.113–19 are identical with IV.613–19.] A few manuscripts omit them in Book XV, and scholars who do not understand Homeric repetition urge their excision. In Book IV, Fitzgerald translates the whole run. (Here, lines 147–48 in the English represent lines 113–14 in the Greek.)

197–225 Omens—natural signs interpreted as messages from the gods—are a consistent feature of ancient epic. Eagles, birds of Zeus, figure prominently in literary omens. Often a professional seer or priest interprets the omen; Kalkhas is one in *The Iliad*. Here it is Helen who is inspired to interpret the sign, which she takes not merely as a positive response to Telémakhos' last word but quite specifically as a prophecy of Odysseus' vengeance on the suitors. For the particular features of this omen and Helen's interpretation, see Penélopê's dream (XIX.620ff.), in which the eagle speaks after slaughtering multiple geese (634ff.), identifying itself as Odysseus. In some regards, both omens and dreams function like epic similes, in that they permit the poet to introduce another perspective, drawn from a field distant from the narrative proper.

198 **off to the right:** The Greeks considered the right side the lucky side for omens. (See 637 and 642 for another good omen on the right, and XX.266 for an evil omen on the left side.)

212–13 In the Greek, Helen is even more explicit that it is the immortal gods who have inspired her with this understanding [172–73].

238 **westward:** There is nothing in the Greek [191] corresponding to a cardinal direction. Likewise "easterner" (276) and "western" (281) are interpolated into the Greek [223–24 and 226, respectively]. All are correct inferences on the basis of the geographical indications given or implied in the Greek (although "western" in line 281 seems to depend on wider geographical knowledge). It is instructive, however, to note that they are modern additions. We recall that Homer's contemporaries, living and navigating before the advent of maps (much less compasses), would not have conceived of movement in terms of the compass points. The rising and setting of the sun were points to steer by, as were the directions of prevailing or notable winds: Boreas, "that wind / out of the north" (XIX.235–36); its opposite number, Notos—the two are opposed as "north" and "south" at XIII.135–37 [110–11, which has the winds' names only] as well as at V.342 [clearly opposed in the Greek, 5.331], where e meet also the East and West winds, Euros and Zephypos [V.332], although it seems that these two were closer to southeast and northwest in orientation.

244 **true friends:** In Greek *xeinoi diamperes* [196]: "*xeinoi* forever." On the "guestfriend" relationship of *xeinoi,* see I.362, above.

246 **partnership:** Greek *homophrosunêisin* [198]. This same likemindedness characterizes the relationship between Odysseus and

Penélopê throughout the epic (see Introduction, p. lvii; VI.194–99, XI.515–17, above, and XIX.158–60 and XXIII.69–73, below).

276–346 Theoklýmenos approaches and begs for passage as a suppliant (345). Homer exploits the opportunity of this incident for variety, telling at some length the story of Theoklýmenos' forebears (282–318), even postponing the name of this descendant of Melampous (until 319–20). Theoklýmenos will play only a marginal role in the final books (most prominently at Book XX.393–416), where as visionary he prophesies the doom hanging over the suitors and takes himself from the palace to safety. (Note that his is the only Homeric name whose first element is "theo-" from *theos,* "god.") Until that point, he serves to provide another opportunity for Telémakhos to display his piety and hospitality, even in straitened circumstances. Homer identifies him as an outlaw fleeing retribution for having spilled blood (277–78), and Theoklýmenos identifies himself to Telémakhos as such, adding the detail that the man he killed was a kinsman (339ff.). See the first version of Odysseus' Kretan tales, told to Athena when Odysseus had just arrived back on Ithaka, in which he claims to have fled after killing Orsílokhos, Idómeneus' son (XIII.331ff.). The disguised Odysseus expected such a story to augment his chances of getting help. In aiding Theoklýmenos here, Telémakhos is thus in a way helping one of the avatars of his father, whom he has just invoked (333).

On "easterner" (276) and "western" (281), see 238, above.

282–318 The highly allusive nature of this summary suggests that stories about the Aeolids were well known to Homer's listeners, even if they seem obscure and esoteric today compared with the better preserved legends about the houses of Thebes and Argos.

289–95 As emerges clearly only in line 295, it is for his brother Bias (who is not mentioned by name) that Melampous undertook to pay Neleus the bride-price he demanded for his daughter, namely, the herd of Íphiklos. Homer names the daughter, Pêro, at Book XI.330. For more bits of the story, see XI.330–43, and the commentary on XI.336, above.

302–7 With Amphiaraos and "the assault on Thebes," we get to parts of the story better preserved today—the battle between the brothers Polyneikes and Eteokles, sons of Oidipous, for dominion over Thebes (see also Aeschylus, *Seven Against Thebes,* or in Latin, Statius, *Thebaid*). "Nor had he ever / to cross the doorsill into dim old age" (304f.) may seem to be a particularly ironic way to refer to the fact that Amphiaraos was cut down in the prime of life. However, the Greeks, even as they honored the wisdom of elders, regarded old age as a grim and ugly time, and avoidance of it by death was generally regarded as good (see 497–99; the image "sill of age" recurs at line 428). The unnamed "woman" (306) was Amphiaraos' wife, Eríphylê, whose ghost Odysseus reported seeing in the nekuia, describing her as "that detested queen, / Erí-phylê, who betrayed her lord for gold" (XI.379–80). The point is not emphasized here, but every treacherous wife may be seen as a counterexample to the faithful Penélopê.

311–13 **For Dawn in silks / of gold carried off Kleitos . . . :** The goddess Dawn was particularly fond of young mortal males, having made off, according to Homer, with Kleitos, Tithonos (V.2), and Orion (V.127, reported by Kalypso).

315 **above all men:** The Greek makes the further qualification "after Amphiaraos died" [253]. This detail is not trivial; we note even in this summary how carefully generations and matters of precedence were observed. It is worth looking back from this point to the run of lines from 299 on to see how adroitly Homer organizes this family tree of stories. Paternity takes precedence over chronology. At lines 299–300, Melampous fathers Antí-phatês and Mantios. Homer first treats Antíphatês' line down to his great-grandson Amphiaraos, whose story he narrates (303–7) and whose two sons he names (308). Note that the last two named are Melampous' great-great-grandsons. Homer then jumps back

(309) to trace the line descending from Melampous' second son, Mantios. Mantios has two sons, Polypheidês and Kleitos. In the long run, Homer wants to highlight Polypheidês (Theoklýmenos' father), so he mentions him first (310), Kleitos second (311), then digresses to tell the latter's story first (311–13), so that he can return to conclude with Polypheidês—putting him in the position of maximum emphasis—and effect a smooth return to Theoklýmenos (319), whose initial entrance (276) provided the opportunity for the entire digression. This is an example of ring composition (see IX.41–43, above). As was the case with the structure of Odysseus' fantastic travels, so in this much briefer passage there are rings within rings. Further analysis would reveal even more rings than I have detailed.

345 **I beg:** The Greek *hiketeusa* [277], "I have made supplication," binds Telémakhos to give holy treatment to the suppliant. (On supplication, see VI.161 and 207, above.)

365 No extant manuscript of *The Odyssey* contains this line [295], but the geographer Strabo (first century C.E.) includes it when he cites the passage, and it was on the basis of his testimony that it was introduced into printed texts of *The Odyssey* in the early eighteenth century. Whether this testifies to the fallibility of the ancient textual tradition or that of modern editors can hardly be decided, but in any case the peculiar odyssey of this line provides a good example of the fluidity of the text (at least in details) even after the poem had long been committed to writing (even to print) and reminds us once again of the history and uncertainty of even the Greek "original" facing any scholar or translator.

372–610 Homer leaves his story of Telémakhos aside until line 599. As Telémakhos and Odysseus get closer to their first meeting, Homer shifts from one to the other. The alternation of night and day appears to have organized the scenes. Night has just fallen on the sailors (366) when we leave them. The scene which begins the segment in Eumaios' hut is clearly a discussion after the evening meal. While Fitzgerald's "that night" (373) is technically an interpolation [301], Odysseus' "At daybreak" (382 [308]) guarantees that we are looking toward the coming of dawn (see also 478–83). When dawn comes at the end of the scene (597 [495]), Homer turns back to Telémakhos and his shipmates to present them making land and breaking fast (599–605). (If "morning" 605, and "of the day" 607, are only hints in the Greek that Fitzgerald has turned into full-fledged temporal markers, Telémakhos' "this evening" 610 [505] provides sufficient justification that this does not defy the Homeric conception.)

377 **observed the swineherd:** Odysseus uses the sort of "testing" here that he had when he told the story of the cloak (XIV.542ff.). In the Greek, the same line describing this testing forms a part of the introduction to both speeches [XV.304 = XIV.459], just as the first lines of both speeches are the same: " 'Listen,' he said, 'Eumaios . . .' " (XV.381 and XIV.546–47 [XV.307 = XIV.462]).

381–99 Homer creates (and Fitzgerald re-creates) a brilliantly calculated speech for Odysseus as he presents a character unashamed of the beggar's station and even the tasks to which he has been reduced. Indeed, he takes pride in his resourcefulness—his boast in line 396 makes him the epic hero of beggars. With great nobility he refuses to become a burden to those who have helped him (383), people themselves in relatively modest circumstances, but with courage, even a show of foolhardiness, he is ready to move on to ingratiate himself with those who have abundance to share.

407 **the rim of heaven:** In Greek, "the iron sky" [329], a phrase that Homer uses only twice, here and at XVII.744 [565]—both times in *The Odyssey* and both times describing the hybris of the suitors. What aspect of iron the poet meant us to think of and apply to the sky is hard to determine. Given the hardness and value of iron in Homer's time, it is clearly in some ways a positive epithet, suggesting the strength and immutability of the heavens, but there may be another thought behind the inert and immuta-

ble nature of steel: namely, that injustice as evident as the suitors'
was falling on "deaf ears," as we might say. The sky is made of
bronze at III.2 and at *Iliad* XVII.425, and the contrast of the
metals provides another opportunity to examine the develop-
ment of the Homeric poems through the transitional period from
Bronze to Iron age. Stanford notes at this juncture: "It is note-
worthy that Homer mentions iron more often in his imagery than
in his direct narrative. When he does mention it in narrative he
generally implies that it was uncommon, potent and valuable.
Bronze is the everyday metal of the *Heroic Age,* but Homer men-
tions it only four times in his imagery in contrast with fifteen
references in it to iron. Apparently the Heroes lived just at the
end of the Bronze Age when iron was still a rarity, while in his
imagery Homer reflects the conditions of his own times when
iron was in full use. . . . Homer's imagery often gives us glimpses
of the poet's own world as distinct from the world of his long-
dead heroes" (2.253 [on XV.329]).

427ff. Odysseus feigns ignorance here, for he already knows of the
death of his mother, with whose ghost he conversed (XI.170–
232). Even though she informed him of his father's sorry state
(XI.210–19), it's not surprising that he should be interested in
hearing Eumaios' assessment as well. Reports of ghosts require
confirmation, and Odysseus is so characteristically suspicious that
he seeks second opinions even for the directives of gods. Of
course, the questions are part of his disguise: Odysseus is portray-
ing a Kretan beggar interested in Odysseus, from whose son he
has been encouraged to expect gifts and aid (415–17).

464ff. If Eumaios was, as he has just claimed (445–50), the constant
childhood companion of Odysseus' younger sister, it's hard to
believe that Odysseus wouldn't have known a good bit about
Eumaios' pedigree, or at least his provenance. (In my reading of
Odysseus' behavior in Eumaios' hut, I have assumed he knows
more than he lets on; see XIV.391–402, above.) Nevertheless, we
can't be completely certain of Eumaios' age, or whether he was

in service as swineherd before Odysseus left for Troy (although that is the most likely construction on XIII.508 and XIV.4: see the notes on these passages, above.)

473 **this landowner's hall:** Who is "this landowner"? It is probably a colloquial reference to either Laërtês or the absent Odysseus. However, the specificity of "this" (in both Greek and English) permits Homer's audience to enjoy it as another daring reference to Odysseus' still undetected presence.

482–84 With great consideration and tact, Eumaios excuses his companions. That they might have heard this tale before is not the point; rather, as working men, they have need of a full night's rest. Furthermore, although little emphasis is put on his supervisory capacity, it is his responsibility to see to it that his assistants are properly rested, even if he is unsparing of himself.

492 **due west:** By this interpretation of *kathuperthen* [404], Fitzgerald makes clear his preference to follow those scholars who identify Eumaios' homeland with the area of Syracuse in Sicily, which is indeed west of Ithaka. However, another school of thought argues for Delos (also known as Ortýgia), which is most definitely not west. (See Fitzgerald's "Delos" in V.130, where the Greek has "Ortýgia," and compare the note there.) In this case, the "turnings of the sun" [*tropai êelioio*, 404] will be the solstices recorded at Delos, site of an important center of worship to Apollo. And as Eumaios will shortly tell us (497ff.), both Apollo and Artemis take particular care of the inhabitants of this land. Both interpretations, however, involve difficulties. Certainty is not possible, and we might be better off accepting that both Odyssean Ortýgias refer to an otherwise unidentifiable land in the east.

497–99 **but when the townsmen reach old age:** Death by divine arrows—Artemis' for the women, Apollo's for the men— would be preferable to suffering in old age; see 302–7, above. (However, that Artemis would kill a woman for reasons other than pity, see 577, below.)

506, 508, 517 On **Phoinikians** mentioned as perennially treach-
erous traders, while their city of Sidon is mentioned in terms of
craftsmanship, see IV.661, above.

517–26 **I am of Sidon town . . . :** The richness of the Phoinikian
woman's parents is a relevant detail. The sailor who brings her
home might well expect a reward. This is no doubt on his mind
(525–26), and may already have been in the back of her mind
(518).

521 This line repeats 473 [429 is identical to 388]. The proximity
of the repetition has led some scholars to suspect the authenticity
of the earlier occurrence. In fact, the line fits well in both places.
And the repetition only underscores the parallel between these
figures, all of whom have suffered comparable fates: not only
Eumaios and the Sidonian maid but also the Kretan.

    The maid, as betrayer of her present master, is a counterexam-
ple to Eumaios himself, who entered servitude under equally
unfortunate circumstances but remains a loyal servant. Insofar as
the Sidonian maid is corrupted by a sexual encounter with a man
from outside the household to which she owes her allegiance, her
behavior foreshadows that of the twelve disloyal serving maids in
Odysseus' own home (see XVI.363–79, XVIII.401–3, XIX.577–
78, XX.8–14, and XXII.472–526). On the ancient household,
see XVI.164, below.

542–47 The maid promises to bring something for her passage, in
particular her master's son. While there may be some hint of tit
for tat, it is more likely that she is thinking that if the sailors have
a good young man to sell into slavery for their own profit, they
will be more inclined to honor the oath she had them swear
(528–31). She is smart enough to know that, oath or no oath, the
sailors might be tempted to sell her and take the money.

562 **by luck:** Homer himself does not have Eumaios say this [466].
We moderns are more embarrassed by strokes of fortune in our
narratives. Admitting that something was a coincidence is a way
for us to apologize for it.

568 **in my bewilderment:** A very daring and interesting inter-
pretation on Fitzgerald's part. The Greek says, more ambigu-
ously, "I followed her in her fickleness" or "in her craziness"
[470]. It would probably be more correct to refer this to her act
of betraying her master, which would turn it into a comment by
the mature Eumaios, who now knows the full meaning and con-
sequences of the maid's actions. Fitzgerald more vividly presents
us the perspective of the child, who will have found his nanny's
behavior most strange. This is a wonderful touch; the only ques-
tion is whether Homer would have had his Eumaios create it.

577 Artemis is using her arrows here not to bring sweet death to
one of Eumaios' fellow countrymen at the "sill of old age" but as
punishment for an outrage against one of her devotees.

611 **When day comes:** Starting tomorrow morning, that is. The
feasting promised is offered to companions and crew as a sort of
reward for a successfully completed voyage.

614–65 The presence of Theoklýmenos permits an episode with
multiple functions. The need to secure hospitality for a man who
happens to be a seer permits Homer to integrate yet another
reminder of the rotten behavior of the suitors with yet another
omen that the house of Odysseus will prevail. Perhaps the most
subtle and important aspect of the segment is the way Teléma-
khos' current state of mind is presented. His first speech (621–35)
begins as we might expect but develops (628–33) in a rather
surprising manner: with great sarcasm, he suggests that Theo-
klýmenos seek hospitality with Eurýmakhos. (Some commenta-
tors, however, take this as a serious suggestion.)

The words he heard from Athena as he lay awake at the
beginning of this book (26–31) obviously still rankle. Or has his
tone crossed from the sarcasm of grim determination to actual
despair: Telémakhos sounds as if he's on the verge of giving up.
This may seem an odd reaction to having returned successfully
from his trip, until we see, as he must too, that his success consists
only in having escaped assassination. He has received no secure

intelligence of his father's whereabouts and is back where he started, with perhaps a greater desire to dislodge the suitors but no more idea how to do so. Telémakhos' intentions and instincts are good, but his faith is as yet shallow. The conclusion to his speech (634–35) shows that he is capable of hope, but it is close to being merely a pious expression. However, the gods are at work to restore Odysseus (and justice) in Ithaka, and at this juncture an omen appears to shore up his son's wavering spirit. Theoklýmenos is at hand to interpret it. With hopes raised (647–52), Telémakhos arranges for Theoklýmenos' lodging with a trusted companion, Peiraios, thus fulfilling his duty as host and as prince (653–65).

637, 642 **on the right:** See 198, above.

640–646 **Theoklýmenos / called him apart . . . :** Theo-klýmenos draws Telémakhos aside to reveal his interpretation of the omen, likely because he has heard enough about the situation in Ithaka to suspect that however well meaning the crew and companions on Telémakhos' voyage, word of such an event, and of his open proclamation of support of the house of Odysseus, would certainly get back to ears who would be less pleased to hear it. Theoklýmenos will interpret this portent later in much more specific terms to Penélopê (XVII.189–202).

BOOK XVI

Father and Son

6–8 **When Telémakhos came, the wolfish troop:** The Greek presents a particularly sharp example of the flexibility of epithets: "the loud-barking dogs fawned on Telémakhos and did not bark as he approached" [4–5]. There is a good bit of sense in what only misguided literal-mindedness would find problematic: the dogs are normally loud barkers—a good characteristic in guard dogs—and thus their not barking at Telémakhos' approach is notable indeed. Homer portrays the nearly infallible sense of animals when it comes to identifications. Note how they, and not Telémakhos, feel Athena's presence (189–90). And Odysseus' own hound will soon prove to be the only creature to pierce his master's total disguise (XVII.375ff.).

17ff. **his tall son stood at the door:** "His" indeed—but with the narrator's matter-of-fact identification of Telémakhos, Homer makes us feel more deeply than if he had described outright what must have been a strong suspicion on Odysseus' part that this is his son. Through this entire scene Homer, unmatched poet of the unspoken, leaves it for us to imagine (and thereby experience) the emotions that rise in Odysseus when it is confirmed that Telémakhos is actually before him. This becomes even more powerful because Odysseus remains unrecognized. He has the opportunity to take full measure of Telémakhos, whose every word and gesture to his retainer and the unknown beggar bespeaks unaffected nobility of character.

Likewise, we are left to gauge once again the mark of Odysseus' self-control by the silence he maintains for nearly a hundred lines. Only after Athena appears (182ff.) and instructs him to make himself known to Telémakhos (197–98) do we have the first great recognition scene, in which the emotions Odysseus has had to keep throttled burst forth. This provides a release point for the audience, too, for whom the strain of watching Odysseus maintain his disguise in the presence of his son is comparably intense. Homer's strategy is emblematized early in the episode by the simile describing Eumaios' joy at seeing Telémakhos (23–26): as no reader or listener could fail to note, the simile would in fact be more nearly adequate for Odysseus. The simile in context does more than describe the swineherd's joy. The way Eumaios' emotions are overtrumped by the presence of a better tenor, Odysseus, underscores the pathos of a situation in which the true father cannot openly claim that role. We note, however, with no prejudice against the estimable Eumaios—o my swineherd!—that it is unlikely Odysseus would ever let bowl and jug fall from his hands, spilling wine in the process (18–20).

40 **Uncle:** *atta* ([31], likewise 67 [57], 152 [130], and XVII.7 [6]). Endearing terms for parents and grandparents often take such sonic shape in children's mouths: "Nonna" for grandmother, Italian "Babbo." (For further examples, see Russo in HWH 3.18–19 [on XVII.6].)

44 **some gloomy spider's weaving:** The image of a spider's web to signify disuse is homespun indeed, but seems uncharacteristically poetic for Telémakhos, who is generally brief and to

the point. We may wonder if Homer wasn't also thinking at this point of Penélopê's weaving, which at least for a time managed to keep the bed unused. (On her ploy, see II.101ff., above.) Clearly, mention of the marriage bed prepares for its importance in Book XXIII.

54 **friend:** *xein'* [44]; on guest-friendship, see VIII.175, above.

55 **our:** Not the "royal we." This indicates instead that he considers himself a member of the household; it is what Stanford calls a "family plural" (2.265 [XVI.44]).

56–58 The couch is made of branches and skins, as we are told most matter-of-factly. This is unself-conscious simplicity and rusticity.

65–67 Telémakhos has politely waited to make inquiry about the guest until after the meal (see also III.46–55 and 75–76, above). It is also proper for him to offer Eumaios, as his official host, the first opportunity to identify his guest rather than ask the stranger directly.

72–78 This might count as yet another version of Odysseus' Kretan tales, though a summary at second hand. The irony of "the truth about him" (72) is broad.

80–84, 99–105 Things are so bad that it seems Odysseus will not be able to enter his own home even disguised as a guest.

108–30 The "stranger" is exceedingly polite as he begins to speak, but almost immediately we see how he goes about gathering intelligence on the attitudes of the other residents of Ithaka and above all Telémakhos' spirit and character. The questions about an oracle or nonexistent brothers of Telémakhos function as part of his patter, but a more subtle point has been drawn from the latter. Odysseus' queries here provoke Telémakhos' explanation that he, like both his father and grandfather (134–39), is a single son. This points up the lack of those who would, in other situations, be ideal and natural allies against the suitors. "But it . . . also requires Odysseus to adopt the kind of clandestine

strategy at which he excels and for which he can get all the glory"
(Murnaghan, 61n.).

160–79 Eumaios expresses concern for Laërtês, who, as we already
know (XV.434–40), has for some time been sick with grief both
for his absent son and for the wife who died of that same grief.
Now we learn that news of Telémakhos' risky trip to the main-
land has caused him to withdraw and worsen. Telémakhos will
have word sent to him discreetly. This small exchange sets up a
pattern with no little relevance for the conclusion of *The Odyssey:*
things cannot be resolved until Laërtês is brought back to full
communion with life. Indeed, Telémakhos mentions the only
balm that would help him: the return of Odysseus himself (172–
73).

164 **his own folk:** Members of his household rather than blood
relatives (unless some of the slaves were his illegitimate children).
In ancient Greek and Roman society, while relations among kin
were carefully tracked and monitored, the "household" in terms
of everyday life was the unit that most closely corresponded to
our "family." The word Eumaios uses for "folk" here [*dmôôn,*
140] is related to words for "house." (In Latin, the word for
"household" is *familia.*)

189–90 See 6–8, above.

195–201 Athena appears in splendor, not in the guise of some local
girl or Ithakan elder. She speaks to Odysseus this time not with
jokes and pleasantries but with impressive solemnity, as her for-
mal salutation indicates (195–96). That the suitors are to die is
her will and command, and she promises our hero that she will
tip the overwhelming odds against him in his favor. The ineluta-
ble movement toward the climactic slaughter in Book XXII has
begun.

211–18 Telémakhos' thought is most likely the first any pious
Greek would have, namely, that the old stranger who now ap-
pears so utterly transformed is a god who has cast off his own

disguise. In other words, this is an epiphany. Telémakhos' piety is clear throughout, particularly in the prayer and promise of gifts with which he concludes his brief speech.

219 **noble:** *Dios* [186]—"divine" or "godlike"—is of course not used casually here. At the very moment Odysseus attempts to reveal himself without disguise, he is, ironically, still taken to be someone other than himself.

223–24 Odysseus is finally free to greet Telémakhos as Eumaios had in lines 21–22. In the Greek the parallel is even clearer: behind Fitzgerald's "embraced" is in fact "he kissed" [*kuse*, 190], so that we have an echo of both kisses and tears.

225–35 Telémakhos' reaction is plausible psychologically (of course!). But Telémakhos never shows himself to be more like his father than when he denies what has just been told him—as suspicious as Odysseus is, for example, in Book XIII. A chip off the old block.

232–33 **unless a god . . . :** Telémakhos has hit upon the truth here, suggesting that he is prepared to believe Odysseus' explanation of his transformation when it is offered at lines 245–51.

238–41 Odysseus assumes the role of father for the first time, giving Telémakhos a mild reproof for behavior unbecoming a prince. He never offers (and never could offer) Telémakhos either a logical argument or a shared token to establish his identity. But emotions here are deeper than logic, and by speaking paternally, Odysseus makes Telémakhos recognize and accept him as his long-desired father. This permits him to let down his own guard and weep as a child can only in the arms of a parent (253ff.).

245–51 This explains only the change of appearance and does not prove his identity (see 232–33 and 238–41, above). The pious proverb with which Odysseus concludes this little speech (250–51)—bromides like this were felt to be fitting caps to a speech—refers to the gods' ability to do much more than change a mortal's clothes or give him a face-lift.

262–66 Telémakhos has sensed that the story Eumaios had been told and had summarized (72–78) is likely not the whole truth.

269–70 **Phaiákians . . . / as they give other wanderers:** Alas, the present tense of "give" [*pempousin*, 228] no longer holds true, because of the disaster Odysseus brought upon them, although he has no way of knowing it (see XIII.171–235, a story that well exemplifies the truth of XVI.250–51). In this small detail, then, what Odysseus tells Telémakhos is not as true as he thinks, although for once Odysseus intends to tell the truth.

273–74 **bronze and gold / and stores of woven things:** Tricolon crescendo, filling one full line in Greek [231]. (See also III.117–20 and XI.294–95, above.)

285–87 Telémakhos could have heard this from many sources, among which were of course the epic songs of bards.

308–19 There is much more to the exchange here than the battle-scarred and ever-victorious veteran talking to an untried and less-than-confident tyro. The point of Odysseus' first response is that Athena and Zeus will be fighting on their side (308–10). Telémakhos, for all his sincere piety, still has doubts—unconscious as he is of having received divine assistance—that the gods actively concern themselves with human affairs (312–15). Odysseus has experienced it, often, and on the field of battle: his response (317–19), brief and to the point, is the most convincing rejoinder he could make. Telémakhos will experience it. There are still many things for father to teach son.

331–32 From Odysseus' point of view, having heard Athena's death sentence on the suitors, he is assured that they are doomed not only in his eyes but in those of the gods. Hence the tone of ineluctable fate, even predestination.

339–52 Odysseus leaves nothing to chance. He is not satisfied to have instructed Telémakhos to remove the arms displayed in the hall (337ff.) but also tells Telémakhos exactly what story to give the suitors if they question him. Odysseus knows that no one can cook up such plausible lies as well as he can. Indeed, he comes up with not one but two lies. Here Odysseus is seeing to Telémakhos' education in rhetoric and, especially, dissembling.

350–51 **Tempered / iron can magnetize a man:** Another proverb to cap a speech (see 245–51, above), translated later as "Iron / itself can draw men's hands" (XIX.16–17). It has long been debated whether Homer, in saying that iron "attracts" or "draws on a man" [294], was actually thinking of the metal's magnetic properties. It's not impossible, but I prefer to take it more figuratively, as we do when we call certain dangers "attractive nuisances." (It can't be entirely literal, for the only men iron could magnetize would be iron men.) I am more sympathetic to the view that sees magnetism as one of the properties of iron which caused the new metal to be regarded as magical (see Russo in HWH 3.75 [on XIX.13]).

357 **our young friends:** In the Greek, simply "them" [297]. Telémakhos of course is younger than the suitors.

359 **If son . . . and blood of mine:** A powerful injunction. Telémakhos will want nothing more than to show himself worthy of his great father.

363–64 **. . . how far the women are corrupted:** This lays the groundwork for the execution of the treacherous maidservants at the end of Book XXII.

380–81 **. . . a scrutiny / of cottagers:** Telémakhos' suggestion to put off testing all the householders of Ithaka is a good one. The bad serving maids are traitors to Odysseus' *house:* not only are they more easily observed and punished, but the status of each— loyal or treacherous—is less susceptible to ambiguities. Although we do not see the testing of all householders carried out in anything like the form implied by Odysseus, the issue of their loyalty is resolved in Book XXIV along with the composition (i.e., settlement) of all the feuds arising from the suitors' mass murder. In their response to Odysseus and Telémakhos' punishment of their relatives, the men of Ithaka test themselves, as it were (see especially the assembly, XXIV.455–520).

382–83 In his last words, Telémakhos shows that he has been moved to defer to Odysseus' living faith in the power of the gods to assist them.

385 We now rejoin Telémakhos' ship, last mentioned at the end of Book XV, when Telémakhos had disembarked to make for Eumaios' hut.

417 **we said he could not:** This has of course a darker undertone: "we declared he would not," in other words, "we would see that he did not."

435 **All others:** An exclusive meeting of the suitors, no other Ithakans allowed (not all the suitors are Ithakan, of course: see 294–300).

449–93 Telémakhos' escape from ambush at sea does not guarantee his future safety. On the contrary, Antínoös seems more resolved than ever to do away with him, and his insistence in this speech that the suitors should murder Telémakhos, and soon, raises the possibility that even as Odysseus and Telémakhos make their plans on the basis of the suitors' well-established habits, the suitors may initiate a new and unpredictable offensive (see XVII.189–202, below). After a speech like this, we are prepared to feel it is only just that Antínoös is the first suitor to die (XXII.8–21).

453–59 **his people are all tired of playing up to us . . . :** For this reason the exclusion of Ithakans was necessary (see 435, above). At the same time, we infer that there are many Ithakans prepared to take Telémakhos' side against the suitors if called to do so, laying the ground for the composition of all quarrels in Book XXIV. Not all of the suitors are prepared to go as far as Antínoös (see 478–92, immediately below).

478–92 Amphínomos has good intentions but not the strength of character to oppose the suitors to the end. He would prefer not to commit murder but doesn't want to fall out with the whole pack. (Note the qualification of 485–88: it's not murder but royal assassination which sticks in his craw.) Hence his proposal: consult an oracle, and if Zeus gives the command to kill Telémakhos, then, so he claims, he'll do it. Such a message from Zeus' oracles is hardly likely. Amphínomos is probably not thinking of that so much as hoping to put off having to take sides. Granted, he is the only man courageous enough to speak up, but for all that he is a coward. It may indeed be fear of the gods that moved him to object in the first place. (For further reflections on this problem, see XVII.631–38, below.) Even lukewarm opposition to evil is punished, and Amphínomos will die at Telémakhos' hand (XXII.98–101).

493 **Now this proposal won them:** It is not that the other suitors are so pious. Rather, Amphínomos' proposal has the advantage of permitting them to postpone action. They may continue to feast without having to commit themselves to act and risk the loss of their places at the trough.

496 **Meanwhile Penélopê the wise:** Homer gives no reason for Penélopê's decision to appear at this juncture. We might imagine that having heard, first, that Telémakhos has returned and escaped one set of risks, and, immediately thereafter, that there is renewed plotting against his life, she might feel sufficiently emboldened and outraged to accuse the suitors to their faces. Unfortunately, from a strategic point of view, this is not a smart move: once accused openly, they have no reason to delay putting their plot into action and every reason to hasten it. Of course, it is Homer who decided that Penélopê would appear, and not merely because her doing so gives him an opportunity for a dramatic scene. More important, her appearance gives him the chance to present the other archvillain among the suitors, Eurýmakhos, in his characteristic role as sweet-talking dissembler. His tongue, ever ready to lie, will do him no good at XXII.47–94.

501 The faithful herald Medôn will be saved (XXII.401–24).

516–23 We learn now that, given Antínoös' family history, his plotting demonstrates outrageous ingratitude. There is a strong family resemblance, so it sounds, between Antínoös and Antínoös' father. We might wonder why Odysseus defended him.

528 Antínoös has no answer. Typically, it is Eurýmakhos who speaks.

538–42 Eurýmakhos can even enumerate the very reasons he ought to be eternally grateful to Odysseus and his house. He recites them and uses them in his carefully constructed rhetorical argument: no man who had received such benefits would wish to harm his benefactor or his benefactor's family; I received such benefits from Odysseus; hence I cannot harbor such thoughts. We know, however, that it is a lie, and, in case we have any doubts, Homer takes care to remove them (546–48). Odysseus is a master rhetorician, as we have had many occasions to observe, but nowhere else in *The Odyssey* does Homer so clearly show us rhetoric's capacity to be used for evil. Clearly, what counts is the character of the person behind the words: Eurýmakhos is a clever but thoroughly evil person. No wonder he can deliver such a speech.

544–45 **Heaven / deals death no man avoids:** Eurýmakhos also caps his speech with a pious bromide (see 245–51, above).

551 **to weep for her dear lord, Odysseus:** It is significant that Penélopê weeps for Odysseus, not Telémakhos, even though she has just voiced explicit concern for her son's life. As we know, Odysseus is soon to reenter their house.

554–92 In this final scene of the book, Homer reunites Eumaios; Odysseus, quickly redisguised by Athena at the approach of the swineherd (558–63); and Telémakhos, now privy to his father's counsels (see esp. 584–86). If Eumaios' answer to Telémakhos' question (of whether or not the suitors who sailed out to ambush Telémakhos have now returned to port, 567–69) is less than decisive (582–83), it is at least quite certain that Telémakhos' return is known to one and all in Ithaka.

BOOK XVII

The Beggar
at the Manor

11–29 Telémakhos is talking about Odysseus, but Eumaios doesn't know that. Nonetheless, Telémakhos doesn't bother to explain to Eumaios why he now suggests a different course of action than he had outlined earlier (XVI.81–105). The ready, enthusiastic assent (20–29) of the "beggar" heads off any reservations Eumaios might have or at least might voice to his young master. Lines 233–39 confirm that he does have reservations.

17 **Plain truth is what I favor:** In other words, "I prefer to speak the truth"—another proverbial cap to a speech (see XVI.245–51, above).

37 **Eurýkleia**, we recall, was of special assistance to Telémakhos as he prepared to depart on his secret journey to Pylos (II.370–403). She will prove indispensable to all three of the major figures—Telémakhos, Odysseus, and Penélopê—in this last third of the epic. She is the faithful servant within the house, as Eumaios is the faithful servant without.

41–43 The mention of Odysseus at this point makes us think of the

differentiation of the maidservants to come and the punishment
reserved for those, fortunately in the minority, who have gone
bad. The "other maidservants" here presumably include none of
the corrupted ones, unless, of course, they are dissembling.

46 "The choice of Artemis and Aphrodite together as a compari-
son for Penelope is especially felicitous. . . . Penelope has been a
chaste Artemis-figure during Odysseus' twenty-year absence, but
she is at the same time a desired sexual object or Aphrodite-figure
every time she appears before the suitors" (Russo, HWH 3.21 [on
XVII.37]). At the close of Book XXIII she comes close to meld-
ing these two radically different views of women. The double
comparison is repeated at XIX.66–67.

59–69 Although Telémakhos puts off giving even a summary re-
port to his mother, line 64 must be a very clear indication to
Penélopê that her son's mood has changed and that something is
likely to be afoot. Telémakhos leaves unstated the reasons ven-
geance is called for. Nonetheless, she carries out Telémakhos'
wishes to the letter (71–75).

65–69 **I am now off . . . :** These lines refer to Theoklýmenos, left
in Peiraios' care at the end of Book XV.

104–7 **But if my hour comes:** While he had only hinted at this
indirectly to Penélopê (64), he speaks more openly to Peiraios.

134–36 **Could you not / tell me . . . / what news:** In Greek
Penélopê adds, "if you have heard anything" [106]. This qualifi-
cation, which may seem a meaningless end-of-line formula, in
fact saves Telémakhos from actually lying in his speech, for he
now knows much more than he heard from Nestor and Mene-
láos—having seen and talked to Odysseus—which he has no
intention of revealing.

141 **of the West:** "Of the flocks" in the Greek [109] (see also
XV.238, above).

157–82 **Intolerable . . . :** That Telémakhos relates large chunks
of Meneláos' speech word for word to Penélopê has of course
more to do with Homeric poetic technique than any obsession

with accuracy in quotation as we know it, based as it is on wide circulation of written texts. For the record, Telémakhos does quote Meneláos (XVII.157–76 [124–41] = IV.358–76 [333–50] and XVII.179–82 [143–46] (Proteus' words to Meneláos as Meneláos reports them to Telémakhos) = IV.593–96 [557–60]).

183–86 As the note above indicates, much of what the audience has just heard it had heard before. Homer uses repetition as a foil against which to mark difference. We must remember that while Telémakhos tells no untruth here, he is of course not telling the whole truth (see also 136, above).

189–202 Theoklýmenos almost falls into the category of stranger who has news of Odysseus, the sort that Eumaios tried to convince the "Kretan" in Book XIV would be regarded with much skepticism in Penélopê's house, so frequently had beggars with similar tales come along. The difference is this: Theoklýmenos claims not to have seen Odysseus but to know things as a seer and reader of portents. As thrilling as Theoklýmenos' prophetic statement is, it presents a new and uncalculated risk: if word of this prophecy gets about, there is more chance the disguise of the "beggar" will be pierced. As carefully as gods and humans plot and as certain as the final outcome seems to be, Homer knows how to throw in new twists and raise at least the possibility of new complications—for example, of new plotting against Telémakhos by the suitors (XVI.449–93, above). And the audience will all along be wondering what role Theoklýmenos will play. The unforeseen possibility that the suitors might get at the weapons even after they have been removed from the hall is developed into a full-scale complication (XXII.143–220).

190 **He** is most likely Meneláos, although there is a manuscript variant that would permit Telémakhos to be understood as the referent.

194–95 See XIV.189–90, above.

200–202 Note that Theoklýmenos' interpretation of the portent of

XV.636–40 is much more specific here than it was at XV.642–46. Largely for this reason, the lines [160–61] were suspected as a later interpolation already by Alexandrian critics. It would, however, have been a very clumsy interpolator who created rather than smoothed an inconsistency, and there is no real reason to reject the lines. (Fitzgerald's "at the ship" rather than "on the ship" [160] silently removes one inconsistency.)

218 **Men:** "Boys" or "noble youths," really [*kouroi*, 174], not without possible sarcasm in Medôn's mind. Medôn is an interesting character: he is well liked by the suitors, whom it is his business to please, but he has chosen to serve Penélopê (see also XVI.501) and what is right.

233–39 Compare 11–29, above. "A master's tongue has a rough edge" (239) has a proverbial ring.

263 If the exact identities of these three remain uncertain, their relative place in the island's history is clear: they are ancestral Ithakans, Ithakos the island's eponymous hero, and the other two nearly as hoary. Nêritos' name seems linked to Mt. Neriton, and the name Polýktor was carried by an Ithakan of more recent memory: the father of the suitor Peisándros (see XVIII.368–69, if, that is, Peisándros is Ithakan, as he seems to be).

267–68 **an altar stone / to the cool nymphs:** The altar dedicated to the nymphs may seem merely a decorative final touch to a picturesque setting, but see lines 308–15. Homer's method is more functional than decorative.

270–333 The encounter with Melánthios, the goatherd, a thoroughly disagreeable character whose abuse of Eumaios and his guest goes far beyond the predictable rivalry between herders of different animals (which seems to surface at line 280), is multifunctional: it gives Odysseus and the audience a foretaste of what he will catch in the hall and Odysseus a first test of patience (304); it provides another opportunity to present Eumaios' piety, this time in striking relief; and it reveals that Eumaios is not so

certain that Odysseus is not alive and cannot return as his re-
marks to the "Kretan" in Book XIV suggested (e.g., 83–88,
161–77). See also 404–17, below.

279 A proverb (confirmed by many ancient quotations) along the
lines of "birds of a feather flock together."

300–304 Typically, when Homeric characters weigh two courses of
action, they execute one. (For example, X.56–61 or XXIV.260–
66, standard cases; or V.369–89, where a higher power inter-
venes.) Here, Odysseus alone, by exercising self-control, chooses
to do neither. The departure from the standard scene of "inner
debate" underlines Odysseus' extraordinary willpower.

319–20 Although this would be a terrible threat and insult to any-
one, Melánthios probably knows that it would be a repetition of
Eumaios' own history. Not only will Melánthios get punishment
fitting a slave (for the final stages, see XXII.527–30) but Eumaios
has the opportunity to begin the torture (XXII.197–212). He is
pious enough to pray for Odysseus' return rather than revenge;
how sweet that he eventually gets the pleasure of having the last
word (see XXII.213–20).

315 **Bad shepherds ruin flocks!:** Obviously proverbial.

321–24 These remarks put Melánthios on the level of the worst
suitors, with whom he has thrown in his lot (Eurýmakhos even,
see 330–32). Such a bow shot as Melánthios mentions will in fact
occur, though with Antínoös, not Telémakhos, as the victim
(XXII.8–16). Here Melánthios imagines Apollo shooting the
arrow; there Odysseus will pray to Apollo for success (XXII.7). In
between comes Penélopê's wish (649–50) of Apollo as archer and
Antínoös as victim.

370–74 Although these lines are calculated by Odysseus to further
his disguise as a beggar, Homer seems to have Odysseus touch on
elementally human experiences. Reentering his own home as a
beggar, he is stripped to bare humanity, not unlike King Lear on
the heath, although Homer does not go so far as Shakespeare and
strip his hero of sanity as well.

375–422 **While he spoke / an old hound:** The man in disguise is recognized only by "man's best friend" (see XVI.6–8, above). This phrase is more apt in its Odysseyan context than in times when the relationship is one of a pet to his owner. Dogs were not regarded as items of luxury but, like other domestic animals, working members of the household: they served as guards (see 253) or aided in the hunt. (They were workers in the latter even if for some members of the society depicted in *The Odyssey* hunting itself was clearly a sport rather than a means to acquire food.)

Argos had been trained by Odysseus to fulfill his function as a necessary auxiliary to one of the standard peacetime pursuits of a man of property and standing. His unappreciated existence had become one of meaningless misery, which demonstrates clearly the impact of Odysseus' twenty-year absence. The rot and waste of a land without its lord, of a house without its master, is reflected here by the life of an animal.

377 **Argos:** The dog's name is based on an adjective that can mean both "shiny" and "swift." Stanford suggests "Flash" as an English approximation (2.289 [on XVII.291ff.]). The name sharpens the indignity of his present bed of manure (384–88).

381 **wild goats . . . hare . . . deer:** Small potatoes, compared with the boar and even lions we imagine Odysseus would have had him track (see 408–409). For the young Odysseus on a memorable boar hunt, see XIX.460–541.

387 **flies:** Or perhaps "fleas" or "ticks."

404–17 **A hunter owned him . . . :** In his response to the disguised Odysseus, Eumaios has returned to the safely pessimistic view that Odysseus is dead. After the outburst at lines 308–15, however, we know what we only suspected before, namely, that this is a calculated self-protective posture.

421–24 Although Homer is capable of abrupt transitions, he often suggests some link. Here it may be in the action of seeing, Argos seeing Odysseus and Telémakhos seeing Eumaios. (In Greek, two forms of the verb appear in consecutive lines: *idont'* [327] and *ide* [328].)

446–47 **This hanging back:** *aidôs* [347] is "sense of shame" or "reserve." The sentiment (relayed by Eumaios with minor variation in 454 [352]) has a proverbial ring, somewhere between "You don't get poor by asking" and "God helps those who help themselves."

457 **Zeus aloft** is plausible, but *Zeu ana* [354] would more likely have been understood as "Lord Zeus."

470–73 **Yes, try the suitors . . . :** It may seem curious to seek to distinguish among the suitors by their qualities if none is to escape death. But it's not pointless for posterity to know that while this man who died was totally worthless, that man died though he had some redeeming qualities. (Lines 550–51 play off the value placed on having someone speak well of a person. That this refers to someone who is still alive does not negate the point: one's reputation after death was all-important.)

482–87 It is not a suitor who first openly questions the beggar's license to beg but a hanger-on, Melánthios, a lowborn man himself, who obviously begrudges the latest arrival any goods he might himself receive and enjoy. This motif is developed at considerably greater length with the arrival of the "scavenger" (XVIII.1ff.), a rival beggar whom Odysseus, egged on by the suitors, routs in a full-fledged contest.

499–514 The gist of Eumaios' speech, which starts to wander before Telémakhos cuts him off, seems to be this: no one seeks beggars for his home, but when they come it is a duty to suffer them and be generous.

503–4 **a healer . . . :** In the list of four desirable foreigners—skilled craftspeople in widely different fields—note that the singer comes last and receives most attention.

522 **What fatherly concern you show me:** Telémakhos' sarcasm is unmistakable. All the suitors would understand part of the point: the very unpaternal Antínoös seeks, like the rest of them, to become Telémakhos' stepfather. Only Telémakhos, Odysseus, and the audience can enjoy the additional irony that these words are being spoken in the presence of Telémakhos' true father. Giving the beggar a loaf because he's the lord of the house will in fact not decrease the house's property (526–27).

552–82 This is the third story the "Kretan" tells, basically a few selections from the version he had given Eumaios (XIV.229–417). For a full list of the accounts, see XIII.327–65, above.

579–82 This is the point at which the Kretan's latest account begins to diverge from the version in Book XIV. Up to now, the episode has not varied by a word: XVII.564–79 [427–41] = XIV.300–314 [258–72]. Here he claims that he too was taken into forced labor (XVII.579 = XIV.314). There, however, he claims that he threw himself on the mercy of the Egyptian king and ultimately prospered (XIV.315–31). The balance of lines 579–82 heads off in an unexpected direction. But before we get to hear any more new information (and before Eumaios has time to wonder whether these new details can be squared with what the Kretan told him—if he remembers it that well), Antínoös speaks and halts the narrative.

595–99 Odysseus makes the obvious point that Antínoös is himself nothing more than a beggar, living off others' wealth.

605–12 The first of three occasions on which Odysseus has something hurled at him by a suitor. The others are XVIII.481–88 and XX.330–36. This is another good example of Homer's mastery of theme and variation. Stanford, building on the analyses of previous scholars, summarizes the differences well: "in the first it is Odysseus who provokes the attack, in the second it is Eurymachus, in the third there is no provocation whatever; in the first Telemachus keeps quiet, in the second he protests, in the third he protests more strongly; in the first the suitors sympathize with Odysseus, in the second they first blame Odysseus and then reluctantly give way to Telémakhos' protest, in the third there is an argument about the suitors' rights" (2.294 [on XVII.462ff.]).

613–14 **One word only, / my lords . . . :** Although such open-
ings tend to be formulaic, we wonder whether Homer, by having
Odysseus begin his speech to the suitors [468] with the very verse
Melánthios had used at lines 482–83 [370], is suggesting that
Odysseus has chosen to echo the goatherd and thus to mock both
him and the suitors.

619 **Here it was otherwise:** Not exactly, but only Telémakhos
knows that absorbing Antínoös' blow here is one of the first stages
in Odysseus' battle for his own property.

625–30 Although his words are still harsh and threatening com-
pared with his former outburst, Antínoös now seems somewhat
abashed, perhaps as a result of the beggar's words, perhaps be-
cause by actually hurling the stool he had vented some of his rage
and now can see how outrageously impious his act was, as at least
one other suitor notes (631–38).

631–38 This unnamed suitor is hardly taking the highest moral
ground, for, according to him, Antínoös' folly consists in attack-
ing someone who may have been a god. It was customary to
expect gods to wander the earth in disguise: compare Telémak-
hos' reaction at XVI.215–18. (For the moral problematic, see
Amphínomos in Book XVI, who is prepared to murder only if
Zeus' oracle has so directed; and, further, XVI.478–92, above.)
In the Homeric world, and for quite a long time after, fear of
divine justice and pious behavior were so closely linked that it
wouldn't have been regarded as a failing if one acted properly just
to avoid divine punishment. What, otherwise, would be the point
of fire-and-brimstone sermons?

649–50 See 321–24, above.

651–55 **And Eurýnome her housekeeper . . . :** This is the first
indication that there are others who wish the destruction of all the
suitors.

672–92 Once again Eumaios summarizes the tale he heard from
Odysseus, this time to Penélopê herself. Here his tone seems

much more optimistic, not at all the sort of prologue his discouraging words to the Kretan in Book XIV would have led us to expect (recall especially XIV.148–60, 421–25, and 452–54). Of course he has just heard Penélopê wonder if the stranger had news of Odysseus (669–70).

675–76 **Three days and nights I kept him . . . :** The swineherd is proud to have been the first to host the beggar and wants to make sure his lady knows it. A charming touch.

709–17 Sneezes were regarded as (minor) incursions of the divine into this world—many people still say "Bless you" to anyone who has just sneezed—and Penélopê interprets Telémakhos' sneeze, coming as it did immediately after her wish (706–8), as a favorable omen (717). Hence her laughter, wonderful amid her cares.

711, 717 **kchaou!:** There is no such word mimicking the sneeze itself in Homer, but Fitzgerald here renders the onomatopoetic sound of the Greek verb meaning "he sneezed" [*eptaren*, 541]. The sounds are picked up even more deliberately when Penélopê uses the verb at line 717: *epeptare pasin epessi* [545]. Not surprisingly, the verb occurs only in this passage in Homeric poetry.

737–54 **Friend . . . :** As Telémakhos had done near the beginning of the book when Penélopê asked him for a report of his trip to Pylos (59–69), Odysseus suggests postponing his interview with the queen. We note how carefully and consistently Odysseus maintains his cover as beggar by (1) speaking ruefully of Telémakhos (747)—though of course Odysseus knew it was part of their plan for Telémakhos to restrain himself when his father was harassed; (2) arranging for his proximity to the fire (751)—this beggar has always been thinking about the wretchedness of his rags and is interested in warmth; and (3) tweaking Eumaios just a tad in his final line with the implied reproach that he had not yet managed to get him outfitted with better clothes (753–54).

744 **rim of heaven:** See XV.407, above.

757–72 **Have you not brought him . . . :** Although Penélopê is most eager to hear what news the beggar has, she recognizes at once the wisdom of his suggestion. Patience is best.

787 **and in the disposition of the gods:** Telémakhos' last words in the book bespeak his characteristic piety.

Blows and a Queen's Beauty

1ff. At the end of Book XVII we are left awaiting the fall of night so that the interview between Penélopê and the disguised Odysseus, which he has postponed until the departure of the suitors from the hall, can take place. The entire action of Book XVIII involves further postponement of the interview. It is of course not the Ithakan night which has delayed it. The narrator has created a series of new episodes to intervene and further prolong his narrative and our pleasure. The first of these is a beggars' contest between a new character, Iros, and Odysseus. The episode, while a comic interlude, is not without significance: even against this laughable braggart Odysseus must win the right to remain in his own hall (56–60).

6–8 **Iros:** The suitors dub Arnaios "Iros" in a play on the name of Iris, the (female) messenger of the gods; Iros was, it seems, always being sent on errands by the suitors (see 87, below)—a Homeric "gofer." His given name, Arnaios, plays either on his acquisitive profession as a beggar or on his sheeplike nature.

29 In the Greek Odysseus calls out his own name: "I don't think you'd be coming a second time to the hall of Odysseus, son of Laërtês" [23–24].

32 **the swine:** The same rather unusual word [*molobros*, 26] was used by Melánthios of Odysseus at XVII.280 [219]. Iros and Melánthios both function as lowlife challengers to the begging Odysseus, and, although they are comparable, Homer (as is his custom) develops two utterly distinct characters, one for each episode.

41–60 Antínoös, playing the role of the hero in this brief parody of epic games, organizes the match and announces the prize. There will be no set of arms or valuable caldron for the victor of this match but rather a blood sausage hot off the grill (54–55). For serious games, in which Odysseus also played an anomalous role, see VIII.107–252. For full-scale games, in epic a traditional way to honor the death of a hero, see the games for Patróklos' funeral in *The Iliad*, Book XXIII.

70–78 As his mother will sharply remind him (270–80), Telémakhos should not have allowed "the stranger" to be subject to such rude treatment and exposed to the possibility of injury. She of course has greater interest in him than in a common beggar, since she believes he bears news of Odysseus and is no ignorant man (XVII.694–95 and 770–72, respectively). If we were to defend Telémakhos' action to his mother, we could cite line 73 here, "if you will stand and fight, as pride requires," which assumes (and thereby establishes) that it is the guest's free decision to take up the challenge, implying that if it weren't, Telémakhos would have to step forward to stop the fight. That is not, however, the defense Telémakhos will make; rather, he will say that he knew what was right and wrong (283–86) but was powerless before the insolent suitors (287–90). And anyhow, as it turned out, the stranger beat Iros (291–94). This is hardly a logical defense, but its illogic reflects the real reasons for Telémakhos' behavior—which is more than he can reveal to his mother: he couldn't have known that *any* stranger would whip Iros, but he did know that Odysseus is virtually certain to best any challenger in single combat. In any event, Telémakhos is not about to gainsay his father. His final remark (77–78) shows that he is willing to participate in his father's grimly jocular mood.

87 **old Iros now retiros:** The wordplay in the Greek juxtaposes Iros and "un-Iros" [*Aïros,* 73]; Fitzgerald gives the joke a Spanish flavor. For the type of wordplay, see XXIII.20–21, below.

95–105 Antínoös had no doubt been hoping, and expecting, that Iros would give this annoying old stranger (XVII.544ff., esp. 595–607) a sound beating. He now tries, as is his wont, to bully him. The reference to King Ékhetos (102) is obscure; note that the punishment Antínoös describes the Epeirote king dealing out to one and all is virtually the same as that meted out to Melánthios (XXII.527–30). (What actually happens to Iros after he exits the scene in this book goes unsaid; although he is mentioned in passing at 412, the last description of him is at 300–303.)

109–14 Again Odysseus holds himself back for the sake of his disguise and his long-term strategy. See XVII.300–304, where the victim spared is Melánthios.

122–23 **half dead / with pangs of laughter:** The idiomatic linking of death and laughter points both to the uncanny and ominous laughing fit to which the suitors are subject in Book XX (386–92) and to their ultimate deaths in Book XXII.

141 **May the gods grant your heart's desire:** Every suitor who says this unwittingly wishes for his own destruction, as Homer suggests in Odysseus' "grim cheer" (146).

150–99 We see Amphínomos once again and recall his intervention in the council of the suitors in Book XVI (476–92), where, perhaps out of a spark of goodness, likely out of cowardice, or perhaps a bit of both, he opposed Antínoös' proposition that the suitors immediately put in motion a new plot to assassinate Telémakhos. At this point he kindly adds to the promised sausage two loaves of bread, wine in a fine cup, and some encouraging words.

A nice gesture—but of course it costs him nothing: the bread, the wine, the cup are all from Odysseus' own store. In turn, Odysseus is moved to warn Amphínomos in general terms, which puts his strategy at risk, based as it is on surprise (see 180–87, esp. 180–81). The libation after the warning speech (188–91) is intended to underline both the seriousness of the warning and the credibility of the speaker. Amphínomos is visibly shaken (191–93) and might have reflected that common beggars are not the sort to make such speeches and solemn libations. Homer tells us unambiguously that Amphínomos "foreknew / the wrath to come, but he could not take flight" (194–95).

At this point we might look at Amphínomos as a man far from bad himself, capable of recognizing good and bad in others, who doesn't have the will or strength of character to separate himself from bad company. Homer does nothing to encourage us to draw ethical lessons of this type; he simply adds that Athena bound him there (196). Despite Odysseus' humane impulse to give this best (or least evil) of suitors a chance to hear a warning and escape, the gods ordain the death of all.

Such an episode may indicate that the poet, however often he presents Odysseus and the other good Ithakans as having no second thoughts about the justice of wholesale slaughter of the suitors, occasionally felt compelled to respond to doubts the story raises in some minds, perhaps in his own. Homer establishes that any attempt by Odysseus to be more humane and give any suitors the benefit of the doubt would be foiled by Athena herself. And lest there be any doubt in this case, Homer tells us explicitly that Amphínomos' fate is to die at Telémakhos' hand (197–98; the death will be described at XXII.95–103). "So he sat down where he had sat before" (199) perfectly describes the ineluctability of his death: his small gesture of kindness and Odysseus' moving speech and warning have changed nothing.

158–60 **so was your father's . . . :** Odysseus' familiarity with

Amphínomos' family nearly gives him away as being an islander at least, so he quickly adds that his knowledge is but hearsay.

188–91 Odysseus' libation and other gestures, presented as part of a formalized ritual, respond to Amphínomos' original gift to him of "wine / in a fine cup of gold" (151–52).

200ff. **And now heart-prompting . . . :** Athena, "the grey-eyed goddess," moves Penélopê to descend to the hall. We might wonder whether Penélopê isn't curious to see this stranger as soon as possible on her own, especially considering how impatient she was when she first learned he would not come to speak to her until nightfall (XVII.756–64). Of course, this is not the reason she gives Eurýnomê (208–13), and we have it on Homer's authority that warning Telémakhos about the crowd is not the real reason, for Penélopê herself has "a craving / I never had at all" (208–9). As it turns out, the most remarkable aspect of the episode—her getting gifts out of the suitors—seems to develop without any preparation or plan.

Scholars have spilt much ink trying to explain Penélopê's "uncharacteristic" descent at this juncture, or—formulated with somewhat more sophistication—Homer's motivation in having her behave in a manner that some have felt is unseemly. There are ancient parallels. The beautiful Queen Esther, in a palace infested with her enemies, also risks offending protocol by appearing before the men, perhaps reckoning that the surprise itself will play into her hand (Esther 5). But perhaps the best course is to believe Homer when he says that "*Athena* meant to set her beauty high / before her husband's eyes, before her son" (204–5, my emphasis), especially since her beauty would be reflected in the inflamed desires of the suitors (202–3). Note that Athena's appearance in the text to motivate Penélopê (and then to beautify her even against her will, 235–48, see below) is prepared by another appearance in line 196.

206 Penélopê laughs at the idea of showing herself to the suitors, as if she were a young unmarried girl eager to attract a husband rather than the ever-grieving wife of a long-lost warrior—a virtual widow. The laughter might also suggest embarrassment—a keen observation, for we often laugh when caught in such a situation. What has Penélopê to be embarrassed about? Quite a bit, if she were thought to be descending in order to enflame the suitors, and if she seemed finally to have decided that she would have to abandon her resolve and choose one of them as her husband. Indeed, contributing to the urgency of Odysseus' return (and the tension of the episodes leading up to Book XXIII) is the real possibility that Penélopê might finally change her mind. The poem loses some of its power if we rule out that possibility entirely.

222 **your boy's a bearded man:** For the specific meaning of this, see 336–37.

235–48 Homer manages to give Odysseus credit for warning Amphínomos, yet, by staging the intervention of Athena, have him die with the other suitors. In the same way, Homer has Penélopê modestly refuse to be beautified (225–29), yet, through the intervention of Athena be "endowed . . . with immortal grace" (241).

252–58 Death as an escape from "heart-ache" is Penélopê's fondest wish, or at least one of them. It wouldn't be thought macabre, simply realistic. This utterance could have aroused in listeners the thought of another plot line, that Penélopê might die of grief while, unbeknownst to her, her husband was in the house.

265–67 **that instant weakness . . . :** Homer is direct (and I daresay accurate) about the powerful physical effect desire can have on those who don't suppress their lust.

268–69 **But speaking for . . . :** The suitors can see that Penélopê and Telémakhos are having a discussion, but they cannot hear the words (see also 304–5).

270–94 **Telémakhos, what has come over you?:** See 70–78, above.

306–13 **Eurýmakhos called out to her:** Eurýmakhos is always the first with honeyed words.

315–48 **Eurýmakhos, my qualities . . . :** This is one of the most moving, and at the same time craftiest, of speeches. First, Penélopê rejects the compliment to her beauty, saying that it departed with Odysseus (315–18). She wishes for his return, for that alone would give her joy; until that time, only grief is her lot (319–21). Then she recalls Odysseus' parting words to her (322–24) and cites them (325–37), although we can imagine she chooses them selectively. They are touching indeed (as is the traditional gesture she describes in line 323). Note in particular the portion of Odysseus' injunctions with which she ends her quotation, thus giving it prominence: "Wait for the beard to darken our boy's cheek; / then marry whom you will, and move away" (336–37). Lest the suitors miss the point of this, she says it straight out, although with as much reluctance as she can muster: "the time has come for me to remarry, as even my absent husband told me" (338–41). That it is her husband's command, so she says, removes any criticism of her. If this was what Odysseus had told her, he would indeed have felt the urgency to get back to Ithaka.

The final lines (342–48) are all based on the assumption that Penélopê has at last, in principle, accepted her suitors, although she never says this explicitly: she simply upbraids them for being bad suitors, and, in particular, for living off her house instead of bringing her gifts. The coyness and feigned wounded pride of "a gentlewoman / daughter of a rich house, if they are rivals," 344–45, are really delicious. All is brilliantly calculated for the suitors, her audience.

Or is the stranger the real audience for this performance? Could she have an inkling, an intuition who it is?

330 **decisive when a battle hangs in doubt:** Or "in battle, the great leveller": the meaning of the Greek [264] is disputed.

351 **she intended none:** If this (i.e., no marriage) is understood as belonging to Odysseus' train of thought, we must ask how he knows what is going on in Penélopê's mind. On the one hand, this may be one of those instances where a main character is made to share in the narrator's omniscience. On the other hand, Odysseus, however, is the only man who can judge the truth, and therefore the meaning, of the speech, including words attributed to him, which she has just delivered (325–37). He may know that she is fooling the suitors and hatching a plot. I prefer this approach to simply claiming that he could intuit the meaning of his like-minded wife, however plausible that may seem.

356–58 Antínoös is not one to leave the condition unspoken, which, in ways the audience can appreciate, Penélopê will be able to fulfill: she will take the best man for her lord—he is present in the person of Odysseus—and then the unsuccessful suitors will go ... elsewhere. (Where exactly they go we'll see at XXIV.1–228.)

359–73 **Pleased at this answer . . . :** Penélopê's speech brings something back into the household coffers from which so much has flowed for so many years. Odysseus appreciates the cleverness of this as well (see 349). Nor is this concern with revenue unepic: we recall the care with which he stashed the treasure he received from the Phaiákians (XIII.454–66): one cannot be a gift- and hospitality-giving lord with nothing in the storehouse.

383–423 Odysseus offers (although at first in a peremptory tone more befitting their master) to take over the task of tending the torches so that the serving maids can withdraw to attend their mistress, which would be more fitting. The response he receives shows both Odysseus and Homer's audience the depths to which some of the women have sunk. They sense (423) the truth of his dire threat (418–20), for that is what he will order Telémakhos to do (XXII.493–94), although Telémakhos will devise his own punishment (XXII.513ff.).

391–92 **offer light / to everyone:** Frequently taken to be a metaphoric or symbolic reference to the victory and release he will soon bring to the house—but the light he will offer to some of the maids will expose their treachery.

394 **patient man:** *polytlêmôn* [319], "much-suffering." As a *poly-*epithet for Odysseus, it fits into the system established in the first verse of the epic [*polytropon*, I.1].

397 Melántho is Melánthios' sister, and, from the sauciness of her response, we see that they share much more than their father, Dólios.

427–514 **They, for their part, could not now be still . . . :** The second of three occasions on which an encounter between the disguised Odysseus and the suitors climaxes in a projectile being hurled at the disguised hero. A comparison of the salient differences (for a summary, see XVII.605–12, above) highlights what characterizes this particular instance, namely, that Eurýmakhos in this case provokes the attack, that this time Telémakhos raises a protest, and that the suitors, while first laying the blame on Odysseus, are in the end forced to accept Telémakhos' criticism. By no means does this exhaust the possibilities for contrasts: for example, this is the only one of the parallel episodes in which Athena's governing intention is thematized (427–29).

434–37 **hear what my heart would have me say . . . :** Eurýmakhos attributes his sudden urge to his "*thumos* in his breast" [*thumos eni stêthessi*, 352]. We know, of course, that Athena put this thought there (see 427–514, immediately above, and 200ff., also above). His blindness, even of his own motivation, is underscored in the next two lines, the irony of which emerges from a more literal rendering: "not without a god does this man come into Odysseus' hall" [*ouk atheei hod' anêr Oduseïon es domon hikei*, 353]. Truer words were never spoke, for Athena is indeed with him.

441 **raider of cities:** A good example of the thematization of a contextually inappropriate epithet. The point is that, unbeknownst to Eurýmakhos, the bald fellow to whom he jokingly offers farm labor is the fierce and famous fighter the epithet so

accurately describes, as Eurýmakhos will discover to his woe in
Book XXII.

443 **to work:** Neither Odysseus nor any member of his family has
any aversion to working the land. This was widely considered
proper and even healthy, in contrast to the work of traders and
merchants, so clearly despised by the Phaiákian Seareach
(VIII.170–74, see VIII.167–73, above). Eurýmakhos expresses
comparable contempt for work Greeks would have regarded in
no way dishonorable in itself by using the verb *thêteuemen* [357],
"to be a *thete*," that is, a day laborer or hired hand, not simply an
agriculturalist. This is yet another sign of the suitors' arrogance
and debauchery. (See IV.689, above, where *thetes* comes dis-
paragingly from Antinoös' mouth.)

449–75 **Oh no . . . :** Eurýmakhos, revealing more about his own
attitudes than about any beggar, assumes that this "beggar"
would refuse his offer of work (449–50). In his response, Odysseus
at least pretends to be prepared to take him up on it, but he
changes the terms of the offer: the case he describes would have
him working not for wages but in a competition with Eurýma-
khos (453–54), a competition which Odysseus skillfully moves
from scything (456–58) and plowing (459–63) to a "competition
in arms" (464ff.) that readily suggests he would be a direct threat
to Eurýmakhos. Just like Odysseus (473–75)! This last section
foreshadows Books XXI and XXII, which will involve a "compe-
tition in arms" (archery) that rapidly develops into Odysseus'
attack on his competitors. There the doors will be closed.

487–97 **"Ai!" they said . . . :** The suitors take Eurýmakhos' side
here, stung equally, we can presume, by the beggar's words
(470–75), which, while addressed to Eurýmakhos, apply to them
all. We know that Athena is about to sway their consciousness too
(see also 428–29). Indeed, Telémakhos pronounces more truth
than even he realizes when he says, "some god / is goading you"
(496–97).

498–99 **I mean when you are moved to . . . :** Telémakhos is not ready to assert full control and pulls back from a direct order, though with evident bitterness. ("Struck by his blithe manner" in line 500 is the translator's modernizing variant on Homer's simple formula "so he spoke" [410].)

502–13 **but now the son of Nísos . . . :** Once again, the counsel of Amphínomos, the "good" suitor, wins the others over. Ironically, it also makes the further plotting of Odysseus and Telémakhos possible—and that will lead to the destruction of all suitors, Amphínomos included.

509–10 **let my own herald wet our cups once more . . . :** The proverbial "one for the road."

Recognitions
and a Dream

1–17 At XVI.333–56, Odysseus gave Telémakhos a full set of
instructions about removing the arms from the hall, saying first
(XVI.334–36) that at Athena's signal to him he would nod to
Telémakhos to indicate that the time had come. In fact, here at
the opening of Book XIX, he gives an only slightly abbreviated
edition of these instructions. If we are inclined to regard this
unexpected repetition as an inconsistency, we could claim that in
Book XVI Odysseus wisely set things up for a situation in which
he didn't expect he would have the opportunity to speak openly
to Telémakhos. But as it turned out, he now has such an opportu-
nity. Without dismissing that argument, it seems more sensible
and more in tune with Homeric aesthetics to see the virtual
repetition—not in this case a variation—as the marker of a new
episode or movement. No wonder that early editors marked this
as the start of a new book, especially since the previous book had
ended with a reference to going to bed (see also I.491, above).

1 **by Athena's side:** Athena's presence is incontrovertible at line

44, and, in the discussion between father and son which then ensues (47–63), the role of the gods is thematized. But in line 1, the Greek is less specific: Odysseus is plotting death for the suitors "with Athena" [*sun Athênêi,* 2], a formulation so transparent that it could suggest Athena's visible presence or, at the other end of the scale, inspire later allegorizers to see Athena as a mere manifestation of Odysseus' own intelligence—a pale concept compared with Homer's vision.

4–17 On the characteristic craftiness of Odysseus, priming Telémakhos at this point with multiple plausible (if false) justifications for his actions—"just in case"—and for the capping proverb, see XVI.339–52 and 350–51, respectively, above.

20–27 **He called Eurýkleia . . . :** In sharp contrast to the other maids, some of whom are traitors, Eurýkleia is the one member of the household proper who is trusted; indeed, she is suffered to learn some facts before even Penélopê does. Nevertheless, in lines 23–26 Telémakhos gives her the substance of the first lie that Odysseus had suggested Telémakhos palm off on the suitors if they called his actions into question.

31–39 Telémakhos shows that he too can improvise.

44–51 This marks a new stage in the degree to which Athena permits her presence to be noticeable to Telémakhos.

53–54 **Be still . . . :** Odysseus continues his instruction of Telémakhos in the ways of the gods and the proper manner for mortals to interact with them. See also XVI.308–19, above.

62–63 **while in the great hall . . . :** These two lines repeat the first two lines of the book exactly [1–2 = 51–52]. This is the classic closure for a "ring" (see IX.41–43 and XV.314, above), marking this as a self-contained, but not therefore necessarily dispensable, compositional building block.

65 **thoughtful beauty:** The comparison with Artemis or Aphroditê that follows (66–67) suggests beauty as well (see also XVII.46, above), but in fact Homer uses only the epithet *periphrôn* [53] for Penélopê in the first line of this new section (see I.379, above). He emphasizes her prudent intelligence, not her physical appearance.

The epithet is repeated frequently at intervals throughout this section, and while it stands behind the modifiers "carefully" (123 [103]), "attentive" (364 [308]), and "grave and wise" (682 [588]), it leaves no distinct trace in the English of lines 73 [59], 108 [89], 146 [123], 409 [349], or 589 [508]. Throughout the same section Odysseus is described with comparable frequency as *polymêtis*, which the translator is more inclined to render, for example, "the great tactician" (52 [41], 579 [499]), "the great master of invention" (194 [164]), "the master improviser" (310 [261])—these last two appear before the longer patches of narrative in the interview—"warily" (392 [335]), "ready for this" (447 [382]), "the master of subtle ways and straight" (643 [554]), although this epithet too is occasionally allowed to pass in silence (86 [70], 127 [106], 262 [220], 674 [582]; see also 678, below).

The treatment of Homeric epithets belongs as well to the history of interpretation of the poem, and it is particularly interesting to note that Odysseus' wiliness somehow seems worthier of emphasis than Penélopê's prudence. It is harder to escape the conclusion that gender must have something to do with the differential treatment.

83 **looking the women over:** Melántho judges the actions of Odysseus according to the behavior of the suitors. She knows where some of this "looking" leads: she herself is involved in an affair with Eurýmakhos.

88–107 **Little devil . . . :** Compare the relative mildness of Odysseus' rebuke of Melántho here with his withering words at XVIII.418–20, after she gave him a comparable challenge. Again, this is technically couched as a warning (100–101). The difference is of course Penélopê's presence, and Odysseus fairly invites his wife to show her sentiments (101–2). Clearly Penélopê is the real audience of this speech, and she once again hears of the stranger's past good fortune and current bad luck, and, above all, an additional reminder that this stranger has reason to think Odysseus' return likely (102–3).

127–45 And he replied . . . : Part of Odysseus' craft is that, like any good politician, he chooses which questions to respond to, and when. Rather than answering Penélopê's standard request for his background (124–26), he launches into an encomium of Penélopê's fame (128–36). His request not to be forced to tell of his (fictive Kretan) woes (137–45) only augments her desire to hear them—as it also increases the likelihood that she will pity him after she has heard them.

Odysseus will soon give the fourth version of his by now familiar Kretan story (see XIII.327–65, above, for a full list), but, as members of Homer's audience, we already note an important difference between this telling and others: although he previously lamented his sad lot, in no instance had he given a full-scale version of the argument "I cannot narrate my story because it involves too much grief"; this was most likely a topos (rhetorical commonplace) at the first performance of *The Odyssey* and certainly became one in its wake. (Compare Aeneas' words to Dido at the opening of *Aeneid* II: "Unspeakable, O queen, the grief you bid me renew," v. 3.)

129–36 It is an interesting commentary on the status of gender roles and on Penélopê's (and to some extent Odysseus') capacity to move slightly beyond them that Odysseus compares Penélopê's fame not to the fame of a queen but to that of a king. Both men and women could be praised for governance. Men were to govern (or to participate in the governance of) the polity, while (free married) women were to exercise comparable skills within the domain of the household. We know much more about the role of women in later Greek societies, and it is worth noting that what differentiates Penélopê from, say, a proper Athenian wife and mother is her fame. In the later city-state of so-called Classical times, at least ideally, the virgin daughters and wives of citizens were to be seen outside a home only in carefully organized rituals, and they were never to be spoken about. To be famous was to be infamous. The representation of heroic women in such a culture required a whole set of strategies, as the extant tragedies of Aeschylus, Sophocles, and Euripides clearly indicate.

132 **black lands:** Rich soil.

146–57 **stranger, my looks, my face . . . :** These phrases and arguments will sound familiar, not only to Homer's audience but to Odysseus himself. Lines 147–53 [124–29] are very similar to the words Penélopê directed to Eurýmakhos, which Odysseus of course overheard (XVIII.315–21 [251–56]). And lines 154–57 [130–33] are virtually identical to XVI.143–46 [122–25], which formed part of Telémakhos' explanation of the situation on Ithaka to the man he still thought only to be a traveler and guest in Eumaios' hut. The variation here is that Penélopê now presents them directly to Odysseus. The ironies arising from the presence of the disguised and unrecognized Odysseus are strongest in this first direct interview between the spouses.

158–60 **Can I give proper heed to guest . . . :** Odysseus and Penélopê share a concern with protocol. Here Penélopê refers to the consequence of the present circumstances in Ithaka, which make it difficult for her to fulfill the proper duties toward guests, suppliants, and heralds. Recall the conclusion of Odysseus' speech (141–45), where rather than focus on whatever personal pain might be behind his tears, he rejects a tearful show of emotions as unseemly "in another's house" (142) because it could be interpreted by observers as the effect of excessive drink (144–45).

It is not surprising that Homer shows them sharing such a concern: the couple are after all models of *homophrosunê* (see VI.194–99, XI.515–17, and XV.246, above). However, it would be more accurate to say that what they share is an ability to employ appeals to protocol in their rhetoric, for they are most similar in their craftiness.

163–82 We have heard of Penélopê's ruse of the web (or shroud) before. Lines 165–78 [139–52] are virtually identical to II.101–15 [94–107], which formed part of Antínoös' rebuttal of Telémakhos. Not surprisingly, the two accounts diverge at the point they relate Penélopê's maid's revelation of her secret (II.116 [108] and XIX.180 [154]). Antínoös and the suitors regard this action as only fair, but Penélopê is bound to view it as rank treachery (see II.116, above). Antínoös specifically says "one of her maids," but Penélopê, who is likely to be less well informed on the particulars of their plotting, merely says "maids," whom she vilifies in the Greek in terms harsher than Fitzgerald's: something like "good-for-nothing bitches" [*kunas ouk alegousas*, 154].

The most substantial variation, however, is one of narrative context: even the lines that are exact repetitions of lines in Book II take on a different tone now that they are Penélopê's own description of the desperate measures to which she had been reduced in order to avoid remarriage—not a reproach of Penélopê's devices by Antínoös to Telémakhos. The present narrative context also involves the disguised Odysseus as a listener. We are free to imagine his delighted admiration of Penélopê's cunning, though his strategy constrains him to conceal any such reaction. (Homer will explicitly ask us to imagine his suppressed reactions at 248–52.)

Along the way I have made reference to Greek traditions of allegorical interpretations of Homer (see VIII.280–392, XIII.127–37, and XIX.1, above). As Stanford notes, the "allegorical interpreters . . . explained Penélopê's ruse as being really a matter of argument—a subtly woven web of dialectic that delayed the Suitors with its prolonged complications" (2.320 [XIX.139]). As always, Homer's image is more compelling if taken literally, but such allegorical interpretations are not without interest, particularly as indicators of the Homeric inventions that later ages found either incredible or embarrassing for one reason or another. Such interpretations form part of a text's "reception history," the story of subsequent readers' responses to an original text. These responses range from explanations and imitations to interpolation and censorship at one extreme, and translation into other languages and media (i.e., painting, sculpture, or film) at another. Even our current preference for "literal" over "allegorical" interpretations in Homer is part of the reception history of the poem. Although once taken as real explanations of cosmic origins, the variations on celestial myths that turn-of-the-century scholars purported to find behind virtually all ancient narratives might themselves be better seen as allegories of the scholars' own historicizing age. Russo relates just such an explanation (HWH 3.82 [on XIX.149–50]), by Van Leeuwen (1917), in which Penélopê represents the moon, the repeatedly woven and unwoven shroud the moon as it waxes and wanes, and the returning hero Odysseus the sun. Like more traditional allegories, such "symbolic" or mythological interpretations are not subject to proof or disproof: they are matters of belief.

183–87 **And now:** We realize that Penélopê has told rather more than is necessary to support her ostensible point—that Odysseus' absence causes her continuing grief and pain (see 147–53). She has also managed to convey that she is virtually bound to remarry in the near future and that all her official suitors are hateful to her. While the first point is of course part of Homer's general strategy of increasing the narrative tension, the second may suggest that Penélopê, who clearly finds this traveler wise and infinitely more to her liking than the suitors, is thinking that it might be good if he entered the competition. This may even be unconscious; in any event, Penélopê would be most subtle in her formulations. Still, she is a prudent woman, and once again presses to learn the traveler's identity (191–93).

195–239 This latest of Odysseus' "Kretan" tales contradicts earlier versions in some details. For example, here he presents himself as Idómeneus' son, whereas he had told the first person he met on Ithaka that he had killed Idómeneus' son Orsílokhos (XIII.331–32). Of course, he need not fear being caught in a contradiction since the lad to whom he told that story turned out to be Athena. The particular connection to the royal Kretan house he presents is an index of his rise. To Eumaios he made himself out to be a prominent Kretan raider who, like Idómeneus, led ships to Troy (XIV.230ff., esp. 273–79). Now he is no less a personage than Idómeneus' younger brother, thereby Minos' grandson and great-grandson of Zeus. Marriageable material indeed! He also finally gives his Kretan disguise a name, "Aithôn" (216), which means "bright" or perhaps "russet-colored" like a fox, so that (some have argued) it could mean "foxy."

Odysseus has always tailored his stories to the situation: to the first person he met in an unknown place, he claimed to have murdered a prominent man—a healthy warning; to Eumaios he presented himself as resourceful and relatively unscrupulous, but utterly needy; now that he has more than a foot in the door, he presents himself to Penélopê as an aristocrat obviously fallen on hard times, in birth Penélopê's and Odysseus' equal.

217–39 Note that in this version the Kretan claims to have seen Odysseus on his way to Troy (221), in other words, some twenty years earlier (compare 264–65). Thus, as Penélopê hopes and expects (see XVII.689–92), if the traveler has intelligence of Odysseus' *recent* travels and whereabouts, he is not yet ready to deliver it. (For a possible rationale of Odysseus' strategy here, see 256–304, below.)

235–36 **that wind out of the north:** Boreas [200]. See XV.238, above.

248–52 Homer underscores the irony of this interview, in which Odysseus' identity is doubled. We are not only to imagine Odysseus' longing for Penélopê and his reactions to her weeping but to appreciate the mental discipline required to suppress them (see 164–82, above).

256–304 Penélopê asks for proof that her interlocutor is telling the truth: he must either produce some token or identify Odysseus' companions. Odysseus has, of course, no problem providing such information, and Penélopê is convinced. Perhaps now it is clear why Odysseus invented this meeting: had he, like other visitors, come out directly with a claim to know Odysseus' present whereabouts, there would be no way for anyone to test it. Odysseus cleverly tells a plausible tale which he knows can be subjected to "proof," and, indeed, he "proves" his report to Penélopê's evident satisfaction. Having established his general credibility, the good rhetorician knows his subsequent claims are more likely to be believed. I write "proves" in quotation marks, because of course no one can really prove that a falsehood is true. The "Kretan"'s tale, however plausible and credible, is a lie. Yet Odysseus' falsehoods mask a higher-level truth: the speaker knows details of Odysseus' clothes and companions not because he hosted Odysseus but because he *is* Odysseus. Likewise, further along in the interview, his claim of Odysseus' whereabouts is not really true, but it points to a more potent truth: Odysseus' actual presence.

Later (sixth-century B.C.E.) Greek sophists might have been thinking of a similar situation when they formulated their characteristically paradoxical claim—that the more an artist deceives, the more accomplished he or she is; and at the same time, that a viewer or reader is wiser to the degree that she or he permits the deception to have its effect. Odysseus, particularly the Odysseus of the Kretan tales, possesses virtues like those that distinguish the good poet.

Hesiod describes the Muses as saying, "We know how to sing both many falsehoods like unto truths, and, when we wish, to pronounce the truth" (*Theogony* 27–28), words which echo those in XIX.240 [203] in astonishing ways.

278–79 **Women there, / many of them . . . :** Women, as weavers of cloth and producers of garments, are the best judges of their quality. The extraordinary quality of Odysseus' garment reflects well on Penélopê, and the speaker's making a special point of mentioning it constitutes a subtle compliment.

280–84 **But I might add . . . :** This is perhaps the most brilliant tack in Odysseus' cunning fabrication. The whole story of this alleged Kretan stop on Odysseus' way to Troy is a feint, intended to prepare the way for Penélopê to believe a more important falsehood. At the same time, Odysseus must not arouse Penélopê's suspicions that he is someone other than the Kretan—a seer, a god, or perhaps Odysseus himself. Hence at the outset of this tack, instead of rushing into an inventory, he lingers a moment, seeming to rack his brains and referring to the difficulties of recalling details at a remove of twenty years (263–66). Here Odysseus quite logically points out that his Kretan persona might err ("I have no notion," 283) were he to assume that these were the garments with which Odysseus set out from home, since they could be gifts he acquired along the way. This assertion of uncertainty is more effective in building credibility than any display of confidence or certitude would be.

Homer and his readers of course can take pleasure in observing that the Kretan puts his finger on the central problem of making inferences, which may be false either because of logical flaws in the deductive process or because the assumptions on which the inferences are made are in fact false. In a move like the famous example of the purloined letter, there is no better way to distract someone from focusing too closely on a possible falsehood than by suggesting another.

Aristotle already cited *ta Niptra*, i.e., "The Episode of the Washing" (the pre-Alexandrian name for the text that later became known as Book XIX) for its exemplification of Homer's clever use of intentionally fallacious logic (*Poetics*, ch. 24 [1460a18–26]). Most scholars believe that the false logic Aristotle refers to is that, since the Kretan can correctly describe Odysseus' outfit, he must have seen Odysseus with these clothes. The second incorrect inference is that, if he can give "true" testimony about Odysseus on his way to the Trojan War, the rest of what he says must also be true.

A minority opinion, going back to ancient times, is that Aristotle is referring to the faulty logic behind Eurýkleia's (in fact correct) recognition (see 454–59, below): since Odysseus was wounded as a boy and would bear a scar if he still lived, and since this man has a scar, he must be the living Odysseus—although it would be possible for more than one man to have a similar scar. However unlikely, and however unlikely that this is what Aristotle meant, it is a good example of the intensity with which ancient Homeric scholars examined every line of the poem.

290–91 It is possible that Eurýbatês, quite vividly described, was of stock we would now call Black or Black African. If the two elements of the Greek word behind "dusky" were rendered by their most basic equivalents, we would get "dark-skinned" or even "black-skinned" [*melanokhroos*, 246]. Of course color terms are highly relative (see IV.146 and VIII.145, above), and compounds present their own complexities: we cannot proceed simply. The description might be of someone with Semitic blood, or even a notably dark-skinned Akhaian. And "woolly-headed" [*oulokarênos*, 246] could refer to tightly curled as well as frizzy hair. Ancient Greek ethnographers and historians certainly knew how Black Africans looked; see M. Bernal, *Black Athena* 2.245ff.

301 **you shall be our respected guest . . . :** Penélopê formally extends her personal hospitality to the stranger, thereby creating that special relationship of guestfriendship which involves each party in making the other's interests his or her own. Among recent scholars who have explored *The Odyssey*, Murnaghan is particularly helpful in analyzing this "guestfriendship" as a "disguised" step toward Penélopê's recognition of Odysseus and his resumption of all his rights and responsibilities as lord of the manor.

305–9 **Gone now:** Again we hear Penélopê speak as Telémakhos and Eumaios have as if she were certain of Odysseus' demise. (On the characteristically self-protective stance, see also I.199–207,

404–7, and III.258–61, above.) However, given her expectations for this interview, these words function as a cue for her guest to provide information he is supposed to have on Odysseus' recent travels. And the Kretan understands the clue as such (311ff.).

309 **that misery at Ilion, unspeakable:** On the Greek behind this line [260], see XXIII.20–21, below, where the wordplay is very clearly reproduced in English.

322 **I heard but lately . . . :** Again, lest he strain his own credibility, the Kretan claims not to have seen Odysseus but to have heard of his whereabouts.

324–49 Continuing to mix true and false, the Kretan now begins to weave into his story elements we know to be true—true within the narrative frame of Homer's *Odyssey:* Odysseus' men did kill Hêlios' kine, his crew did drown, and he was washed up on the shore of the Phaiákians, who gave him hospitality, gifts, and a passage homeward.

328 **held it against:** *Odusanto* [275], a form of the verb meaning "to be angry at" (here, as often, the gods at Odysseus), which is often linked with the hero's name (see further 477–81, below). Note that among the contrasts drawn between the heroes of *The Iliad* and those of *The Odyssey,* it is Akhilleus' role to *be* angry beyond the measure of mortals, while it is Odysseus' to be the *object* of divine anger.

334–62 It may seem incredible to Penélopê that Odysseus, offered passage home, might choose to delay his homecoming. Yet this too is a hint of a truth: what the real Odysseus delays is not his coming home but his public homecoming, involving the revelation of his identity. Indeed, when he says "playing the vagabond" or "beggar" (336) [*agurtazein*, 284], the Kretan comes close to describing what Odysseus is really doing. A bit further on he claims that Odysseus has gone to consult Zeus' oracle at Dodona, to know "how to return to Ithaka / after so many years—by stealth or openly" (351–52). If there is a message here for Penélopê, it is that Odysseus has not ceased strategizing, and he will appear in his good time and on his own terms, perhaps even in secret.

367 **You would soon know our love!:** Indeed. The Greek for "love" here, *philotês* [310], ranges from friendship, especially friendly hospitality, the explicit context of Penélopê's words, to sexual love.

369–74 Although we have yet to reach the conclusion of Penélopê's speech, this effectively marks the end of one episode, or subepisode—the interview—and the beginning of another—the footbath. Note the renewed expression of Penélopê's pessimism; her emphasis on the lack of a master to see to her guest's journey recalls lines 158–60, near the beginning of the interview.

386–91 **Men's lives:** And women's, too. The Greek of line 386 properly means "humans" [*anthrôpoi*, 328]; the same is true of "men" in line 391 [334]. If there is a grammatically masculine form in the Greek behind "him" (389 [332]), it would have been understood to refer to either a man or a woman, the "unmarked" usage universally accepted in English until recently and still not uncommon among some writers and speakers even in American English. Penélopê certainly meant it this way, for it is her fame that is at issue in this passage.

413–20 **I have an old maidservant . . . :** As Eurýkleia was Telémakhos' nurse, so, a generation earlier, was she Odysseus'. Here, as Homer has Penélopê play with the identity of the Kretan and Odysseus (418–19), the narration returns to the moment of Odysseus' birth. Soon Homer will tell us of a significant episode from Odysseus' youth, and at epic length (460–541).

416–17 The English broadens Homer's toying with his audience. A more literal rendering of the line would yield "wash your master's contemporary . . ." [358]. The frequent mention of footwashing in the preceding lines will have set listeners to expect "feet" to follow "master's" rather than the unexpected and more abstract "contemporary" (even if this would be an odd construction in Greek, the syntax of which would read "I wash you your feet" [356 and 376]).

421 **Men grow old soon in hardship:** On the speech-ending proverb, see also XVI.245–51 and other examples, above.

425 **Oh, my child!:** Intended as an apostrophe of the absent Odysseus, this is, unbeknownst to Eurýkleia, a direct address. *Apostrophe* (an address of someone or something not present, or someone who is dead), refers to a performance practice in which the speaker, facing his or her audience, would turn away (*apostrophê*) from the listeners to mime the invocation of the absent person or object.

429 **who plays in lightning:** Zeus "rejoices in lightning" (the epithet is *terpsikeraunos* [365]) in the sense that he takes pleasure in casting thunderbolts, one of his mythical roles.

433–37 Although the Kretan did not specify why he did not want to be bathed by any of the younger maids, Eurýkleia plausibly assumes his reasons.

448–50 On the one hand, Odysseus admitting openly that "that is what they say" is meant to dispel her suspicions. Eurýkleia and Penélopê, after registering their wonder at the uncanny resemblance between the Kretan and Odysseus, may be got to reason as follows: if people who know Odysseus much more superficially than we do see a resemblance, the resemblance must be superficial. Eurýkleia now, and Penélopê much later, will see and hear things that would not be significant to other people. On the other hand, Odysseus is playing with the identity of the two: strictly speaking, no one has "seen / the two of us" (448–49), for there are not two to be seen—only one.

454–59 Homer has a surprise for us, not the least part of which is that even the cunning Odysseus he has created can make a mistake. This could be an even greater (if less arrogant) mistake than revealing his real name to Polyphêmos (IX.551–52). Here Odysseus has agreed to a footbath and suddenly discovered that he has forgotten about the scar, a sign he knows will give him away to Eurýkleia. It is too late to feign a change of mind and escape the bath. Almost like a child, he must submit. He slips back as far as he can into the dark, in the vain hope that Eurýkleia may overlook the mark and that whatever revelations come out have a chance of being kept from Penélopê.

456–59 We will never know whether the nurse's recognition of Odysseus by means of the scar was a feature of all versions of Odysseus' homecoming or a special innovation of the Homeric *Odyssey*. It is thus impossible to say what expectations the first audience of *The Odyssey* had at this moment in the narrative. But even those who know the episode of the scar are free to imagine the experience of a first-night audience or first-time reader. Such a listener or reader will surmise from lines 456–67 that the scar was a telltale sign and will want to know about it: where did it come from? How does Eurýkleia know of it? But Homer refuses to satisfy that desire all at once. First we return to the preparations for the bath and are told that Eurýkleia "knew the groove at once" (459). At this point, when we are burning to know how Eurýkleia will react and how Odysseus will handle her recognition, Homer expands what is in Greek a simple relative clause modifying "scar" or "wound" (*oulên*, 393) into a flashback narrative of some 180 lines. When we return to the aged Eurýkleia, we discover that Homer has left her in a state of suspended animation: at lines 542–43 Eurýkleia is still feeling the scar and recognizing it. Only at the end of line 543 has she understood what this familiar scar really reveals: at this point she lets Odysseus' leg fall into the basin (543–44). But, as we will see, this is only the beginning of the suspense and excitement.

460–62 **An old wound . . . :** This would have sufficed to identify the wound as one dating from a hunting party before Odysseus went to Troy, which would have explained how Eurýkleia could have known about it. Homer, however, wishes to give a fuller version of this incident. Display is one of the most important reasons for this grand episode, but it isn't the only one. There are significant thematic cycles to be developed.

463ff. Autólykos, his mother's father, is central to this episode and to Odysseus' identity. The hunting wound has long since healed to become a scar. But it is only the first of the grooves in a narrative with several more insets or wounds, each of which has left its scar (or groove). Homer mentions that the young Odysseus went on the hunting expedition on Parnassos with Autólykos (463). This in turn leads quite naturally to a brief consideration of Autólykos as thief and trickster (464–66)—an important component of Odysseus' inheritance—and to an even earlier scene, shortly after Odysseus' birth. We meet a younger Eurýkleia here, the nurse who sets the baby Odysseus on Autólykos' lap and conveys to him that it will be his duty to name his grandson (471–75). The name is of course "Odysseus," a play on the word "odium" (480 [407]; see also 477–81 immediately below). The promise of gifts to be bestowed when he visits Parnassos (481–84) is followed immediately by the visit, the gifts bridging the years (484–85). At this point we have a more leisurely description of Odysseus' reception by his grandparents (486–89) followed by feasting organized by his uncles (490–99). The hunt itself occupies lines 500–533, during which Odysseus comes of age—by killing his first boar—but not without a cost: the wound in his thigh. After an indeterminate time of care and recovery (533–34), he is sent back to Ithaka with his gifts (534–36), and Homer concludes the episode by mentioning the youthful Odysseus' narration of the hunt to his parents (538–41), bringing this narrative to an end with the end of one of his hero's earliest tales.

This constant in Odysseus' character is thus highlighted, raising the possibility, however outrageous, that since the etiology—an account of origins—of the wound is Odysseus' own response to his parents' request for a story, it might not be true! *If* this is the case (and I underscore the fact that we have no way of knowing if it is), then (1) not only does Odysseus' history of inventing his self by storytelling go back to his childhood but (2) there would be no firm bottom to any level of narrative in *The Odyssey* and (3) Homer would be presenting himself as a dupe of his own character's lies. A narrative structure of this sort, which plays with the possibility of infinite regression, is generally known to narratologists by the French phrase *mise en abîme*. How fitting for it to be one of Homer's ruses. For another example of infinite regress, in the logical realm, compare "All Kretans are liars," and see XIII.327, above.

477–81 Homer tells the story of Autólykos' naming of Odysseus, of obvious significance in *The Odyssey*. But why is it part of the narrative of the boar hunt and wounding? It is the scar that leads Eurýkleia to address Odysseus by his name (*"You are Odysseus!"* 550 [474]). To take it further, a hero's name is like a deep wound: he can no more escape the fate of his name (a victim of odium and suffering) than erase the trace left by the wound, the scar.

But Homer may have connected the two in Odysseus' case by another of his characteristic wordplays: Autólykos gives him the name "Odysseus," explicitly derived by his grandfather from *odussamenos* [407–9] (see also 328, above). But in other regions and other traditions, his name was *Oulixes,* Latinized as *Ulixes* (the English version of his name, "Ulysses," derives ultimately from this tradition via the Latin). He receives this name, after a fashion, when the boar gives him his "wound" (*oulê*). The argument here is one not of historical etymology but of etymological play on the poet's part, and we know that the poet of *The Odyssey* is entirely capable of bringing the words into conjunction. From the historical perspective, the major objection would be the now invisible digamma ("w" sound) with which *oulê* at one time began (compare the Latin *uulnus*), but the poet of *The Odyssey* only fitfully preserves the digamma, already a fossil remnant in the language of his day. (See also I.448 and VIII.70, above.)

480 **odium . . . Odysseus:** This now standard solution to the problem of finding wordplay in English to correspond to Homer's is on the whole satisfactory. Odysseus' name itself would mean "child of woe" or "one who is hated," but it suggests as well that Odysseus would deal out his share of woe to others (as the Trojans, the suitors, and Polyphêmos could testify). In this very scene, he is inflicting pain, however temporary and strategic, on Penélopê, and his treatment of Euríkleia, though expedient, will be harsh (557–69).

Autólykos grounds the name in his experience, but of course Odysseus fills out the fate of his name in his own career. Both ancient Greeks and Latins memorialized the widely assumed connection between a person's name and his or her destiny in proverbs which mean, in essence, "one's name is a prophetic sign" (*onoma ornis,* Greek; *nomen omen,* Latin).

482–89 The delight grandparents have in their grandchildren's visits seems universal. Recall that before the advent of mass travel, any visit of over a few miles would have been astonishingly rare: Odysseus' maternal grandfather had not seen him since he was in swaddling clothes, his maternal grandmother never. Neither could Penélopê send her parents photographs or put baby Odysseus on the phone to chat. No regular and reliable postal service existed: one relied on news carried by either messengers or the chance wayfarer, such as the Kretan in these books or the young Odysseus himself as described at the end of this passage. Stories of one's heritage and family were of more importance for the Greeks, not less, amid a lack of communication that would appear to us today a frightening silence.

490–95 The men of the house, Odysseus' uncles, prepare the ritual meal. See XIV.494–514 for the shape of this "typical scene," of which this is a highly compressed version.

531 **rune:** A spell or incantation. Reports of the efficacy of a spell to stop a flow of blood circulate even in our own century, but the practice was obviously more common in ancient times.

540–41 **...boar's white tusk...:** At this point exact repetition of the Greek behind Fitzgerald's lines 461–63 marks the formal closure of the boar-wound tale's compositional ring. In Greek, the repeated material consists of one line including the last two metrical feet of the preceding line [393b–94, 465b–66]. In English, the text would run something like "with a white tusk, coming to Parnassos with the sons of Autólykos."

553–54 **Her eyes turned to Penélopê . . . :** Homer's gift for compellingly detailed descriptions of things, of movements, of physical consequences in all their materiality could be pointed out throughout the poem, but it leaps out in moments like this, when a lesser poet, or lesser school of poets, would focus only on the high drama and emotion. The drama is in the clang of bronze and the spilling of water. As if to signal a return to normality (and formally, to close the ring), after the intense whispered exchanges between Odysseus and Eurýkleia (549–82), Eurýkleia fetches "more water, / her basin being all split" (583–84). Note too the characteristically Homeric economy, not only in the sense of the spare means with which he achieves his effects but in the sense of disposition or arrangement: he can play with the possibility of greater recognition of Odysseus by Penélopê at this point, but instead he gives us a lesser one, and keeps us waiting for the grand moment we all want. Before that, however, more than a bronze basin will clang, and more than water will be spilt.

580–81 Odysseus is master and will give up none of his authority, not even to Eurýkleia, particularly when the issue is a judgment of life or death over other servants. In fact, when he has gained control of the house, he does consult Eurýkleia (XXII.467–68).

590–642 Penélopê has made the Kretan her own guest (see 301, above), and she addresses him now as the valued friend and adviser she would expect her guestfriend to be. In lines 608–19 she asks straight out whether he thinks she should persevere in her current course or whether she should marry the "noblest" (613) of the suitors or, as the Greek has it, "the best of the Akhaians" [528], a term that, since the death of Akhilleus, best describes Odysseus himself. "Now," she tells this Kretan noble, "my son is of age; I can remarry."

601–7 Think how Pandáreos' daughter . . . : Penélopê turns to legend for an example for her grief. The daughter of the Kretan king Pandáreos was Aedon, who had one son, Itylos, from her Theban husband, Zêthos. She was so jealous of her sister-in-law Niobe, who had many children, that she attempted to kill Niobe's oldest son. But in the dark she killed her own, Itylos (in some versions Itys), instead. Zeus transformed her into a nightingale to sing her lament unceasingly.

606–19 mourning for Itylos . . . : The linkage of legend and her present situation is virtually explicit: if Penélopê does not accede to the suitors' pressure and marry soon, she may inadvertently cause the death of "her and her lord's only child" (compare 607), who as the adult male of the household (617) must either give her away or face the suitors' wrath alone.

620–42 Listen: / interpret me this dream . . . : On dreams, oracles, and their interpretation, see XV.197–225, above. Of course it is possible that Penélopê suspects the true identity of her Kretan guest and makes up this dream narrative to see if he might be willing to reveal himself (see 678–99 and XX.69ff., below). There is no way either to confirm such a hypothesis or to prove it false. "Intuit" may be a better word than "suspect."

630 killed my geese: As often is the case in dreams and oracles, there is a grammatical or semantic equivocation that could be resolved in two ways. The Greek [543] could bear either "killed my geese" or "killed the geese for my benefit." Fitzgerald, forced to choose, as a translator always is, rightly picks the first, which is what provoked Penélopê's wailing (could the geese stand for her son?) until the eagle corrects her. Russo presents "[a] third and more submerged association" by construing the sentence so that it yields "my eagle," which he analyzes as "an irony in that Penélopê does not yet know that the eagle is more truly hers than the geese are" (HWH 3.102 [on XIX.543]).

652–59 **The two gates for ghostly dreams** have inspired both poets (e.g., Vergil, *Aeneid* VI.893–99) and generations of interpreters. For Homer, "honest horn" and "ivory" are likely assigned to false and true dreams—true in the sense that they will come true—on the basis of etymological play: "Horn" [*keraessi*, 563] sounds like a word meaning "to fulfill, to come to pass" [*krainousi*, 566–67]; "ivory" [*elephas*, 563–64] like a word meaning "to deceive" [*elephairontai*, 565], although Homer's exact understanding of both etymologies is still debated.

662–73 Without waiting for a further response, although she has made clear what her hopes are, Penélopê decrees a contest. In the fashion of a fairy tale, aspirants for the hand of the queen must compete in a contest. (On the much-debated particulars of the contest of the twelve ax heads, see XXI.132–37, below.) By her introduction (note "listen / carefully" 660–61), it seems clear that she wants her guest to compete, or at least consider competing.

673 **But I'll remember, though I dream it only:** Although Penélopê is ostensibly referring to the fact that once remarried and departed she will look back at her time in Ithaka, in Odysseus' home, as a dream, by referring to dreams at the end of this speech (*oneirôi* is in fact the very last word [581]), she recalls the dream she had narrated just above, thereby expressing her true hope.

678–99 **Odysseus . . . / will be here:** It is also a fairy-tale motif that the lady's champion arrives just in time for the contest. If Penélopê has been exploring her suspicions by a sort of code, the Kretan responds in kind. She will recognize that this is the only form an affirmative answer could take, and understanding that, she withdraws for the night (admirable and wise restraint). But there is no certainty, and she remains at best unsure, still weeping as Homer tells us for her husband (697–98). Again, rather than speaking in terms of the suspicions she has articulated in her mind and the tests she has devised, it is better to think of Penélopê's actions in Books XIX–XXIII in terms of a shifting set of motivations, at times a contradictory mix of suspicion, intuition, hope, desperation, inspiration, and divine direction.

678 **who knows the shifts of combat:** Here the disguised Odysseus makes striking use of *polymêtis* [585] to describe the real Odysseus (see 65, above).

693 On the Greek wordplay behind "that misery at Ilion, unspeakable" [597], which also appears at 309, see XXIII.20–21, below, where the wordplay is most clearly reproduced in English: "ill wind / to Ilion."

BOOK XX

Signs and a Vision

8ff. **Now came a covey of women:** The opportunity to observe exactly which maids are traitors to the house, of which Odysseus spoke to Eurýkleia (XIX.581), comes now.

11–24 **and anger took him:** As in Book XVII.300–304 and 608–11, the challenge to which Odysseus must rise is still to restrain his anger and to postpone action until the proper time.

14–17 **His heart cried out . . . :** Homer frequently uses a word metaphorically—in the Greek, Odysseus' heart "growls" [*hulaktei,* 13]—which Homer then explains by a simile ("the way a brach with whelps . . ."). Fitzgerald has done virtually the same thing, only it is worth remarking that Homer's style keeps the two parts more distinct, his method being (as often noted) additive. Homer builds in blocks. Another poet, or Homer on another occasion, might omit the simile and retain merely the metaphor—perhaps if his lord's stomach, or his own, were already growling (out of hunger). To make his point clearer, Homer also uses the verb or a closely related verb twice in the lines in question [*hulaei*, 15; *hulaktei*, 16]; Fitzgerald, writing for an entirely different sensibility, avoids repetition, striving for rich variety ("cried out," 14; "would howl," 16).

21 **Nobody** [*mêtis*, 20]: This word doubles the reference to the encounter with Polyphémos. (See esp. IX.394ff., above.) Here as well, "being a nobody" and "guile" are both required.

25–28 **rocked, rolling** (25) and **rolled** (28) on either side of this even more striking simile conveys the sense of Homer's repetition of *helisseto* [24, 28].

45–49 Odysseus, politician as well as warrior, already foresees the difficulties he will have in Ithaka because of the slaughter of the suitors: their families will be hot for vengeance. Homer shows him thinking ahead, and the poet himself prepares the audience to expect a treatment of events beyond the slaughter of Book XXII and the recognition of Book XXIII. Does Odysseus seem less than confident, even in Athena, as the goddess implies (51–57)? If so, it is an interesting contrast with the facade of strong faith he presents to and seeks to inculcate in his son.

69ff. Here we see a desperate Penélopê; at this juncture she is obviously not convinced, and doesn't suspect, that the Kretan is Odysseus, for if she did, she wouldn't pray for death. A different plot shape, a tragic one, might see her wish granted while her husband slept on her doorstep.

74 **tides:** Homer seems to refer to larger changes of flow in what the ancients imagined to be the encircling River Ocean. But the translator is right not to distract his audience at this point—the original audience was not given a lesson in the history of science—and only a pedantic commentator writes a note such as this.

75–88 **Pandáreos' daughters:** Penélopê alluded to the fate of one of Pandáreos' daughters at XIX.601–7, but that tale seems irrelevant here. The story described here has left no other trace in literature. Even as we remain in the dark, we can ponder how many stories well known to Homer's audiences are utterly lost to us.

79 **wit:** Or "prudence," "good sense" [*pinutê*, 71]; a gift Penélopê particularly appreciates (see 149, below).

91–92 These are particularly ironic lines: Homer's audience knows that Odysseus saw the shades only as a visitor and doesn't dwell in the underworld yet. It is wise on the poet's part to keep in our minds the theme of shades gathering in the underworld—although it is standard epic fare—for the first part of Book XXIV will show us the suitors in hell.

99–101 Another case where dreams approach truth more nearly than what a character takes to be reality.

100 **as I remember him with troops:** Not of course *at* Troy but as he went off to that war or some earlier conflict. In the field of the dream's fulfillment, the "troops" will consist of Telémakhos, Eumaios, and Philoítios.

110–138 **O Father Zeus . . . :** Ancient heroes frequently ask the gods for a sign or omen—and in literature they never draw a blank. In the Greek tradition, there is no injunction against tempting the Lord as there is in the Judeo-Christian one (Deuteronomy 6:16, quoted by Jesus at Matthew 4:7 and Luke 4:12).

122–38 In contrast to the wanton maidservants, here is one—and not the only one—of Odysseus' household to be true to him. It is not accidental that she is old: *The Odyssey* is a celebration of maturity and staying power, the wisdom of lived experience over hot youth.

134–35 **They've made me work . . . :** Note the realistic touch that this aged laborer's resentment at the suitors focuses on the fact that their feasting forces her to grind overtime, so to speak.

148–51 **My mother is like that:** This seems quite odd in Telémakhos' mouth, but it is said with no little irony on his part. He of course knows who the guest is and is no doubt proud to be sole possessor of the knowledge—so he thinks (see 153–61, below). At lines 150–51 Telémakhos voices the suspicion that his mother has not recognized that the beggar, taken as "riff-raff" by the suitors, is in fact a "solid man." Or he pretends to suspect this: the entire remark may be intended to function as part of the smoke screen around the guest's true identity.

149 **perverse for all her cleverness:** Or "though she be prudent" [*pinutê*, 131] (see 79, above).

153–61 Eurýkleia responds, and of course by this exchange Homer can engage us in an irony much subtler than Telémakhos' almost rude joke. We are witness to an exchange between two persons each of whom thinks that he or she alone knows the guest's identity, and neither of whom would dream of letting it on to the other. Note one major bit of hospitality Eurýkleia quite consciously omits: the footbath she gave Odysseus.

174 **holiday** catches part of the tone of the Greek "festival" [156], although it misses the religious overtones of "holy day" (see XXI.293). Festivals had ceremonial and cultic aspects. It is doubtful that most household slaves ever had the leisure time "holiday" implies; if anything, they would have had more work to do on such days. Stanford adds, "We may guess that part of [Eurýkleia's] excitement was also due to her knowledge of Odysseus' presence now" (2.348 [XV.149ff.]).

Ancient scholars suggested that the festival was that of the new moon, holy to Apollo. However fitting it might be for the archery contest to follow, and however closely the new moon festival can be made to square with a reconstructed chronology of the days of Odysseus' return (see XIV.539), if Homer had expected his audience to make such a connection, it is hard to believe that he wouldn't have made a more explicit reference than the delayed mention of Apollo at 305–6 (see 305–6, below).

175ff. Dawn had come at line 102. Here Homer depicts the practical break of day, as servants begin to bustle about their chores and members of the household who live on the land and others arrive, bringing—or driving—their produce to the great house.

194–201 Once again Odysseus must restrain his anger.

202 **A third man came up now . . . :** In contrast to the nasty Melánthios, a new man, Philoítios, a much more agreeable sort, arrives. There are honest people alongside the rotten. His name means something like "desirable fate."

203 **the cattle foreman:** We now have assembled a swineherd, a goatherd, and a cowherd. For a complete quartet of ancient herdsmen, we lack only a shepherd. Rivalries between and among representatives of each group are traditional in Greek poetry and presumably reflect the competition for grazing space in which the real-life counterparts of these literary herdsmen engaged. Goatherds are usually presented as the rudest and crudest of the lot, and Melánthios stands at the head of this literary tradition. (After Homer, swineherds appear less frequently than the others; indeed, swine tended to be kept closer to home.)

219–48 **Welcome, Sir . . . :** Philoítios' speech shows him to be a pious man and above all a loyal and courageous retainer of his master, courageous because he shows his loyalty to Odysseus before establishing what if any ties the stranger has to the suitors. In Greek, his first words (219–20 [199–200]) are identical to those spoken in Book XVIII (154–55 [122–23]).

230–33 The multiplication of Odysseus' herds Philoítios describes is an indication both of his good husbandry and of Odysseus' prosperity, itself a token of good kingship.

252–54 This oath recalls the words Odysseus spoke to Eumaios in Book XIV (189–90 [XX.230–31 = XIV.158–59]). They are also twice addressed to Penélopê (XVII.194–95 [155–56] and XIX.356–58 [303–4], the last time slightly varied).

260 The point of the introduction of Philoítios at this juncture now becomes clear: Homer is gathering a group of loyal retainers, fit but few, to join Odysseus and Telémakhos in the fight. Even though Athena has assured Odysseus that her aid alone would guarantee him victory (see 54–57), it is characteristic of both Odysseus and Homer to recruit a few more characters: characteristic of the former, because, as Athena herself noted (e.g., in the same spot), he never puts his trust entirely in her—no doubt one of the reasons she is so fond of him, according to the principle that "God helps those who help themselves." And it is characteristic of a Homer who seeks opportunities of variety and movement: as we will see, the battle with four against the massed suitors is more interesting and varied than it could have been with only two champions. It is also slightly more credible, a significant factor, although perhaps the least important of the ones mentioned here.

266–71 **for Telémakhos?** . . . : Once again (as at XVI.483–93), Amphínomos' combination of real or feigned piety and cowardice saves the day for Telémakhos. The other suitors, however, are only too happy to continue feasting (271). On the significance of "from the left" (266), see XV.197, above.

294–300 Antínoös, bolder than ever, alludes to designs on Telémakhos' life not only in public but in Telémakhos' presence.

305–6 The reference to Apollo the Archer, while a traditional epithet [*hekatêbolou,* 278], is not accidental here. Odysseus will invoke Apollo just before he shoots the first of the suitors (XXII.7). Indeed, the entire scene of the animals being led to sacrifice (303–4; see Eurýkleia's "holiday," 174, above) seems to have a largely symbolic significance: note the juxtaposition of islanders sacrificing beasts (303–6) with the suitors eating meat (306–8). Soon the suitors will be slaughtered (if not technically sacrificed), many dying by Odysseus' and Telémakhos' arrows.

312–14 **But Athena / had no desire** . . . : Compare XVIII.194–96. Athena, in other words Homer, wants the injuries against Odysseus and outrages against the gods to be fresh in the minds of one and all, so that retribution appears both swift and just.

315–55 The third in the series of scenes of objects being hurled at Odysseus (compare XVII.605–12 and XVIII.481–88). The distinguishing features of this episode are that the assault is unprovoked and that it leads to a heated debate about the suitors' prerogatives (see also XVII.605–12, above). Ktésippos' sarcasm is memorable, and not very appealing.

340 This foreshadows the general action of Book XXII, even if in the end it is Philoítios who kills Ktésippos (XXII.315–22), where the justice of the cowherd acting as Odysseus' avenger is made abundantly clear.

351–55 **Granted you mean at last to cut me down:** Telémakhos openly acknowledges the threats against his life, a provocative and generally risky maneuver, since it removes secrecy as a reason for the suitors to delay their plot to assassinate him. Yet it is a calculated risk and provocation. Is he hoping that open conflict will break out at once?

360 **like a fishwife:** A comparison introduced by the translator. The original is less colorful ["with hostile words," 323].

386–92 The suitors' fit of laughter does not follow logically on Telémakhos' speech. Some have argued that the "natural glee" of the suitors, who "have just heard what sounds like the fulfillment of their long-deferred hope" (Stanford 2.353 [on XX.345ff.]), is the starting point of the laughter which ensues, but that mistakes the situation. First, while Telémakhos says he will not oppose the marriage, he leaves the decision to Penélopê: he will not force her (384–85). This isn't substantially different from the position he told the suitors he would adopt after at most a year of hearing nothing about his father (II.229–34). Rather, it is the disjunction of Telémakhos' speech and the suitors' reaction which is the point of this memorable and uncanny episode. Athena inspires this crazed laughter, a sign less of the suitors' folly than of their impending doom. This is the reading of the prophet Theoklýmenos, whose function in the poem is to pronounce sentence on the suitors.

388 **uncontrollable:** Or "unextinguishable," as of flame or light [*asbeston*, 346].

393–427 Theoklýmenos, "the visionary," sees clearly the doom of the suitors and leaves. There is plenty of drama in the scene, but

Homer opts for realistic rather than melodramatic touches by having the suitors continue their joking (402–6, 417–27). They make fun of the seer's vision—the motivation of their laughter (402) is once again in the realm of the comprehensible—yet it is clear that they are the ones who are blind. (For a Biblical analogue with full melodramatic development, see Daniel at Belshazzar's feast, Daniel 5.)

404 In the Greek, Eurýmakhos adds the xenophobic charge "from another country" [*allothen eilêlouthas*, 360].

427 The **Sikels** were the "natives" whom the Greeks of Homer's day, during the first era of intensive Hellenic westward expansion and colonization, encountered in Sicily. (Modern scholars doubt they were indigenous Sicilians but rather believe they had come to Sicily from elsewhere; then again, there are few truly indigenous—in the sense of autochthonous or aboriginal—peoples in historic times.)

428–29 Homer keeps us in suspense: how will the battle begin? Telémakhos doesn't know, and it may be that Odysseus doesn't either—yet.

433 **father and son:** In fact true, but she can only think "newly arrived guest whom I very much admire and son." Once again, the often described narrative device of Homer sharing his omniscient perspective with a major character may also function as a means to convey intuitions or thoughts held just below the level of what we call consciousness (see XVIII.351, above, and XXI.5 and XXIII.94–100, below).

BOOK XXI

The Test of the Bow

1ff. Penélopê acts according to the plan she herself devised and
described to the disguised Odysseus in Book XIX (660–73).
Athena's role is to prompt her at the advantageous moment.

5 **to usher bloody slaughter in:** This is of course not Penélopê's
thought, although she might wish it (see **XVIII.**351 and **XX.**433,
above, and **XXIII.**94–100, below).

12 **double-torsion bow:** The Greek word Homer uses to de-
scribe the bow at this point, *palintonon* [11], means "stretching
back" and seems less technical than Fitzgerald's rendering. Odys-
seus' bow is unusual, and describing it is almost as difficult as
stringing it. It was certainly a composite bow, constructed of
wood, animal sinews, and horn. (The word Fitzgerald translates
"weapon" at 449 is in fact "horn" in Greek [*kera*, 395].) Due to
the combination and shaping of materials "such bows . . . are
more powerful than the ordinary bow: to string them is difficult,
and it cannot be accomplished by one pair of hands unless the
stringer sits or squats and braces the bow under one thigh and

over the other knee. The type was familiar in classical Greece as the characteristic weapon of the Scythians" and was known earlier "as a foreign weapon. . . . The suitors could not string Odysseus' bow because it was of this unfamiliar type. They stood up to try, and failed. Odysseus did it sitting down—not because he was stronger, but because he knew the way" (Frank H. Stubbings, in W&S, pp. 520–21; see also HWH 3.138–40; both have helpful sketches of such a bow). On Odysseus' seated position for the shot, see 480. There may be a hint of the bow's Scythian provenance, or at least its foreign connotations, in "polished bowcase" (see 56, below).

15–41 Like Odysseus' wound (see XIX.456–541), his bow and arrows have a history—as the weapons of epic heroes often do.

20–23 This raid sounds almost state sponsored. The Ithakans sent Prince Odysseus as a representative to settle the dispute. In those days, Odysseus was in the position Telémakhos is now, a young man who must learn by doing.

24–41 **But Íphitos . . . :** The chronology of this seems confused because of lines 26–31, a note on Íphitos' fate, sparked by mention of the mares and colts (25). His fate does not come to pass until he continues tracking the mares and is killed by Heraklês (36–37). Íphitos was a guest at Messenia at the same time as Odysseus and gave the future hero the bow of his own father, Eurýtos. (On further complications involving Messênê, see under "Messenians" in Who's Who, below).

41 **It served him well at home in Ithaka:** litotes (see IV.215, above).

46–53 Perhaps because of the heightened drama of the context, this is the fullest treatment of the unlocking of a door, complete with simile (51). For a description of the actual mechanics of the Homeric lock and key, see IV.854, above.

53–63 Homer heightens the implausibility of this death-dealing weapon (symbol of the male's role in war and hunt) in Penélopê's hands, emphasizing her pale arms (54)—a sign of beauty and a

marker that the woman is a proper lady, not a worker. After she
weeps at the memories of Odysseus the bow brings her (57–60),
she shoulders the bow—an intentionally incongruous image—
and proceeds to the hall. The only females regularly depicted
with weapons are goddesses (e.g., Artemis) and Amazons; Penél-
opê is neither.

56 **its own polished bowcase:** the Greek for "bowcase" (*gôrytos*,
54) is *hapax* and "refer[s] to the case of metal"—"polished" is
literally "shiny" (*phaeinos*)—"carried by the Scythians and other
nomad tribes to protect their bows in cold northern climates"
(Fernández-Galiano, HWH 3.137). On the possible significance
of a Scythian provenance for the bow, see XXI.12, above.

71–83 **My lords, hear me:** The opening part of Penélopê's
speech (71–76), in which she once again upbraids the suitors,
hardly sounds like a preamble to the second part ("Stand up,
then," 76–81), in which she establishes the terms by which one
of the men can win her as bride. The concluding lines (79–83
[75–79]) repeat her original description of the contest (XIX.669–
73 [577–81]) and underscore her reluctance to proceed on her
present course. Conspicuously and intentionally absent is any
remark between parts one and two to the effect of "But now that
my Lord Odysseus is surely dead, never to return," which the
suitors would probably infer.

87–104 **Tears came to the swineherd's eyes . . . :** Eumaios
and Philoítios sob. Antínoös, surprisingly, seems concerned for
Penélopê's feelings. A nice touch: perhaps he's a lady's man. Yet
he may care less for Penélopê's feelings than for the fact that the
retainers' tears might give her pause and lead her to change her
mind again about remarrying. Indeed, after his modest words
(101–4), Homer confirms that it has all been for show (105).

105–12 Homer prepares us again for Book XXII, here referring
explicitly to XXII.5–21.

112–14 **Now they heard a gay snort . . . :** Fitzgerald follows a
long line of scholars who assume that Telémakhos laughs or

smiles openly at the ironies implicit in Antínoös' speech and the thought of the suitors' imminent comeuppance. To explain this Telémakhos devises the speech that follows ("A queer thing, that!," 115ff.); hence also Fitzgerald's "brilliantly" (114).

115–31 A queer thing, that! . . . : Telémakhos' praise of his mother, as if he were an auctioneer talking up his wares to inspire a lukewarm audience of bidders, would be quite odd were it not spoken with the knowledge that Odysseus himself is in the hall.

132–37 Telémakhos sets up the blades for the contest. There has been much controversy about exactly what the shot consisted of, controversy based on difficulties in interpreting the Greek, which the translator has quite rightly smoothed. Even more than a commentator, at controversial points a translator must decide on one interpretation and present it coherently. Fitzgerald has discussed the difficulties of the passage in his "Postscript" (pp. 474–78). In short, he agrees with those who argue that twelve ax heads, handles removed, are set up in a long earthen barrow, so that the sockets in which handles would be fit form what Denys Page fairly describes (though he is criticizing the view) as "a discontinuous tunnel" (*Folktales*, 99). For a sketch of this, see Figure 8. This is a view of great antiquity, recently championed with great intelligence and learning by Fernández-Galiano (HWH 3.143–47; readers may consult his "Introduction to Book XXI" in HWH 3.131–47, esp. 140ff., for a full recent discussion with several line drawings). But I am not inclined to accept it, largely because it involves too much special pleading to get Homer's words to describe such a contest.

There are some controversies on which the book will never be closed, and Odysseus' shot is likely to belong to that group. Nonetheless, Page makes a case for two other explanations—neither of them original with him, as he makes clear—which do less violence to the Greek. In both the axes have handles attached. In the one, the successful shot goes through all twelve ax handles, that is, it pierces the wood and goes out the other side with enough strength to do the same thing eleven more times. Of course this is physically impossible, and no one who had any experience of archery even as spectator would think otherwise. Nonetheless, remarkably similar parallels in ancient Sanskrit epics support this theory. Part of the persuasive power of these analogues comes from the similarity of contexts: in the Indian *Mahābhārata*, a disguised suitor is required to make an amazing shot to win the hand of a princess; in the *Rāmāyana*, Rāma bends and strings a fantastically large and powerful bow (thereby winning a king's daughter). Rāma then takes this bow and shoots an arrow through the trunks of seven palm trees.

The existence of these analogues makes us entertain a hypothesis for the shot in *The Odyssey* that we would otherwise throw out on the ground of improbability. There is no reason why in this episode traces of more fairy-tale–like stories (which *The Odyssey* presents in Books IX–XII but generally not elsewhere) cannot be present. Scholars of Indo-European folklore often hypothesize on the basis of such parallels that there was a very old tale in circulation among the "Indo-European" peoples which descended in parallel lines in Sanskrit and Greek; while this is entirely possible, students of folklore know that there are many other explanations for similarities, ranging from borrowing of stories to polygenesis. Nearer home are legendary shots by Egyptian pharoahs..

There is another, more rational explanation, perhaps quite old, bolstered with more up-to-date archeological evidence in the version championed by Page. In this account, the axes would be cult axes, of the sort displayed in abundance in Minoan and Mycenaean palaces. Most of these are entirely of metal, and many have a ring at the base of the handle from which they could be suspended (see Figure 7). If a series of these cult axes were arranged with ax blade down and handle up, a series of rings would be on top, through which a truly outstanding archer could make a prize shot (Page, *Folktales,* pp. 103–13).

Of course, enjoyment of the shot and our understanding of its place in the larger narrative is not dependent on our having an absolutely clear, much less a certain, picture of the technical details.

137–39 More than an indication that Telémakhos was to the manor born, this uncanny knowledge suggests divine guidance.

145–46 **all but strung— / when a stiffening in Odysseus:** The implication here is that Telémakhos could have strung the bow on the fourth try—he is now the equal of his father in strength. But at a sign from Odysseus, he feigns failure. The communication between father and son is wonderful: by the sign itself Odysseus acknowledges that he knows Telémakhos was about to do it and asks him not to, primarily—we infer—because it is not the time. It would also compromise the plan as it is developing in Odysseus' mind. And we can speculate that Odysseus is not prepared for a public demonstration that his son is his equal and ready to displace his father.

147–54 **Blast and damn it . . . :** Aware that the truth is known to those who matter, Telémakhos ostentatiously "fails" with words of ironic self-deprecation.

153 **elders:** This does not strictly appear in the Greek, although it suggests the translator also has something in mind like the speculation about Odysseus at the end of the note on 145–46, above.

163–209 Leódês is the first of over a hundred suitors to try the bow. Homer customarily handles such scenes by varying the speeches and attitudes of each. The first is usually one of the longer (often the longest) cells in the larger structure, and there is nothing at this point in the text to suggest that Homer will depart from this practice: the introduction of Leódês (otherwise a minor suitor), his attempt, failure, and speech, and Antínoös' reaction to the speech, occupy thirty-four lines (163–96). However, Homer's solution to what could have been a wearisome catalog of failed attempts is radical. It turns out that by clever manipulation Leódês' attempt is made to stand for those of all the suitors, with the exception of Eurýmakhos' at the end.

Antínoös, somewhat unfairly to Leódês (it seems to me), declares that henceforth the bow will be greased and heated before each attempt. After Melánthios effects this operation (198–206; the fullest description of the procedure is postponed to 275–76; see the commentary on these lines, below), Homer summarizes all attempts with "one by one" (205–6), each ending in failure (207). The two ringleaders hold off (208–9). The way Homer presents the action, the attempts are ended (all but one, at 209) and the process is suspended while Homer directs our attention to a scene he stages outside the hall (210–73). But this is merely the way Homer presents simultaneous action. We are led to understand that Odysseus follows Eumaios and Philoítios outside and speaks to them while the long series of vain attempts is proceeding in repetitive fashion.

There is one other reason why Homer has chosen this radical compression of the series in Book XXI: he plans to recount the activities of many more suitors in much greater detail in Book XXII, when they are struggling, equally in vain, to avoid death at the hands of Odysseus, Telémakhos, Eumaios, and Philoítios.

210–12 The two loyal retainers leave the hall, unable to bear the sight of the suitors handling Odysseus' bow. For all they know, one of them is on the verge of winning their lady's hand, putting an end to the life of their household as they know it.

215–25 **You, herdsman, / and you, too, swineherd . . . :** Odysseus reveals himself to Eumaios and Philoítios. The questions he asks (219–23) bear such obvious hints that they seem intended more to prepare the two men—and the audience—for the revelation than to be serious queries. Odysseus already knows the loyalties of these two. Curiously enough, when he gets to the identification, Homer is very straightforward. Other recognitions, both prior and to come, are treated with more complexity and at greater length. Odysseus states that he is home and promises rewards if he proves victorious (240–43). Before there can be any exclamations of wonder—we might imagine a treatment in which Eumaios comments on his having been deceived, or saying that he sensed it all along—Odysseus shows them the scar from the boar's wound, which we know well from Book XIX, where it prompted Eurýkleia's recognition of him.

255–58 **Break off, no more of this . . . :** Odysseus is always the clever strategist and dissembler.

271 **took the stool:** A very important detail. Odysseus will remain seated both to string the bow (see XXI.12, above) and to shoot (480).

274ff. The bow has now made its way around to all the suitors save Eurýmakhos and Antínoös (see 163–209, above).

275–76 **He turned it around . . . :** Even though the suitors had been greasing and warming the bow ever since the second suitor's vain attempt to string it (198–207), this is the fullest description of the process itself.

290–94 **Antínoös said:** It is never stated directly whether Antínoös tried the bow and failed. One inference from the management of the scene is that he suffered his failure just before Eurýmakhos' attempt (274ff., compare 207: "Antínoös held off; so did Eurýmakhos"). While arguments claiming to prove his attempt "from silence" are rightly suspect, had Antínoös alone ducked the contest, Homer would hardly have missed the opportunity to point to his cowardice, if only in passing. Or is the subtle point of the present speech Antínoös' all-too-transparent attempt to wriggle out of trying, so as to avoid ignominy.

316–17 **Apollo . . . :** A pious prayer. Odysseus means other than the suitors will, as he knows, take it.

323 **since they were nagged by fear:** Note the suitors' sense of weakness. They had already witnessed this beggar's thrashing of Iros (XVIII.1–147). Antínoös of course casts his refusal in other terms, first as an affront to the suitors' dignity given the station of a beggar (325–29) and then as an example of folly spurred by drunkenness, for which he cites a mythological exemplum (331–42).

349–59 Penélopê, significantly, speaks before Telémakhos has a chance to open his mouth. Note how cleverly she puts her finger on the true reason (353, "What are you afraid of?"), although she, even more cleverly, takes this imaginary fear one step further: not merely that the suitors will be shown up but that they fear the beggar as an actual rival. We are again left to wonder, especially at 357–59, if Penélopê isn't saying this to inspire just this ambition in the "noble Kretan" 's heart. "Analytical" scholars argue that this speech is a remnant of a version of *The Odyssey* in which Penélopê is clearly in on the plot.

361–69 Eurýmakhos, less subtle than Antínoös, sees no reason not to admit they fear for their reputations.

371–75 **Eurýmakhos, you have no good repute . . . :** Penélopê's words are an insult and an argument at once, both unanswerable.

388–97 Telémakhos finally speaks. He is gruff because his goal is not merely to get the bow in Odysseus' hands—it looks as if Penélopê were on the verge of effecting this—but to get Penélopê and the other women ("maids," 395) out of harm's way.

404–39 **The swineherd had the horned bow in his hands . . . :** Eumaios undertakes to execute Odysseus' directive (from lines 262–63) but is so used to taking orders that he falters when challenged (414). It requires Telémakhos' countermand to get him moving again, with language that seems dangerously provocative of the suitors (422–24). Telémakhos is excited, and his youthful rashness surfaces. Homer doesn't ignore this but has the exaggeration provoke nothing but a storm of laughter (425–27). This resembles but differs from the laughter that Athena inspired (XX.386ff.). Eumaios then delivers the bow to Odysseus and immediately (430–39) fulfills the rest of Odysseus' commands (264–67).

440–45 Philoítios now sets out to do as Odysseus bade him (268–69).

446–49 The beggar will of course appear to be handling the bow for the first time, but Homer lets us know that Odysseus is clearheaded enough to think of eventualities that would never occur to a lesser man. Odysseus must be certain that the bow will still withstand his full strength and be fit for the battle to follow.

450–59 The sight of the beggar taking his time clearly unnerves the suitors, and they vent their nervousness in jesting.

462–71 **like a musician . . . :** The simile of the harper is of course of particular interest, drawing as it does on Homer's own profession. Left unsaid is a fuller elaboration of the comparison, whereby the harper's music and bard's songs fly into the audience's hearts as do archer's shafts when they are as well aimed as Odysseus' will be. Apollo is after all the god of both song and archery and of other areas of human endeavor as well, for example, healing. For the moment, the bow literally becomes a harp, and the plucked string sends a note into the suitors' hearts.

473 **laughed within him:** The suitors jest openly and lamely. Odysseus conceals *his* laughter.

475–91 **He picked one ready arrow . . . :** So long has Homer kept us focused on the trial of stringing the bow that it comes almost as a surprise to be reminded that the stringing is but a preliminary to the trial of the axes. This arrow is not yet for the suitors, but for the ax heads. Reference to the "rest" of the arrows (476b–77) might suggest that, now that the bow has been strung, the suitors could try the shot. But of course Homer and his audience will be thinking of the rather different way in which the young men will make trial of the arrows in Book XXII.

480 **sat upon the stool:** While great strength is also needed, this too is part of the trick of stringing this unusual bow (see XXI.12, above).

492–95 **The hour has come to cook . . . :** Whether the code was prearranged or not—and Homer has not told us that it was— these ambiguous words are the signal to Telémakhos that the time for vengeance is at hand. I take it that the very fact that they seem to be code suffices to convey the message whether it was prearranged or not, given the context in conjunction with a head signal (495).

495–99 **He dropped his eyes and nodded . . . :** After the carefully strategized delaying economy of the test of the bow, Homer, like Odysseus, once the bow is strung and in his hands, is for action. The change of tempo is remarkable and makes for an exciting book ending.

BOOK XXII

Death in the Great Hall

1ff. Homer continues at the rapid rate with which Book XXI concluded. Odysseus is ready for action, and after a brief but equivocal prayer to Apollo (7)—equivocal because the suitors will not take it the way Odysseus intends it—the slaughter begins. Antínoös is first, which is not only just but good strategy: Odysseus will get off only one shot without opposition, and he uses it to take out the most dangerous suitor, and the subtler and in that way more Odysseus-like of the two ringleaders. Eurýmakhos' death will be the second (87–94).

24–26 Each detail of Odysseus' plotting now falls into place.

31 **You killed the best on Ithaka:** Obviously far from true, since Odysseus is there, although this is the last instant Homer can evoke that irony. The suitors are about to learn what the audience has known all along: Odysseus is back. Note another advantage of the (eminently practical) removal of Penélopê from the hall: Homer will be able to treat the reaction to the news of Odysseus' return by the suitors and by her in different scenes.

47–57 **Eurýmakhos alone could speak . . . :** Now that Antínoös lies dead in a pool of his own blood, no one is swifter than Eurýmakhos in attempting to lay all the blame on him.

58–71 Eurýmakhos offers a "deal." It is not entirely unreasonable, but Odysseus rejects it. This is not the novelistic world of business, as the suitors would like to believe, but heroic epic. They wanted the honor and glory of occupying Odysseus' place in Ithaka; they will now have to pay for their ambitions in epic terms.

79 **Swords out!:** Odysseus was able to have the javelins and shields removed, but each man still has a sword as personal armor.

131–34 Scenes of heroes arming themselves are conventional. This is an abbreviated, "express" version, with mention made of only shield, helmet, and spears. More extensive versions describe the donning of greaves, breastplate, and sword. (For comparisons, not surprisingly mostly from *The Iliad*, see Fernández-Galiano in HWH 3.243–44 [on XXII.122–25]).

137–58 **a window . . . / lighting the passage to the storeroom . . . :** On the best, or at least most satisfactory, solution to the controversy about this much-disputed feature of Odysseus' house, the inner passage to the storeroom, see Fitzgerald's Postscript (pp. 478–81 of the translation).

158–64 Homer knows that nothing grips an audience's attention more than the introduction of unforeseen complications. Odysseus excels not only at devising plots but at responding impromptu to the unexpected. This turn of events could completely destroy Odysseus. Already twelve men have shields and spears. There is every danger that more hostile weapons will get into the hall: hence Eumaios and Philoítios are sent on their foray (190–97) and surprise Melánthios. His punishment is reserved until lines 527–30.

191 **for all their urge to leave:** Another instance of grim understatement (litotes), one of the most characteristic and pleasurable features of epic style. Like irony, it permits the listener to share the sovereign superiority of both hero and narrator.

226–28 Homer so far has not made it possible for us to tell how many suitors have been slain by either Odysseus' arrows or the odd spear cast, such as the one by which Telémakhos dispatched Amphínomos (98–100). As we settle in for more standard hacking and the typical scene (even into modern adventure movies) of one or a few against many, we learn that the count is now four versus forty. The odds were worse before, but now some of the "bad guys" are armed. Athena's appearance is timely.

233 **For he guessed it was Athena:** Homer doesn't leave us to wonder if Odysseus took "Mentor" to be the venerable Ithakan elder or Athena. Of course, the suitors remain in the dark (236ff.).

244–46 **Your sons . . . :** A terrible threat: this imagined vengeance would fall not only on Mentor but on his entire family.

247–67 **Athena's anger grew like a storm wind:** At this point Athena is there only to inspire the courage inherent in Odysseus and Telémakhos. Her abusive words are meant to fire them up, to challenge them—a technique still practiced in the ritual half-time tongue-lashing that coaches give their teams (at least in all popular depictions; the "halftime harangue" is one of film and TV's "typical scenes," and if it is also true to life, it may be impossible to determine whether art is imitating life or life imitating art). Note lines 262–64, especially. No one—in our hero's band, among the suitors, or Homer—mentions that the transformation of "Mentor" into a bird would have convinced one and all of the goddess' presence. If anything, Ageláos' remark shows him to be not only impious but obtuse (275).

268–85 A group of suitors is now shown to act in concert, and Homer presents a brief huddle. This also makes it possible for Homer to sort and shape the carnage. Here, for example, only six take on the four. Were all forty to band together, it would likely have taxed Odysseus and Homer both. Athena is now giving more than encouraging words.

297 **As these lay dying:** At this point thirty-six suitors remain opposed to Odysseus. (For a thorough review of the ever-diminishing census, see Fernández-Galiano in HWH 3.263–64 [on XXII.241–329]).

301–24 With the death of Ktésippos, the opponents are reduced to thirty-two. This time, for variety's sake, both Telémakhos and Eumaios have experienced superficial wounds. Because it was a "cow's hoof" that Ktésippos hurled at Odysseus (see XX.330–32), the privilege of avenging that insult is transferred from Odysseus, the victim of the outrage, to the good cowherd, Philoítios. Of course, from the poet's point of view, credibility is the only limit to the number of victories ascribable to the hero himself, and Homer must have been seeking to create opportunities for the other characters to have particular men to "waste." Fernández-Galiano, articulating an important structural principle of all action narratives, notes that "the author is careful to apportion the fourteen killings he describes according to a strict order of precedence: six to Odysseus, four to Telemachus, and two each to Eumaeus and Philoetius" (263).

330ff. **that unmanning thunder cloud . . . :** Having seen Odysseus and company reduce the odds from forty-to-four to thirty-to-four, Athena weighs in, the appearance of her shield (aegis) driving the suitors mad. Now undisciplined, they are much easier to eliminate, as the simile suggests (334–42), and at lines 344–46 we lose count of the dead.

347–428 **Now there was one . . . :** Homer initiates a series of scenes focusing on individuals begging for mercy. (For other examples in *The Odyssey,* see Book X.361ff.: Odysseus threatening Kirkê; and there are battlefield instances in *The Iliad,* for example, Lykaon's entreaties of Akhilleus, XXI.74ff.) The first of the scenes ends in Odysseus' rejection of Leódês' request (347–70). We met Leódês when he was the first to attempt and fail to string Odysseus' bow (XXI.163–87).

371–400 In contrast, the next suppliant, Phêmios the minstrel, is saved by the testimony of Telémakhos (400), but we feel that it is primarily by virtue of his singing, so nobly described by Telémakhos and Homer (388–93). (On Phêmios' name and genealogy, see Who's Who in *The Odyssey*, p.338.)

401–28 **And we should let our herald live:** Telémakhos himself thinks to seek the herald Medôn, who hears the offer and emerges from his hiding place beneath the table (406ff.). This is a moment of comic relief amid the exaltation of battle and the grim carnage, and a notable variation on the theme of universal slaughter.

432–38 **In blood and dust / he saw that crowd all fallen:** All the suitors are now dead. Homer has given us a variety of scenes and is not at all pedantically concerned that we can catalog each and every one of the corpses. The scene is capped with a simile drawn from the world of fishing, a decidedly homespun and antiheroic field (434–38). The suitors, who feasted in so lordly a manner on vast quantities of animal meat, are now reduced to fish, much humbler fare.

455–66 **As she gazed . . . :** Eurýkleia's reaction—to raise a cry of triumph—is completely understandable, even natural, we might say, considering the oppression all the loyal members of the household have suffered for so long. But Odysseus checks her, demanding a more pious response (460–66). The suitors brought destruction upon themselves by their folly, he says, and the victory belongs to the gods and to justice itself.

469–83 Eurýkleia reports that twelve of the fifty household women have been disloyal. It is clear that she is very eager for Penélopê to be told of the astounding events in the hall. But Odysseus, and Homer of course, wish this moment to be postponed (482–83). Without revealing how he plans to punish the guilty maidservants, he tells Eurýkleia to have the twelve sent in.

474–75 **taught / to be submissive:** Or, by another interpretation, "not to participate in the sexual service usually demanded of slaves."

480 **her:** Homer significantly has Eurýkleia say, "your wife," literally "your bedmate" [*sêi alokhôi*, 429].

487–96 The disloyal servants are made to do most of the dirty work, helping remove the bodies of the suitors with whom they betrayed the house and then cleaning the gore. A cruel punishment, but one that fits the crime, as the phrase goes. Then they will be executed by Telémakhos and the two herdsmen.

514–26 **The clean death of a beast** would be the swift butchering with swords that Odysseus had prescribed (493–94). Here Telémakhos acts on his own and gives the twelve a death more ignominious and protracted than death by sword blade: he hangs them. Telémakhos probably also thinks that his sword should be reserved for worthier enemies, such as male opponents or animals prized in hunting. Hanging was clearly thought to be a fitting death for women: in Greek literature at least—of which virtually all that survives was written by men—when women commit suicide they do so by hanging themselves (e.g., Neobule, insulted by Arkhilokhos; Jocasta in Sophokles' *Oidipous Tyrannos*).

527–30 The final act of meting out justice is the mutilation and death—although the latter goes undescribed—of the goatherd Melánthios, who had been left trussed up and hanging from the beams (see 206–22). This not only brings to a conclusion the lives of all Odysseus' opponents within the house but avenges the very first wrong done to Odysseus (by Melánthios) as he approached his home in Book XVII (270–333). A great compositional ring is thus closed. The mutilation and feeding of body parts to animals is the worst fate that could befall a Greek upon dying (see also XVIII.95–105, above).

531 . . . **called for a washing:** To whatever degree the hanging of the maidservants and the mutilation of Melánthios might be thought unholy and unclean, the poet has taken care that Odysseus not be implicated. Indeed, he is shown to be concerned only about ritual purity (see 545–46).

555 **nodding to every one:** Or "he recognized each one of them in his heart" [501]. It is with this half line that Homer closes Book XXII. Fernández-Galiano surmises (and even at the risk of over-reading, it is a nice touch) that "Odysseus had forgotten the names after" so many years, "but now, as he runs his eyes over the crowd of faces, he brings to mind each individual's name" (HWH 3.310 [on XXII.501]).

BOOK XXIII

The Trunk of the Olive Tree

12–25 Penélopê rejects Eurýkleia's report. While her initial response is one that anyone in a comparable situation might have uttered in sheer astonishment and disbelief, it in fact establishes the issue of the coming book. Few of Homer's (first-time) listeners or readers will have imagined at this point how much effort it will take to bring Penélopê around to a complete and public acceptance of the identity of the new arrival, for only in this book do we experience the full depth of her prudence and craft. As Eurýkleia will say, reproachfully, "You always were mistrustful" (80, for more on which, see below).

20–21 **ill wind / to Ilion:** An English equivalent of Homer's "Evil-" or "Ill-Ilion" [*Kakoïlion*, 19]. As she's done twice before (XIX.309 [260] and XIX.693 [597]), here Penélopê avoids the word "Ilium" in its pure form as one that is ill-omened, as she herself says, adding "not to be named" [*ouk onomastên*, 19]. Such "taboo deformation" is still current in the by-forms of what (to the orthodox at least) would be blasphemous oaths, such as

"Jiminy Cricket" or "Judas Priest" (for "Jesus Christ") or to replace what would be unacceptable diction in certain contexts, such as "shoot" or "darn." It is interesting that *Kakoïlion* occurs only in Penélopê's speech, although Telémakhos will shortly coin a comparable term for her (see 110–11, below; also XVIII.87, above).

30–39 We may imagine a thought passing through Penélopê's mind at lines 30–32: if this is Odysseus, why did he trust Telémakhos and not trust me? Homer gives no hint of this but describes her as full of joy and questions (33–39). That understandable joyousness is important, too: all the caution that follows is enforced by her powerful will and prudence winning over her natural desire to want Odysseus' return to be true.

41–44 Though brief, this is a wonderful revisitation of the events of the preceding book, which Homer presented to us in such vivid directness. Now we relive this time as it was experienced by those locked in silence in the neighboring rooms.

55 **Then he sent me here to you:** As he bade her at XXI.537.

56 **embark** may seem like an odd word, reminiscent of the sea voyage that has so long separated the couple. Perhaps Euríkleia's idea is that the new "voyage" her word evokes will erase the memories of the old. Yet Odysseus will have another trip to take in his final trial. (See XI.133–52, Teirêsias' prophecy, and XXIII.281–318, where Homer shows that it is very much on Odysseus' mind. On the question of his "seaborne death," see XI.148, above.)

67 **your notion:** Or "story"—the Greek is *muthos* [62], source of our word "myth," although the Greek didn't have the implication of "falsehood" or "fantasy" that English "myth" now does.

69–73 **Some god has killed the suitors . . . :** Even as she denies Euríkleia's report, Penélopê expresses a truth that Euríkleia has omitted—for a god was involved in the punishment of the suitors—and expresses a profound piety. Giving voice to the same kind of piety as Odysseus' (XXII.460–66, words also spoken to

Eurýkleia), Penélopê unwittingly (but Homer quite carefully) displays the depth of *homophrosunê,* "agreement" or "harmony of mind," that characterizes the couple.

80 **Child, you always were mistrustful:** Heubeck (HWH 3.319 [on XXIII.70–72]) reminds us to recall Kalypso's and then Athena's response to Odysseus' characteristically cautious skepticism (V.193–94 and XIII.417–22, respectively). This is yet another instance of the couple's "harmony of minds."

81–93 The nurse reports to Penélopê how she came upon the "sure mark" (81) of the scar, revealing that, like Telémakhos, she has believed that the stranger is Odysseus for some time. She explains that she was restrained from telling Penélopê. This must have a profound effect on Penélopê, but at least in her response to Eurýkleia she maintains the facade of cool resolve. Immortals frequently do appear disguised as mortals in *The Odyssey,* and Penélopê's pious husband and son at various junctures also allow for this possibility (VI.161–64 and XVI.211–35, respectively, although the first instance is likely only rhetorical). Homer's audience may well have known of the story of Heraklês' engendering, when Zeus appeared to Alkmênê disguised as her mortal husband, Amphitryon, returning from foreign wars and travels. If the audience recalled this, Odysseus' return would be a tacit counterexample, but not before the poet has played with the possibility of it being a true model (see 272–77, below).

93 **and that strange one:** Homer says only "and who" [84].

94–100 **She turned then . . . :** Homer tells us that Penélopê's heart is now "in tumult" (94–95). Still uncertain of what course to take and no doubt fearing that she may be swept away by the joy so long anticipated and make some terrible mistake of judgment, she holds to her course of prudence. Homer's style is such that we cannot definitively determine if "her husband" (96) conveys what listeners have known for some time or if it represents Penélopê's own thought to herself. If the latter is the case, it would be an early example of what is called "indirect free style"—which historians of narrative generally regard Flaubert to have invented, or to have definitively exemplified in *Madame Bovary*. Note that although the name "Odysseus" in line 100 would logically be open to the same analysis, because it lacks the emotive and personal force of "her husband" [*philon posin,* 86] it is clear that it fits into the language of the objective narrator (see also XVIII.351, XX.433, and XXI.5, above).

101–38 Odysseus, of one mind and spirit with his wife, understands her caution perfectly. Telémakhos, however, is disappointed; in some ways a child again, he longs to see his parents united, something he never experienced as a boy, and he breaks the highly charged silence. He accuses his mother of being hard-hearted (110–17). Penélopê ably justifies her position: she will demand her own signs (119–25). Odysseus not only concurs (129–32) but is content to let her come to her recognition of him at her own pace. He tactfully reduces the pressure on Penélopê by changing the subject to another issue: the political problems Odysseus and Telémakhos face as the murderers of the suitors, especially the Ithakans among them (133–38). This is no mere conversational diversion: even as Homer is about to complete a major pattern in his design with the long-awaited reunion of Odysseus and Penélopê, he opens up a new design element that will demand resolution. The issue is not resolved until the final book, which his listeners will now feel is required.

104 **wife:** Homer attaches an epithet to the word, calling her "strong" or "excellent" [*iphthimê,* 92].

110–11 **Mother, / cruel mother:** With his *mêter emê, dusmêter* [97], Telémakhos coins a term comparable to Penélopê's "Ill-Ilion" (see 20–21, above).

142 **foresighted in combat:** Telémakhos refers to general "cunning," or *mêtis* [125]. (See also IX.394 and XX.21, above, and the following note.)

149–58 **Here is our best maneuver ... :** Odysseus is ever-ready with a ruse, in this case one calculated not to solve the problem but to buy time. Perhaps the greatest mark of a strategist is not whether or not he or she can devise complex plots, because the best strategists know that many elements are out of their control. Rather, the key is to remain flexible and be prepared to improvise in whatever situation develops. Note also that this is the first time that Penélopê will be seeing "the stranger" acting as the lord of the house, giving orders. She will now see that Telémakhos and the servants obey him as if he were Odysseus. This might be sufficient to persuade another person, but Penélopê, equal in strategies to her husband, keeps her own counsel and sets her own tests.

154–55 **wedding feast:** Not that this matters for the credibility of the ruse, but there is a certain truth to it. There will be rejoicing at the reunion of a married couple, if, that is, Penélopê consents to recognize Odysseus. We should never underestimate either Homer or Odysseus and deny that this remark might be not cast with an eye to Penélopê, who, as we're all very well aware, is sitting by silently and pondering. Of course, for the passerby or neighbor whom Odysseus mentions, unaware of the unexpected turn of events, the "wedding feast" would be interpreted as that of one of the suitors with Penélopê, who has finally been won over. That is just the reaction Homer describes in lines 167–70. The two plots—of Odysseus' return and of the suitors' long wait—had been gradually approaching each other and came together in Book XXI, when Odysseus completed the test required of a victorious suitor.

185–94 Odysseus had told Telémakhos that Penélopê's reserve was understandable since he was at that point still in tatters and covered with grime and gore: no wonder he was unrecognizable (130–33). Now that he has been bathed, given clean garments, and been beautified by Athena, he reproaches Penélopê in practically the same terms Telémakhos had moments earlier (in fact, 189–92 [168–70] = 114–16 [100–102]). Has he forgotten that Penélopê herself said that she would be convinced by signs known only to the two of them (122–25)? Probably not, given the nature of his recognition of Penélopê's cleverness at that very point (126–27). More likely, Odysseus speaks here (and particularly at 193–94) to provoke the test and precipitate the moment of ultimate reconciliation.

187, 197 **Strange woman . . . Strange man:** The echo [in Greek, *daimoniê,* 166, and *daimoni',* 174] is intentional on the part of Penélopê, who wants Odysseus to understand that he seems as strange to her as she does to him, a doubled "like-mindedness" on the level of appearance and perception as well as on that of the real.

202–58 **Make up his bed . . . :** The secret Odysseus knows, and knowledge of which Penélopê accepts as a sure sign, is that Odysseus' bed is immovable without destroying the structure of the house itself. That knowledge of this fact should convince Penélopê that the man before her is indeed Odysseus—rather than some immortal—is not terribly logical: immortals could have access to information mortals could not. The most convincing point, albeit unstated, is the nature of Odysseus' reaction.

First of all, it is essential to note that Penélopê does not set a riddle, as so often happens in folk- and fairy-tales. Rather, she gives an order that only someone who knows the secret of Odysseus' bed would understand is impossible. Nor does Odysseus calmly respond, "Don't be silly, woman. What you say is impossible." His response is outrage and anger. Only the mortal Odysseus would react with such passion. And while it is not stated explicitly as a factor in Penélopê's reasoning, Homer certainly emphasizes the emotional aspect of Odysseus' outburst, both at the introduction to his speech (207) and with the first words of Penélopê's response—"do not rage at me, Odysseus" (236).

It is worth noting that this time Odysseus reacts with complete spontaneity and without guile—Penélopê's words have touched him to the quick—and that, correspondingly, Homer introduces this speech without any of the usual formulae referring to his prudence or craft (see Stanford 2.398–99 [on XXIII.182]). It is the humanity of the emotional reaction more than the information known which guarantees Odysseus' identity as Penélopê's husband. Moreover, only in the course of the outburst does it become clear to Odysseus that this is the token he will be able to use to convince Penélopê.

237 It is wise of Penélopê to say (actually, of Homer to show Penélopê's wisdom by having her say), "No one ever matched your caution" when she might more accurately say, "Consider how cautious I have been."

241–52 **I could not / welcome you with love on sight . . . :** In her defense, Penélopê very cleverly presents as counterexample the case of Helen, who welcomed the blandishments of Paris without considering the consequences. While the correspondences between the two situations aren't extremely close—to begin with, one would have thought that one of Paris' attractions is that he looked very unlike Helen's husband, Meneláos—it is an argument with poetic attractions. For according to Penélopê's reading, her restraint (unlike Helen's action) would metaphorically reverse the effect of the war Helen had sparked by running off with Paris, for Penélopê and Odysseus at least. Purely on the logical level, Penélopê emphasizes two aspects of Helen's actions: she would not have acted as she did had she known the outcome, and she was likely deceived by an immortal. (On Helen and Penélopê, see Introduction pp. lxi–lxiii, above.)

256 **Aktoris:** Not otherwise mentioned. If she were now dead, as seems likely, it would not have been possible for her to pass her knowledge to the "stranger." Some scholars have suggested that Aktoris is Eurýnomê, here referred to as "daughter of Aktor," but no one could infer this with confidence from the information in *The Odyssey.*

263–70 **a swimmer / spent in rough water . . . :** This simile is so apt for Odysseus, pursued by Poseidon and returned after such disastrous sea voyages. Indeed, its very language recalls Odysseus' struggle in Book V (405–88). But it is all the more surprising when the listener or reader of Homer's Greek is made to realize that the simile refers to Penélopê's emotions, not Odysseus'. Fitzgerald's English fits it more neatly with Odysseus' feelings (described in lines 259–61). The Greek, although it flirts with the more banal reading, is unambiguous [233–40]. "This poetic relocation of experiences like Odysseus' in Penelope's emotional life not only suggests an internalized version of the withdrawal and return plot that is basic to heroic narrative but also evokes the necessarily . . . notional kinship on which their marriage is based: Penélopê's ability to experience Odysseus' trials in her imagination is a sign of their *homophrosynê,* their 'likeness of mind' " (Murnaghan, 46).

272–77 It is frequently noted that a divine lengthening of the night also occurred when Zeus lay with Alkmênê to beget Heraklês. Less frequently noted is that this same story underlay Penélopê's suspicions that it was a god in disguise, and not Odysseus, who was appearing before her. Homer and his audience were clearly capable of keeping such models in the backs of their minds throughout a whole segment of narrative (see also 81–93, above).

333 **opening glad arms to one another:** Some of the most prominent Alexandrian critics regarded this verse [296] as the true "end" or "goal" of *The Odyssey,* by which they most likely meant the "climax" of the story—an opinion in which many modern critics follow them. It is less likely that they actually believed the poem ought to stop at this juncture. Both ancient and modern critics recognize a phase of "tying up the loose ends," although in the case of *The Odyssey,* careful reading convinces us that the "ends" are in no sense "loose" but have been carefully prepared.

337–38 Homer clearly enjoyed using different forms of the same verb (infinitive *terpein*) in successive lines [300, 301; also 308] to refer to the pleasures of lovemaking and of storytelling, respectively.

348–83 We now get a recapitulation and summary of Odysseus'
travels, this time in strict chronological order, without the com-
plex narrative displacement of *The Odyssey* itself, which sets Books
IX–XII as an inset narrative or flashback. This new narrative,
perhaps significantly a Homeric report of Odysseus' own narra-
tive to his wife, corrects (as it were) the many and ever-shifting
tales the "Kretan" told about "his" travels since he arrived in
Ithaka.

403 **scores I'll get on raids:** On the acceptability of such piracy,
see III.79–81, above.

408 **My noble father, for he missed me sorely:** Odysseus has
heard of the depths of his father's grief, both from the shade of
his dead mother (XI.210–19) and more recently from Eumaios
(XVI.161–68).

409–10 Odysseus is tactful: as lord of the house, it is his duty to give
orders, but he realizes that he is addressing a woman who has
managed things quite competently without him through twenty
trying years. He tries to be diplomatic, but see the following note.

414 This is the last we see of Penélopê, and although we learn of
no subsequent actions on her part, we certainly hear much of her
prior actions in the last book of the poem (XXIV.141–67, 187–
89, 218–23). Her last words turn out to have been "trials will end
in peace" (321), as fine and pious a wish as anyone could want.
Still, it is hard, from a modern perspective, not to register dismay
that, having had her moment in the sun, Penélopê is ordered to
retire to her quarters with her women and stay out of sight
(412–14). Would it be stretching too far to compare the late 1940s
and '50s, when those women who had served so well in the
factories of wartime economies were encouraged, in some cases
virtually ordered, to disappear into their homes and concern
themselves once more solely with domestic affairs and consump-
tion (perhaps a little charity work), so that the men returning from
the war could resume sole possession of paid labor outside the

home? I think not, so long as we remember the different historical contexts of both the poem before us and our own period.

421–22 **Athena,** having beautified Odysseus at lines 176–84, has been manipulating the progress of night and day since line 272, and Homer emphasizes her continued assistance in the final lines of the book. Her prominence at the close of Book XXIII prefigures her even more direct presence at the close of Book XXIV and the entire epic.

BOOK XXIV

Warriors, Farewell

1–230 Hermês, who guides the souls of the dead to the beyond, is performing his function for the suitors. In many ways this is a totally unexpected opening of this final book, yet upon reflection it is a satisfying novelty. While we left the suitors as a pile of corpses in the hall, we have also been alerted to the storm that is about to break when their relatives discover what has happened to them. So this scene, which presents their souls in Hades, does more than simply recall the presentation of the shades in Book XI. In that episode, Odysseus received important information and prophecies from his mother and Teirêsias, and he engaged in discussions with some of the heroes of *The Iliad*, which, if not strictly important for the plot of *The Odyssey*, serve as a commentary and counterpoint to the theme of return. The ghosts of the suitors, as they meet and interact with the ghosts we met in Book XI, confirm that Odysseus not only reached Ithaka but also bested the rivals who had been waiting for him there. All that remains is for him to neutralize the new enemies he has made on Ithaka by liquidating the suitors.

In ancient times, prominent critics already condemned this entire episode as a post-Homeric interpolation. This is not the place to consider or even list the range of their arguments, nor the support or dissent of more modern scholars. It is worth noting, however, that a number of the objections have to do with purported inconsistencies with *The Iliad,* which ancient and modern "analysts" (on whom, see Introduction, p. xlii) attribute to a poet other than the poet of *The Odyssey;* very few of the arguments mounted against Book XXIV are based on either the coherence or the logic of *The Odyssey* itself.

8 rock-hung chain: Of bats, that is.

16–111 The exchange between Akhilleus and Agamémnon provides the poet of *The Odyssey* an opportunity to revisit and recast, in a minor key, the quarrel between the two most important Greeks in *The Iliad.* This would certainly not be less attractive, and perhaps it would be even more attractive to a poet of *The Odyssey* who had himself not created *The Iliad,* but who certainly knew *The Iliad,* presumably having sung it countless times.

The very idea of the shades of the suitors in the presence of the shades of the great heroes of the Trojan War reminds us of what might be called the post-Iliadic theme of *The Odyssey:* these are the men who stayed behind, who did not go to Troy. It may be that in part they belonged to a later generation not old enough to go to the war, and that if they had had the chance they would have acted no less heroically than the Akhaians who went to Troy. But emotionally, this is no satisfying argument: until it has proved itself in war, no generation of men—I use "men" to mean "males"—feels that it has lived up to the veterans of the preceding war, and no veteran of any war feels that even the veterans of later wars, much less those who didn't serve, have provided an equivalent proof of their "manliness." Consider the continued importance of military service in the careers and campaigns of the men who run or are considered for the offices of president and vice-president, or the mileage the opposition makes if there is something to criticize about the service record of a candidate— or the president.

25–36 **My lord Atreidês . . . :** Akhilleus' speech to Agamémnon is clearly devised to raise the important thematic issues in *The Odyssey* and once again point to the fate of Agamémnon as the counterexample par excellence to the career of Odysseus.

30 **in the morning of your life:** This expression isn't particularly apt, and it becomes less so when at lines 32–36 Akhilleus says it would have been better had Agamémnon died at Troy, at an even earlier point than he did. The Greek here is "early" [28], and insofar as death is almost always "early" relative to one's hopes and expectations, we might think of it as meaning "untimely." Alternatively, we could see this as just one of the illogical juxtapositions that oral composition often leads to. Drama rather than logic (if the beyond is subject to logic) has already led the poet to present at this point what appears to be the first encounter of the souls of Agamémnon and Akhilleus, although both have been dead for some ten years.

35 **your son:** Orestês, once again Telémakhos' opposite in the scheme of counterexamples (see Introduction, and I.45–46, above).

38–111 **Fortunate hero . . . :** Almost all of Agamémnon's response (38–107) refers to the death and burial of Akhilleus, which, it is important to remember, occurred after the end of the Homeric *Iliad* and was not recounted there. Such stories circulated in Homer's time, even if the "cyclic epics" (which we know only from fragments and summaries) that recounted these episodes in full were written later. Only in the last four lines (108–11; three in Greek [95–97]) does Agamémnon refer to his fate at the hands of his wife and her usurping lover.

Taken together, Akhilleus' and Agamémnon's speeches describe the deaths and burial honors (or lack thereof) of two of the "best of the Akhaians," a category to which Odysseus belongs as well. Odysseus' death can be foretold but not narrated in *The Odyssey* as Homer has shaped it, and indeed, near the end of the preceding book (XXIII.314–17), Odysseus told Penélopê about the death Teirêsias prophesied for him (XI.148–51). In more ways than one, then, Book XXIV is about "ends," ends of lives as well as the end of a story. Perhaps we can see the stories of the death and burial of Akhilleus (told in great detail) and Agamémnon as in some way standing in for the unnarrated death of Odysseus. Fitzgerald seems to have intuited something like this when he gave Book XXIV the title "Warriors, Farewell." (However "un-Homeric" the titles may be, they can be appreciated as part of the understanding of a fine Homeric scholar.) Odysseus' death, readers of *The Odyssey* may surmise from indications in Books XI and XXIII, will be the best of all in Greek eyes: at home and in peace. (Later legend devised violent alternatives, a clear example of epic deflation: the greater the hero, the greater the fall. There have always been, and will always be, revisionists.)

52–104 The apparition of Thetis and the Nereids, the song of the Muses, the divine amphora and trophies—all this evokes, as does the entire underworld episode in Book XXIV, a number of aspects of the "fairy-tale" world in which Odysseus' own travels took place. Indeed, steady intercourse with the gods is one of the characteristics that marks the age of the heroes, Odysseus included. This human-divine interaction becomes less frequent thereafter, and such latecomers as the suitors have no share in it. The communion of heroes and gods is no better evidenced than by their common grief and communal mourning (72; in the Greek, gods and mortals are even on equal grammatical footing [*athanatoi te theoi thnêtoi t'anthrôpoi*, 64]).

68 **in nine immortal voices:** The Greek refers unambiguously to nine muses [60], which some critics take as a sign (in their eyes, a further sign) that the "second nekuia" did not belong to the original, authentic *Odyssey*. Elsewhere in the poem the Muse is singular (I.1, VIII.68, 79, 513, and 521). Nine as the canonical number of Muses is next mentioned by Hesiod (*Theogony*, 60, 77–79, 916–17, "next," that is, unless the *Theogony* predates this patch of *The Odyssey*). However, the Muses are frequently multiple already in *The Iliad*, which is certainly earlier.

74–78 Though a small detail, it is significant for the career of Odysseus that contrary to standard practice (see XI.83, XII.14–15), Akhilleus' battle gear was not burned with his body but made into a contest prize at his funeral games. In the contest for these arms Odysseus bested Aîas, earning him Aîas' literally undying anger (see XI.646–74). Akhilleus' arms were themselves "immortal," made for him at his mother's request by Hephaistos (see *Iliad* XVIII.369–617).

112 **Wayfinder:** Hermês (see 1–230, above).

119–27 It is a nice touch that Agamémnon addresses questions to the suitors (123–27 [109–13]) that Odysseus had addressed to Agamémnon (when Odysseus encountered him, much to his surprise, among the shades), with only minor variations (XI.462–69, esp. 465–69 [399–403]). The irony of the same questions being asked here of Odysseus' victims is telling. Certainty about Homer's intent is clouded, as it so often is, by the nature of formulaic language. On the one hand, in both places the likely causes of death for a warrior are molded into a typical pattern of a triple question. On the other hand, the author of *The Odyssey* does seem to be in control of formulae and typical scenes more often than not, and it is likely that this is the case here.

144 **ever bent on our defeat:** Homer's Amphímedon forcefully claims that Penélopê plotted for the suitors' death [127]. This may be an exaggeration, but Amphímedon, as victims often do after the fact, imagines and narrates a plot more organized and coherent than it really was. In what follows, note especially lines 188–90, where Amphímedon says that Odysseus "assigned his wife her part: next day / she brought his bow and iron axeheads out / to make a contest." This would be a natural inference, but we know very well that (at least in the text of *The Odyssey* that we have) this is not at all how it occurred (see XIX.660–73). Even more: Amphímedon's narrative presumes either that Penélopê knew the identity of the beggar from the outset (a major, even paranoid misreading) or that she learned it considerably earlier than she actually did.

145–67 **Here is one of her tricks . . . :** Different narrators' differing perspectives and situations account for the differences among the three accounts of the ruse of the shroud: II.96–118 (Antínoös), XIX.163–82 (Penélopê), and the present one (the ghost of Amphímedon). See also II.101ff., above.

170–80 Unless we invent an informant, this too must be pure inference. But the inferences are correct, with the possible exception of lines 176–77 [156–58] which suggest that Amphímedon believes that Eumaios too was already in on the secret of the beggar's identity when he led him to town to beg in the hall (in Book XVII). Actually, Eumaios learned the beggar's identity four books later (XXI.233–54).

183–90 **That night . . . :** Note, in addition to his mistaken assumptions that Penélopê knew the identity of the beggar and arranged the contest of the bow on Odysseus' command (see 144, above), Amphímedon's other inaccuracies. One is minor: "Zeus" did not give Odysseus the idea of moving the arms "that night"; rather, in his wisdom—whether divinely inspired or not—Odysseus instructed Telémakhos to prepare for this when they were still in Eumaios' hut (XVI.333–51). The second is of fairly major proportions: the storeroom was not locked (see XXII.152–220). We can see Amphímedon's self-serving purpose in spreading this untruth: it is hardly to his or any of his fellow suitors' credit to admit that they were unable to exploit this potentially fatal oversight on Telémakhos' part.

194 **Only Telémakhos:** Not entirely true, since Penélopê also urged that the beggar be given the bow (XXI.349–86, esp. 379).

Given his eagerness above to make Penélopê part of the plot, it is somewhat odd that he obscures her role here. Perhaps while he can stomach giving a woman a role of co-conspirator who follows out her husband's commands or who devises her own acts of deception (the trick of the shroud, described at 145–67, above), he would prefer not to memorialize a scene in which she boldly rebuffed the suitors in the hall.

202–7 Amphímedon's summary of Book XXII is also self-serving. He describes a monumentally heroic Odysseus aided only by "some god" (204), who slaughtered suitors by the dozen. We know that although Athena was of great help in encouraging Odysseus, four fighters, managed skillfully by the master strategist Odysseus, step by step reduced the number of their opponents, who had some arms and acquired a few more during the course of the battle. Of course, Amphímedon suppresses this; he never reveals the great number of suitors who were present.

209–13 **Now in Odysseus' hall . . . :** Reference to the unburied bodies and the suitors' uninformed kin is a reminder in the midst of this episode of the danger and difficulty Odysseus has to resolve before the epic can be concluded.

216–28 **O fortunate Odysseus . . . :** Amphímedon's narrative had been calculated to win sympathy, never more so than at its conclusion, and he certainly won't have expected a response like Agamémnon's. To call it unsympathetic would be an understatement. Of course it is a nice touch that the ghost of Agamémnon not only gives the final version of the frequent comparison between Klytaimnéstra and Penélopê but in so doing also pronounces the final commendation of Penélopê.

218–20 **The girl you brought home . . . :** Fitzgerald's blended translation [of 193–96a] ascribes Penélopê's virtue both to her and to Odysseus' credit (to him for bringing home so "valiant" a wife). This is true to the spirit of the Greek, even if scholars still argue whether the "virtue" of the first line [*aretê*, 193] belongs to

Penélopê or Odysseus, or even both. Fitzgerald's translation is a diplomatic solution of the controversy.

219 Homer has Agamémnon give Odysseus the epithet *kouridios* [*kouridiou,* 196], which may be translated "wedded." He uses the word again at line 226, which, if the Greek were translated literally, would involve the seemingly redundant "her wedded husband" [200]. *Kouridios* suggests all the aspects of one's life which are consequences of being mated to a partner. The state of being in a good partnership with his wife is as essential to Odysseus' character as it is to the triumphant story of *The Odyssey*. And it is essential to the tragic story of Agamémnon that he is the kind of man who would have a Klytaimnéstra as his wife (which I've phrased in this way to suggest that he's as responsible as she).

221–22 **The very gods themselves will sing her story . . . :** Might Homer expect his listeners to think of his own poem, sung by the Muse to him (I.1)? Though oblique—because *The Odyssey* is about much more than Penélopê—it seems very possible, if not inevitable.

226–28 Without the least inkling of the insights of modern feminist theory, Homer captures with unblinking clarity the illogic of the misogynistic perspective: even though Agamémnon has said that Penélopê and Klytaimnéstra will both be the subjects of songs (in other words, they are the archetypes for "good" and "bad" women), for him it is the bad woman who represents the true essence of womanhood, the essence of "even the best."

Does Homer him- or herself undermine this position by (1) presenting it so blatantly in the mouth of one of the heroes who falls far short of the Odyssean ideal and (2) even more subtly, having Agamémnon, in defiance of his own logic, attribute the song about Penélopê to the gods while making no such claim for the song about Klytaimnéstra? (In this context it is worth noting that "forever" (227) is an interpolation on the translator's part of which the Greek is innocent [201]). Not without cause have some

wanted to argue that the poet of *The Odyssey* was a woman, as
Samuel Butler did in *The Authoress of the Odyssey* (1897). While his
book has long been considered a quaint curiosity by most Hom-
erists, some of the best recent work is finding new ways to talk
about female perspectives on and in *The Odyssey*.

236 **Sikel:** See note XX.427, above, and 338, below.

246 Penélopê had sent her "orchard keeper" Dólios to inform
Laërtês of the suitors' plot to assassinate Telémakhos (IV.786–89;
see lines 430–54, below, for further details about Dólios).

250–56 The picture of Laërtês is another powerful example of
what Homer can achieve through the quiet accumulation of
detail: he is alone, concentrating on performing a simple task,
wearing shabby and patched clothes. His distance from the he-
roic is marked by the word "leggings" (253): Homer uses no term
specific to the farm but the very word employed frequently in *The
Iliad* for warriors' "greaves" or "shin guards" [*knêmidas*, 229], an
element of their armor. These leather leggings are Laërtês' armor
now in the old man's battle for survival and dignity. Without
launching into an epic simile, which could only end in bathos
here, Homer sets up an entire metaphoric field with one old word
in a new context.

259–65 Why does Odysseus feel he needs to "test" his father? Why
subject him to "sharp words" or taunts? Is he joking with his
father? It seems unnecessarily cruel. There appears to be no
satisfactory answer. Perhaps that is the point: even weeping at the
sight of Laërtês, Odysseus cannot stop, cannot escape being
Odysseus. Our actions appear as the habits and essential charac-
ter traits they are, especially when they serve no real function:
Odysseus is at bottom always tricky, he can never let well enough
alone, never just trust, never just act on his emotions, unless he
is emboldened (as when he boasted over his escape from the
Kyklops) or angry (as in Book XXIII). Of course it is possible that
even while admitting this, Homer's audience could choose to
enjoy this trick on Laërtês rather than overidentify with and

indulge their sympathy for the old man. The irony and mockery of Odysseus' speech is gentle and loving, and listeners and readers can take comfort in knowing that the poet can produce an unadulterated "happy ending" within a few lines.

Heubeck, who would call the words "calculated" rather than sharp describes the entire anonymous presentation Odysseus makes (270–306) thus: "by posing questions, awaking memories, and stirring long-suppressed feelings, Odysseus forces his father . . . [first] to answer, . . . [then] to ask questions . . . , and so, step by step, to emerge from his self-inflicted isolation and apathy" (HWH 3.390 [on XXIV.244–79]; see also 396–97 [on XXIV.315–17]). Murnaghan offers an explanation which covers structural as well as therapeutic motifs. While too subtle to be summarized in a few words (see Murnaghan 26–34 for the full argument), it runs along these lines: "the imbalance in their [Odysseus' and Laërtês'] relationship" is emphasized both by "the extremity of Laërtês' destitution, which is expressed in the transfer of the motifs of disguise [patches and rags] to him, and [by] the placement of the episode late in the narrative, which gives it a belated and tacked-on quality. . . . [Only] late in the story when his return is virtually complete . . . is Odysseus' presence sufficiently powerful to bring Laërtes out of the decline that has been his response to the suitors' presence" (31).

278–85 **your master:** As part of his pose, Odysseus pretends to take Laërtês for a slave (note esp. 285). Assuming this, he indulges in the further irony of saying that this slave looks more like a king.

294–98 **I entertained the men . . . :** Odysseus as an anonymous stranger pretends to Laërtês to have hosted his son.

316 Laërtês does not make a big production about revealing that he is Odysseus' father. He clearly has no interest in excusing his shabby appearance or even describing his personal distress, as the shade of his wife and Eumaios had.

333–45 In response to the formulaic questions (328–31), Odysseus tells yet another tale of origins. This final one is not the nth variant on the Kretan story but a completely new fib. The names are all significant, which explains Fitzgerald's choice of interpretive translation over transliteration. There is particular poignance in Odysseus, once again as "stranger," telling his own grief-stricken father that he is the only son of a king named "Allwoes." (In Greek, there are actually three generations in this fictitious genealogy, which in literal translation would run something like "I am the son of Unstinting, himself the son of King Allwoes" [305]; in rendering it into English, Fitzgerald wisely prunes the family tree.)

338 **Sikania:** The place sounds temptingly close to Sicily, and some ancient accounts speak of both Sikans and Sikels living on that island.

346–49 Laërtês' grief is too great for words, and he reacts precisely as Akhilleus does when he learns of the death of Patróklos [315–317a are identical to *Iliad* XVIII.22–24a].

The mourning and displays of grief described of Biblical characters is comparably extravagant. For example, Jacob rends his clothes and dons sackcloth at the (false) report of his son Joseph's death (Gen. 37.34; recall the comparison of Odysseus to Joseph at XIV.320–23, above). Mordecai does the same upon hearing news of the Persian king's edict to destroy all the Jews (Esther 4.1), and upon hearing a prophecy against his city, the King of Nineveh fasts, puts on sackcloth, and sits in ashes (Jonah 3.6; reinforced by Matthew 11.21, "sackcloth and ashes" became proverbial in English). David rends his garments, fasts, and laments the deaths of Saul and Jonathan (2 Samuel 1.11ff.), and puts on sackcloth and laments the death of Abner (2 Samuel 3.31ff.). This is another instance in which the Homeric world takes its place alongside the other cultures of the ancient Near East.

361–63 Like Penélopê, Laërtês is cautious not to let emotions cloud his prudence. He too demands a sign.

365–79 The wound is exhibited again as a sign. Likewise, Eurýkleia had hoped to persuade Penélopê by mention of the scar (XXIII.81–85). As he had to do with Penélopê, so Odysseus here offers further proof: that he possesses some bit of detailed knowledge that only he and Laërtês share.

388–90 **But now the fear is in me . . . :** Laërtês demonstrates that he has lost nothing of his wits, thinking immediately of the problem facing Odysseus.

430–54 Odysseus' shifting tone indicates the possibilities of stickiness in dealing with Dólios—first honeyed words ("hit an easy tone," 432) then abruptness ("Odysseus gruffly said," 446–48). By means of his verbal craft he manages to avoid revealing what has actually gone on in the hall any earlier than he has to. All of this makes sense if this Dólios is the same as the father of Melánthios and Melántho (see XVII.270 and XVIII.398), both of whom Odysseus knows have been executed along with the suitors. As noted on line 246, above, Penélopê had sent Dólios the orchard keeper to Laërtês in Book IV. Stanford speculates that "after he had come to Laertes' farm . . . and had seen the old king's pitiful condition, [he] may well have summoned his less depraved sons and stayed to help the old man. With regard to Melanthius and Melanthô, there is no reason why in life or in letters a good father should not have wicked children" (2.420 [on XXIV.222]). If Laërtês' companion Dólios has lost two children in the slaughter, however depraved they may have been, it only increases the pathos of the pairing of these two old men, one a slave, the other a king almost sunk as low as a slave, and their children. Whether knowing their fate or ignorant of it, Dólios and his sons aid Odysseus and Laërtês when the matter comes to arms (552–53).

462–539 In its formal aspects, the assembly of the grieving kin mirrors the assembly Telémakhos summoned in Book II (7–272), but in tone and intent it resembles the slightly more relaxed plotting sessions of the suitors themselves (IV.706–22 and XVI.411–95). To complete the ring, just as the poem had opened with a council of the gods (Book I) followed by a lengthy council of Ithakans (Book II), in the final sections of Book XXIV we have a briefer council of Ithakans (462–520) followed by an abbreviated council of the gods (521–39). Note the reverse or chiastic order, an element of proper rings (ab . . . b'a').

464–82 **Eupeithês**, Antínoös' father, takes as prominent a role in this assembly as his son was wont to in the suitors' meetings. At lines 474–75 we have a good measure of the man's cowardice: projecting onto Odysseus what he (or his son) would have done in a comparable situation, he imagines that Odysseus is on the verge of flight.

488–96 **Medôn's** brief but accurate testimony before the suitors' kin not only counters Eupeithês' speech but mirrors and corrects the lengthier, misleadingly tendentious narrative of Amphímedon (136–213).

498–510 **Halithérsês** had indeed interpreted an omen for the suitors during the first Ithakan assembly, in which he prophesied Odysseus' return (II.166–86).

522–39 Only the gods, and in particular Zeus by his declaration of his intent to "blot out the memory / of sons and brothers slain" (536–37), can put an end to what would otherwise be an ongoing series of acts of vengeance and retribution. Heubeck sees in Zeus' settlement "nothing less than the abolition of the law of the blood-feud, which had hitherto prevailed without qualification; in its place is established a new political order based on justice and law, and validated by the gods, in which a just and benevolent king ensures wealth and freedom" (HWH 3.412 [on XXIV.482–85]). "Is established" as an ideal, that is, in and by this poem.

570–85 It is wonderfully satisfying in this final book, the first in which we meet Laërtês face-to-face, for Athena to encourage and empower him to strike the first blow, a successful one at that. *The Odyssey* is an epic of maturity, as I've mentioned (see on XIX.122–38, above), and, even if only for a moment, Grandpa regains his former glory. Just as Odysseus had killed Antínoös first of all the suitors (XXII.8–21), Antínoös' father, Eupeithês, is the first to die in this skirmish by the spear of the father of his son's executioner. Such a parallel is no accident. Homer reminded his listeners that Antínoös was the first to die when his father rose to speak (466).

600–609 Odysseus is in no way frightened or abashed at Athena's appearance and intervention. Indeed, accustomed to having her fight as his ally, he is ready to press the advantage. Only Zeus' bolt and his will as interpreted by Athena stay Odysseus.

614 **though she still kept the form and voice of Mentor:** The last line [548] repeats line 558 [503]. It seems an odd and unimportant detail. Perhaps we shouldn't put too much weight on final things. Still, by the repetition of this formulaic verse in this spot, the last line of the poem refers to divine ventriloquism, and the last word in the Greek turns out to be "voice" [*audên*]. Athena appears in the guise and speaks in the voice of Mentor, who is an older man, not, we might imagine, unlike the bard before his audience.

WHO'S WHO IN THE ODYSSEY

BIBLIOGRAPHY: SUGGESTIONS FOR FURTHER READING

ACKNOWLEDGMENTS

Who's Who in
The Odyssey

The following list identifies virtually all of the people and places in Fitzgerald's *Odyssey*. Names of figures who appear only once and have no significant connections with important characters are generally omitted (e.g., Laerkês, the Pylian goldsmith of III.460, or Alektor, father of Megápenthês' bride). I have also omitted all of the invented names whose meanings would have been clear to Homer's original audience and which Fitzgerald quite properly translates, names like "Tipmast," "Tiderace," "Hullman," "Sternman." The largest number of these names are those of Phaiákian sailors (VIII.118ff., whence the above examples), but also of this type are "King Allwoes," "Quarrelman," and the place-name "Rover's Passage" (XXIV.334–35). The amount of detail is not necessarily indicative of the importance of the character or place; for example, for the central characters of the epic (e.g., Odysseus, Penélopê, Telémakhos) I give little more than basic genealogical information. I have striven to provide what I thought important or potentially interesting for readers of *The Odyssey* and what would best complement the information in the preceding commentary. Thus I often provide geographical identifications not made in the commentary.

I follow the translator's spelling throughout.[1] In cases where a cross reference would be valuable, I use the abbreviation "q.v.," Latin for "which see." Also, in the few cases where more than one character has the same name, I have distinguished them by number (1), (2).

Readers should keep in mind that stories about Greek gods and heroes developed over time and varied widely from place to place. Poets and mythographers attempted to adjudicate between or to harmonize inconsistent versions, the former often inventing new stories in the process, the latter aiming, considerably later, at pan-Hellenic systematization. No universally recognized canon of myth was ever established, and hence there is no "right" version of any myth. Even if such a consensus had emerged, it would be anachronistic to apply it to Homer. Hence my identifications and mythological explanations refer to the imaginary universe of *The Odyssey* and *The Iliad*. Thus Oidipous' mother is called Epikastê, not Jocasta (as in the Sophoclean tragedy), and Elektra is not listed as one of Agamémnon's daughters. Exceptions are clearly noted. For example, the story of Tithonos as the lover of Dawn who attained immortality without everlasting youth, is identified as dating only from the Homeric (i.e., post-Homeric) *Hymn to Aphrodite*.

---

[1]The translator's spellings are meant as a guide to readers' pronunciation, not as consistent transliterations. For example, Fitzgerald writes "Kikonês" to indicate that the word should be pronounced as a three- (i.e., Ki-kō-nes) rather than a two-syllable word (Ki-kōnz), as English speakers might otherwise have done. Likewise, "Gigantês," "Kyklopês," and "Laistrygonês." A strict system of transliteration would have demanded that he represent the final vowel of all three words as an "e," since in Greek it is a short "e" [*epsilon*], not a long "e" [*êta*].

This of course means only that no earlier version is extant: Homer's silence does not prove that the story was not already in circulation and known to his audience.

Adrastê: female attendant of Helen.

Agamémnon: son of Atreus, king of Mykênai, leader of the Akhaians in *The Iliad;* husband of Klytaimnéstra, whose lover Aigísthos (Agamémnon's own first cousin) murders him; father of Khrysothemis, Laodikê, Iphianassa (later versions call her Iphigenia), and Orestês, who avenges his father's murder.

Ageláos: suitor, son of Damástor.

Aiaia: Kirkê's island, known in the stories about Jason and the Argonauts as Aia.

Aíakos: son of Zeus and Aigina, grandfather of Akhilleus. See also Myrmidons. (Fitzgerald once spells it "Aíakhos.")

Aias and Aîas: (1) Aias son of Oïleus and impious ravisher of the Trojan princess Kassandra: his actions brought the wrath of the gods, and of Athena in particular, on the victorious Greek army at Troy as it was about to embark on its way home. (2) Aîas, son of Télamon and one of the greatest Greek warriors at Troy; he contended with Odysseus for the right to wear the arms of the slain Akhilleus, lost the debate, went mad, and committed suicide. (On both Aiases, see note on IV.533–34.)

Aiêtês: son of Hêlios and Persê, brother of Kirkê. (Though his role as Medea's father and opponent of Jason is now extant only in later literature, it may well have been known to the first audience of *The Odyssey;* compare "baleful Aiêtês" in X.151 [139]. It is clear that versions of Jason's journey in the *Argo* predate *The Odyssey;* on this, see further under Artakía, below.)

Aigai: locale closely associated with Poseidon. Its exact geographical site, even in Homer's mind, is difficult to determine: in Akhaia or on (or near) Euboia are possibilities.

Aigísthos: son of Thyestês, nephew of Atreus, first cousin of Agamémnon; lover of Klytaimnéstra, usurper and then murderer of Agamémnon, murdered by Orestês.

Aigýptios: Ithakan elder.

Aigýptos: Egypt or the Nile. See note on IV.511.

Aiolos: lord of the winds, ruler of the floating island Aiolia; as son of Hippotês, his patronymic is Hippotadês.

Aison: king of Iolkos, son of Krêtheus and Tyro, father of Jason.

Aithôn: the name Odysseus gives himself when speaking to Penélopê and claiming to be a Kretan prince. "Aithôn" claims to be the younger brother of Idómeneus and the grandson of Minos. See note on XIX.195–239.

Akastos: king of Doulíkhion, island near Ithaka.

Akhaians: most common Homeric name for the Greeks.

Akhilleus: son of Pêleus and Thetis, hero of *The Iliad*, the greatest Greek warrior, slayer of Hektor but himself victim of Paris (aided by Apollo). His ghost appears in both underworld scenes in *The Odyssey* (Books XI and XXIV).

Akroneus: a Phaiákian.

Aktoris: a slave of Penélopê, "daughter of Aktor" possibly Eurýnomê. See note on XXIII.256.

Alkandrê: wife of Pólybos 1, host of Meneláos and Helen in Egyptian Thebes, she gave Helen precious gifts.

Álkimos: father of Mentor.

Alkínoös: king of the Phaiákians, grandson of Poseidon, brother of Rhêxênor, father of Nausikaa by Arêtê, his wife.

Alkippê: female attendant of Helen.

Alkmáon: son of Amphiaraos and Erίphylê, brother to Amphílokhos.

Alkmênê: wife of Amphitrion; deceived by Zeus, disguised as Amphitrion, she conceived Heraklês; her shade appeared to Odysseus.

Alpheios: river god, named after a river in Arkadia and Elis near Olympia, father of Ortílokhos, grandfather of Dióklês.

Ámnisos: port-city in Krete near Knossos and the location of the holy cave of Eileithuía, where Odysseus, bound for Troy, dropped anchor.

Amphialos: a Phaiákian.

Amphiaraos: seer of Argos, son of Oikleiês, grandson of Antíphatês; through the treachery of his wife, Erίphylê, he was fatally involved in the campaign against Thebes ("Seven Against Thebes").

Amphílokhos: seer of Argos, son of Amphiaraos and Erίphylê, brother of Alkmáon.

Amphímedon: suitor, slain by Telémakhos, but not before wounding Telémakhos slightly.

Amphínomos: suitor from Doulíkhion, son of Nísos, slain by Telémakhos.

Amphion: (1) son of Zeus and Antiopê, husband of Niobe; with his brother Zêthos he built the walls of Thebes; (2) king of Orkhómenos in Boiotia, son of Iasos, father of Khloris.

Amphithéa: wife of Autólykos, maternal grandmother of Odysseus.

Amphitrion: king of Tiryns, husband of Alkmênê; Zeus, disguised as Amphitrion, deceived Alkmênê and engendered Heraklês, making Amphitrion Heraklês' mortal or foster-father. (Note: "Amphitryon" would be a preferable transliteration, and elsewhere Fitzgerald reproduces Greek upsilon with "y"; however, on the sonic basis of his spellings, see the note to this section.)

Amphitritê: sea goddess.

Amytháon: son of Krêtheus and Tyro, expert charioteer.

Anabesineus: a Phaiákian.

Andraimon: king of the Aetolians in Kalydon, father of Thoas.

Ankhíalos: father of Mentês of Taphos.

Antikleía: daughter of the archthief Autólykos, wife of Laërtês, mother of Odysseus and Ktimenê; her shade appears and speaks to Odysseus in Book XI.

Antiklos: Greek warrior at Troy and one of those enclosed in the wooden horse; hearing Helen imitating the voices of the wives of Greek heroes, he was on the verge of responding when Odysseus stifled him.

Antílokhos: son of Nestor, killed in the Trojan War by Memnon.

Antínoös: leader of the suitors, son of Eupeithês, he is the victim of Odysseus' first arrow.

Antiopê: daughter of Ásopos, mother of Amphion and Zêthos by Zeus; her shade appears to Odysseus.

Antíphatês: (1) king of the man-eating Laistrygonês, he drank the blood of strangers visiting his land; (2) Greek commander, son of Melampous, brother of Mantios, father of Oikleiês, grandfather of Amphiaraos.

Ántiphos: (1) Ithakan spearman, son of Aigýptios, comrade of

Odysseus, the last man eaten by Kyklops; (2) friend of Odysseus (clearly distinct from the first Ántiphos, since this one is still alive for Telémakhos to speak to in Book XVII).

Aphroditê: Olympian goddess, particularly of love in its erotic manifestations, daughter of Zeus and Dione, wife of Hephaistos, paramour of Arês.

Apollo: Olympian god, son of Zeus and Lêto, brother of Artemis; god of prophecy and music (he himself played the lyre); the epithet "far-darter" refers to the fact that he is a keen archer, whose arrows bring swift and painless death; the epithet "Phoibos" may refer to his brilliance, although a strong association with the sun seems not to have been part of his original nature (which is exceedingly complex).

Arês: an Olympian god, son of Zeus and Hêra, god of war, bloody and violent; adulterous lover of Aphroditê.

Arêtê: queen of Phaiákia, wife of Alkínoös, mother of Nausikaa, only daughter of Rhêxênor.

Arethousa: spring on Ithaka.

Arêtós: one of Nestor's sons.

Argo: ship of the Argonauts.

Argos: (1) important city in the eastern Peloponnese, often used to denote the realm of Agamémnon, who actually ruled in Mykênai, and sometimes even the entire Peloponnese (q.v.); (2) Pelasgian Argos: Akhilleus' domain; (3) Odysseus' dog, left behind in Ithaka, who does not die before he sees his master return home; (4) monster slain by Hermês, not mentioned directly in Homer unless his epithet "Argeiphontês" refers to the deed; see further under Hermês, below.

Ariadnê: Kretan princess, daughter of Minos and Pasiphaae; helped Theseus escape the Labyrinth; Theseus took her with him, but she was killed by Artemis on the island of Dia; her shade appears to Odysseus.

Arkesilaos: son of Lyeus, leader of the Boeotians.

Arkeíos: son of Zeus, father of Laërtês, grandfather of Odysseus; hence "Arkeísiadês" as the patronymic of Laërtês.

Arnaios, nicknamed "Iros": a public tramp and beggar in Ithaka, bested by Odysseus in a wrestling match.

Artakía: spring in the land of the Laistrygonês. Known also from the *Argonautica*, a fact which, along with other evidence, has lead scholars to argue that the Laistrygonian episode was transferred by the poet of *The Odyssey* to Odysseus' story from the cycle of tales about Jason.

Artemis: Olympian god, daughter of Zeus and Lêto, sister of Apollo, famed for the hunt and archery.

Arubas Pasha: father of a Phoinikian woman who was captured by Taphian pirates and sold as a slave to the father of the then still-free Eumaios.

Ásopos: father of Antiopê, grandfather of Amphion and Zêthos.

Athena: Olympian god, daughter of Zeus, greatest champion of Odysseus.

Atlas: titan who holds up pillars of heaven, Kalypso's father.

Atreus: son of Pelops and Hippodamia, brother of Thyestês, father of Agamémnon and Meneláos, the two brothers who are hence known as the Atreidai.

Attika: region of mainland Greece where Athens is located.

Autólykos: father of Antikleía, grandfather of Odysseus; thief and archtrickster under Hermês' protection (later tradition makes

Autólykos Hermês' son); the name means "the wolf himself." See also under Sísyphos, below.

Autonoë: female attendant of Penélopê.

Boiotia: large state on the mainland of Greece, north of Attika and the Gulf of Corinth, to its west lay Phokis, to its east the strait separating Euboia from the mainland.

Cape Malea: see Malea.

Damástor: father of Ageláos, who was one of the suitors.

Danaans: along with Akhaians and Argives, a third general name Homer applies to the Greeks, especially the host assembled at Troy. Although there may have been real tribal differences among them at an earlier stage, and although later commentators invented differences, Homer uses them without any apparent distinction.

Dawn: goddess; her Greek name is Eos; she precedes Hêlios' chariot as the sun god traverses the heavens. In *The Odyssey*, she is presented as having a lusty appetite for mortal males, e.g., Tithonos (who became her spouse), Orion, and Kleitos, qq. vv.

Deïphobos: prince of Troy, son of Priam and Hekabê; after the death of Paris, Helen lived with him. In the sack of Troy, he was killed by Meneláos.

Delos: Aegean island, also known as Ortýgia, q.v.; birthplace of Apollo and Artemis, for further on which see under Lêto.

Dêmêtêr: Olympian goddess, "earth mother," mother of Perséphonê; because she made love with the mortal Iasion, Zeus killed him.

Demódokos: blind Phaiákian minstrel.

Demoptólemos: suitor, killed by Odysseus.

Deukálion: son of Minos, father of Idómeneus and "Aithôn."

Dia: Aegean island where Theseus abandoned Ariadnê and Artemis slew her. The name applied to several islands in antiquity. The most likely candidate for the original Dia is a small island just off the north coast of Krete (Sandia today), though it was soon identified with the more important Naxos, the largest of the Kyklades.

Dióklês: son of Ortílokhos, q.v., and father of two sons, another Ortílokhos and Krethon, both of whom died at Aeneas' hand in *The Iliad* (V.541). He lived at Phêrai, where he gave hospitality to Telémakhos and Peisístratos both on their way from Pylos to Sparta and on the return trip.

Diomêdês: Greek, captain of some of the ships sailing home from Troy, he made land at Argos.

Dmêtor: a name invented by Odysseus in one of his Kretan tales for a traveler, son of Iasos; the name means "Tamer."

Dodona: oracle of Zeus in northwestern Greece.

Dólios: (1) father of the nasty Ithakan goatherd Melánthios and the nasty maidservant Melántho; (2) slave and companion of Laërtês. The two Dólios' are likely one and the same person (see note on XXIV.430–54).

Dorians: in Homer, listed as one of the races inhabiting Krete. They were a Greek-speaking people who invaded the Mycenaean world from the north (c. 1150–1000 B.C.E.), occupying most of the Peloponnese and some Aegean islands.

Doulíkhion: island near Ithaka. This is clear in Homer's conception, but its geographical identity has been controversial since antiquity. It may well be Leukas, a Greek island or peninsula in the Ionian Sea to the northeast of Ithaka. Leukas is separated from the mainland by a shallow lagoon and connected to it by so narrow a strip of land (a feature we still call by a word derived from the Greek, "isthmus") that it is often reckoned a true island ("peninsula" deriving after all from the Latin for "almost island"). Ancient tradition has it that it was unambiguously a peninsula until Corinthian settlers dug a canal across the isthmus.

Dymas: Phaiákian shipman, in the shape of whose daughter Athena appears to Nausikaa at night.

Eidothea: daughter of Proteus, she gives the advice to Meneláos that is necessary for him to force her father to answer the Greek's questions.

Eileithuía: goddess of childbirth; the "Kretan," speaking to Penélopê, claims that Odysseus, bound for Troy, dropped anchor in a cave holy to her.

Ekhenêos: eldest of the Phaiákians, he speaks first in Alkínoös' hall after Odysseus has made his supplication to Arêtê.

Ekhéphron: one of Nestor's sons.

Ékhetos: fierce king of Epeíros, he flays all strangers who come to his kingdom alive.

Élatos: suitor, killed by the swineherd.

Elis: coastal region in the northwestern Peloponnesos rich in pasture, where Ithakans such as Noêmon kept horses.

Elpênor: Ithakan, companion of Odysseus, who dies by falling from the roof of Kirkê's house; unnoticed, he receives no burial rites; his shade appears to Odysseus.

Elysion: location in, or aspect of, the world of the dead; it was conceived as a pleasant meadow (see also note on IV.599ff.).

Enipeus: river in Thessaly or the northern Peloponnesos; equally, the river god, beloved of Tyro.

Epeioi: inhabitants of Elis.

Epeios: builder of the wooden horse.

Epeiros: northwestern region of mainland Greece, with the Ionian Sea on its west and Macedonia and Thessaly to the east. See also Thesprótia, below.

Ephialtês: giant, son of Iphimedeia and Poseidon; with his brother, Otos, he constituted a threat to the Olympian gods, so while still young, he was slain by Apollo.

Ephyra: site of indeterminate location (some scholars claim the Ephyra in Thesprótia is meant, others, an Ephyra in northern Elis); all that can be said with certainty is that it was known as a source of poisonous plants. Odysseus once stopped here.

Epikastê: mother of Oidipous, whom she unwittingly married; her shade appeared to Odysseus. Later tradition knows her as Jocasta.

Érebos: a name for Hades or a particularly dark place within Hades.

Erekhtheus: legendary hero and early king of Athens, son of the earth and foster son of Athena.

Eríphylê: treacherous wife of Amphiaraos, who betrayed her lord for gold; her shade appeared to Odysseus.

Erymanthos: large mountainous massif in the northern Peloponnese, one of Artemis' favorite hunting grounds.

Eteóneus: companion in arms to Meneláos.

Euboia: longish island off the east coast of Greece, separated from mainland Greece by a narrow strait.

Eumaios: born free but captured by slave traders, raised by Odysseus' family, now Odysseus' loyal swineherd, who hosts the disguised Odysseus on his first night back in Ithaka; one of the four who slay the suitors.

Eupeithês: father of Antínoös; mustered others to avenge the death of his son and all the suitors.

Eurýadês: suitor, killed by Telémakhos.

Eurýbâtes: according to the "Kretan," Odysseus' herald (see also note on XIX.290–91).

Eurýdamas: suitor, struck down by Odysseus.

Eurydíkê: wife of Nestor, eldest daughter of Klyménos.

Eurýkleia: daughter of Ops, granddaughter of Peisênor 2; while still a girl purchased by Laërtês, who kept her as a wife but never touched her; nurse to Odysseus and later Telémakhos. It is she who gives the "Kretan" a footbath and recognizes Odysseus by the scar on his thigh. As ordered, and on pain of death, she keeps the news to herself.

Eurýlokhos: relative of Odysseus, he stands out among Odysseus' companions through his important role in several episodes (the approach to Kirkê's house, the sacrifices before the first nekuia, the safe passage by the Sêirênes, and the slaughter of Hêlios' cattle). See also note on XII.357.

Eurýmakhos: suitor, son of Pólybos 3.

Eurymedon: father of Periboia 1, grandfather of Nausíthoös, king of the Gigantês.

Eurymedousa: Nausikaa's nurse.

Eurymos: one of the Kyklopês, father of Télemos.

Eurýnomê: housekeeper of Penélopê.

Eurýnomos: a suitor, son of Ántiphos.

Eurýpulos: son of Télephos, Keteian (q.v.) ally of the Trojans, killed by Neoptólemos.

Eurýtion: Thessalian centaur who, wine-crazed, initiated the rape and battle in Peiríthoös' hall among the Lapíthai.

Eurytos: father of Íphitos of Oikhalía; vied with the gods in bowmanship but was killed by Apollo.

Gaia: the goddess Earth.

Gerênia: Spartan locale associated with Nestor (although the connection is probably bogus, Nestor's epithet "Gerênios" originally having nothing to do with Gerênia).

Gigantês: giants, unsuccessful rebels against the Olympian gods.

Gortyn: Kretan city, about ten miles inland from the southern coast.

Gyrai: rocky outcropping in the Aegean Sea near Naxos, on which Aias, son of Oileus (see Aias 1, above), was shipwrecked, while Poseidon made it a safe haven for Agamémnon.

Halios: Phaiákian prince, one of the sons of Alkínoös and Arêtê.

Halithérsês: son of Mastor (hence the patronymic Mastóridês), soothsayer, friend of the house of Odysseus.

Hêbê: daughter of Zeus and Hêra, goddess of youth; Odysseus sees her with Heraklês' phantom in the underworld.

Hektor: Trojan prince, son of Priam, greatest of Trojan warriors; as *The Iliad* reports, after slaying Akhilleus' friend Patróklos, he is killed by Akhilleus, who drags his body around the citadel. In the final book of *The Iliad*, Priam comes to Akhilleus to ransom his corpse.

Helen: daughter of Lêda and Zeus or Tyndareus (the latter is her human foster-father if not her real father), wife of Meneláos, mother of Hermionê; as the most beautiful woman, she is Aphroditê's gift to Paris of Troy, whence the Trojan War.

Hêlios: the sun as divine being, son of Hyperion, consort of the Oceanid Persê, who bore him Aiêtês and Kirkê; owner of sacred cattle which he grazes on the island Thrinákia, some of which Odysseus' companions, in contravention of their captain's strictest orders, slay and eat.

Hellas: from the time of Hesiod, immediately after Homer, the name for all of Greece (as it is in modern Greek). In *The Odyssey* it appears most frequently paired with "the Argive midlands" (e.g., I.395, IV.777, 869, XV.106), so that in these instances Hellas would seem to refer to central Greece. The pairing "Hellas and Phthia" appears frequently in *The Iliad* to denote the kingdom of Pêleus, Akhilleus' father, and so once in *The Odyssey* (XI.587, where in fact it is the shade of Akhilleus speaking about his father).

Hephaistos: son of Zeus and Hêra, divine smith, husband of Aphroditê, cuckolded by Arês—but he gets his revenge.

Hêra: Olympian goddess, daughter of Kronos, at once Zeus' sister and consort; implacable enemy of the Trojans and supporter of the besieging Akhaians, she saved Agamémnon from the storm on the ocean which ravaged Aias.

Heraklês: hero, son of Zeus and Alkmênê, foster-son of Amphitrion, husband of Megarê.

Hermês: Olympian god, son of Zeus and Maia, divine messenger and escort of the souls of the dead to the underworld. Hermês frequently is given the epithet "Argeiphontês," the original sense of which is uncertain: traditionally explained as "killer of [the monster] Argos," that exploit may well have been invented to make sense of the epithet; other scholars interpret it as "brilliant" or "shining."

Hermionê: daughter of Helen and Meneláos, bride of Neoptólemos. (Later tradition has her marry Orestês, and out of this contradiction it seems poets and other mythographers created a fierce rivalry between the sons of Akhilleus and Agamémnon for Hermionê, which continues the fierce rivalry between the fathers celebrated in *The Iliad*.)

Hippodameía: female attendant of Penélopê.

Hippotadês: patronymic of Aiolos (q.v.).

Hypereia: previous homeland of the Phaiákians, whence, after being driven out by the Kyklopês, they migrated under the command of Nausíthoös.

Iardanos: a river in western Krete, now called the Platanias.

Iasion: mortal briefly united with the goddess Dêmêtêr until Zeus blasted him with a thunderbolt.

Iasos: father of Amphion and Dmêtor, grandfather of Khloris; in *The Iliad*, commander of the Athenians at the siege of Troy.

Idómeneus: Kretan king who fought at Troy, son of Deukálion, grandson of Minos, brother to "Aithôn."

Iêson: Jason, commander of the *Argo* and leader of the Argonauts. See also under Aiêtês, above.

Ikários: descendant of the royal family in Sparta, father of Penélopê.

Ikmálios: famed craftsman, maker of a chair and footrest in Odysseus' home; not otherwise known.

Ilos: son of Mérmeris, who (according to Athena/Mentês) refused Odysseus' request for poison for his arrows when he visited him in Ephyra.

Ino: daughter of Kadmos, once mortal, now a nereid with the name Leukothea, q.v.

Iolkos: home to Pelias.

Íphiklos: son of Phylakos, giant; with his steers he infested the land of Phylakê; Pêro's father, Neleus, set the removal of these steers as a task for her suitors.

Iphimedeia: wife of Aloeus, mother of Otos and Ephialtês by Poseidon; her shade appears to Odysseus.

Íphitos: son of Eurýtos, king of Oikhalía, who gives Odysseus his famous bow; he is killed by Heraklês (compare XXI.15–37).

Iphthimê: daughter of Ikários and sister of Penélopê, wife of Eumêlos of Phêrai.

Iros: nickname for Arnaios, q.v.

Ismaros: city in the land of the Kikonês.

Ithaka: island home of Odysseus in the Ionian Sea off the west coast of mainland Greece, most likely present-day Thiaki.

Ithakos: one of Ithaka's early residents; he built a spring house on Ithaka near Clearwater with Nêritos and Polýktor.

Itylos: son of Zêthos, killed by his mother, Aedon (whose name is the same as the word for "nightingale").

Kadmos: founder of Thebes, father of Ino.

Kalypso: lesser goddess, daughter of Atlas, detained Odysseus on her island, Ogýgia, for seven years in the vain hope he would renounce Penélopê and a homecoming in Ithaka for immortal life with her. Her name plays on the Greek for "to hide" (see note on V.16, above).

Kassandra: Trojan princess, daughter of Priam and Hekabê, brought home as concubine by Agamémnon, murdered with her master by Klytaimnéstra. (Homer does not mention the prophetic abilities given her by her ravisher Apollo, which are so important in subsequent representations.)

Kastor: famous horseman, son of Tyndáreus and Lêda, brother of Helen and Klytaimnéstra, he shares immortality with his brother Polydeukês. Later it was believed that one or both of Kastor and Polydeukês (also known as Pollux) had Zeus for father; as a pair, they were known and worshiped as the Dioskouroi, "sons of Zeus."

Kaukonians: people inhabiting a portion of western Peloponnese.

Kephallênia: island near Ithaka, also called Samos and Samê, the latter the name of the island's largest settlement. Largest of all the Ionian islands and much larger than Ithaka, Homer refers to all those under command of the house of Odysseus as "Kephallênians" (XXIV.415 [and elsewhere in the Greek]).

Keteians: allies of the Trojans, their home was in Mysia in northwest Asia Minor.

Kharybdis: whirlpool opposite Skylla, q.v. Later mythology makes her the daughter of Poseidon and Gê whom Zeus blasted with a thunderbolt to punish her gluttony.

Khloris: youngest daughter of Amphion, wife of Neleus, queen of Pylos, mother of Nestor and Pêro, among other children; her shade appears to Odysseus.

Khromios: son of Neleus and Khloris.

Kikonês: allies of the Trojans, they lived on the Aegean coast of

Thrace; a raid on their territory was, according to Odysseus (IX.44–73), the first incident on his homeward journey from Troy.

Kirkê: goddess, daughter of Hêlios and Persê, sister of Aiêtês. Initially malign—she turns a good number of Odysseus' companions into swine—Odysseus is able to counter her magic thanks to Hermês' advice and the herb *molü*. After that she offers rich hospitality, and Odysseus remains one year on her island, Aiaia, sharing her bed and board, and receiving important instructions before he sails on. (The epic cycle introduces children born of their union, a son—Telegonos, and a daughter, Kassiphonê. As an example of the un-Odysseyan nature of subsequent plots, note that Telegonos kills Odysseus, Kirkê resurrects Odysseus, and Kassiphonê marries her half-brother Telémakhos.)

Kleitos: beautiful mortal in the family of Theoklýmenos, son of Mantios, grandson of Melampous, carried off by Dawn to live among the gods.

Klymênê: daughter of Minyas and Euryalê, mother of Íphiklos; her shade appears to Odysseus.

Klytaimnéstra: daughter of Tyndáreus and Lêda, sister of Helen, Kastor, and Polydeukês, wife of Agamémnon, mother of Iphianassa and Orestês, paramour of Aigísthos; she is complicit in the murder of Agamémnon and the actual slayer of Kassandra. She is slain by her son, Orestês. (In later myth, she has other daughters besides Iphianassa/Iphigenia.)

Klytóneus: Phaiákian prince, one of the sons of Alkínoös and Arêtê, winner of the footrace.

Knossos: the most important of the ninety towns found on Krete, about two and a half miles inland from the island's north coast, site of palace of King Minos. Indeed, it was the center of Minoan culture.

Kreon: ruler in Thebes after the departure of Oidipous, father of Megarê.

Krete: modern Crete, by far the largest of the Greek islands, it had been home to the lavish and powerful Minoan culture in the second millennium B.C.E. (see also under Knossos, above). In the Homeric poems, it is still rich and populous, renowned for its ninety cities and mingling of tongues.

Krêtheus: son of Aiolos, husband of Tyro, father of Aison, Pherês, and Amythaón.

Kronos: pre-Olympian god, his role was usurped by his son, Zeus; hence Zeus' patronymics Kronidês and Kroníon.

Ktêsios: ruler of the island of Syriê, son of Orménos, father of Eumaios.

Ktésippos: wealthy Samian suitor of Penélopê, he throws a cow's foot at the disguised Odysseus' head; killed by the cowherd.

Ktimenê: youngest daughter of Antikleía and Laërtês, sister of Odysseus, playmate of Eumaios.

Kydonians: people inhabiting the western part of Krete. Their city Kydonia is today called Canea.

Kyklopês: man-eating giants dwelling in a land far to the west; by occupying Hypereia they forced the Phaiákians to migrate.

Kyllênê: mountain in Arkadia; birthplace of Hermês and thus an important site of his cult.

Kypros: the eastern Mediterranean island Cyprus, birthplace and favorite haunt of Aphroditê. Rich in copper, in ancient times it was a critical source of the mineral, which takes its name from the island.

Kythera: island off the south coast of the Peloponnese, southwest of Cape Malea, home to the important cult of Aphroditê Ourania (Celestial Aphroditê). In some traditions, Kythera rather than Kypros is claimed to be the goddess' birthplace.

Kythereia: epithet of Aphroditê, often used as a name for the goddess. It was assumed already in ancient times to have been derived from Kythera, q.v., but that is not certain.

Laërtês: son of Arkeísios, husband of Antikleía, father of Odysseus and Ktimenê. He had already turned over control of all affairs to Odysseus and retired to the country before the latter was called away to the Trojan War.

Laistrygonês: man-eating giants who destroyed all the ships of Odysseus' fleet—with the exception of Odysseus' own—and ate the crew.

Lakedaimon: Sparta and its territory, ruled in the Homeric poems by Meneláos.

Lamos: earlier king of the Laistrygonês, later said to be a son of Poseidon.

Lampetía: nymph, daughter of Hêlios and Neaira, with her sister Phaëthousa she guarded her father's flocks and reported to him their slaughter at the hands of Odysseus' men.

Laódamas: Phaiákian prince, favorite son of Alkínoös, winner of the boxing match.

Lêda: wife of Tyndáreus, mother of Kastor, Polydeukês, Klytaim-néstra, and Helen (the last a child of Zeus); her shade appeared to Odysseus (XI.343).

Lemnos: Aegean island with associations with the god Hephaistos, who had a cult there.

Leódês: one of Penélopê's less boorish suitors and their soothsayer, son of Oinops, he was the first to try to string Odysseus' bow and the first to fail.

Leókritos: one of Penélopê's suitors, son of Euênor, his is the final speech in the Ithakan assembly in Book II; he dies by Telémakhos' spear.

Lesbos: relatively large Aegean island not far from the coast of Asia Minor. *The Iliad* reports that it had belonged to Priam's kingdom before Akhilleus took it. It was a natural staging point for the Greeks on their way back from Troy: in *The Odyssey* we hear that Nestor, Meneláos, and Diomêdês stopped there before setting out across the open sea for home. On an earlier occasion, Odysseus bested Lesbos' king, Philoméleidês, at wrestling.

Lêto: lesser goddess, mother of Artemis and Apollo, whom she bore to Zeus on the island of Delos after long wandering; she was raped by the giant Títyos, for which he suffers unceasing torment in Hades.

Leukothea: "the bright goddess," a sea nymph, the divine avatar of Ino (q.v.); it is she who gives her magic scarf to Odysseus, adrift in the sea after a shipwreck, to ensure him safe landfall.

Lotos Eaters: peaceful people whose land Odysseus reached after being driven by a storm ten days past Kythera. Their placidity seems to derive from the properties of the herb they consume, and those of Odysseus' companions who partook of it lost their will to return home.

Maira: in Homer only a name—her shade appears to Odysseus—but from other sources we hear that she was a companion of Artemis, who shot her when she bore Lokros to Zeus.

Malea: Cape Malea, a promontory which forms the southeast tip of the Peloponnese; its treacherous winds posed a problem to sailors attempting to round it.

Mantios: grandfather of Theoklýmenos' forebears, son of the seer Melampous, father of Polypheidês and Kleitos.

Marathon: village in Attica on Athena's itinerary from Skhería to Athens. In 490 B.C.E. it was the site of a famous battle, in which the Athenian general Miltiades, commanding ca. 9,000 Athenians and ca. 1,000 Plataians, turned back a much larger army of Persians.

Maron: son of Euanthês, priest of Apollo at Ismaros in the land of the Kikonês; he gave Odysseus the potent wine with which the hero drugs Polyphêmos.

Mastor: father of Halithérsês, q.v.

Medôn: herald or crier in Ithaka; spared in the general slaughter of the suitors, of whose crimes he was innocent.

Megapénthês: illegitimate son of Meneláos (the mother was not Helen but a slave), he married the daughter of the Spartan Alektor in a double wedding ceremony which took place on the day Telémakhos arrived in Sparta. The other couple in the ceremony was his (legitimate) half-sister, Hermionê, and Neoptólemos.

Megarê: daughter of Kreon, wife of Heraklês; her shade appears to Odysseus.

Melampous: Pylian lord who after many travails won Neleus' daughter, Pêro, to be his brother Bias' bride (see XV.282–300 for the story). He was the father of Antíphatês and Mantios, and great-grandfather of Theoklýmenos.

Melánthios: Ithakan goatherd and hanger-on of the suitors, son of Dólios, q.v., and brother of Melántho. Impudent to Odysseus upon meeting him, in disguise, approaching his own home, and on the verge of helping the besieged suitors regain their arms, he is caught by Eumaios and Philoítios, trussed up, and ultimately given an ignominious death.

Melántho: most outspoken of the treacherous maidservants in Odysseus' home and sister of Melánthios, she is sleeping with the suitor Eurýmakhos; she is hanged along with the other maidservants by Telémakhos.

Memnon: well known from the epic cycle (especially the *Aithiopis*, which follows *The Iliad* and tells of subsequent battles for Troy), he was the king of the Aithiopians, the son of Dawn (Eos) and Tithonos, and nephew of Priam; after the death of Hektor and then of the Amazon Penthesileia (the latter also in the *Aithiopis*), he was the last best hope of Troy. He killed Nestor's son Antílokhos but was himself killed by Akhilleus, who like Memnon was the son of a goddess and bore arms crafted by Hephaistos. Zeus granted Memnon immortality after death.

Meneláos: son of Atreus, brother of Agamémnon, king of Sparta, husband of Helen, whose abduction by the Trojan prince Paris (also called Alexander) sparked the Trojan War. With Agamémnon, he convinced Odysseus to join the Greek expeditionary force (see XXIV.130–35).

Mentês: Taphian captain, son of Ankhíalos; in his guise Athena first appears to Telémakhos.

Mentor: Ithakan, son of Álkimos, contemporary of Odysseus; it is to him that Odysseus entrusted his home and family when he went to Troy, and he remains a staunch ally. Athena disguises herself as Mentor more than once.

Mesaúlios: assistant of Eumaios, bought from Taphian slavers by the swineherd on his own out of his own earnings.

Messenians: residents of Messênê, which does not solve the problem. Debate still rages about the exact location or locations Homer meant, since the confusion of multiple Messênês is augmented by the multiple Ortílokhos' and Phêrais involved in any argument. It is probably simplest to think of Messênê as a region in the southwestern or south central part of the Peloponnese. Even if this were some day proved to be wrong, doing so would hardly have impeded appreciation of *The Odyssey*.

Minos: king of Krete, brother of Rhadamanthos, husband of Pasiphaae, father of Ariadnê and Deukálion, and in later accounts other children, i.e., Phaidra; also later is the story that he had Pasiphaae's offspring, the minotaur, enclosed in the labyrinth. The Homeric Minos is particularly dear to Zeus: after his death he became a judge in Hades and he is received by Zeus every ninth year in private council. (On a possible Egyptian prehistory for Minos, his brother, and the Minotaur, see Bernal, *Black Athena* 2.171–86.)

Minyai: a legendary Greek people at Orkhómenos, ruled by Amphion.

Moulios: soldier from Doulíkhion and herald of Amphínomos.

Muse: daughter(s) of Zeus and Mnemosynê (memory), at an early but not certain point conceived of as nine in number; the Muse is or the Muses are source and guarantor of the memories and stories sung by poets (see notes on I.1 and XXIV.63, above).

Mykênai: Mycenae, one of the oldest cities in the district belonging to Argos, in *The Odyssey* sometimes used interchangeably with Argos. It was the center of the all-important Mycenaean culture; archeology (with Schliemann at Mycenae from 1874) and documentary evidence now suggests a chronology of Mycenaean culture developing from perhaps as early as the late eighteenth center B.C.E.—dating remains controversial— to a high point (ca. 1470–1230 B.C.E.) only to suffer a swift collapse (by ca. 1150 B.C.E.).

Mykênê: daughter of Inakhos, she is clearly the eponymous heroine of Mykênai, but we have information neither on her connection to that city nor on the story of her "coronet" (II.128).

Myrmidons: name of a people from Thessaly, the men constitute the vassals of Pêleus and the troops of his son, Akhilleus. In Homer, their home was described as "Hellas and Phthia" (on which, see under Hellas, above). Slightly later tradition has the Myrmidons arise from ants [Greek *myrmêkes*] when Zeus responded to the prayers of Aíakos (q.v.) for human companions, Aíakos having been left alone on the island Aigina, named after his mother, whom Zeus had seduced and abandoned there.

Naiadês: water nymphs.

Neaira: nymph who bore Phaëthousa and Lampetía to Hêlios.

Nausikaa: Phaiákian princess, daughter of Alkínoös and Arêtê. At Athena's prompting she takes her companions to the shore to wash her linens, arriving there just in time to aid the shipwrecked Odysseus. Like her ancestor Nausithoös, she has a name beginning with an element which means "ship," appropriate for the Phaiákians, who were renowned for their sailing.

Nausíthoös: king of Phaiákia, father of Rhêxênor and Alkínoös, grandfather of Arêtê; under his leadership, the Phaiákians migrated from Hypereia to Skhería.

Neion: mountain on Ithaka mentioned only by Homer; it remains uncertain to what actual topographic feature of Ithaka it refers. The same is also true of an Ithakan mountain called Nêriton in the Greek behind IX.25 and XIII.440; rather than prolonging this double confusion, Fitzgerald has called both mountains "Neion" in his translation. (In the catalog of ships in *The Iliad*, Nêriton is an island or city near Ithaka [II.632]; since Nérikos, q.v., is on Leukas, this Nêriton is often taken to be on or the same as Leukas.)

Neleus: son of Poseidon and Tyro, brother of Pelias, he lived at Pylos and, with Khloris, his wife, he had many children, among who were Nestor and Pêro.

Neoptólemos: son of Akhilleus and Deidamia, bridegroom of Hermionê, q.v. (later tradition knows him as Pyrrhos/Pyrrhus as well).

Nérikos: coastal town on Leukas conquered by Laërtês in his heyday.

Nêritos: one of Ithaka's early residents, he built a spring house near Clearwater with Ithakos and Polýktor (the name is clearly related to Nêriton, on which, see under Neion, above).

Nestor: king of Pylos, son of Neleus and Khloris, husband of Eurydíkê, father of seven sons (i.e., Antílokhos) and two daughters. Already in *The Iliad* he is presented as old and wise, treasured for his advice, which he spiced with lengthy reminiscences of the deeds of his youth; yet he is still an active and effective member of the Greek fighting force. Also called Lord of Gerênia, q.v.

Nísos: father of the suitor Amphínomos, son of Arêtos (hence his patronymic, Aretíadês).

Noêmon: wealthy Ithakan, son of Phronios, keeps a dozen mares at pasture on the mainland at Elis (q.v.), lends his ship to Telémakhos (at the request of Athena disguised as Telémakhos). He unwittingly endangers Telémakhos' safe return when his innocent but untimely question about Telémakhos tips off the suitors to their young opponent's sea voyage.

Odysseus: son of Laërtês and Antikleía, husband of Penélopê, father of Telémakhos.

Ogýgia: island home of the nymph Kalypso.

Oidipous: son of Epikastê, whom he marries (see note on XI.315–16).

Oikhalía: locale near Trikka in Thessaly, home of Eurytos, but not otherwise identifiable.

Oikleiês: grandson of the seer Melampous, son of Antíphatês, father of the famous seer Amphiaraos, and thus part of the illustrious heritage of the seer Theoklýmenos.

Olympos: mountain in northeastern Greece, the country's tallest (9,573'), legendary home of the Olympian gods.

Ops: father of Odysseus' and later Telémakhos' nurse, Eurýkleia, son of Peisênor 2, hence the patronymic "Peisonórídês."

Orestês: son of Agamémnon and Klytaimnéstra; as avenger of his father's death at the hands of his mother and her lover, Aigísthos, constantly presented in *The Odyssey* as a model for Telémakhos (for some of the later tradition associated with him, see under Hermionê, above).

Orion: legendary hunter, giant, famed for his beauty, loved by the goddess Dawn, who took him to Ortýgia; the gods, envious of her happiness, had Artemis kill him; also, a constellation named after him.

Orkhómenos: city in Boiotia northwest of Lake Copais, seat of the Minyai, famed for great wealth; by Homer's time its historical and political importance already lay in the past.

Orménos: father of Ktêsios, grandfather of Eumaios.

Orsílokhos: according to the fiction of the disguised Odysseus, a courier, son of Idómeneus, whom the "Kretan" killed (XIII.332).

Ortílokhos: son of the river god Alpheios, father of Dióklês. Like Dióklês, he lived at Phêrai in Messênê, where he was host to Odysseus. (His name is often spelled Orsílokhos, which makes for confusion not so much with the "Kretan Orsílokhos"—the immediately preceding entry—as with his own grandson of the same name, son of Dióklês, q.v., who appears in *The Iliad*. Already ancient scholars debated the point, trying, vainly, to use spelling to distinguish between the grandson and the grandfather, but the manuscripts did not cooperate.)

Ortýgia: literally "Quail Island." It may (but then again may not) define two different islands in *The Odyssey:* (1) home of Dawn/Eos, which Fitzgerald identifies as Delos (V.130 [121]); (2) island near Eumaios' home island, Syriê (XV.491). See the note on XV.491.

Ossa: mountain south of Olympos. The giants Otos and Ephialtês planned to pile another mountain, Pelion, on Ossa, in order to assault Olympos, hence the proverbial "to pile Pelion on Ossa."

Otos: giant, son of Iphimedeia and Poseidon. With his brother Ephialtês, he constituted a threat to the Olympian gods—see Ossa—and hence, while still a youth, was shot down by Apollo.

Paian: god of healing and music, later associated with both Apollo and Asklepios.

Pallas: epithet of the goddess Athena, the word itself may mean "maiden." Alternatively, "Pallas" may have been an earlier god worshiped at Athens whom Athena superseded.

Pandáreos: father of Aedon, grandfather of Itylos, q.v.

Panopeus: southwestern city in the region of Phokis (on the Greek mainland just north of the Gulf of Corinth), lying on the plain of the river Kephissos.

Paphos: city on the south coast of Kypros, frequented by and center of a cult to Aphroditê, q.v.

Parnassos: one of the highest and most important mountain ranges of Greece, it was frequently associated with Delphi, which lies on its southern flank. It is prominent in *The Odyssey* as the site of the boarhunt described in flashback in Book XIX, during which the boy Odysseus received a notable wound.

Patróklos: dearest companion of Akhilleus; killed at Troy when he donned Akhilleus' armor and led the Akhaians into battle; in *The Iliad*, it is his death that finally rouses Akhilleus to return to war and to slay Hektor.

Peiraios: Ithakan, son of Klytios, friend of Telémakhos; accompanies Telémakhos to Pylos and is Theoklýmenos' host after their return to Ithaka, it being impossible for Telémakhos to guarantee fitting hospitality to Theoklýmenos in his own hall.

Peirithoös: hero, son of Ixion and king of the Lapiths. It was at his wedding with Hippodameia that the Centaur Eurytion's misconduct led to the famous battle of the Centaurs and the Lapiths. The hero Theseus aided Peirithoös, and the two friends began a whole career of adventures together, the most sensational being their descent to Hades in the attempt to take Persephonê to be Peirithoös' wife. Heraklês freed Theseus, but Peirithoös was forced to remain. After seeing the phantom of Heraklês, Odysseus looked forward to seeing both Peirithoös and Theseus, but the press of shades forced him to flee.

Peisándros: one of the suitors of Penélopê, he gives her a gift in Book XVIII, son of Polýktor 2, slain by Philoítios.

Peisênor: (1) Ithakan herald; (2) father of Ops, grandfather of Eurýkleia.

Peisístratos: youngest son of Nestor, accompanies Telémakhos from Pylos to Sparta.

Pêleus: son of Aíakos, king of the Myrmidons, hero of many adventures, but most important for the Homeric poems as husband of the nymph Thetis and father of Akhilleus.

Pelias: son of Poseidon and Tyro, ruler of Iolkos, brother of Neleus, husband of Kretheus.

Pelion: mountain peak south of Otos, q.v.

Peloponnese or Peloponnesos: the entire southern portion of Greece south of the isthmus of Korinth (cut early on by a canal). The land connection notwithstanding, it was regarded as a virtual island already in ancient times; "Peloponnesos" means "Pelop's island." The two parts of Greece are distinct in many ways, and it is common to this day to use the phrase "Greek mainland" to mean that part of Greece north of the Peloponnese. The name itself is not used by Homer, for whom Argos comes closest to a designation of the region.

Penélopê: daughter of Ikários and Periboia or Polykástê (her mother's name is not given by Homer; see under Periboia 2), wife of Odysseus, mother of Telémakhos. The etymology of Penélopê's name is debated (see note on I.268, above).

Periboia: (1) daughter of Eurymedon, by Poseidon mother of Nausíthoös, grandmother of Alkínoös; (2) though never mentioned by Homer, Periboia is elsewhere transmitted as the name of Penélopê's mother. She was according to these stories a naiad. Periboia is, however, a frequent name for Greek heroines. (Yet other sources give Polykástê as the name of Penélopê's mother.)

Periklýmenos: son of Neleus and Khloris, grandson of Poseidon, brother of Nestor.

Perimêdês: second most frequently named of Odysseus' companions—after Eurýlokhos, with whom he is often described as acting, e.g., making a sacrifice, binding Odysseus fast so that he can safely hear the song of the Seirênês.

Pêro: daughter of Neleus and Khloris; the successful suitor for her hand would have to drive the steers of the giant Íphiklos from Phylakê.

Persê: daughter of Okeanos, consort of Hêlios and mother of Hêlios and Kirkê.

Perséphonê: daughter of Dêmêtêr, consort of Hades and thus queen of the underworld.

Perseus: one of Nestor's sons (and not the famous hero, son of Zeus and Danae, who beheaded Medusa).

Phaëthousa: nymph, daughter of Hêlios and Neaira, with her sister Lampetía she guarded her father's flocks and reported to him their slaughter at the hands of Odysseus' men.

Phaiákia: land of the Phaiákians, also called Skhería, whither they migrated under the leadership of Nausíthoös when the Kyklopês drove them from their former home, Hypereia. The current ruler is Alkínoös, who has as vassals twelve subkings.

Phaidimos: king of Sidon, Meneláos' host on the latter's journey homeward, he gave a precious mixing bowl to Meneláos, which he in turn gives Telémakhos.

Phaidôn: variant spelling of Pheidon, q.v.

Phaidra: Kretan princess, daughter of Minos and Pasiphaae; her shade appears to Odysseus.

Phaistos: port city on the south coast of Krete, just east of Gortyn.

Pharos: a small Mediterranean island just off the coast of Egypt near (what later became known as) Alexandria.

Pheidon: king of Thesprótia (q.v.) mentioned as helping Odysseus. (Spelled thus at XVIII.345, but written Phaidôn at XIX.339–45.)

Phêmios: singer and harpist in Ithaka. His name means something like "Bestower of fame"; in XXII.372 he is called "son of Terpis," i.e., "son of the Pleasure-giver." The attribution of such a fanciful genealogy was another way to add a significant name to describe an aspect of the bard's character.

Phêrai: town between Pylos and Sparta, now Kalamata, in southern Messênia, where Dióklês hosted Telémakhos and Peisístratos both on their way from Pylos to Sparta and on their way back.

Pherês: son of Krêtheus and Tyro.

Philoítios: cowherd, loyal to Odysseus and Telémakhos, with Eumaios he becomes the fourth fighter against the suitors.

Philoktêtês: from Magnesia in Thessaly, son of Poias, one of the Greek commanders in the expedition against Troy. He never reached Troy, however, since en route he received an incurable but not fatal snake bite; the Greeks, unable to stand the stench of the wound, left him on Lemnos. According to a prophecy, Troy could not fall without him (and/or Heraklês bow, of which he was the possessor), and Odysseus, along with Diomêdês, had a major role in effecting his return. (Odysseus' part in this drama attracted treatments by the three great tragedians, of which Sophocles' *Philoctetes* alone is extant.) According to Nestor, Philoktêtês has a safe return from Troy.

Philomeleidês: king and champion of Lesbos, bested by Odysseus in a wrestling match.

Phoinikians: Phoenicians, a Punic people inhabiting Phoenicia (Phoinikia), on the eastern shore of the Mediterranean, their major cities were Sidon and Tyre. Already famed as sea-going merchants in Homer's day (with concomitant negative connotations: mercenary, untrustworthy, tricky), they established trading posts and later colonies throughout the Mediterranean as far west as Spain. Carthage was the most famous of Phoenician colonies, eventually far surpassing either Tyre or Sidon in wealth and military power.

Phorkys: a sea god, father of Thoösa and thus grandfather of Poly-phêmos. He has a cave on Ithaka, giving his name to one of the island's harbors or coves.

Phronios: Ithakan, father of Noêmon.

Phrontis: steersman of Meneláos' ship, son of Orêtor, died near Cape Sunion by falling from the ship. Meneláos lands to give him proper burial.

Phthia: kingdom of Pêleus and Akhilleus, home of the Myrmidons. Its Homeric site is in the east central portion of the Greek main-land, but traces in legends and names suggest that it originally referred to most or all of Thessaly.

Phylakê: district ruled by Neleus. Its location cannot be identified precisely, but in Homer it seems to be a city on mainland Greece, in Achaia Phthiotis.

Phylakos: father of Íphiklos, q.v.

Phylo: female servant of Helen.

Pleiadês: one of the constellations by which sailors steered by night, and Odysseus is no exception. It is still known as the seven sisters, although today only six can be seen with the naked eye.

Politês: companion of Odysseus who lead several of his fellows right into Kirkê's trap.

Pólybos: literally "many oxen," so frequently a name for minor characters it could, in other registers, be translated "so and so" or "Mr. Smith." In *The Odyssey* it is applied to four characters: (1) a citizen of Thebes in Egypt, who gave Meneláos costly presents, while his wife, Alkandrê, gave gold and silver gifts to Helen, all of which is now in the couple's possession in Sparta (IV.137); (2) a Phaiákian craftsman, who has carved the ball with which

Halios and Laódamas dance (VIII.400); (3) an Ithakan, father of Eurýmakhos (XV.630); and (4) one of the suitors (XXII.270).

Polydamna: consort of the Egyptian lord Thôn, she supplied Helen with the soothing drug she adds to the wine served to Meneláos and their guests.

Polydeukês: famous boxer, son of Tyndáreus (or Zeus) and Lêda, brother of Helen, he shares immortality with his brother Kastor, q.v. An alternate form of his name is Pollux.

Polykástê: youngest daughter of Nestor and Eurydikê, she gives a bath to Telémakhos. See also note on III.506. (For Polykastê as the name of Penélopê's mother, see under Periboia 2.)

Polýktor: (1) one of Ithaka's early residents, he built a springhouse near Clearwater with Ithakos and Nêritos; (2) father of the suitor Peisándros.

Polypheidês: prophet, son of Mantios, grandson of Melampous, father of Theoklýmenos.

Polyphêmos: one of the Kyklopês, one-eyed man-eating giant, son of Poseidon and Thoösa, in whose cave Odysseus and his companions find gruesome hospitality and whose blinding, however justified, earns Odysseus Poseidon's enmity, which dogs him through *The Odyssey*.

Pontónoös: royal squire of the Phaiákians.

Poseidon: an Olympian god with powers over the seas and earthquakes (earth shaker); father of Polyphêmos, he pursued Odysseus with enmity after Odysseus blinded his one-eyed son.

Priam: king of Troy during the Trojan War, father of fifty sons and daughters (not all by his consort Hekabê), among whom were Paris, Helen's abductor or seducer, Hektor, Troy's greatest fighter, Kassandra, and Deïphobos. In the final movement of *The Iliad,* he goes behind enemy lines to Akhilleus' tent in order to ransom the now mangled corpse of Hektor from the Greek hero who slew him.

Prokris: Kretan princess, daughter of Minos and Pasiphaae; her shade appeared to Odysseus (XI.372).

Proteus: ancient sea god, shape changer, father of Eidothea, associated with Pharos, the island off the coast of Egypt, where under compulsion he shares his wisdom with Meneláos.

Pylos: Nestor's home in southwestern Peloponnese. See note on III.6.

Pytho: ancient name of Apollo's oracle at Delphi. (Later, the name Python was given to the monster Apollo slew at the site of the oracle.)

Reithron Bight: Ithakan harbor or bay (not mentioned elsewhere).

Rhadamanthos: legendary Kretan, son of Zeus and Europa and brother of Minos, he led the Phaiákians on their search for Títyos and is now enjoying afterlife in Elysion. (More properly spelled "Rhadamanthys"; see note on IV.599ff.) His role as one of the judges in afterlife is not known before Plato.

Rhêxênor: son of Nausíthoös, brother of Alkínoös, father of Arêtê.

Raven's Rock: home of the swineherd.

Salmoneus: father of Tyro.

Samê: an island near Ithaka, usually called Kephallênia, and/or the major settlement on Kephallênia, q.v..

Seirênês: singing sisters, two in Homer (but later three), who lured passing sailors to approach their rock, on which, however, it was impossible to land without shipwreck. Warned by Kirkê, Odysseus both manages to get his sailors past the seduction and to hear their song himself.

Sidon: coastal city of the Phoinikians, ruled by Phaidimos. It was associated with crafts and metalworking, especially bronze. See note on IV.661.

Sikania: place, possibly identical to Sicily (see note on XXIV.338).

Sikel: native Sicilian. See note on XX.427.

Sísyphos: known from *The Iliad* as the son of Aiolos (eponymous hero of the Aiolians and not the king of the winds) and the father of Glaukos, in *The Odyssey* he appears in Odysseus' vision of the underworld, his torment being to push a boulder to the top of a hill only to have it roll back down. Such labor is ever since known as "Sisyphean." Only later accounts try to explain what the crime was for which he was punished. In some of these accounts he is directly entwined in Odysseus' family: for example, he is supposed to have stolen the cattle of Odysseus' grandfather Autólykos and to have abducted his daughter Antikleía, so that in some accounts it is Sísyphos who is in fact Odysseus' father.

Skylla: cave-dwelling monster inhabiting a cliff across a narrow strait from Kharybdis (q.v.). Skylla barks like a dog and with each of her six mouths grabs one of Odysseus' companions as they sail past. Ancient geographers already identified this strait with the Strait of Messina, which divides Sicily from the toe of the Italian boot.

Skhería: home of the Phaiákians. Later Greek tradition identified it with Korkyra or Korfu, but in Homer it is not certain that it is even an island. See note on VI.11.

Skyros: island east of Euboia with legendary connections to Akhilleus. After Akhilleus' death, Odysseus reports that he brought

Akhilleus' son, Neoptólemos, from Skyros to join the Akhaian siege of Troy.

Sparta: major city-state in the Peloponnese, center of Lakedaimon, seat of Meneláos and Helen.

Stratíos: one of Nestor's sons.

Styx: river in Hades; the strongest oath an immortal could make was to swear by the River Styx.

Sunion Point: promontory forming the southeast point of Attika and commanding a wide vista of the Aegean Sea.

Syriê: island home of Eumaios, near Ortýgia. Its true location is uncertain.

Tálemos: one of the Kyklopês.

Tántalos: king of Sipylos, he appears in Odysseus' vision of the underworld, his torment to be unable to drink of the water in which he stands or to eat of the fruit that hangs over his head. As with the case of Sísyphos, genealogy and explanation of the crime which merited this punishment postdate *The Odyssey*. According to the most widespread accounts he is a son of Zeus and the father of Pelops, and his crime was an offense against the gods, either the theft from their table of the divine nectar and ambrosia their favor had permitted him to share or a revelation of their secrets.

Taphians: inhabitants of the island(s) of Taphos, between Leukas and Akarnia. (The major island is probably to be identified with Meganisi.) Ruled by Mentês, they were a seafaring people, and as is true of many such people in *The Odyssey*, pirates and slave-traders. See under Arubas Pasha and Mesaúlios, above, for instances of such activity.

Taÿgetos: mountain range dividing Lakonia and Messênia, one of Artemis' favored hunting grounds.

Teirêsias: blind seer of Thebes, dead by the time of the events narrated in *The Odyssey*. Odysseus consults him in the underworld. Teirêsias alone among the buried dead is able to remember, know things of the world, and speak without drinking the blood Odysseus offers to the other ghosts.

Télamon: father of Aîas 2 ("Télamonian Aîas"), famed in other sources both as one of the Argonauts and as a participant in that earlier siege, under Heraklês' command, of Troy, at the time ruled by Laomedon.

Telémakhos: son of Odysseus and Penélopê.

Télemos: wizard among the Kyklopês, son of Eurymos, who had foretold that Polyphêmos would lose his eye at Odysseus' hand.

Télephos: father of Eurýpulos, q.v.

Témesê: Tamassos, important center of copper production on Kypros (q.v.), south of present-day Nikosia.

Ténedos: small island just across from Troy, first staging point of the Greek forces before they set out for their homes.

Terpis: "father" of Phêmios, q.v.

Thebes: (1) most important city of Boiotia, according to the legends founded by Kadmos and fortified with walls built by Amphion and Zêthos; (2) city in upper Egypt, famous in Greek sources for its wealth and "hundred gates."

Theoklýmenos: an Argive seer, with many seers among his forebears, i.a. his father, Polypheidês, and his great-grandfather Melampous. Exiled for having killed a cousin, he takes passage with Telémakhos in Pylos and sails to Ithaka with him. Once there, he proclaims to a doubting Penélopê that Odysseus is already in Ithaka and to the suitors that they are a doomed lot (Books XVII and XX, respectively).

Thesprótia: coastal region of western mainland Greece, part of Epeiros roughly across from the island of Korkyra; to Eumaios, Odysseus as the Kretan describes being washed up on the shore and given shelter by the king, Pheidon, q.v. Thesprótia is sometimes used to stand for all of Epeiros, and Dodona is also described as being in Thesprótia.

Thessaly: northern region of mainland Greece west of Mounts Olympos, Ossa, and Pelion and south of Macedonia.

Thetis: nereid (i.e., daughter of the sea god Nereus), she bore Akhilleus to Pêleus. This pairing was arranged by Zeus, who would himself have liked to lie with Thetis but renounced her when informed of the prophecy that the son of Thetis would be stronger than his father.

Thoösa: nymph, daughter of Phorkys, Polyphêmos' mother by Poseidon.

Thrace: Greece's far north, on the northern coast of the Aegean and running north to the Black Sea, with Macedonia to the west.

Thrasymêdês: one of Nestor's sons.

Thrinákia: island sacred to Hêlios, where the sun god pastured his herd of cattle, which Odysseus' companions, acting against dire warnings, slaughtered.

Thyestês: father of Aigísthos, brother of Atreus and thus uncle of Agamémnon and Meneláos. The enmity between Thyestês and his brother, with whom he contested the right to the throne in Argos, is continued by his son Aigísthos and Atreus' son Agamémnon (first cousin of Aigísthos, q.v.).

Tithonos: son of Laomedon, mortal beloved by Dawn, he became her consort; their son was Memnon. According to later elaboration of the myth (*Homeric Hymn* 4), Dawn requested immortality for her lover but forgot to ask for eternal youth, condemning Tithonos to age without ever being able to die.

Títyos: giant, son of Gaia, violator of Lêto, slain by Apollo and Artemis and now suffering eternal punishment in Hades. The story that Rhadamanthos visited him in Euboia (see VII.345–48) seems a trace of an earlier tradition according to which Títyos was no giant, "son of earth," but a hero, son of Zeus and Elare, who dwelt in a Euboian cave.

Troy: important city on the northwest coast of Asia Minor, less than four miles inland from the coast and less than three miles from the Dardanelles. The nearest modern settlement is Hissarlik. Like most ancient citadels, it was built on a mound, which grew higher as new cities were constructed on the ruins of earlier cities. Modern archeology (Heinrich Schliemann began excavations in 1870, Wilhelm Dörpfeld taking over in 1882 and working through 1894; a team from the University of Cincinnati under Carl Blegen worked in the 1930s; excavations continue to produce important discoveries today) has established a series of multiple Troys, with the earliest dating back to the late fourth millennium B.C.E. The most important Troys are Troy VI (1900–1340 B.C.E.—all dates approximate), which marked a major leap in the size of the settlement area, and Troy VII, both with subphases. These phases and subphases are distinguished by differences in material culture. Some of the discontinuities suggest an earthquake or a fire and a peaceful change of populations.

Do any of these transitions reflect a real Trojan War? The Trojan War was traditionally dated between 1250 and 1170 B.C.E. Recent scholarship seems to support Troy VIIa, burned ca. 1220–1210 B.C.E, as the prime candidate for the Iliadic Troy. On the other hand, it is likely that the "Trojan War" represents many sieges and campaigns. Troy would be an attractive anchor for such stories, for a number of reasons. Given its commanding position on the northern Aegean trade routes, particularly those running through the Dardanelles into the Black Sea, it was likely to have been rich and very much hated by all those whose free trade it tried to encumber. Stories of its true wealth, exaggerated as stories always are, no doubt attracted storytellers as it all along attracted marauding forces. And finally, its position on the eastern edge of the Greek sphere meant, particularly as Greece was expanding and colonizing in a westerly direction, that it could be inflected as an "eastern" city and could bear all the connotations the "East" (i.e., Orient) always has had for the "West": rich, luxurious, tyrannical, less than manly, and inevitably conquerable.

What is ultimately most important for a reading of *The Odyssey* is the Troy of *The Iliad* and the epic-cycle. From the extant *Iliad* we know of a rich and nearly impregnable citadel—*The Iliad* is the best source of the architectural and topographical details— ruled by Priam and ably defended for a decade by his sons, sons-in-law, and the troops he could rely on from allies and vassal states throughout Asia Minor. While the details are to some extent fictionalized, from everything we know about the period, this must be an essentially accurate picture of the way a city would withstand the assault of a besieging army. In sum, memories of a historical expedition and sack are possibly buried in *The Iliad*, but they are transformed, likely beyond recognition, by epic convention.

Tyndáreus: husband of Lêda, father of Klytaimnéstra, father or foster-father of Kastor and Polydeukês (at least later Zeus was claimed to be the true father of one or both boys, the so-called Dioskouroi; see note under Kastor, above), and foster-father of Helen, whom Homer calls Zeus' daughter (although at times he also calls her Tyndáreus' daughter). As brother of Ikários, he is Penélopê's uncle.

Tyro: daughter of Salmoneus, wife of Krêtheus, she is mother of Pelias and Neleus by Poseidon, who appeared to her in the figure of the river god Enipeus, with whom she was infatuated; she later bore her mortal husband three children, Aison, Pherês, and Amytháon; her shade appears to Odysseus.

Zakýnthos: wooded island near Ithaka, so named to this day.

Zêthos: son of Zeus and Antiopê; with his brother, Amphion, he built the walls of Thebes; his wife, Aedon, killed his only child, Itylos.

Zeus: chief of the Olympian gods, son of Kronos, brother and consort of Hêra, father of Athena, Apollo, Hermês, Heraklês, Helen, and many other gods and heroes.

Bibliography
Suggestions for Further Reading

The secondary literature on Homer is vast, and it would be easier to list far too much than too little. I have emphasized books and (a very few) articles of recent vintage; each of the items will give access to earlier scholarship, much of which is still of great value. With an eye on the requirements of most users of this volume, I have restricted these "suggestions for further reading" to material in English, at the same time taking comfort in the fact that, again, the notes and bibliographies of the works cited will give readers access to the richly international world of Homeric scholarship. Finally, I have arranged the list in categories; needless to say, many of the books could be placed under more than one heading.

I. COMMENTARIES

Heubeck, Alfred, et al. *A Commentary on Homer's Odyssey:* Alfred Heubeck, Stephanie West, and J. B. Hainsworth, *Volume I: Introduction and Books I–VIII;* Alfred Heubeck and Arie Hoekstra, *Volume II: Books IX–XVI;* Joseph Russo, Manuel Fernández-Galiano, and

Alfred Heubeck, *Volume III: Books XVII–XXIV*. Oxford, 1988, 1989, and 1992, respectively. [Referred to in the Commentary as HWH 1, HWH 2, and HWH 3.]

Stanford, W. B. *The Odyssey of Homer*, vol. 1, Books I–XII; vol. 2, Books XIII–XXIV. 2nd edition. London: Macmillan, 1959 and 1958, respectively (both volumes frequently reprinted, with addenda, through 1971).

Note: These two commentaries on the Greek text have been indispensable in my work on *The Odyssey*, Stanford my constant companion in reading the poem for some twenty years now, and the Oxford commentary more recently. Both are excellent in very different ways. They may also be of great value to readers of *The Odyssey* with little or no Greek. Both have helpful introductory sections, and indexes to lead users to longer notes on specific issues. Finally, the line numbers of the Greek originals of the translated passages appear in the running heads of the Fitzgerald translation, and these should be sufficient to get users to the appropriate pages in the commentaries for detailed analysis.

II. GENERAL AND SELECTED DETAILED STUDIES ON *THE ODYSSEY*

Austin, Norman. *Archery at the Dark of the Moon: Poetic Problems in Homer's Odyssey*. Berkeley and Los Angeles, 1975.

Bergren, Ann. "Helen's 'Good Drug': *Odyssey* IV 1–305." In S. Kresic, ed. *Contemporary Literary Hermeneutics and Interpretation of Classical Texts*. Ottawa, 1981. Pp. 201–14.

Clarke, Howard W. *The Art of the Odyssey*. Englewood Cliffs, N.J., 1967.

———, ed. *Twentieth Century Interpretations of the Odyssey: A Collection of Critical Essays*. Englewood Cliffs, N.J., 1983.

Clay, Jenny Strauss. *The Wrath of Athena: Gods and Men in the Odyssey.* Princeton, 1983.

Dimock, George E. *The Unity of the Odyssey.* Amherst, 1989.

Fenik, Bernard. *Studies in the Odyssey.* Hermes Einzelschriften 30. Wiesbaden, 1974.

Finley, John. *Homer's Odyssey.* Cambridge, Mass., 1978.

Finley, Moses I. *The World of Odysseus.* Rev. ed. New York, 1978.

Foley, Helene. " 'Reverse Similes' and Sex Roles in the *Odyssey.*" *Arethusa* 11 (1978), 7–26.

Griffin, Jasper. *Homer: The Odyssey.* Cambridge, 1987.

Katz, Marylin Arthur. *Penelope's Renown: Meaning and Indeterminacy in Homer's Odysseus.* Princeton, 1991.

Murnaghan, Sheila. *Disguise and Recognition in the Odyssey.* Princeton, 1987.

Page, Denys L. *Folktales in Homer's Odyssey.* Cambridge, Mass., 1973.

Peradotto, John. *Man in the Middle Voice: Name and Narration in the Odyssey.* Princeton, 1990.

Pucci, Pietro. *Odysseus Polutropos: Intertextual Readings in the Odyssey and Iliad.* Ithaca, 1987.

Schein, Seth L. "Odysseus and Polyphemus in the *Odyssey.*" *Greek, Roman and Byzantine Studies* 11 (1970), 73–83.

Segal, Charles. *"Kleos* and Its Ironies in the *Odyssey.*" *L'antiquité classique* 52 (1983), 22–47.

———. "The Phaeacians and the Symbolism of Odysseus' Return." *Arion* 1 (1962), 17–64.

Thornton, A. *People and Themes in Homer's Odyssey.* Dunedin and London, 1970.

Winkler, John J. "Penelope's Cunning and Homer's." In *The Constraints of Desire*. New York, 1990. Pp. 129–61.

Woodhouse, W. J. *The Composition of Homer's Odyssey*. Oxford, 1930; rpt. 1969.

III. HOMER, THE HOMERIC POEMS, ISSUES OF COMPOSITION

Carpenter, Rhys. *Folk Tale, Fiction and Saga in the Homeric Epics*. Berkeley and Los Angeles, 1946.

Clarke, Howard. *Homer's Readers: A Historical Introduction to the Iliad and the Odyssey*. Brunswick, N.J., 1981.

De Jong, Irene J. F. *Narrators and Focalizers: The Presentation of the Story in the Iliad*. Amsterdam, 1987.

Fenik, Bernard. *Typical Battle Scenes in the Iliad: Studies in the Narrative Techniques of Homeric Battle Descriptions*. Hermes Einzelschriften 21. Wiesbaden, 1968.

Ford, Andrew. *Homer: The Poetry of the Past*. Ithaca, 1992.

Griffin, Jasper. *Homer on Life and Death*. Oxford, 1980.

———. "Homeric Words and Speakers." *Journal of Hellenic Studies* 106 (1986), 36–57.

Hainsworth, J. B. *The Flexibility of the Homeric Formula*. Oxford, 1968.

Hoekstra, Arie. *Homeric Modifications of Formulaic Prototypes*. Amsterdam, 1965.

Janko, Richard. *Homer, Hesiod and the Hymns: Diachronic Development in Epic Diction*. Cambridge, 1982.

Kirk, Geoffrey. *The Songs of Homer*. Cambridge, 1962.

Lord, Albert B. *The Singer of Tales*. Cambridge, Mass., 1960.

Lüthi, Max. *The European Folktale: Form and Nature*. Tr. John D. Niles. Philadelphia, 1982.

Martin, Richard P. *The Language of Heroes: Speech and Performance in the Iliad*. Ithaca, 1989.

Moulton, Carroll. *Similes in the Homeric Poems*. Hypomnemata 49. Göttingen, 1977.

Nagler, Michael N. *Spontaneity and Tradition: A Study in the Oral Art of Homer*. Berkeley and Los Angeles, 1974.

Nagy, Gregory. *The Best of the Achaeans: Concepts of the Hero in Archaic Greek Poetry*. Baltimore, 1979.

————. *Pindar's Homer: The Lyric Possession of an Epic Past*. Baltimore, 1990.

Page, Denys L. *History and the Homeric Iliad*. Berkeley and Los Angeles, 1959.

Parry, Adam. "Have We Homer's *Iliad*?" *Yale Classical Studies* 20 (1966), 177–216.

————. "Language and Characterization in Homer." *Harvard Studies in Classical Philology* 76 (1972), 1–22.

————. "The Language of Achilles." *Transactions of the American Philological Association* 87 (1956), 1–7.

————. *The Language of Achilles and Other Papers*. Oxford, 1989.

Parry, Anne Amory. *Blameless Aegisthus*. Leiden, 1973.

Parry, Milman. *The Making of Homeric Verse: The Collected Papers of Milman Parry*. Ed. and with introduction by Adam Parry. Oxford, 1971; rpt. 1987.

Propp, Vladimir. *Morphology of the Folktale.* Tr. Laurence Scott. 2nd ed. Austin, Texas, 1968; rpt. 1977.

Redfield, James. *Nature and Culture in the Iliad: The Tragedy of Hector.* Chicago, 1975.

Sacks, Richard. *The Traditional Phrase in Homer: Two Studies in Form, Meaning and Interpretation.* Leiden, 1987.

Schein, Seth. *The Mortal Hero.* Berkeley and Los Angeles, 1984.

Scott, William C. *The Oral Nature of the Homeric Simile.* Leiden, 1974.

Shive, David M. *Naming Achilles.* Oxford, 1987.

Vivante, Paolo. *The Epithets in Homer.* New Haven, 1982.

―――. *The Homeric Imagination: A Study of Homer's Poetic Perception of Reality.* Bloomington, 1970.

Whitman, Cedric. *Homer and the Heroic Tradition.* Cambridge, Mass., 1958; rpt. New York, 1965.

IV. THE WORLD OF HOMER AND HIS HEROES: ARCHEOLOGY, ''EVERYDAY LIFE,'' LINGUISTICS

Bernal, Martin. *Black Athena: The Afroasiatic Roots of Classical Civilization.* Vol. II: *The Archaeological and Documentary Evidence.* New Brunswick, N.J., 1991.

Blegen, C. W., et al. *The Palace of Nestor at Pylos in Western Messenia.* Princeton, 1966–73.

Boardman, John. *The Greeks Overseas.* 2nd ed. London, 1980.

Casson, L. *Ships and Seamanship in the Ancient World.* Princeton, 1971.

Crouwel, J. H. *Chariots and Other Means of Land Transport in Bronze Age Greece.* Amsterdam, 1981.

Dicks, D. R. *Early Greek Astronomy to Aristotle*. London, 1970.

Finley, Moses I. "Homer and Mycenae: Property and Tenure." *Historia* 6 (1957), 133–59. Reprinted in Geoffrey S. Kirk, ed. *Language and Background of Homer*. Cambridge, 1964. Pp. 191–217.

Havelock, Eric. *The Muse Learns to Write: Reflections on Orality and Literacy from Antiquity to the Present*. New Haven, 1986.

———. *Preface to Plato*. Cambridge, Mass., 1963.

Lorimer, H. L. *Homer and the Monuments*. London, 1950.

Morrison, J. S., and R. T. Williams. *Greek Oared Ships*. Cambridge, 1968.

Nilsson, Martin P. *Minoan-Mycenaean Religion*. 2nd ed. Lund, 1950.

Powell, Barry. *Homer and the Origin of the Greek Alphabet*. Cambridge, 1991.

Renfrew, Colin. *Archaeology and Language: The Puzzle of Indo-European Origins*. Cambridge, 1987.

Simpson, R. Hope, and J. F. Lazenby. *The Catalogue of the Ships in Homer's Iliad*. Oxford, 1970.

Snodgrass, A. M. *The Dark Age of Greece: An Archaeological Survey of the Eleventh to the Eighth Centuries B.C.* Edinburgh, 1971.

———. *Early Greek Armour and Weapons*. Edinburgh, 1964.

Ventris, Michael, and J. Chadwick. *Documents in Mycenaean Greek*. 2nd ed. Cambridge, 1973.

Wace, Alan J. B., and Frank H. Stubbings, eds. *A Companion to Homer*. London and New York, 1962 (abbreviated as W&S).

Webster, T. B. L. *From Mycenae to Homer*. London, 1958.

V. THE WORLD OF HOMER AND HIS AUDIENCE: THOUGHT, CULTURE

Adkins, Arthur. *Merit and Responsibility: A Study in Greek Values.* Oxford, 1960.

Burkert, W. *Greek Religion: Archaic and Classical.* Tr. John Raffan. Oxford, 1985.

————. *Homo Necans.* Tr. Peter Bing. Berkeley and Los Angeles, 1983.

Detienne, Marcel, and Jean-Pierre Vernant. *Cunning Intelligence in Greek Culture and Society.* Tr. Janet Lloyd. Hassocks, 1978.

Dodds, E. R. *The Greeks and the Irrational.* Berkeley and Los Angeles, 1951; rpt. 1964.

Lloyd-Jones, Hugh. *The Justice of Zeus.* Berkeley and Los Angeles, 1971.

Long, A. A. "Morals and Values in Homer." *Journal of Hellenic Studies* 90 (1970), 121–39.

Onians, R. B. *The Origins of European Thought.* Cambridge, 1951.

Vermeule, Emily Townsend. *Aspects of Death in Early Greek Art and Poetry.* Berkeley and Los Angeles, 1979.

Vernant, Jean-Pierre. *Myth and Society in Ancient Greece.* Tr. Janet Lloyd. Brighton and Atlantic Highlands, N.J. 1980.

————. *The Origins of Greek Thought.* Tr. Janet Lloyd. Ithaca, 1982.

VI. THE LEGACY OF HOMER: THE HOMERIC POEMS, ODYSSEUS, TRANSLATING HOMER

Arnold, Matthew. "On Translating Homer." In R. H. Super, ed. *The Complete Prose Works of Matthew Arnold*. Vol. 1, *On the Classical Tradition*. Ann Arbor, 1960. Pp. 97–216.

King, Katherine Callen. *Achilles: Paradigms of the War Hero from Homer to the Middle Ages*. Berkeley and Los Angeles, 1987.

Mason, Harold A. *To Homer Through Pope: An Introduction to Homer's Iliad and Pope's Translation*. New York, 1972.

Pavlock, Barbara. *Eros, Imitation, and the Epic Tradition*. Ithaca, 1990.

Porphyry. *Porphyry on the Cave of the Nymphs*. Tr. Robert Lamberton. Barrytown, N.Y., 1983.

Reynolds, L. D., and N. G. Wilson. *Scribes and Scholars: A Guide to the Transmission of Greek and Latin Literature*. 3d ed. Oxford, 1991.

Scherer, Margaret R. *The Legends of Troy in Art and Literature*. 2d ed. New York, 1964.

Simonsuuri, Kirsti. *Homer's Original Genius: Eighteenth-Century Notions of the Early Greek Epic (1688–1798)*. Cambridge, 1979.

Stanford, W. B. *The Ulysses Theme: A Study in the Adaptability of a Traditional Hero*. 2d ed. Oxford, 1963; rev. 1968.

Suzuki, Mihoko. *Metamorphoses of Helen: Authority, Difference, and the Epic*. Ithaca, 1990.

Williams, Carolyn D. *Pope, Homer, and Manliness: Some Aspects of Eighteenth-Century Classical Learning*. London and New York, 1993.

Wolf, F. A. *Prolegomena to Homer [1795]*. Tr. with introduction and notes by Anthony Grafton, Glenn W. Most, and James Zetzel. Princeton, 1985.

Acknowledgments

During my last two years of college (many years ago), I read for the first time in their original languages Homer's *Odyssey*, Vergil's *Aeneid*, *Beowulf*, and Gottfried von Strassburg's *Tristan*. This intense exposure to the ancient and medieval European epics at a formative period of my studies deepened what was already a long-standing love affair with epic and romance. Homer's poetry and the story of Odysseus have been special delights over the years, even if I have devoted my research and scholarly writing more often to Homer's—and Odysseus'—descendants than to the originals. For that reason it has been a great pleasure to undertake the present *Guide to The Odyssey*, which I have done not as a specialist in the Homeric epics (which I am not) but as a classicist and comparatist, as a lover of the poem, and above all as a teacher of literature both ancient and modern.

Every commentary passes on a large proportion of inherited material. It would not have been appropriate, given the intended audience of the present guide, for me to cite previous authorities at every point where I agree with one or more of them, nor I believe would this have been expected in a "school" commentary, where originality is rarely a virtue. I refer readers at important junctures to W. B. Stanford's two-volume commentary and the collaborative three-volume commentary recently issued by Oxford University Press, and I cite other scholars when their formulation of a particular point seems unusually valuable or thought-provoking. I have suggested a large number of books for further study in the Bibliography, but I have not attempted to list all the items users might find interesting or all those which helped form my views. For example, it is unlikely that I would have developed in the Introduction my concept of the "archeological reader" had I not read (as most literary scholars do today) the works of Michel Foucault. However, it would have served little purpose to distract readers of this guide with a discussion of the similarities and differences between my "archeological reader" and Foucauldian archeology. Nor will I apologize for all the matters of substance I chose *not* to address: for the crafter of a commentary, exclusion is a more difficult discipline than inclusion.

My list of debts is a long one. Given the purpose of this guide, it is right for me to begin with those teachers who inspired in me a love of literature and who taught me, at various stages of my schooling, how to read: my family, Jean and Burton Randall, Frank Warnement, Jean Slingerland, Betsy Walsh, B. J. Whiting, Morton Bloomfield, Zeph Stewart, Margaret Howatson, Thomas Greene, Lowry Nelson, Jr., Jack Winkler, and Paul de Man. As a classicist, I am grateful for encouragement and insight to many—teachers, colleagues, students, too many to name. I owe a great debt of thanks to my first teacher of Greek, Gregory Nagy. Special thanks to those who have seen me through this project: Penelope Laurans and LuAnn Walther, for their trust and patience; Alecia Dantico, who helped me with some of the technical aspects of preparing the manuscript in Boulder, as Stephen Wolf and Sally Arteseros did in New York and Susan Brown did in Belmont; John Boswell, Joe

Gordon, and Daniel Selden, for inspiration and encouragement; Sheila Murnaghan and Matthew Gumpert for that and for so generously offering improvements and corrections at short notice; and Manfred Kollmeier, for unwavering confidence. I made important progress on parts of the Commentary during the academic year 1991–92, when, supported by a grant from the National Endowment for the Humanities, I was at the Harvard University Center for Italian Renaissance Studies, the Villa I Tatti in Florence. I thank the NEH for their support of all my projects that year, the director of Villa I Tatti, Walter Kaiser, its staff, and my fellow fellows for making this year a wonderful intellectual odyssey. I also thank Salvatore and Diane Vacca, my "Alkinoös" and "Arêtê," whose hospitality permitted me to write some of the final pages on Capri, gazing out on waters some believe Odysseus sailed in his travels, before I too returned home.

About the Author

Ralph Hexter is Professor of Classics and Director of the Graduate Program in Comparative Literature at the University of Colorado at Boulder. He has also taught at Yale University, where he received his Ph.D., was a guest lecturer at the Folger Institute, and in 1991–92 was a fellow of the Villa i Tatti, Harvard Center for Studies in the Italian Renaissance, in Florence. He is the author of books and articles on Virgil, Horace, a variety of topics in medieval Latin, and Goethe. He is co-editor of *Innovations of Antiquity,* published in 1992 in Routledge's series "The New Ancient World." His current projects include Homer and Virgil, classical and medieval literary history, Renaissance Latin drama, and the development of comparative literature.